MW01092597

The Deleuze Reader

The Deleuze Reader

Edited
with an Introduction by
Constantin V. Boundas

Columbia University Press
New York

*The editor of this volume wishes to dedicate it
to Linda Carol Conway.*

*Columbia University Press
New York   Oxford*

Editor's Introduction and its notes and English translations for
essays 15, 22, 23, and 25 copyright © 1993 Columbia
University Press
All rights reserved

Library of Congress Cataloging-in-Publication Data

Deleuze, Gilles.
    [Selections. English. 1993]
      The Deleuze reader / edited with an introduction by
Constantin V. Boundas.
      p.   cm.
      Includes bibliographical references and index.
      ISBN 0-231-07268-6
      1. Philosophy.   2. Aesthetics.   3. Psychoanalysis and
    philosophy.
I. Boundas, Constantin V.   II. Title.
B2430.D452E54   1993
194—dc20   92–30237
                                                      CIP

⊚

Casebound editions of
Columbia University Press books
are Smyth-sewn and printed
on permanent and durable
acid-free paper.

Printed in the United States of America

c   10   9   8   7   6   5   4   3   2   1

Contents

Acknowledgments

Essays 1, 4, 5, 14, 17, 19, 24, and 27 reprinted from *A Thousand Plateaus: Capitalism and Schizophrenia* by permission of the University of Minnesota Press; copyright 1987 by the University of Minnesota Press. Essays 2, 3, 6, and 8 reprinted from *The Logic of Sense* by permission of Columbia University Press; copyright 1990 by Columbia University Press. Essay 7 reprinted from *Spinoza: Practical Philosophy* by permission of City Lights Books; copyright 1988 by Robert Hurley. Essay 9 reprinted from *Difference and Repetition* by permission of The Athlone Press; copyright forthcoming by The Athlone Press. Essays 10 and 28 reprinted from *Nietzsche and Philosophy* by permission of Columbia University Press; copyright 1983 by Columbia University Press. Essay 11 reprinted from *Foucault* by permission of the University of Minnesota Press; copyright 1988 by the University of Minnesota Press. Essays 12, 16, 26, and 29 reprinted from *Dialogues* by permission of Columbia University Press; copyright 1987 by The Athlone Press. Essay 13 reprinted from *Anti-Oedipus: Capitalism and Schizophrenia* by permission of The Viking Press; copyright 1977 by Viking Penguin, Inc. Essay 15 translated from *Proust et les signes* by permission of Presses Universitaires de France: copyright 1975 (fifth edition) by Presses Universitaires de France. Essay 18 reprinted from *Kafka: For a Minor Literature* by permission of the University of Minnesota Press; copyright 1986 by the University of Minnesota Press. Essay 20 reprinted from *Cinema 1: The Movement-Image* by permission of the University of Minnesota Press; copyright 1986 by The Athlone Press. Essay 21 reprinted from *Cinema 2: The Time Image* by permission of The Athlone Press; copyright 1989 by The Athlone Press. Essays 22 and 23 translated from *Francis Bacon: Logique de la sensation* by permission of Editions de la Différence; copyright 1981 by Editions de la Différence. Essay 25 translated from *Superpositions* by permission of Les Editions de Minuit; copyright 1979 by Les Editions de Minuit.

Editor's Introduction
Constantin V. Boundas

Gilles Deleuze will be remembered as a philosopher, that is, as a creator of concepts. This has been his way of imposing a bit of order upon the menacing chaos. But he will also be remembered as a "stutterer," as someone who stutters as he speaks and writes, in his effort to make speech and, even more important, language, begin to stutter. Finally, he will be remembered as the thinker of "the outside." His moving references to those he reads and loves can easily be returned and attributed to him: "a little fresh air," "a gust of air," "a thinker of an outside." *Philosopher, stutterer, thinker of an outside.* How do these link?

Closed upon itself, and holding the lid down on its own discipline, philosophy has often mistaken vacuity and ineptness for wisdom and rigor and the foul odors of inbreeding for signs of intellectual and moral integrity. To open the lid, so that a gust of fresh air may come in from the outside, is not to waste time deciphering the signs of an upcoming end of philosophy. Although the problems of philosophy are problems of the outside, the outside is not a space for the preserve of disciplines *different from* philosophy; it is the space where philosophy begins to differ *in itself*.

In laboratories of research adjacent to the philosopher's, the scientist, the painter, the cinematographer experiment with their own materials.

Sometimes the porousness of the vessels' walls permits us to see that we have all been working with the same problems. But more often, an outside, which is the outside of all these laboratories and all these vessels, asserts itself and allows an unstable resonant "communication," which does not wipe out the differences or the discordance of the "regional" concerns. I will come back to this "absolute" outside later and stress again the role it plays in Deleuze's work. But a provisional characterization of it may already be possible. Deleuze does not mean to say that problems and issues outside the philosopher's laboratory are what cause the philosopher or her philosophy to develop as she or it does. Philosophy does not reflect or represent an outside that is merely relative to it. Rather, the philosopher creates concepts— nobody else can create concepts in her stead. But to create a powerful concept is to trace and to follow the line that makes the various regions communicate at the same time that these regions diverge and retain their differences. To trace such a line, say, between philosophy and music, is not to orchestrate a philosophical theme or to talk with philosophical expertise about the form and the content of a piece of music. It is to find a third term, in between the two, which would facilitate the "becoming-music" of philosophy and the "becoming-philosophy" of music.

It is this "becoming-x" that offers a possibility of explaining Deleuze's predilection for the stuttering philosopher. The concepts that Deleuze creates are the result of three interrelated imperatives that motivate and inform his philosophical experimentations with difference, repetition, and productive desire: to reverse Platonism without trading one structure of domination for another; to dismantle foundationalism without permitting the consensus of our Northwestern ethnicity to become the new foundation; and to deconstruct affirmatively, not for the sake of the Other-in-general, but rather for the sake of the "minoritarian" Other. But a moment's reflection shows that any creator of concepts who experiments with such operational rules in mind will be placing herself in a vulnerable position: her own concepts, along with the narratives within which they are embedded, will be problematic, both in the sense of problem-raising and in the sense of being essentially contestable and controversial. And problems and opposition will multiply because of the resistance of those who already occupy the regions and the territories that the philosopher-experimenter wishes to transform. It may be true that a powerful concept can be created only as regions begin to vibrate and to resonate together. It may also be true that vibrating and resonating occur along "nomadic" itineraries which cause those who travel to "become-other" than themselves. But sedentarism, being the law of the regions, along with its rules of identity, resemblance, and analogy, create a formidable "majority," armed with the kind of moral uprightness which is ready to pounce at, and crush, the stutterer who dares them. Becoming or transformation here is possible only when the stuttering of the philosopher "hooks up" with the stuttering of the "majority" and begins to dissolve stubborn resistances and to clear up existing blockages (after all, every "majority" has a stuttering impediment of its own).

Philosopher, stutterer, thinker of an outside—but never marginal or parasitic. His philosophical apprenticeship and, later on, his career as a "public professor" have been in accordance with France's best and time-honored ways: *La Sorbonne, Professeur de Lycée, Professeur de l'Université en Provence,* researcher at the *Centre national des recherches scientifiques, Professeur de l'Université de Paris VIII,* first at Vincennes and, later on, at Saint Denis. But this rather orthodox French academic career—this molar, segmented line, as he would call it—never managed to conceal a certain taste for the outside, a desire for nomadic displacements, an openness to encounters which could cause the molar line to deviate and the rhizome to grow by the middle, or a kind of humor with which to displace the philosopher's old irony.

François Châtelet, for example, has retained, from his student days at Sorbonne, the memory of an oral presentation that Deleuze made on Malebranche's theory in a seminar led by a scholarly and meticulous historian of philosophy. Châtelet recalls how the erudite professor first paled, then got hold of himself, and finally expressed his respect and admiration as he sat listening to Deleuze's argument, backed by impeccable textual references and premised squarely on . . . the "principle of the irreducibility of Adam's rib."[1] As for Deleuze's own references to the postwar period in France, which coincides with his student days, they show the same early preference for the outside. He tells us how the new scholasticism that descended upon the Sorbonne after the liberation was made somewhat bearable thanks to the presence of Sartre. "Sartre was our Outside," he writes in his *Dialogues* with Claire Parnet. "He was really the breath of fresh air from the backyard. . . . Among all the Sorbonne's probabilities, it was his unique combination which gave us the strength to tolerate the new restoration of order."[2] In 1964 Deleuze will praise Sartre, private thinker and never public professor, for having introduced philosophy to new themes, for choosing a new style and for preferring a new, polemic and aggressive way of raising problems. In a way that speaks as much about himself as he does about Sartre, Deleuze goes on to remind us that, like every other private thinker, Sartre demonstrated how much thought needs a world with a grain of disorder in it, a bit of agitation and a dash of solitude. Stressing, with admiration, Sartre's opposition to all modes of representation and his love for speaking in his own name, Deleuze, in 1964, hailed Sartre as his own teacher—a teacher of the outside.[3]

Historico-Philosophical Stutterings

Deleuze's love for the outside is also evident in his historico-philosophical work. Nobody can accuse him of not having labored hard and long in the fields of the history of philosophy before he came to write books in his own name. ("How can you think without having read Plato, Descartes, Kant and Heidegger, and so-and-so's book about them?" Deleuze mused with irony in *Dialogues*.)[4] His impressive monographs on Hume, Nietzsche, Bergson, Kant, Spinoza, and Leibniz, his discussions of Plato, the Stoics, and the Epicureans, betray his partiality for those fellow stutterers "who seemed to be part of the history of philosophy, but who escaped from it in one respect, or altogether."[5] His way of reading them is not a search for hidden signifieds. Rather, Deleuze tries to get hold of their texts "by the middle," refusing to follow them step after step according to the order of their argumentation or according to "the order of reasons." He forces arguments and reasons, he precipitates them toward their vanishing point, he accelerates and decelerates them the way that we accelerate or decelerate a liquid in an experimental vessel, until he gets hold of the machine that generates the problems and the questions—the stuttering—of the thinker.

Deleuze's thought cannot be contained within the problematics of the now fashionable textual allegory. The main thrust of his theoretical intervention is in the articulation of a theory of transformation and change or, as he likes to say, of a theory of *pure becoming* which, together with a language adequate to it, would be sufficiently strong to resist all identitarian pressures. It is this relentless effort to articulate a theory of transformation and change (and not the obsession with the diacritic nature of the linguistic sign) that motivates Deleuze to replace Being with difference, and linear time with a difference-making repetition.

It is precisely for the sake of a theory of transformation that Deleuze will reflect, throughout his work, on the nature of the event (see this volume, part II, essays 2 and 3), the structure of multiplicity (part II, essay 4), the requirements of individuation (part II, essay 5), the lure of the other (part II, essay 6), the ethics of the event (part II, essays 7 and 8), and the enabling and selecting force of repetition in the eternal return (part II, essays 9 and 10). To his theory of transformation, he will subordinate the results of his investigation of the agonistic relations between major and minor languages (part IV) and, later on, his elucidation of mobile nomadic differences, situated half way between migrant and sedentary political strategies (part V).

Hume

Hume gives Deleuze a method, the method of *transcendental empiricism,* which allows him to dissolve the organic compounds of idealism and to reach for the anorganic subsoil of the atomic and the distinct. *Empiricism and Subjectivity: An Essay on Hume's Theory of Human Nature,* is among Deleuze's earlier writings.[6] True to his own reading "by the middle," Deleuze refuses to define empiricism on the basis of the postulate that the validity of ideas depends strictly on corresponding impressions of sensation or reflection. He rather believes that the principle of empiricism rests with Hume's doctrine of the externality of all relations: relations are always external to the terms they relate (even in the case of analytic relations). The principle of empiricism, therefore—Deleuze will argue—is a principle of differentiation and of difference: ideas are different because they are external to, and separable from one another; and they are separable, that is, external to one another, because they are different. It is easy to understand, therefore, why the question "how to relate or associate entities which are different" finds in Hume, and in Deleuze, an urgency that it never had before. Hume's associationism leads Deleuze, in the final analysis, to a theory of inclusive disjunctions and a theory of paratactic discourse, that is, to the triumph of the conjunction AND (*et*) over the predicative IS (*est*).

Spinoza

Deleuze wrote two books on Spinoza: *Expressionism in Philosophy: Spinoza*[7] and *Spinoza: Practical Philosophy.*[8] In them, he expressed his admiration for Spinoza's way of addressing the old problem of the One and the many. It was the Platonic paradigm that bequeathed us the problem embedded in the metaphor of participation, and that, in its effort to preserve the identity of the One, hardened the ontological difference between Being and becoming. Later on, the neoPlatonic shift of metaphors, from participation to emanation and gift, did little to decrease the cost of the moral and political choice involved. In either paradigm, a vertical axis of power relations was instituted, and whether the Despot was the self-identical Form or the One beyond Being and knowledge, the suitors had to rally around the center or face excommunication from the Republic of man or from the City of God.

But as Deleuze reads Spinoza, all this changes. To read Spinoza "by the middle" is to make the notion of expression the "vanishing point" of his text. The One (which here is not a number) has the coherence of an open-ended differentiated whole, and expresses its essence by means of an infinity of attributes. Or again, the One expresses itself by means of an infinity of attributes in modes. The essence and the modes are the "explications" or "unfoldings" of all that which is "implicated" or enveloped inside the One. Deleuze suggests that we must learn to admire in this *implicatio/explicatio* the total absence of hierarchical powers and the freedom from vertical axes of descending grace. Being is univocal, equal to itself, and offers itself equally to all beings.

There is more, of course, in Spinoza's "minor" philosophy that attracts Deleuze's attention: there are bodies and affects specified in terms of their active and reactive forces; there is desire linked up with joy; there is opposition to representationalism, critique of negation, deconstruction of analogy and identity; there is opposition to teleological deferral, an entire phenomenology of joyful modes of life, and a discipline aimed at preventing sadness, loss of energy, and *ressentiment;* but, above all, there is *isonomia* among beings and compossible yet diverging lines inside the One, universal Being.

Bergson

Bergson is Deleuze's ally in his displacement of phenomenology and of the privilege that phenomenology assigns to natural perception. In *Bergsonism,*[9] *Difference and Repetition,*[10] and *Cinema 1: the Movement-Image,*[11] Deleuze argues that to be serious about the notion of the "worlding of the world," the mind must strive to sense a world behind appearances, a world in perpetual motion and change, without anchorage, without assignable points of reference, and without solid bodies or rigid lines. For empiricism to become transcendental, and for Spinozism to overcome the last vestiges of the One, the mind must transcend the *sensible* in the direction of the *sentiendum* (= that which ought to be sensed), in search of lines of (f)light traveling without resistance, an eye situated inside things, and consciousness understood as epiphenomenal opacity. What Deleuze admires in Bergson is his resolve to speak about the "originary" world of intensive magnitudes and forces—or, more accurately, about this originary world being in the process of "explicating" itself in extended surfaces.

Nietzsche

Bergson's theory of intensive time carries profound implications for memory and repetition. Memory as repetition of the past inside the interval of the present presupposes the irreducible *écart* (interval) between past and present and foregrounds the "originary delay" upon which Derrida already fastened the dissemination of the *gramma*. And yet Deleuze is not convinced. Bergson's memory/repetition, without the time of the eternal return, would tend to immobilize past and present and to disempower the intuition of the irreducible multiplicity that, nevertheless, animates Bergson's texts. Isn't Plato's recollection, after all, a sufficient warning against putting our trust in *mnemosyne* and letting it chase after the shadow of the One?

As a result, Deleuze shifts his attention to Nietzsche's eternal return, and asks it to carry the weight of the move from *Being and Time* to *Difference and Repetition* (see this volume, part II, essays 9, 10 and 11). But for this move to be convincing, Deleuze must distinguish between the repetition/recycling of the tradition and the repetition which makes the difference. He pursues the project in *Nietzsche and Philosophy*[12] and *Nietzsche*.[13] Traditional repetition works with identical entities forming the extension of the same concept, with only their numerical difference to separate them from one another. Deleuze calls this difference a difference extrinsic to the concept.

The repetition that "makes the difference" is intensive, whereas the recycling repetitions of the present and the past are extensive. The concept is the shadow of the Idea-problem, because a concept has extension, that is, a range of particulars that instantiate it. But an Idea, being a structure, is an intensive magnitude whose nature changes as the Idea is divided or subdivided. The Idea-problem circulates in repetition and differentiates itself in concepts-solutions. But, as Deleuze has argued, no concept is ever adequate to the Idea, recycling repetitions can never exhaust or represent the nature of the difference that is intrinsic to the Idea. It is the Idea, with no intuition adequate to it, that generates problems and offers provisional solutions; the latter crystallize for a while around concepts and their extensions, only to be overthrown again by new intensities and new problems.

The conclusion that Deleuze draws from these examples, and from his reflection on Nietzsche's eternal return, is that to repeat is to behave in a certain way, but always in relation to something unique, without likeness or equivalence. Repetition, in Nietzsche's sense, is exception, transgression, difference. Like Kant's aesthetic Idea, repetition is a singular intuition, without a concept adequate to it. It was Nietzsche's privilege and fate to get a glimpse at this unique, transgressive, and a-centered center; he named it "will to power."

The will to power, as Nietzsche understands it, is not an intentional pursuit of power by forces deprived of it, but rather the expression of the kind of power that the force itself is. "Will *of* power," in the sense that power itself wills, is the correct reading of the will to power. The traditional, intentional reading makes power the object of a representation, a wanting to acquire that which a force lacks, and therefore something incompatible with Nietzsche's theory of forces. According to Deleuze, it is a falsification of Nietzsche's views on the subject to expect values to come to light as a result of the struggle for recognition or the power-grabbing that such a representationalist reading of the will to power would necessitate.[14]

The Stoics

The articulation of a theory of pure becoming presupposes the overthrow of Platonism and the repudiation of the ethical choice that such difference supports. But a theory of pure becoming and transformation can only be a theory of paradoxes and of series-formation. "It is at the same moment that one becomes larger than one was and smaller than one becomes."[15] Predicative logic is not equipped to handle pure becoming. Deleuze needs a logic of the event, a sense-generating logic, and he sets out in earnest to give himself one in *The Logic of Sense*.

In this work, Deleuze discusses the Stoics extensively. With the Stoics, as Deleuze reads them, the overthrow of Platonism is undertaken seriously: philosophy thinks the event and gives itself the right tools for the discussion of change, transformation, and becoming. Since Zeno of Elea, philosophy had known that becoming cannot be thought of as a mere juxtaposition of immobile slices of extension and time. It was the Stoics, Deleuze argues, who made the first, correct move: to think of becoming is to think of the event (this volume, part II, essay 3).

Events are caused by bodies, but they are not states of affairs or Aristotelian accidents, which also affect substances or are caused by substances. Deleuze stresses the importance of the Stoic ontological difference traced between bodies, their qualities, mixtures, *and* "incorporeal events." Bodies and their mixtures are actual; they exist in the present, and they causally affect other bodies and bring about new mixtures. But bodies also cause events that are virtual and that, in turn, take toward bodies a kind of "quasi-causal efficacy." Events, as the Stoics and Deleuze understand them, elude the present: an event is never what is happening in the present, but always what has just happened or what is about to happen. It is best, Deleuze concludes, to denote them by means of infinitives: to green, to cut, to grow, to die. Without being subjective or objective, infinitives are determinate and specific and guarantee reversibility between future and past. And this is important for the designation of events, because the latter, by eluding the present, affirm simultaneously future and past, becoming thereby responsible for the passing of the present. Events, rather than denoting substances or qualities, stand for forces, intensities, and actions. They do not preexist bodies; they rather inhere, insist, and subsist in them.

A central chapter in the Stoic overthrow of Platonism—a chapter that Deleuze discusses extensively in *The Logic of Sense*—is the *ethics of the event*.[16] No longer do the Stoics attempt to articulate an ethical system on the basis of imitation of, and participation in, an ideal model. The ethical question is how individuals can be worthy of what is happening to them. Deleuze's reading of the Stoics, in the context of Spinoza (part II, essay 7) and Nietzsche (part II, essay 10) makes it clear that the quietist overtones of this ethical question are, in fact, deceptive. The ethics of the event is not the ethics of the accident. No one is suggesting that to acquiesce, without demurring, to whatever happens is the right thing to do. Moreover, events do not happen to a subject; they are presubjective and preindividual. Events decenter subjects—they are never responsible for the formation of the subject. To the extent that events are still future and always past, the ethics of the event presupposes a will that seeks in the state of affairs the eternal truth of events. Real *amor fati* is not in the acceptance of the actual state of affairs but in the "counteractualization" of the actual, so that the virtual event that inheres in it may be, for the first time, thought and willed.

To be worthy of what is happening to us, Deleuze concludes, means to will what is always both different and the same in each moment of our lives, to raise the banal and mundane into the remarkable and singular, the wound into a wound that heals, war against war, death against death. This is what it takes to will repetition as the task of freedom.

Leibniz

From his reading of Leibniz (*Le Pli. Leibniz et le baroque*;[17] *Expressionism in Philosophy: Spinoza*) Deleuze forges a powerful concept—the fold—and uses it extensively and as a fulcrum to make the questions of Leibniz resonate, but also to define the baroque as a style and as a period and to elaborate the theory of power and subjectivity that he shares with the late Foucault.

Leibniz's world resembles a building with two floors: on the upper floor, windowless monads, distinct from one another and without interaction, express the world, each one of them from a singular point of view. On the lower floor, organic and inorganic matter becomes subject to forces of the world that govern, and account for, its movement. The two floors communicate through the world, which is virtual, albeit actualized, in the monads and realized in matter. The world is *the fold* that separates the floors as it links them together. The concept of the fold and the power of the virtual link up with each other in Leibniz, and make him diverge sharply from the expressionism of Spinoza where everything is subjected to an uninterrupted causal "explication." As for the centrality that the concept *fold* acquires in Deleuze's thought, its constant recurrence in his works, under different names and masks, establishes it beyond any doubt: it is the "somber precursor" of *Difference and Repetition*,[18] the "esoteric word" of *The Logic of Sense*,[19] the "outside" of *Foucault*,[20] the "line of death" of the *Dialogues*[21] and *A Thousand Plateaus*.[22] It is the entity or agent that holds diverging series together and makes possible a theory of inclusive disjunctions: Deleuze is fond of calling it "the differentiator of the differends."

Leibniz, of course, is not Deleuze; he remains the uncompromising theorist of convergence—not of divergence. But a more labyrinthine world than his, with an infinity of floors, can still be imagined—a world of incompossible strata. Of course, Leibniz thinks of his world of converging series as the best possible. But the reason this world is the best possible is no longer its optimal participation in the ideal model of the Good. The "best possible" presupposes and witnesses the erosion of Platonism. The world is the best possible as a result of a divine selection and play.[23] But then one more daring step is still possible: God can be "replaced by Baphomet, the 'prince of all modifications,' and himself modification of all modifications. . . . Rather than signifying that a certain number of predicates are excluded from a thing in virtue of the identity of the corresponding concept, the disjunction now signifies that each thing is opened up to the infinity of predicates through which it passes, on the condition that it lose its identity as concept and as self."[24] And Deleuze does take this step.

Kant

In 1963 Deleuze published a book on Kant, *Kant's Critical Philosophy: The Doctrine of the Faculties*,[25] whose brevity and clarity have proven to be deceptive. Very few noticed this important "minor" deconstructive reading of Kant. And yet the most fruitful way to receive Deleuze's *Difference and Repetition* is in its aspiration to be the critique of the *Critique of Pure Reason*. (I often wondered whether *Capitalism and Schizophrenia* is most profitably read as the critique of the *Critique of Practical Reason*—a critique clearly motivated by the *aporias* of Kant's third critique.)

Kant's love for all-rounded architectonic structures is well known: his theory of rationality based on the consensual harmony of all mental faculties and his attempt to coordinate cognitive praxiological and ludic interests belong here. Deleuze decides to pry open these structures by dislodging the cornerstone: the presumed harmony and cooperation among mental faculties. He states, before Lyotard made this point popular among us, that for this cooperation to become possible, imagination must be assigned the task of training sensibility, memory, and understanding. Therefore, the lifting of the barriers that Kant placed between cognitive, practical, and aesthetic interests is what Deleuze will advocate, along with the coordination of the *aisthesis* (= sensation) of the first Critique and the *aisthesis* (= artistic, aesthetic sense) of the third.

We are now in a better position to advance a global characterization of Deleuze's theory of difference and repetition, the best source for which is his 1968 book bearing this very title. The *idée mère* of this theory is that fusion and fission are the external limits of all functioning assemblages, natural or man-made.[26] Despite the difference in degrees of contraction or dilation, the final result of fusion and fission is the same: the apparent numerical difference between the one (fusion) and the many (fission) disappears, since time, qualitative difference, and change no longer exist in either state. Assemblages, however, that are still in operational order avoid these absolute external limits through the preventive mechanism of a controlled repetition: they repeat the very conditions the extremes of which would have brought about their entropic *stasis* and death. Contraction *and* dilation constitute therefore the inclusive, disjunctive law of all systems. This does not mean, Deleuze will argue, that contraction and dilation are opposite forces in the service of homeostatic systems. Nor is dilation (extension) the founding stratum of systems. The world of extended things, in extended space and time, is the result of the dilation of intensive quanta of energy, captured in the process of slowing down and becoming cooler. And this process is "always already" reversible through new irruptions of intensity.

Now, to say that transformation, change, and motion implicate at least two differential, intensive forces or magnitudes is no longer surprising or new. But what is not so obvious is Deleuze's definition of an intensive magnitude in terms of incommensurability, inequality, and indivisibility. For, although intensive forces seem to be divisible into parts, the parts obtained through division differ *in nature* from one another. In an important sense, therefore, intensive forces are indivisible, because, unlike extended magnitudes, no one of their parts preexists the division or retains the nature that it used to have before its division.[27]

Thus, Deleuze concludes, the sufficient reason for transformation and becoming is the interaction of differential intensities, incommensurable with respect to each other, indivisible in themselves, but not at all for these reasons, indeterminate. Intensive forces are perfectly determinable and determinate in relation to each other. Distance, inequality, and difference are positive characteristics of the intensive manifold. Negation has no primacy. Only in the process of its deployment, difference tends to cancel itself out in extension, and distance, to transform itself into length. But the cancellation of difference in extension and length does not make it any less the *sentiendum* of sensibility: difference/intensity is that which constitutes the sensible.

Without understanding, however, sensibility is blind, and understanding without sensibility is empty. This cornerstone of the Kantian idealism is due for a radical revision in the texts of Deleuze. The revision will attempt to establish the primacy of the Idea over the concept, with the understanding that, if this move succeeds, the traditional image of a recognitive and representative understanding will have to surrender its constitutive function to the differentiating role of the *cogitandum*—to that which ought to be thought.

Desire and Its Politics

Poised against the totalizing ambitions of the modern and the ineffectual celebration/lament of the postmodern, Deleuze orchestrated an untimely project for desire. The two volumes of *Capitalism and Schizophrenia*[28] and his *Dialogues*[29] are the repositories of this project. Rather than being a generator of phantasms, desire, according to Deleuze, produces connections and arrangements that are real in their function and revolutionary in their sprawling multiplicity. A process without *telos*, intensity without intention, desire (like the Aristotelian pleasure) has its "specific perfection" within itself at each moment of its duration. Desire is *energeia*—not *kinesis*. The fault of the modern and the postmodern alike is to have overlooked the energetic model of Aristotle, Spinoza, and Nietzsche and to have appropriated instead the kinetic and mimetic model of Plato (see part III, essay 16).

An energetic, constructivist, productive, and revolutionary model of desire such as Deleuze's is inevitably on a collision course with the psychoanalytic version of the unconscious and its subjection to Oedipus (part III, essay 12). Indeed, the twin volumes of *Capitalism and Schizophrenia* deploy a critique of psychoanalysis that is no longer a mere revisionism, like Marcuse's, Ricoeur's, or Habermas's.[30] Oedipus is no longer the phantasm that haunts the child; he is the paranoid obsession that torments the adult. The child must not expect her becoming-adult from her forced participation in the order of the father; the adult must build her becoming-child with the blocks of childhood she carries along with her. Deleuze (and coauthor Félix Guattari) denounce the Freudian Oedipus for having captured and confined desire. But the *Anti-Oedipus,* the first volume of *Capitalism and Schizophrenia,* published in 1972, is not exactly placated by the Lacanian recasting of the Freudian drama either; nor does it conceal its opposition to the ominous transformation of psychoanalysis that the *École Freudienne* brought about.[31] When the signifier is substituted for the signified, Deleuze and Guattari argue, psychoanalysis turns its back to any experimental scientific aspiration that it might have entertained and opts for the invincibility of axiomatic systems. As a result of this shift, it articulates a daunting official language and places it at the service of the established order.

Instead of the Oedipus-dominated psychoanalysis, Deleuze and Guattari have been advocating schizoanalytic theory and practice.[32] Schizoanalysis takes psychoanalysis to task for insulating the libido and its investments against the flights of masses and the marauding of packs. It suggests that all desiring investments are social and have necessary relations to concrete historical conjunctures (see part III, essay 13). The unconscious, for Deleuze and Guattari, is a social and political space to conquer—not a prodigious memory to nurture and protect.

As for death, Deleuze and Guattari argue, it is the limit of extreme, opposite investments of desire, but the fact is that schizoanalysis and psychoanalysis do not invoke the same death. One does not need the postulate of a death drive to account for catatonic states. The "black hole" of the paranoid fusion, being the outcome of the collapse of desiring arrangements, has nothing in common with the active schizoid desire of becoming-Other, which shatters the "sphere of ownness" and ushers in the death of the subject.[33] They have nothing in common except the "body without organs," the unextended, zero-intensity body of Deleuze and Guattari's schizoanalysis. Neither an organism nor a "lived body," the body without organs is a series without organs, with indeterminate organs, or with temporary, transitory organs. Being the site of anarchy (its political function), of a Nirvana-like release from excitements and irritations (its schizoanalytic function), and the surface for the inscription of inclusive disjunctions (its ontological function), it appropriates organs in order to function, makes use of them, but also repudiates and takes its revenge upon them whenever it has enough of their aggression. It is clear that "body without organs" is a portmanteau word, the sign of an originary disjunction, the "somber precursor" that gives rise to two distinct series, organic and anorganic, and brings them together in a resonant association—nonsense generating sense.[34]

Deleuze and Guattari's political theory and strategy loathe models—models for *the* revolution—and work instead with "localized" principles of intelligibility, allowing concrete social conjunctures to be assessed in terms of their molar and molecular tendencies.[35] Once again, the ritornello of their minor deconstruction coordinates the manifesto of their radical pluralism: fusion and fission are the absolute external limits of society. Centralizing hyperorganizations and political atomism are the two poles that tend toward, without ever reaching, the state of political immobility. They are the exclusive disjunctions of the body politic marking the paranoid and clinically schizophrenic poles of the social investment of desire.

But the emphasis on local principles of intelligibility does not always prevent Deleuze and Guattari from advancing bold hypotheses. Take, for example, their nomadology and the way it centers on the *Urstaat* hypothesis: the State, they argue, is not the result of a long and laborious evolution. It comes about, ready-made and all of a sudden, as the prototype of all sedentary arrangements.[36] The State always already exists, but it exists only in relation to an *outside* and cannot be conceived apart from this relation. The outside of the State are nomads and their constant struggle to fend off the sedentarism that the State threatens to impose upon them. But once again, this outside is not a relation of externality. Sedentaries and nomads are simultaneously present within the State. The State, with its appropriative powers, incorporates lines of flight that were not made for it. Once captured, these "alien to the State lines" may mobilize forces of transformation and change that cannot be overlooked by any political analyst and strategist.

In the nomads' capacity for transformation and flight, Deleuze and Guattari situate their difference from Foucault: "for him," they say, "a social field is run through by strategies; for us it flees from all its edges."[37] Indeed, this difference may well be the basis for the guarded optimism that permeates the following passage: "The choice is not between the State and its other—the nomad—. . . . We should dream no more about the disappearance of the State; we should rather choose . . . between blocking becomings or endowing ourselves with a war machine and making ourselves nomad"[38] (see part V, essay 25). In the last analysis, Deleuze and Guattari's wager on the nomads is due to their conviction that the outside is ultimately an irrecuperable and inexhaustible source of neg-entropic energy and capture-resisting subjectivity.

This point was recently made by one subtle reader of Deleuze, Monique Scheepers. According to her, the correct reception of Deleuze's politics depends on our ability to coordinate skillfully his political theory with his theory of subjectivity. In fact, as Scheepers goes on to argue, subjectivity, for Deleuze, is essentially a political dimension, to the extent that it folds and unfolds in an ever-renewed contact with the "outside"; thanks to this contact, subjectivity is able to resist standardization and harnessing.[39] When the traditional subject of interiority is bracketed, subjectivity is not lost. On the contrary, it is then that it reveals itself for the first time as a process and as a special operation on the outside. But what is this "outside," and what is this special operation that merits the name "subjectivity"? Moreover, what is the political significance of subjectivity linked to this "outside"?

The outside is not another site, but rather an out-of-site that erodes and dissolves all other sites. Its logic, therefore, is like the logic of difference, provided that the latter is understood in its transcendental and not in its empirical dimension: instead of difference between x and y, we must now conceive the difference of x from itself. Like the structure of supplementarity whose logic it follows, the outside is never exhausted; every attempt to capture it generates an excess or a supplement that in turn feeds anew the flows of deterritorialization, and releases new lines of flight. As P. Levoyer and P. Encrenaz have recently argued, the outside is Deleuze-Leibniz's virtual that is always more than the actual; it is the virtual that haunts the actual and, as it haunts it, makes it flow and change.[40] A Heideggerian *"es gibt"* bestows upon forces the role of the subject *and* the object of forming and unforming processes. This same *"es gibt"* permits Deleuze to endorse Foucault's claim about the primacy of resistances: "There will always be a relation to oneself which resists codes and powers; the relation to oneself is even one of the origins of their points of resistance."[41] To the extent that the subject, for Deleuze, is the result of the folding of the outside, that is, of the bending of forces and making them relate to one another, the subject is the individual who, through practice and discipline, has become the site of a bent force, that is, the folded inside of an outside. Foucault's position could not have been any closer.

This move seals the priority and inexhaustibility of resistances, but, as far as I can see, it paints resistances as resistances to form and as objections to stratification. A politics of transgression can certainly find its place and justification here, but a differentiation between smart, progressive resistances and mere conservative, resentful, or even fascist oppositions cannot. Must we then conclude that the theoretical usefulness of the coordination between Deleuze's theory of subjectivity and his politics has run its course? I do not think so. The question is this: Once the Kantian categorical imperative is no longer available, how can the compossibility of diverging wills chart a passage between the politics of fusion and the politics of fission? Such questions invite us to take a more serious look at Deleuze's studies of Hume, Spinoza, and Nietzsche (this volume, part V, essay 28) and at the discussions of subjectivity and its politics found in them: *Hume*— subjectivity and politics as an artifice, that is, as the result and the agent of experimentation; *Spinoza*—subjectivity and politics as the artifice of desire that dissipates sad passions and restores the healing power of joyous affects; *Nietzsche*—subjectivity and politics as the bent and folded forces of the outside that create an inside already always deeper than any other kind of inte-riority.[42]

Minor Languages and Nomad Arts

Derrida's theory of the deconstructive efficacy of language and the practice that this theory entails are by now fairly well-known moves in our fin de siècle manic depression. But, on the other hand, Deleuze and Guattari's "minor deconstructive" approaches to language are more timidly invoked in the context of our local discussions, and the timidity begins to lose its initial innocence. The truth of the matter is that Deleuze (and Guattari) have written extensively on the subject: *Capitalism and Schizophrenia*,[43] *Kafka: Toward a Minor Literature*,[44] and *Superpositions*,[45] are the main sources.

Minor deconstruction does not propose to determine majorities and mi-norities statistically. On the contrary, the dominant linguistic model that postulates that the intelligibility of minor languages depends on the epis-temic priority of standard languages is in collusion with the political model for a homogeneous, centralized, and dominant language of power (see part IV, essays 17 and 18). Minor languages have their own internal homoge-neity and consistency. In fact, as minor languages strive for recognition, they tend to become locally major. On the other hand, the more major a language becomes, the more it is evident that its innermost lines of flight transform it from within and deterritorialize it toward a minor position. It follows that "major" and "minor" languages or literatures enter into com-plex disjunctive syntheses that disallow the simplistic oppositional distribu-tion of them into "high" and "low." It is preferable, therefore, to read "ma-jor" and "minor" as the qualifiers of two different tendencies or functions of every language. Major is the tendency toward standardization and fixed identity by means of homogenization, overcoding, and centralization: the *langue/parole* distinction, the pragmatic presuppositions of the dominant theory of the speech acts, the differentiation between ideal speech situation and distorted communication, the pre-predicative founding stratum of op-erating intentionality, are some of the many different strategies for the pro-duction of such an identity. "Minor," on the other hand, is not the mark of the quantitative or qualitative marginality of a dialect, but rather the index of transformative forces inherent in language and literature (semiotic, se-mantic, stylistic, pragmatic, etc.), and especially of the transformative forces that facilitate "transversal" alliances of equivalence. "Major" and "minor," in this sense, qualify different experiences of language, distribute in different ways the space of politics, and give rise to different linguistic theories. In the last analysis, it may be argued that they are anchored in different experiences of the body.

With Derridean deconstruction, minor deconstruction shares the initial premise that language is *anarchic,* provided, of course, that "anarchic" is heard in a very special way: it is not from the "lived" or the "sensed" that one reaches the "said," but rather one "said" always engenders another. Deconstructive minorities, in holding language to be "anarchic," intend indeed to denounce all attempts to fasten language onto referents whose identity is guaranteed by "good" and "common" sense, reliable hard science, required competences, or entrenched conventions. But at the same time they are uneasy with the defensive Derridean strategies that reproduce in the space of language the Freudian dream of an interminable analysis. If emancipation from the reproductive proliferation of the dominant signifier is to become possible, if deconstruction is to intervene, not for the sake of the Other-in-general, but rather for the sake of the Other for whom *la prise de la parole* is an urgent task, then the circulation of the signifier—whether atheist, parodic, performative or whether devout, somber, and assertive—must be circumscribed by a purposiveness without purpose, even if one is convinced that the final hour of the Other and of the pure emancipatory utterance will never come. Against, therefore, defensive strategies aimed at preventing the conservative foreclosure of language through anaphoric identities and against the endless relay of signifiers through metaphoric differences, Deleuze and Guattari opt for the stuttering intervention of the minoritarian.

Order-words and passwords, for Deleuze and Guattari, are the contractions and dilations of language.[46] Order-words and passwords, without being coextensive with imperatives or commands, are the staging orders of discourse, without which no utterance can function. Radicalizing the work of Austin, Searle, and Apel, Deleuze and Guattari show that order-words and passwords are regulatory and verdictive. They are the implicit presuppositions of discursive practices, distinct from presuppositions that become explicit when utterances are interpreted by other utterances, and also distinct from actions that are extrinsic to them. Without these regulatory presuppositions, the articulation of the semiotic, semantic, pragmatic, and procedural features of language-games would not account for "pragmatic contradictions" or for the materiality of language. Deleuze insists that order-words and passwords depend upon concrete political spaces. To argue, therefore, as is often done, that politics is external to language is to turn a blind eye to the way language functions. Not only vocabulary but also syntax and semantics are transformed as order-words change and shift.

Deleuze and Guattari know of course that order-words and passwords do not have the same function. Order-words attempt to fuse language and to eliminate the space or the interval between types in order to bring the flight of signifiers to an abrupt halt. Consequently, they are techno-political devices that bring about conjunctive syntheses, exclusive disjunctions, hypotactic formations, and molar or subjugated groups. But at the other end of the linguistic continuum, the password "names the flight" and "speaks the things." The password functions as it breaks the blocks of identity, as it creates intervals, and as it makes language move (see part IV, essay 25). Its performativeness is reminiscent of the "estrangement-effect" that Russian formalists used to talk about.[47]

Order-words and passwords alike annex Being, and the annexation of Being is, in the Kantian project, the trace of politico-libidinal desires. But they do not annex Being in the same way. Order-words annex Being through identity-formation and subjection. Passwords annex Being through the repetition of differences. The fact is, though, that language is simultaneously crisscrossed by order-words and passwords without this fact disabling the evaluation of semiotic systems according to the preponderance of either order-words or passwords in them.

In *A Thousand Plateaus*, Deleuze and Guattari gave us a lengthy characterization of "nomad" (as opposed to "royal") sciences, and I find in this characterization a helpful access to the problematic of "nomad" arts as well.[48] Nomad arts mobilize material and forces instead of matter and form. Royal arts, being law oriented, strive to establish constants and, by means of an unchanging form, to discipline and control a supposedly reticent and unruly matter. Nomad arts, on the contrary, strive to put variables in a state of constant variation. The model for royal arts is hylomorphic, imposing form on secondary matter, that is, on matter that is already prepared to accept form. But in the case of nomad arts, matter is never prepared in advance, nor is it homogenized. It is rather "a vehicle of singularities which constitutes the form of the content. As for the expression, instead of being formal, it is inseparable from the pertinent characteristics, which constitute the matter of the expression."

In *Difference and Repetition*, Deleuze argued that the Idea-problem (or the *cogitandum*), in order to be grasped, requires a chain reaction of levels of intensity that must begin with sensible encounters.[49] Only the violence of the *sentiendum* would stand a chance of bringing about the resonance and the compossibility of all Ideas-problems. In 1981 Deleuze decided to face this violence seriously, choosing this time as his laboratory the paintings of the Irish artist Francis Bacon[50] (see part IV, essays 22 and 23). Struck by the powerful tensions that run through these paintings (tensions between figuration and defiguration; between disequilibrating, convulsive forces and an emerging balance; between motion and rest; contraction and expansion; destruction and creation) Deleuze concluded that their function is "to produce resemblances with non-resembling means." The violence of sensation tormenting Bacon's canvases trades off representation for the exploration of a world never before seen, yet strangely familiar and near. In his effort to escape the figurative and representative modes of narration and illustration and also the abstractness of pure form, Bacon aims at the liberation of the figure through iconic isolation. Through iconic isolation, that is, the neutralization of the background and the enclosure of figures in well-defined spaces, it prevents the figure from telling a story or from representing forms external to the canvas. Deleuze, faithful to his principle of transcendental empiricism, applauds the techniques of iconic isolation that turn figures into "matters of fact" and prevent their becoming situated inside a network of intelligible relations. Iconic isolation is the best training possible for those who look for an alternative to the phenomenology of natural perception in order to raise sensibility to its suprasensible destiny. It is also the best training possible for all those who, in Klee's happy phrase, want "not to render the visible, but to render visible."[51]

Instead of many sensations of different orders, Deleuze credits Bacon's painting with the ability to display different orders of one and the same sensation. Sensation, in his painting, is what happens between orders and levels. Indeed, Deleuze finds it more appropriate to talk of sensation and not of sensations, because sensations are extensive and contiguous, whereas sensation is intensive. Sensation is the figure, understood as the difference *of* the canvas.

None of this would be possible if sensation were to be thought of as a mere representation of the interaction of an eye and an object. But sensation is not the response to a form any more than Bacon's painting is a form-giving gesture. Sensation, contends Deleuze, is intimately related, not to forms but to forces, just as Bacon's painting aims at the capturing of force. And since a force must exert itself on a body for sensation to exist, force is the necessary condition of sensation, provided of course that sensation is not supposed to represent the force. It is "form . . . that subjugates force to a function, turns it against itself and transforms it into an energy of reproduction and conservation of forms."[52] Sensation, like force, brings things together in the very process of separating them. Now we understand what allows Deleuze to think of sensation in terms of different orders and levels: it is the fact that forces are intensities and therefore qualified as either high or low. Intensity permits us to talk about the multiplicity of sensation without having to appeal to many sensations. "Sensation," says Deleuze following Cézanne, "has one face turned toward the subject . . . and another, turned toward the object ('the fact,' the place, the event). Or rather, it does not have faces at all, it is both things at once; it is the being-in-the-world of the phenomenologists: *I become* in sensation, and at the same time *something happens* because of it. In the last analysis, the same body gives it and receives it, and this body is both object and subject."[53]

Painting, to be sure, is not the only fine art. Deleuze and Guattari find in music additional confirmation for their nomadic choice (see part IV, 24). Indeed, *A Thousand Plateaus* devotes some very intriguing pages to music and to the place that music has within the cosmos:[54] an entire chapter on "rhizomusicosmology"[55] defends a nontraditional approach to music, connecting it with molecular becomings, studying it for the sake of its "ametrical rhythms of the incommensurable and the unequal," and gleaning from it a method of experimentation with "the floating time of haecceities."

It is not the expression or the content of a work of art that capture the attention of Deleuze and Guattari. It is the form of the expression and the form of the content,[56] the parallelism established between the two, and their resonant association. A brief look at Deleuze's impressive work on cinema—*Cinema 1: The Movement-Image* and *Cinema 2: The Time-Image*[57]—makes this very clear. In these two volumes, Deleuze invites Bergson, the philosopher, to the movies in order to show him that his dismissal of the "cinematographic illusion," that is, of the reconstitution of movement on the basis of immobile slices or cuts, was in fact all too hasty. Cinema today, argues Deleuze, successfully meets Bergson's challenge, because the age of the camera verifies the system of universal variation that Bergson tried to articulate. Moreover, the eye of the camera transcends human perception toward another perception, which is the genetic element of every possible perception.

As they sample a wide variety of films—from silent to experimental—Deleuze and Bergson stop to savor the new image of thought that the filmmaker, experimenting with her new material, has also begun to articulate: the need for a nonhuman eye, an eye between and inside things, that only montage can satisfy in its quest for the "originary" world; the organic arrangement of movement-images of the American cinema, with D. W. Griffith setting the parts in binary oppositions and, through alternating or parallel montage, making the image of one part succeed the image of another according to a certain rhythm; the oppositional montage of the Russian Eisenstein under the dialectical law of the one divided into two in order to form a higher unity; the mathematical sublime of the classic French cinema, interested primarily in the quantity of movement and in the metric relations that would allow its determination; the dynamic sublime of German expressionism, which substitutes light for movement and ushers in intensity as the tremendous force that annihilates organic being, strikes it with terror, but also gives birth to a thinking faculty that makes us feel superior to the forces that annihilate us. The cinema is replete with movement-images, representing mobile "slices" of duration, with time-images, change-images, relation-images, action-images, and affect-images. There is framing and deframing (see part 4, essay 20), intervals operating with the force of intensive time (part 4, essay 21), spatial singularities and, above all, the Whole that is the Open—not the frame of all frames, but the unseen and the unrepresented that links frames together at the same time that it separates and differentiates them.

One word now about this *Reader:* it is the child of a frustration and the response to a challenge. Judging by recent publications and conferences, our Anglo-American discussions on "poststructuralism," "postmodernism," and "deconstruction" seem to be running out of steam. But the curious thing is that epitaphs and eulogies alike tend to bypass Gilles Deleuze, one of the most fertile minds of the last forty years. The name is mentioned—often with admiration—but Deleuze's texts are seldom used. This embarrassing silence is the source of the frustration from which this *Reader* was born.

Perhaps the silence is overdetermined. In the 1970s and 1980s the center of gravity of theoretical encounters of the "minor" kind shifted toward literary theory, feminist theory, and "dissident" sociology. But the space within which these encounters took place was already striated with exclusive disjunctions of North American vintage: pagan pluralism *or* hermeneutic pietas, phallogocentricism *or* being woman, positivist superficiality *or* genealogical investigations. On the other hand, the long and intimidating philosophical lineage of Deleuze's project, the long-standing reticence of the North American Freudo-Marxism even to entertain the suspicion that its war machine may have bred a "capture apparatus," the inoculation of our analysts with the Marcuse vaccine, and, last but not least, the fear of being identified with the "marginals" of the 1960s, have all contributed to the silence.

But to overlook Deleuze's theory of difference and repetition is to surrender the deconstructive space to the jejune logophobia of the epigoni: to refuse to name the Other on whose body power is inscribed in figures of cruelty, subjection, and forced reterritorialization is to silence the agent constantly mobilized in all deconstructive practices. To ignore Deleuze's theory of productive desire is to allow the Foucauldian emancipatory interest to fritter away in positivist investigations without ever revealing the "body without organs" that supports and sustains it. Finally, not to heed minor languages and minor deconstructive practices is to think wishfully that catachresic transgressions suffice by themselves to produce the event of speech and the *prise de la parole*.

With the selections included in this *Reader,* I have tried to trace a diagram zigzagging from one concept of Deleuze's to another, without obliterating the outline of his own canvas. In order to counterbalance, as much as possible, the arborescent (orderly and organic) tendencies of the *Reader,* or, at least, in order to remind the reader of the precautions s/he must take as s/he goes through this collection, I chose as my prefatory text long excerpts from Deleuze and Guattari's "Rhizome," the well-known introduction to *A Thousand Plateaus* (see part I, essay 1). Rather than "book-trees" and the arborescent reading that helps them grow taller, Deleuze and Guattari prefer book-rhizomes, rhizomatic writing, and schizoanalytic reading. Rhizomes may be broken at any point of their growth, without being prevented from spreading through a multitude of alternate lines. Rhizomatic writing and reading are therefore preferable for turning a text into a problem and for tracing its active lines of transformation, stuttering, and flight, or for preventing its canonization. Lines of flight help transform a text and deconstruct the primacy of its signifiers or signifieds. This *Reader* grows around the textual lines of flight marked "intensity," "desire," "power," "becoming-minoritarian," and "becoming-nomad." It counts on these lines to bring the anthologized texts to their decline, and writing with its authorial responsibility, to its demise or, at least, face to face with the kind of alterity that would no longer circulate and exchange or inspire and enshrine meaning.

The choice of the "Rhizome" as the opening statement of this *Reader* is also governed by another consideration. In 1968, when nomadic desire took its affirmation to the streets, Deleuze met Guattari. From 1970 to 1980 they wrote and grew together, giving us samples of writing that are convincingly rhizomatic. After eleven years of separate growth, with the publication of *Qu'est-ce que la philosophie?*[58] with both their names on the jacket, their active cooperation has been renewed. This *Reader* includes many texts from the earlier period of the *écriture à deux* and makes any attempt to draw lines of demarcation between the rhizome "Deleuze" and the rhizome "Guattari" pointless. Here is how Deleuze talks about his work with Guattari:

> My encounter with Félix Guattari changed a lot of things. Félix already had a long history of political involvement and of psychiatric work. . . . In my earlier books, I tried to describe a certain exercise of thought; but describing it was not yet exercising thought in that way. . . . With Félix, all that became possible, even if we failed. We were only two, but what was

important for us was less our working together than this strange fact of working between the two of us. And these "between-the-twos" referred back to other people, who were different on one side from on the other. The desert expanded, but in so doing became more populous.[59]

This *Reader* assumes a number of challenges: to bring to the center of our critical discussions Deleuze's philosophical references to the nomadic itinerary of Ideas, always already at war with the sedentary "image of thought"; to highlight texts that could prevent misreadings of rhizomatic desire from becoming canonic; to distinguish the minor deconstructive practices of Deleuze from the dominant "restrained" deconstruction of Derrida; to offer a sample of Deleuze's writings on nomad arts in search of the aesthetic Idea that has no intuition adequate to it; and to sketch the diagram of the political dilations and contractions of the body without organs. Whether accepting this challenge was a successful throw of the dice is not for me to say. Instead, it will be determined by the reader's desire to go beyond this volume, to the rhizome named "Deleuze," outside of the solarium that I, the editor, prepared for it. My only solace is that this selection was made as a labor of love and with the humiliating awareness that a *Reader* may not easily cast out its own arborescent tendencies.

Part One

. . .

Rhizome

Part One

Rhizoma

1
. . .
Rhizome Versus Trees

A first type of book is the root-book. The tree is already the image of the world, or the root the image of the world-tree. This is the classical book, as noble, signifying, and subjective organic interiority (the strata of the book). The book imitates the world, as art imitates nature: by procedures specific to it that accomplish what nature cannot or can no longer do. The law of the book is the law of reflection, the One that becomes two. How could the law of the book reside in nature, when it is what presides over the very division between world and book, nature and art? One becomes two: whenever we encounter this formula, even stated strategically by Mao or understood in the most "dialectical" way possible, what we have before us is the most classical and well reflected, oldest, and weariest kind of thought. Nature doesn't work that way: in nature, roots are taproots with a more multiple, lateral, and circular system of ramification, rather than a dichotomous one. Thought lags behind nature. Even the book as a natural reality is a taproot, with its pivotal spine and surrounding leaves. But the book as a spiritual reality, the Tree or Root as an image, endlessly develops the law of the One that becomes two, then of the two that become four . . . Binary logic is the spiritual reality of the root-tree. Even a discipline as "advanced" as linguistics retains the root-tree as its fundamental image, and thus remains wedded to classical reflection (for example, Chomsky and his grammatical trees, which begin at a point S and proceed by dichotomy). This is as much as to say that this system of thought has never reached an understanding of multiplicity: in order to arrive at two following a spiritual method it must assume a strong principal unity. On the side of the object, it is no doubt possible, following the natural method, to go directly from One to three, four, or five, but only if there is a strong principal unity available, that of the pivotal taproot supporting the secondary roots. That doesn't get us very far. The binary logic of dichotomy has simply been replaced by biunivocal relationships between successive circles. The pivotal taproot provides no better understanding of multiplicity than the dichotomous root. One operates in the object, the other in the subject. Binary logic and biunivocal relationships still dominate psychoanalysis (the tree of delusion in the Freudian interpretation of Schreber's case), linguistics, structuralism, and even information science.

The radicle-system, or fascicular root, is the second figure of the book, to which our modernity pays willing allegiance. This time, the principal root has aborted, or its tip has been destroyed; an immediate, indefinite multiplicity of secondary roots grafts onto it and undergoes a flourishing development. This time, natural reality is what aborts the principal root, but the root's unity subsists, as past or yet to come, as possible. We must ask if reflexive, spiritual reality does not compensate for this state of things by demanding an even more comprehensive secret unity, or a more extensive totality. Take William Burroughs's cut-up method: the folding of one text onto another, which constitutes multiple and even adventitious roots (like a cutting), implies a supplementary dimension to that of the texts under consideration. In this supplementary dimension of folding, unity continues its spiritual labor. That is why the most resolutely fragmented work can also be presented as the Total Work or Magnum Opus. Most modern methods for making series proliferate or a multiplicity grow are perfectly valid in one direction, for example, a linear direction, whereas a unity of totalization asserts itself even more firmly in another, circular or cyclic, dimension. Whenever a multiplicity is taken up in a structure, its growth is offset by a reduction in its laws of combination. The abortionists of unity are indeed angel makers, *doctores angelici*, because they affirm a properly angelic and superior unity. Joyce's words, accurately described as having "multiple roots," shatter the linear unity of the word, even of language, only to posit a cyclic unity of the sentence, text, or knowledge. Nietzsche's aphorisms shatter the linear unity of knowledge, only to invoke the cyclic unity of the eternal return, present as the nonknown in thought. This is as much as to say that the fascicular system does not really break with dualism, with the complementarity between a subject and an object, a natural reality and a spiritual reality:

unity is consistently thwarted and obstructed in the object, while a new type of unity triumphs in the subject. The world has lost its pivot; the subject can no longer even dichotomize, but accedes to a higher unity, of ambivalence or overdetermination, in an always supplementary dimension to that of its object. The world has become chaos, but the book remains the image of the world: radicle-chaosmos rather than root-cosmos. A strange mystification: a book all the more total for being fragmented. At any rate, what a vapid idea, the book as the image of the world. In truth, it is not enough to say, "Long live the multiple," difficult as it is to raise that cry. No typographical, lexical, or even syntactical cleverness is enough to make it heard. The multiple *must be made,* not by always adding a higher dimension, but rather in the simplest of ways, by dint of sobriety, with the number of dimensions one already has available—always $n - 1$ (the only way the one belongs to the multiple: always subtracted). Subtract the unique from the multiplicity to be constituted; write at $n - 1$ dimensions. A system of this kind could be called a rhizome. A rhizome as subterranean stem is absolutely different from roots and radicles. Bulbs and tubers are rhizomes. Plants with roots or radicles may be rhizomorphic in other respects altogether: the question is whether plant life in its specificity is not entirely rhizomatic. Even some animals are, in their pack form. Rats are rhizomes. Burrows are too, in all of their functions of shelter, supply, movement, evasion, and breakout. The rhizome itself assumes very diverse forms, from ramified surface extension in all directions to concretion into bulbs and tubers. When rats swarm over each other. The rhizome includes the best and the worst: potato and couchgrass, or the weed. Animal and plant, couchgrass is crabgrass. We get the distinct feeling that we will convince no one unless we enumerate certain approximate characteristics of the rhizome.

  1 and 2. Principles of connection and heterogeneity: any point of a rhizome can be connected to anything other, and must be. This is very different from the tree or root, which plots a point, fixes an order. The linguistic tree on the Chomsky model still begins at a point S and proceeds by dichotomy. On the contrary, not every trait in a rhizome is necessarily linked to a linguistic feature: semiotic chains of every nature are connected to very diverse modes of coding (biological, political, economic, etc.) that bring into play not only different regimes of signs but also states of things of differing status. *Collective assemblages of enunciation* function directly within *machinic assemblages;* it is not impossible to make a radical break between regimes of signs and their objects. Even when linguistics claims to confine itself to what is explicit and to make no presuppositions about language, it is still in the sphere of a discourse implying

particular modes of assemblage and types of social power. Chomsky's grammaticality, the categorical S symbol that dominates every sentence, is more fundamentally a marker of power than a syntactic marker: you will construct grammatically correct sentences, you will divide each statement into a noun phrase and a verb phrase (first dichotomy. . .). Our criticism of these linguistic models is not that they are too abstract but, on the contrary, that they are not abstract enough, that they do not reach the *abstract machine* that connects a language to the semantic and pragmatic contents of statements, to collective assemblages of enunciation, to a whole micropolitics of the social field. A rhizome ceaselessly establishes connections between semiotic chains, organizations of power, and circumstances relative to the arts, sciences, and social struggles. A semiotic chain is like a tuber agglomerating very diverse acts, not only linguistic, but also perceptive, mimetic, gestural, and cognitive: there is no language in itself, nor are there any linguistic universals, only a throng of dialects, patois, slangs, and specialized languages. There is no ideal speaker-listener, any more than there is a homogeneous linguistic community. Language is, in Weinreich's words, "an essentially heterogeneous reality."[1] There is no mother tongue, only a power takeover by a dominant language within a political multiplicity. Language stabilizes around a parish, a bishopric, a capital. It forms a bulb. It evolves by subterranean stems and flows, along river valleys or train tracks; it spreads like a patch of oil.[2] It is always possible to break a language down into internal structural elements, an undertaking not fundamentally different from a search for roots. There is always something genealogical about a tree. It is not a method for the people. A method of the rhizome type, on the contrary, can analyze language only by decentering it onto other dimensions and other registers. A language is never closed upon itself, except as a function of impotence.

3. Principle of multiplicity: it is only when the multiple is effectively treated as a substantive, "multiplicity," that it ceases to have any relation to the One as subject or object, natural or spiritual reality, image and world. Multiplicities are rhizomatic, and expose arborescent pseudomultiplicities for what they are. There is no unity to serve as a pivot in the object, or to divide in the subject. There is not even the unity to abort in the object or "return" in the subject. A multiplicity has neither subject nor object, only determinations, magnitudes, and dimensions that cannot increase in number without the multiplicity changing in nature (the laws of combination therefore increase in number as the multiplicity grows). Puppet strings, as a rhizome or multiplicity, are tied not to the supposed will of an artist or puppeteer but to a multiplicity of nerve fi-

bers, which form another puppet in other dimensions connected to the first: "Call the strings or rods that move the puppet the weave. It might be objected that *its multiplicity* resides in the person of the actor, who projects it into the text. Granted; but the actor's nerve fibers in turn form a weave. And they fall through the gray matter, the grid, into the undifferentiated. . . . The interplay approximates the pure activity of weavers attributed in myth to the Fates or Norns."[3] An assemblage is precisely this increase in the dimensions of a multiplicity that necessarily changes in nature as it expands its connections. There are no points or positions in a rhizome, such as those found in a structure, tree, or root. There are only lines. When Glenn Gould speeds up the performance of a piece, he is not just displaying virtuosity, he is transforming the musical points into lines, he is making the whole piece proliferate. The number is no longer a universal concept measuring elements according to their emplacement in a given dimension, but has itself become a multiplicity that varies according to the dimensions considered (the primacy of the domain over a complex of numbers attached to that domain). We do not have units [*unités*] of measure, only multiplicities or varieties of measurement. The notion of unity [*unité*] appears only when there is a power takeover in the multiplicity by the signifier or a corresponding subjectification proceeding: This is the case for a pivot-unity forming the basis for a set of biunivocal relationships between objective elements or points, or for the One that divides following the law of a binary logic of differentiation in the subject. Unity always operates in an empty dimension supplementary to that of the system considered (overcoding). The point is that a rhizome or multiplicity never allows itself to be overcoded, never has available a supplementary dimension over and above its number of lines, that is, over and above the multiplicity of numbers attached to those lines. All multiplicities are flat, in the sense that they fill or occupy all of their dimensions: we will therefore speak of a *plane of consistency* of multiplicities, even though the dimensions of this "plane" increase with the number of connections that are made on it. Multiplicities are defined by the outside: by the abstract line, the line of flight or deterritorialization according to which they change in nature and connect with other multiplicities. The plane of consistency (grid) is the outside of all multiplicities. The line of flight marks: the reality of a finite number of dimensions that the multiplicity effectively fills; the impossibility of a supplementary dimension, unless the multiplicity is transformed by the line of flight; the possibility and necessity of flattening all of the multiplicities on a single plane of consistency or exteriority, regardless of their number of dimensions. The ideal for a book would be to lay everything out on a plane of exteriority of this kind, on a single page, the same sheet: lived events, historical determinations, concepts, individuals, groups, social formations. Kleist invented a writing of this type, a broken chain of affects and variable speeds, with accelerations and transformations, always in a relation with the outside. Open rings. His texts, therefore, are opposed in every way to the classical or romantic book constituted by the interiority of a substance or subject. The war machine–book against the State apparatus–book. *Flat multiplicities of n dimensions* are asignifying and asubjective. They are designated by indefinite articles, or rather by partitives (*some* couchgrass, *some* of a rhizome. . .).

4. Principle of asignifying rupture: against the oversignifying breaks separating structures or cutting across a single structure. A rhizome may be broken, shattered at a given spot, but it will start up again on one of its old lines, or on new lines. You can never get rid of ants because they form an animal rhizome that can rebound time and again after most of it has been destroyed. Every rhizome contains lines of segmentarity according to which it is stratified, territorialized, organized, signified, attributed, etc., as well as lines of deterritorialization down which it constantly flees. There is a rupture in the rhizome whenever segmentary lines explode into a line of flight, but the line of flight is part of the rhizome. These lines always tie back to one another. That is why one can never posit a dualism or a dichotomy, even in the rudimentary form of the good and the bad. You may make a rupture, draw a line of flight, yet there is still a danger that you will reencounter organizations that restratify everything, formations that restore power to a signifier, attributions that reconstitute a subject—anything you like, from Oedipal resurgences to fascist concretions. Groups and individuals contain microfascisms just waiting to crystallize. Yes, couchgrass is also a rhizome. Good and bad are only the products of an active and temporary selection, which must be renewed.

How could movements of deterritorialization and processes of reterritorialization not be relative, always connected, caught up in one another? The orchid deterritorializes by forming an image, a tracing of a wasp; but the wasp reterritorializes on that image. The wasp is nevertheless deterritorialized, becoming a piece in the orchid's reproductive apparatus. But it reterritorializes the orchid by transporting its pollen. Wasp and orchid, as heterogeneous elements, form a rhizome. It could be said that the orchid imitates the wasp, reproducing its image in a signifying fashion (mimesis, mimicry, lure, etc.). But this is true only on the level of the strata—a parallelism between two strata such that a plant organization on one imitates an animal organization on the other. At the same time, something else entirely is going on: not imitation at all but a capture of code, surplus value of code, an increase in valence, a veritable becoming, a becoming-wasp of the orchid and a becoming-orchid of the wasp. Each of these becomings brings about the deterritorialization of one term and the reterritorialization of the other; the two becomings interlink and form relays in a circulation of intensities pushing the deterritorialization ever further. There is neither imitation nor resemblance, only an exploding of two heterogeneous series on the line of flight composed by a common rhizome that can no longer be attributed to or subjugated by anything signifying. Rémy Chauvin expresses it well: "the *aparallel evolution* of two beings that have absolutely nothing to do with each other."[4] More generally, evolutionary schemas may be forced to abandon the old model of the tree and descent. Under certain conditions, a virus can connect to germ cells and transmit itself as the cellular gene of a complex species; moreover, it can take flight, move into the cells of an entirely different species, but not without bringing with it "genetic information" from the first host (for example, Benveniste and Todaro's current research on a type C virus, with its double connection to baboon DNA and the DNA of certain kinds of domestic cats). Evolutionary schemas would no longer follow models of arborescent descent going from the least to the most differentiated, but instead a rhizome operating immediately in the heterogeneous and jumping from one already differentiated line to another.[5] Once again, there is *aparallel evolution,* of the baboon and the cat; it is obvious that they are not models or copies of each other (a becoming-baboon in the cat does not mean that the cat "plays" baboon). We form a rhizome with our viruses, or rather our viruses cause us to form a rhizome with other animals. As François Jacob says, transfers of genetic material by viruses or through other procedures, fusions of cells originating in different species, have results analogous to those of "the abominable couplings dear to antiquity and the Middle Ages."[6] Transversal communications between different lines scramble the genealogical trees. Always look for the molecular, or even submolecular, particle with which we are allied. We evolve and die more from our polymorphous and rhizomatic flus than from hereditary diseases, or diseases that have their own line of descent. The rhizome is an antigenealogy.

The same applies to the book and the world: contrary to a deeply rooted belief, the book is not an image of the world. It forms a rhizome with the world, there is an aparallel evolution of the book and the world; the book assures the deterritorialization of the world, but the world effects a reterritorialization of the book, which in turn deterritorializes itself in the world (if it is capable, if it can). Mimicry is a very bad concept, since it relies on binary logic to describe phenomena of an entirely different nature. The crocodile does not reproduce a tree trunk, any more than the chameleon reproduces the colors of its surroundings. The Pink Panther imitates nothing, it reproduces nothing, it paints the world its color, pink on pink; this is its becoming-world, carried out in such a way that it becomes imperceptible itself, asignifying, makes its rupture, its own line of flight, follows its "aparallel evolution" through to the end. The wisdom of the plants: even when they have roots, there is always an outside where they form a rhizome with something else—with the wind, an animal, human beings (and there is also an aspect under which animals themselves form rhizomes, as do people, etc.). "Drunkenness as a triumphant irruption of the plant in us." Always follow the rhizome by rupture; lengthen, prolong, and relay the line of flight; make it vary, until you have produced the most abstract and tortuous of lines of n dimensions and broken directions. Conjugate deterritorialized flows. Follow the plants: you start by delimiting a first line consisting of circles of convergence around successive singularities; then you see whether inside that line new circles of convergence establish themselves, with new points located outside the limits and in other directions. Write, form a rhizome, increase your territory by deterritorialization, extend the line of flight to the point where it becomes an abstract machine covering the entire plane of consistency. "Go first to your old plant and watch carefully the watercourse made by the rain. By now the rain must have carried the seeds far away. Watch the crevices made by the runoff, and from them determine the direction of the flow. Then find the plant that is growing at the farthest point from your plant. All the devil's weed plants that are growing in between are yours. Later . . . you can extend the size of your territory by following the watercourse from each point along the way."[7] Music has always sent out lines of flight, like so many "transformational multiplicities," even overturning the very codes that structure or arborify it; that is why musical form, right down to its ruptures and proliferations, is comparable to a weed, a rhizome.[8]

5 and 6. Principle of cartography and decalcomania: a rhizome is not amenable to any structural or generative model. It is a stranger to any idea of genetic axis or deep structure. A genetic axis is like an objective pivotal unity upon which successive stages are organized; a deep structure is more like a base sequence that can be broken down into immediate constituents, while the unity of the product passes into another, transformational and subjective, dimensions. This does not constitute a departure from the representative model of the tree, or root—pivotal taproot or fascicles (for example, Chomsky's "tree" is associated with a base sequence and represents the process of its own generation in terms

of binary logic). A variation on the oldest form of thought. It is our view that genetic axis and profound structure are above all infinitely reproducible principles of *tracing*. All of tree logic is a logic of tracing and reproduction. In linguistics as in psychoanalysis, its object is an unconscious that is itself representative, crystallized into codified complexes, laid out along a genetic axis and distributed within a syntagmatic structure. Its goal is to describe a de facto state, to maintain balance in intersubjective relations, or to explore an unconscious that is already there from the start, lurking in the dark recesses of memory and language. It consists of tracing, on the basis of an overcoding structure or supporting axis, something that comes ready-made. The tree articulates and hierarchizes tracings; tracings are like the leaves of a tree.

The rhizome is altogether different, a *map and not a tracing*. Make a map, not a tracing. The orchid does not reproduce the tracing of the wasp; it forms a map with the wasp, in a rhizome. What distinguishes the map from the tracing is that it is entirely oriented toward an experimentation in contact with the real. The map does not reproduce an unconscious closed in upon itself; it constructs the unconscious. It fosters connections between fields, the removal of blockages on bodies without organs, the maximum opening of bodies without organs onto a plane of consistency. It is itself a part of the rhizome. The map is open and connectable in all of its dimensions; it is detachable, reversible, susceptible to constant modification. It can be torn, reversed, adapted to any kind of mounting, reworked by an individual, group, or social formation. It can be drawn on a wall, conceived of as a work of art, constructed as a political action or as a meditation. Perhaps one of the most important characteristics of the rhizome is that it always has multiple entryways; in this sense, the burrow is an animal rhizome, and sometimes maintains a clear distinction between the line of flight as passageway and storage or living strata (cf. the muskrat). A map has multiple entryways, as opposed to the tracing, which always comes back "to the same." The map has to do with performance, whereas the tracing always involves an alleged "competence." . . .

Let us summarize the principal characteristics of a rhizome: unlike trees or their roots, the rhizome connects any point to any other point, and its traits are not necessarily linked to traits of the same nature; it brings into play very different regimes of signs, and even nonsign states. The rhizome is reducible neither to the One nor the multiple. It is not the One that becomes Two or even directly three, four, five, etc. It is not a multiple derived from the One, or to which One is added ($n + 1$). It is composed not of units but of dimensions, or rather directions in motion. It has neither beginning nor end, but always a middle [*milieu*] from which it grows and which it over-spills. It constitutes linear multiplicities with n dimensions having neither subject nor object, which can be laid out on a plane of consistency, and from which the One is always subtracted $(n - 1)$. When a multiplicity of this kind changes dimensions, it necessarily changes in nature as well, undergoes a metamorphosis. Unlike a structure, which is defined by a set of points and positions, with binary relations between the points and biunivocal relation-ships between the positions, the rhizome is made only of lines: lines of seg-mentarity and stratification as its dimensions, and the line of flight or deter-ritorialization as the maximum dimension after which the multiplicity undergoes metamorphosis, changes in nature. These lines, or lineaments, should not be confused with lineages of the arborescent type, which are merely localizable linkages between points and positions. Unlike the tree, the rhizome is not the object of reproduction: neither external reproduction as image-tree nor internal reproduction as tree-structure. The rhizome is an antigenealogy. It is a short-term memory, or antimemory. The rhizome op-erates by variation, expansion, conquest, capture, offshoots. Unlike the graphic arts, drawing, or photography, unlike tracings, the rhizome per-tains to a map that must be produced, constructed, a map that is always detachable, connectable, reversible, modifiable, and has multiple en-tryways and exits and its own lines of flight. It is tracings that must be put on the map, not the opposite. In contrast to centered (even polycentric) sys-tems with hierarchical modes of communication and preestablished paths, the rhizome is an acentered, nonhierarchical, nonsignifying system without a General and without an organizing memory or central automaton, de-fined solely by a circulation of states. What is at question in the rhizome is a relation to sexuality—but also to the animal, the vegetal, the world, poli-tics, the book, things natural and artificial—that is totally different from the arborescent relation: all manner of "becomings."

Part Two

. . .

Difference and Repetition

2

. . .

What Is Becoming?

Alice and *Through the Looking-Glass* involve a category of very special things: events, pure events. When I say "Alice becomes larger," I mean that she becomes larger than she was. By the same token, however, she becomes smaller than she is now. Certainly, she is not bigger and smaller at the same time. She is larger now; she was smaller before. But it is at the same moment that one becomes larger than one was and smaller than one becomes. This is the simultaneity of a becoming whose characteristic is to elude the present. Insofar as it eludes the present, becoming does not tolerate the separation or the distinction of before and after, or of past and future. It pertains to the essence of becoming to move and to pull in both directions at once: Alice does not grow without shrinking, and vice versa. Good sense affirms that in all things there is a determinable sense or direction [*sens*]; but paradox is the affirmation of both senses or directions at the same time.

Plato invites us to distinguish between two dimensions: (1) that of limit- ed and measured things, of fixed qualities, permanent or temporary which always presuppose pauses and rests, the fixing of presents, and the assigna- tion of subjects (for example, a particular subject having a particular large- ness or a particular smallness at a particular moment); and (2) a pure be- coming without measure, a veritable becoming-mad, which never rests. It moves in both directions at once. It always eludes the present, causing future and past, more and less, too much and not enough to coincide in the simultaneity of a rebellious matter. " 'Hotter' never stops where it is but is always going a point further, and the same applies to 'colder,' where as definite quality is something that has stopped going on and is fixed"; ". . . the younger becoming older than the older, the older becoming younger than the younger—but they can never finally become so; if they did they would no longer be becoming, but would be so."[1]

We recognize this Platonic dualism. It is not at all the dualism of the intelligible and the sensible, of Idea and matter, or of Ideas and bodies. It is a more profound and secret dualism hidden in sensible and material bodies themselves. It is a subterranean dualism between that which receives the action of the Idea and that which eludes this action. It is not the distinction between the Model and the copy, but rather between copies and simulacra. Pure becoming, the unlimited, is the matter of the simulacrum insofar as it eludes the action of the Idea and insofar as it contests *both* model *and* copy at once. Limited things lie beneath the Ideas; but even beneath things, is there not still this mad element which subsists and occurs on the other side of the order that Ideas impose and things receive? Sometimes Plato wonders whether this pure becoming might not have a very peculiar relation to language. This seems to be one of the principal meanings of the *Cratylus*. Could this relation be, perhaps, essential to language, as in the case of a "flow" of speech, or a wild discourse which would incessantly slide over its referent, without ever stopping? Or might there not be two languages and two sorts of "names," one designating the pauses and rests which receive the action of the Idea, the other expressing the movements or rebel becomings?[2] Or further still, is it not possible that there are two distinct dimensions internal to language in general—one always concealed by the other, yet continuously coming to the aid of, or subsisting under, the other?

The paradox of this pure becoming, with its capacity to elude the present, is the paradox of infinite identity (the infinite identity of both directions or senses at the same time—of future and past, of the day before and the day after, of more and less, of too much and not enough, of active and passive, and of cause and effect). It is language which fixes the limits (the moment, for example, at which the excess begins), but it is language as well which transcends the limits and restores them to the infinite equivalence of an unlimited becoming ("A red-hot poker will burn you if you hold it too long; and . . . if you cut your finger *very* deeply with a knife, it usually bleeds"). Hence the reversals which constitute Alice's adventures: the reversal of becoming larger and becoming smaller—"which way, which way?" asks Alice, sensing that it is always in both directions at the same time, so that for once she stays the same, through an optical illusion; the reversal of the day before and the day after, the present always being eluded—"jam tomorrow and jam yesterday—but never jam *to-day*"; the reversal of more and less: five nights are five times hotter than a single one, "but they must be five times as cold for the same reason"; the reversal of active and passive: "do cats eat bats?" is as good as "do bats eat cats?"; the reversal of cause and effect: to be punished before having committed a fault, to cry before having pricked oneself, to serve before having divided up the servings.

All these reversals as they appear in infinite identity have one consequence: the contesting of Alice's personal identity and the loss of her proper name. The loss of the proper name is the adventure which is repeated throughout all Alice's adventures. For the proper or singular name is guaranteed by the permanence of *savoir*. The latter is embodied in general names designating pauses and rests, in substantives and adjectives, with which the proper name maintains a constant connection. Thus the personal self requires God and the world in general. But when substantives and adjectives begin to dissolve, when the names of pause and rest are carried away by the verbs of pure becoming and slide into the language of events, all identity disappears from the self, the world, and God. This is the test of *savoir* and recitation which strips Alice of her identity. In it words may go awry, being obliquely swept away by the verbs. It is as if events enjoyed an irreality which is communicated through language to the *savoir* and to persons. For personal uncertainty is not a doubt foreign to what is happening, but rather an objective structure of the event itself, insofar as it moves in two directions at once, and insofar as it fragments the subject following this double direction. Paradox is initially that which destroys good sense as the only direction, but it is also that which destroys common sense as the assignation of fixed identities.

3
. . .
What Is an Event?

The Stoics also distinguish between two kinds of things. First, there are bodies with their tensions, physical qualities, actions and passions, and the corresponding "states of affairs." These states of affairs, actions and passions, are determined by the mixtures of bodies. At the limit, there is a unity of all bodies in virtue of a primordial Fire into which they become absorbed and from which they develop according to their respective tensions. The only time of bodies and states of affairs is the present. For the living present is the temporal extension which accompanies the act, expresses and measures the action of the agent and the passion of the patient. But to the degree that there is a unity of bodies among themselves, to the degree that there is a unity of active and passive principles, a cosmic present embraces the entire universe: only bodies exist in space, and only the present exists in time. There are no causes *and* effects among bodies. Rather, all bodies are causes—causes in relation to each other and for each other. In the scope of the cosmic present, the unity is called Destiny.

Second, all bodies are causes in relation to each other, and causes for each other—but causes of what? They are causes of certain things of an entirely different nature. These *effects* are not bodies, but, properly speaking, "incorporeal" entities. They are not physical qualities and properties, but rather logical or dialectical attributes. They are not things or facts, but events. We can not say that they exist, but rather that they subsist or insist (having this minimum of being which is appropriate to that which is not a thing, a nonexisting entity). They are not substantives or adjectives but verbs. They are neither agents nor patients, but results of actions and passions. They are "impassive" entities—impassive results. They are not living presents, but infinities: the unlimited Aeon, the becoming which divides itself infinitely in past and future and always eludes the present. Thus time must be grasped twice, in two complementary though mutually exclusive fashions. First, it must be grasped entirely as the living present in bodies which act and are acted upon. Second, it must be grasped entirely as an entity infinitely divisible into past and future, and into the incorporeal effects which result from bodies, their actions and their passions. Only the present exists in time and gathers together or absorbs the past and future. But only the past and future insist in time and divide each present infinitely. These are not three successive dimensions, but two simultaneous readings of time.

In his fine reconstruction of Stoic thought, Emile Bréhier says:

> When the scalpel cuts through the flesh, the first body produces upon the second not a new property but a new attribute, that of being cut. The *attribute* does not designate any real *quality* . . . , it is, to the contrary, always expressed by the verb, which means that it is not a being, but a way of being. . . . This way of being finds itself somehow at the limit, at the surface of being, the nature of which it is not able to change: it is, in fact, neither active nor passive, for passivity would presuppose a corporeal nature which undergoes an action. It is purely and simply a result, or an effect which is not to be classified among beings. . . . [The Stoics distinguished] radically two planes of being, something that no one had done before them: on the one hand, real and profound being, force; on the other, the plane of facts, which frolic on the surface of being, and constitute an endless multiplicity of incorporeal beings.[1]

Yet, what is more intimate or essential to bodies than events such as growing, becoming smaller, or being cut? What do the Stoics mean when they contrast the thickness of bodies with these incorporeal events which would play only on the surface, like a mist over the prairie (even less than a mist, since a mist is after all a body)? Mixtures are in bodies, and in the depth of bodies: a body penetrates another and coexists with it in all of its parts, like a drop of wine in the ocean, or fire in iron. One body withdraws from another, like liquid from a vase. Mixtures in general determine the quantitative and qualitative states of affairs: the dimensions of an ensemble—the red of iron, the green of a tree. But what we mean by "to grow," "to diminish," "to become red," "to become green," "to cut," and "to be cut," etc., is something entirely different. These are no longer states of affairs—mixtures deep inside bodies—but incorporeal events at the surface which are the results of these mixtures. The tree "greens." . . .[2] The genius of a philosophy must first be measured by the new distribution which it imposes on beings and concepts. The Stoics are in the process of tracing out and of forming a frontier where there had not been one before. In this sense they displace all reflection.

They are in the process of bringing about, first, an entirely new cleavage of the causal relation. They dismember this relation, even at the risk of re-creating a unity on each side. They refer causes to causes and place a bond of causes between them (destiny). They refer effects to effects and pose certain bonds of effects between them. But these two operations are not accomplished in the same manner. Incorporeal effects are never themselves causes in relation to each other; rather, they are only "quasi-causes" following laws which perhaps express in each case the relative unity or mixture of bodies on which they depend for their real causes. Thus freedom is preserved in two complementary manners: once in the interiority of destiny as a connection between causes, and once more in the exteriority of events as a bond of effects. For this reason the Stoics can oppose destiny and necessity.[3] The Epicureans formulated another cleavage of causality, which also grounds freedom. They conserve the homogeneity of cause and effect, but cut up causality according to atomic series whose respective independence is guaranteed by the *clinamen*—no longer destiny without necessity, but causality without destiny.[4] In either case, one begins by splitting the causal relation, instead of distinguishing types of causality as Aristotle had done and Kant would do. And this split always refers us back to language, either to the existence of a *declension* of causes or, as we shall see, to the existence of a *conjugation* of effects.

This new dualism of bodies or states of affairs and effects or incorporeal events entails an upheaval in philosophy. In Aristotle, for example, all categories are said of Being; and difference is present in Being, between substance as the primary sense and the other categories which are related to it as accidents. For the Stoics, on the other hand, states of affairs, quantities, and qualities are no less beings (or bodies) than substance is; they are a part of substance, and in this sense they are contrasted with an *extra-Being* which constitutes the incorporeal as a nonexisting entity. The highest term therefore is not Being, but *Something (aliquid)*, insofar as it subsumes being and nonbeing, existence and inherence.[5] Moreover, the Stoics are the first to reverse Platonism and to bring about a radical inversion. For if bodies with their states, qualities, and quantities, assume all the characteristics of substance and cause, conversely, the characteristics of the Idea are relegated to the other side, that is to this impassive extra-Being which is sterile, inefficacious, and on the surface of things: *the ideational or the incorporeal can no longer be anything other than an "effect."*

These consequences are extremely important. In Plato, an obscure debate was raging in the depth of things, in the depth of the earth, between that which undergoes the action of the Idea and that which eludes this action (copies and simulacra). An echo of this debate resonates when Socrates asks: is there an Idea of everything, even of hair, dirt, and mud—or rather is there something which always and obstinately escapes the Idea? In Plato, however, this something is never sufficiently hidden, driven back, pushed deeply into the depth of the body, or drowned in the ocean. *Everything now returns to the surface.* This is the result of the Stoic operation: the unlimited returns. Becoming-mad, becoming unlimited is no longer a ground which rumbles. It climbs to the surface of things and becomes impassive. It is no longer a question of simulacra which elude the ground and insinuate themselves everywhere, but rather a question of effects which manifest themselves and act in their place. These are effects in the causal sense, but also sonorous, optical, or linguistic "effects"—and even less, or much more, since they are no longer corporeal entities, but rather form the entire Idea. What was eluding the Idea climbed up to the surface, that is, the incorporeal limit, and represents now all possible *ideality,* the latter being stripped of its causal and spiritual efficacy. The Stoics discovered surface effects. Simulacra cease to be subterranean rebels and make the most of their effects (that is, what might be called "phantasms," independently of the Stoic terminology). The most concealed becomes the most manifest. All the old paradoxes of becoming must again take shape in a new youthfulness—transmutation.

Becoming unlimited comes to be the ideational and incorporeal event, with all of its characteristic reversals between future and past, active and passive, cause and effect, more and less, too much and not enough, already and not yet. The infinitely divisible event is always *both at once.* It is eternally that which has just happened and that which is about to happen, but never that which is happening (to cut too deeply and not enough). The event, being itself impassive, allows the active and the passive to be interchanged more easily, since it is *neither the one nor the other,* but rather their common result (to cut—to be cut). Concerning the cause and the effect, events, *being always only effects,* are better able to form among themselves functions of quasi-causes or relations of quasi-causality which are always reversible (the wound and the scar).

The Stoics are amateurs and inventors of paradoxes. It is necessary to reread the astonishing portrait of Chrysippus given in several pages written by Diogenes Laertius. Perhaps the Stoics used the paradox in a completely new manner—both as an instrument for the analysis of language and as a means of synthesizing events. *Dialectics* is precisely this science of incorporeal events as they are expressed in propositions, and of the connections between events as they are expressed in relations between propositions. Dialectics is, indeed, the art of *conjugation* (see the *confatalia* or series of events which depend on one another). But it is the task of language both to establish limits and to go beyond them. Therefore language includes terms which do not cease to displace their extension and which make possible a reversal of the connection in a given series (thus too much and not enough, few and many). The event is coextensive with becoming, and becoming is itself coextensive with language; the paradox is thus essentially a "sorites," that is, a series of interrogative propositions which, following becoming, proceed through successive additions and retrenchments. Everything happens at the boundary between things and propositions. Chrysippus taught: "If you say something, it passes through your lips; so, if you say 'chariot,' a chariot passes through your lips." Here is a use of paradox the only equivalents of which are to be found in Zen Buddhism, on one hand, and in English or American *nonsense,* on the other. In one case, that which is most profound is the immediate, in the other, the immediate is found in language. Paradox appears as a dismissal of depth, a display of events at the surface, and a deployment of language along this limit. Humor is the art of the surface, which is opposed to the old irony, the art of depths and heights. The Sophists and Cynics had already made humor a philosophical weapon against Socratic irony; but with the Stoics, humor found its dialectics, its dialectical principle or its natural place and its pure philosophical concept.

Lewis Carroll carries out this operation, inaugurated by the Stoics, or rather, he takes it up again. In all his works, Carroll examines the difference between events, things, and states of affairs. But the entire first half of *Alice* still seeks the secret of events and of the becoming unlimited which they imply, in the depths of the earth, in dug out shafts and holes which plunge beneath, and in the mixture of bodies which interpenetrate and coexist. As one advances in the story, however, the digging and hiding gives way to a lateral sliding from right to left and left to right. The animals below ground become secondary, giving way to *card figures* which have no thickness. One could say that the old depth having been spread out became width. The becoming unlimited is maintained entirely within this inverted width. "Depth" is no longer a complement. Only animals are deep, and they are not the noblest for that; the noblest are the flat animals. Events are like crystals, they become and grow only out of the edges, or on the edge. This is, indeed, the first secret of the stammerer or of the left-handed person: no longer to sink, but to slide the whole length in such a way that the old depth no longer exists at all, having been reduced to the opposite side of the surface. By sliding, one passes to the other side, since the other side is nothing but the opposite direction. If there is nothing to see behind the curtain, it is because everything is visible, or rather all possible science is along the length of the curtain. It suffices to follow it far enough, precisely enough, and superficially enough, in order to reverse sides and to make the right side become the left or vice versa. It is not therefore a question of *the adventures* of Alice, but of Alice's *adventure:* her climb to the surface, her disavowal of false depth and her discovery that everything happens at the border. This is why Carroll abandons the original title of the book: *Alice's Adventures Underground.*

This is the case—even more so—in *Through the Looking-Glass.* Here events, differing radically from things, are no longer sought in the depths, but at the surface, in the faint incorporeal mist which escapes from bodies, a film without volume which envelops them, a mirror which reflects them, a chessboard on which they are organized according to plan. Alice is no longer able to make her way through to the depths. Instead, she releases her incorporeal double. *It is by following the border, by skirting the surface, that one passes from bodies to the incorporeal.* Paul Valéry had a profound idea: what is most deep is the skin. This is a Stoic discovery, which presupposes a great deal of wisdom and entails an entire ethic. It is the discovery of the little girl, who grows and diminishes only from the edges—a surface which reddens and becomes green. She knows that the more the events traverse the entire, depthless extension, the more they affect bodies which they cut and bruise. Later, the adults are snapped up by the ground, fall again, and, being too deep, they no longer understand. Why do the same Stoic examples continue to inspire Lewis Carroll?—the tree greens, the scalpel cuts, the battle will or will not take place. . . . It is in front of the trees that Alice loses her name. It is a tree which Humpty Dumpty addresses without looking at Alice. Recitations announce battles, and everywhere there are injuries and cuts. But are these examples? Or rather, is it the case that every event is of this type— forest, battle, and wound—all the more profound since *it* occurs at the surface? The more it skirts bodies, the more incorporeal it is. History teaches us that sound roads have no foundation, and geography that only a thin layer of the earth is fertile.

This rediscovery of the Stoic sage is not reserved to the little girl. Indeed, it is true that Lewis Carroll detests boys in general. They have too much depth, and false depth at that, false wisdom, and animality. The male baby in *Alice* is transformed into a pig. As a general rule, only little girls understand Stoicism; they have the sense of the event and release an incorporeal double. But it happens sometimes that a little boy is a stutterer and lefthanded, and thus conquers sense as the double sense or direction of the surface. Carroll's hatred of boys is not attributable to a deep ambivalence, but rather to a superficial inversion, a properly Carrollian concept. In *Sylvie and Bruno*, it is the little boy who has the inventive role, learning his lessons in all manners, inside-out, outside-in, above and below, but never "in depth." This important novel pushes to the extreme the evolution which had begun in *Alice,* and which continued in *Through the Looking-Glass.* The admirable conclusion of the first part is to the glory of the East, from which comes all that is good, "the substance of things hoped for, and the existence of things not seen." Here even the barometer neither rises nor falls, but goes lengthwise, sideways, and gives a horizontal weather. A stretching machine even lengthens songs. And Fortunatus' purse, presented as a Möbius strip, is made of handkerchiefs sewn *in the wrong way,* in such a manner that its outer surface is continuous with its inner surface: it envelops the entire world, and makes that which is inside be on the outside and vice versa.[6] In *Sylvie and Bruno,* the technique of passing from reality to dream, and from bodies to the incorporeal, is multiplied, completely renewed, and carried out to perfection. It is, however, still by skirting the surface, or the border, that one passes to the other side, by virtue of the strip. The continuity between reverse and right side replaces all the levels of depth; and the surface effects in one and the same Event, which would hold for all events, bring to language becoming and its paradoxes.[7] As Carroll says in an article entitled "The Dynamics of a Parti-cle": "Plain Superficiality is the character of a speech. . . ."

4
. . .
What Is a Multiplicity?

Let us summarize the principal characteristics of a punctual system: (1) Systems of this kind comprise two base lines, horizontal and vertical: they serve as coordinates for assigning points. (2) The horizontal line can be superposed vertically and the vertical line can be moved horizontally, in such a way that new points are produced or reproduced, under conditions of horizontal frequency and vertical resonance. (3) From one point to another, a line can (or cannot) be drawn, but if it can it takes the form of a localizable connection; diagonals thus play the role of connectors between points of different levels or moments, instituting in their turn frequencies and resonances on the basis of these points of variable horizon or verticon, contiguous or distant.[1] These systems are arborescent, mnemonic, molar, structural: they are systems of territorialization or reterritorialization. The line and the diagonal remain totally subordinated to the point because they serve as coordinates for a point or as localizable connections for two points, running from one point to another.

Opposed to the punctual system are linear, or rather multilinear, systems. Free the line, free the diagonal: every musician or painter has this intention. One elaborates a punctual system or a didactic representation, but with the aim of making it snap, of sending a tremor through it. A punctual system is most interesting when there is a musician, painter, writer, philosopher to oppose it, who even fabricates it in order to oppose it, like a springboard to jump from. History is made only by those who oppose history (not by those who insert themselves into it, or even reshape it). This is not done for provocation but happens because the punctual system they found ready-made, or themselves invented, must have allowed this operation: free the line and the diagonal, draw the line instead of plotting a point, produce an imperceptible diagonal instead of clinging to an even elaborated or reformed vertical or horizontal. When this is done it always goes down in history but never comes from it. History may try to break its ties to memory; it may make the schemas of memory more elaborate, superpose and shift coordinates, emphasize connections, or deepen breaks. The dividing line, however, is not there. The dividing line passes not between history and memory but between punctual "history-memory" systems and diagonal or multilinear assemblages, which are in no way eternal: they have to do with becoming; they are a bit of becoming in the pure state; they are transhistorical. There is no act of creation that is not transhistorical and does not come up from behind or proceed by way of a liberated line. Nietzsche opposes history not to the eternal but to the subhistorical or superhistorical: the Untimely, which is another name for haecceity, becoming, the innocence of becoming (in other words, forgetting as opposed to memory, geography as opposed to history, the map as opposed to the tracing, the rhizome as opposed to arborescence). "The unhistorical is like an atmosphere within which alone life can germinate and with the destruction of which it must vanish. . . . What deed would man be capable of if he had not first entered into that vaporous region of the unhistorical?"[2] Creations are like mutant abstract lines that have detached themselves from the task of representing a world, precisely because they assemble a new type of reality that history can only recontain or relocate in punctual systems.

When Boulez casts himself in the role of historian of music, he does so in order to show how a great musician, in a very different manner in each case, invents a kind of diagonal running between the harmonic vertical and the melodic horizon. And in each case it is a different diagonal, a different technique, a creation. Moving along this transversal line, which is really a line of deterritorialization, there is a *sound block* that no longer has a point of origin, since it is always and already in the middle of the line; and no longer has horizontal and vertical coordinates, since it creates its own coordinates; and no longer forms a localizable connection from one point to another, since it is in "nonpulsed time": a deterritorialized rhythmic block that has abandoned points, coordinates, and measure, like a drunken boat that melds with the line or draws a plane of consistency. Speeds and slownesses inject themselves into musical form, sometimes impelling it to proliferation, linear microproliferations, and sometimes to extinction, sonorous abolition, involution, or both at once. The musician is in the best position to say: "I hate the faculty of memory, I hate memories." And that is because he or she affirms the power of becoming. The Viennese school is exemplary of this kind of diagonal, this kind of line-block. But it can equally be said that the Viennese school found a new system of territorialization, of points, verticals, and horizontals that position it in history. Another attempt, another creative act, came after it. The important thing is that all musicians have always proceeded in this way: drawing their own diagonal, however fragile, outside points, outside coordinates and localizable connections, in order to float a sound block down a created, liberated line, in order to unleash in space this mobile and mutant sound bloc,, a haecceity (for example, chromaticism, aggregates, and complex notes, but already the resources and possibilities of polyphony, etc.).[3] Some have spoken of "oblique vectors" with respect to the organ. The diagonal is often composed of extremely complex lines and spaces of sound. Is that the secret of a little phrase or a rhythmic block? Undoubtedly, the point now assumes a new and essential creative function. It is no longer simply a question of an inevitable destiny reconstituting a punctual system; on the contrary, it is now the point that is subordinated to the line, the point now marks the proliferation of the line, or its sudden deviation, its acceleration, its slowdown, its furor or agony. Mozart's "microblocks." The block may even be reduced to a point, as though to a single note (point-block): Berg's B in *Wozzeck*, Schumann's A. Homage to Schumann, the madness of Schumann: the cello wanders across the grid of the orchestration, drawing its diagonal, along which the deterritorialized sound block moves; or an extremely sober kind of refrain is "treated" by a very elaborate melodic line and polyphonic architecture.

In a multilinear system, everything happens at once: the line breaks free of the point as origin; the diagonal breaks free of the vertical and the horizontal as coordinates; and the transversal breaks free of the diagonal as a localizable connection between two points. In short, a block-line passes amid [*au milieu des*] sounds and propels itself by its own nonlocalizable middle [*milieu*]. The sound block is the *intermezzo*. It is a body without organs, an antimemory pervading musical organization, and is all the more sonorous:

> The Schumannian body does not stay in place. . . . The intermezzo [is] consubstantial with the entire Schumannian oeuvre. . . . At the limit, there are only intermezzi. . . . The Schumannian body knows only bifur-

cations; it does not construct itself, it keeps diverging according to an accumulation of interludes. . . . Schumannian beating is panic, but it is also coded . . . and it is because the panic of the blows apparently keeps within the limits of a docile language that it is ordinarily not perceived. . . . Let us imagine for tonality two contradictory (and yet concomitant) statuses. On the one hand . . . a screen, a language intended to articulate the body . . . according to a known organization. . . . On the other hand, contradictorily . . . tonality becomes the ready servant of the beats within another level it claims to domesticate.[4]

Does the same thing, strictly the same thing, apply to painting? In effect, the point does not make the line; the line sweeps away the deterritorialized point, carries it off under its outside influence; the line does not go from one point to another, but runs *between points* in a different direction that renders them indiscernible. The line has become the diagonal, which has broken free from the vertical and the horizontal. But the diagonal has already become the transversal, the semidiagonal or free straight line, the broken or angular line, or the curve—always in the midst of themselves. Between the white vertical and the black horizontal lie Klee's gray, Kandinsky's red, Monet's purple; each forms a block of color. This line is without origin, since it always begins off the painting, which only holds it by the middle; it is without coordinates, because it melds with a plane of consistency upon which it floats and that it creates; it is without localizable connection, because it has lost not only its representative function but any function of outlining a form of any kind—by this token, the line has become abstract, truly abstract and mutant, a visual block; and under these conditions the point assumes creative functions again, as a color-point or line-point.[5] The line is between points, in their midst, and no longer goes from one point to another. It does not outline a shape. "He did not paint things, he painted between things." There is no falser problem in painting than depth and, in particular, perspective. For perspective is only a historical manner of *occupying* diagonals or transversals, lines of flight [*lignes de fuite:* here, the lines in a painting moving toward the vanishing point, or *point de fuite*—Trans.], in other words, of reterritorializing the moving visual block. We use the word "occupy" in the sense of "giving an occupation to," fixing a memory and a code, assigning a function. But the lines of flight, the transversals, are suitable for many other functions besides this molar function. Lines of flight as perspective lines, far from being made to represent depth, themselves invent the possibility of such a representation, which occupies them only for an instant, at a given moment. Perspective, and even depth, are the reterritorialization of lines of flight, which alone created painting by carrying it farther. What is called central perspective in particular plunged the multiplicity of escapes and the dynamism of lines into a punctual black hole. Conversely, it is true that problems of perspective triggered a whole profusion of creative lines, a mass release of visual blocks, at the very moment they claimed to have gained mastery over them. Is painting, in each of its acts of creation, engaged in a becoming as intense as that of music?

5
. . .
Individuation

There is a mode of individuation very different from that of a person, subject, thing, or substance. We reserve the name *haecceity* for it.[1] A season, a winter, a summer, an hour, a date have a perfect individuality lacking nothing, even though this individuality is different from that of a thing or a subject. They are haecceities in the sense that they consist entirely of relations of movement and rest between molecules or particles, capacities to affect and be affected. When demonology expounds upon the diabolical art of local movements and transports of affect, it also notes the importance of rain, hail, wind, pestilential air, or air polluted by noxious particles, favorable conditions for these transports. Tales must contain haecceities that are not simply emplacements, but concrete individuations that have a status of their own and direct the metamorphosis of things and subjects. Among types of civilizations, the Orient has many more individuations by haecceity than by subjectivity or substantiality: the haiku, for example, must include indicators as so many floating lines constituting a complex individual. In Charlotte Brontë, everything is in terms of *wind*, things, people, faces, loves, words. Lorca's "five in the evening," when love falls and fascism rises. That awful five in the evening! We say, "What a story!" "What heat!" "What a life!" to designate a very singular individuation. The hours of the day in Lawrence, in Faulkner. A degree of heat, an intensity of white, are perfect individualities; and a degree of heat can combine in latitude with another degree to form a new individual, as in a body that is cold here and hot there depending on its longitude. Norwegian omelette. A degree of heat can combine with an intensity of white, as in certain white skies of a hot summer. This is in no way an individuality of the instant, as opposed to the individuality of permanences or durations. A tear-off calendar has just as much time as a perpetual calendar, although the time in question is not the same. There are animals that live no longer than a day or an hour; conversely, a group of years can be as long as the most durable subject or object. We can conceive of an abstract time that is equal for haecceities and for subjects or things. Between the extreme slownesses and vertiginous speeds of geology and astronomy, Michel Tournier places meteorology, where meteors live at our pace: "A cloud forms in the sky like an image in my brain, the wind blows like I breathe, a rainbow spans the horizon for as long as my heart needs to reconcile itself to life, the summer passes like vacation drifts by." But is it by chance that in Tournier's novel this certitude can come only to a twin hero who is deformed and desubjectified, and has acquired a certain ubiquity?[2] Even when times are abstractly equal, the individuation of a life is not the same as the individuation of the subject that leads it or serves as its support. It is not the same Plane: in the first case, it is the plane of consistency or of composition of haecceities, which knows only speeds and affects; and in the second case, it is the altogether different plane of forms, substances, and subjects. And it is not in the same time, the same temporality. *Aeon:* the indefinite time of the event, the floating line that knows only speeds and continually divides that which transpires into an already-there that is at the same time not-yet-here, a simultaneous too-late and too-early, a something that is both going to happen and has just happened. *Chronos:* the time of measure that situates things and persons, develops a form, and determines a subject.[3] Boulez distinguishes tempo and nontempo in music: the "pulsed time" of a formal and functional music based on values versus the "nonpulsed time" of a floating music, both floating *and* machinic, which has nothing but speeds or differences in dynamic.[4] In short, the difference is not at all between the ephemeral and the durable, nor even between the regular and the irregular, but between two modes of individuation, two modes of temporality.

We must avoid an oversimplified conciliation, as though there were on the one hand formed subjects, of the thing or person type, and on the other hand spatiotemporal coordinates of the haecceity type. For you will yield nothing to haecceities unless you realize that that is what you are, and that you are nothing but that. When the face becomes a haecceity: "It seemed a curious mixture that simply made do with time, weather and these people."[5] You are longitude and latitude, a set of speeds and slownesses between unformed particles, a set of nonsubjectified affects. You have the individuality of a day, a season, a year, a *life* (regardless of its duration)—a climate, a wind, a fog, a swarm, a pack (regardless of its regularity). Or at least you can have it, you can reach it. A cloud of locusts carried in by the wind at five in the evening; a vampire who goes out at night, a werewolf at full moon. It should not be thought that a haecceity consists simply of a decor or backdrop that situates subjects, or of appendages that hold things and people to the ground. It is the entire assemblage in its individuated aggregate that is a haecceity; it is this assemblage that is defined by a longitude and a latitude, by speeds and affects, independently of forms and subjects, which belong to another plane. It is the wolf itself, and the horse, and the child, that cease to be subjects to become events, in assemblages that are inseparable from an hour, a season, an atmosphere, an air, a life. The street enters into composition with the horse, just as the dying rat enters into composition with the air, and the beast and the full moon enter into composition with each other. At most, we may distinguish assemblage haecceities (a body considered only as longitude and latitude) and interassemblage haecceities, which also mark the potentialities of becoming within each assemblage (the milieu of intersection of the longitudes and latitudes). But the two are strictly inseparable. Climate, wind, season, hour are not of another nature than the things, animals, or people that populate them, follow them, sleep and awaken within them. This should be read without a pause: the animal-stalks-at-five-o'clock. The becoming-evening, becoming-night of an animal, blood nuptials. Five o'clock is this animal! This animal is this place! "The thin dog is running in the road, this dog is the road," cries Virginia Woolf. That is how we need to feel. Spatiotemporal relations, determinations, are not predicates of the thing but dimensions of multiplicities. The street is as much a part of the omnibus-horse assemblage as the Hans assemblage the becoming-horse of which it initiates. We are all five o'clock in the evening, or another hour, or rather two hours simultaneously, the optimal and the pessimal, noon-midnight, but distributed in a variable fashion. The plane of consistency contains only haecceities, along intersecting lines. Forms and subjects are not of that world. Virginia Woolf's walk through the crowd, among the taxis. Taking a walk is a haecceity; never again will Mrs. Dalloway say to herself, "I am this, I am that, he is this, he is that." And "She felt very young; at the same time unspeakably aged. She sliced like a knife through everything; at the same time was outside, looking on. . . . She always had the feeling that it was very, very dangerous to live even one day."[6] Haecceity, fog, glare. A haecceity has neither beginning nor end, origin nor destination; it is always in the middle. It is not made of points, only of lines. It is a rhizome.

And it is not the same language, at least not the same usage of language. For if the plane of consistency only has haecceities for content, it also has its own particular semiotic to serve as expression. A plane of content and a plane of expression. This semiotic is composed above all of proper names, verbs in the infinitive and indefinite articles or pronouns. *Indefinite article + proper name + infinitive verb* constitutes the basic chain of expression, correlative to the least formalized contents, from the standpoint of a semiotic that has freed itself from both formal significances and personal subjectifications. In the first place, the verb in the infinitive is in no way indeterminate with respect to time; it expresses the floating, nonpulsed time proper to Aeon, in other words, the time of the pure event or of becoming, which articulates relative speeds and slownesses independently of the chronometric or chronological values that time assumes in the other modes. There is good reason to oppose the infinitive as mode and tense of becoming to all of the other modes and tenses, which pertain to Chronos since they form pulsations or values of being (the verb "to be" is precisely the only one that has no infinitive, or rather the infinitive of which is only an indeterminate, empty expression, taken abstractly to designate the sum total of definite modes and tenses).[7] Second, the proper name is no way the indicator of a subject; thus it seems useless to ask whether its operation resembles the nomination of a species, according to whether the subject is considered to be of another nature than that of the Form under which it is classified, or only the ultimate act of that Form, the limit of classification.[8] The proper name does not indicate a subject; nor does a noun take on the value of a proper name as a function of a form or a species. The proper name fundamentally designates something that is of the order of the event, of becoming or of the haecceity. It is the military men and meteorologists who hold the secret of proper names, when they give them to a strategic operation or a hurricane. The proper name is not the subject of a tense but the agent of an infinitive. It marks a longitude and a latitude. If Tick, Wolf, Horse, etc., are true proper names, they are so not by virtue of the specific and generic denominators that characterize them but of the speeds that compose them and the affects that fill them; it is by virtue of the event they are in themselves and in the assemblages—the becoming-horse of Little Hans, the becoming-wolf of the Were [which etymologically means "man"—Trans.], the becoming-tick of the Stoic (other proper names).

Third, the indefinite article and the indefinite pronoun are no more indeterminate than the infinitive. Or rather they are lacking a determination only insofar as they are applied to a form that is itself indeterminate, or to a determinable subject. On the other hand, they lack nothing when they introduce haecceities, events, the individuation of which does not pass into a form and is not effected by a subject. The indefinite then has maximum determination: once upon a time; a child is being beaten; a horse is falling . . . Here, the elements in play find their individuation in the assemblage of which they are a part, independent of the form of their concept and the subjectivity of their person. We have remarked several times the extent to which children use the indefinite not as something indeterminate but, on the contrary, as an individuating function within a collectivity. That is why we are dumbfounded by the efforts of psychoanalysis, which desperately wants there to be something definite hidden behind the indefinite, a possessive, a person. When the child says "*a* belly," "*a* horse," "how do *people* grow up?" "*someone* is beating *a* child," the psychoanalyst hears "my belly," "the father," "will I grow up to be like daddy?" The psychoanalyst asks: who is being beaten, and by whom?[9] Even linguistics is not immune from the same prejudice, inasmuch as it is inseparable from a personology; according to linguistics, in addition to the indefinite article and the pronoun, the third-person pronoun also lacks the determination of subjectivity that is proper to the first two persons and is supposedly the necessary condition for all enunciation.[10]

We believe on the contrary that the third-person indefinite, HE, THEY, implies no indetermination from this point of view; it ties the statement to a collective assemblage, as its necessary condition, rather than to a subject of the enunciation. Blanchot is correct in saying that ONE and HE—*one* is dying, *he* is unhappy—in no way take the place of a subject, but instead do away with any subject in favor of an assemblage of the haecceity type that carries or brings out the event insofar as it is unformed and incapable of being effectuated by persons ("something happens to them that they can only get a grip on again by letting go of their ability to say I").[11] The HE does not represent a subject but rather makes a diagram of an assemblage. It does not overcode statements, it does not transcend them as do the first two persons: on the contrary, it prevents them from falling under the tyranny of subjective or signifying constellations, under the regime of empty redundancies. The contents of the chains of expression it articulates are those that can be assembled for a maximum number of occurrences and becomings. "They arrive like fate . . . where do they come from, how have they pushed this far?"[12] He or one, indefinite article, proper name, infinitive verb: A HANS TO BECOME HORSE, A PACK NAMED WOLF TO LOOK AT HE, ONE TO DIE, WASP TO MEET ORCHID, THEY ARRIVE HUNS. Classified ads, telegraphic machines on the plane of consistency (once again, we are reminded of the procedures of Chinese poetry and the rules for translation suggested by the best commentators).[13]

6
. . .
A Theory of the Other

By comparing the primary effects of the Other's presence and those of his absence, we are in a position to say what the Other is. The error of philosophical theories is to reduce the Other sometimes to a particular object, and sometimes to another subject. (Even a conception like Sartre's, in *Being and Nothingness*, was satisfied with the union of the two determinations, making of the Other an object of my gaze, even if he in turn gazes at me and transforms me into an object.) But the Other is neither an object in the field of my perception nor a subject who perceives me: the Other is initially a structure of the perceptual field, without which the entire field could not function as it does. That this structure may be actualized by real characters, by variable subjects—me for you and you for me—does not prevent its pre-existence, as the condition of organization in general, to the terms which actualize it in each organized perceptual field—yours and mine. Thus the *a priori Other*, as the absolute structure, establishes the relativity of others as terms actualizing the structure within each field. But what is this structure? It is the structure of the possible. A frightened countenance is the expression of a frightening possible world, or of something frightening in the world—something I do not yet see. Let it be understood that the possible is not here an abstract category designating something which does not exist: the expressed possible world certainly exists, but it does not exist (actually) outside of that which expresses it. The terrified countenance bears no resemblance to the terrifying thing. It implicates it, it envelops it as something else, in a kind of torsion which situates what is expressed in the expressing. When I, in turn, and for my part, grasp the reality of what the Other was expressing, I do nothing but explicate the Other, as I develop and realize the corresponding possible world. It is true that the Other already bestows a certain reality on the possibilities which he encompasses—especially by speaking. The Other is the existence of the encompassed possible. Language is the reality of the possible as such. The self is the development and the explication of what is possible, the process of its realization in the actual. Proust says of the perceived Albertine that she encompasses or expresses the beach and the breaking of the waves: "If she had seen me, what could I have represented for her? At the heart of what universe was she perceiving me?" Love and jealousy will be the attempt to develop and to unfold this possible world named "Albertine." In short, the Other, as structure, is *the expression of a possible world:* it is the expressed, grasped as not yet existing outside of that which expresses it.

> Each of these men was a *possible* world, having its own coherence, its values, its sources of attraction and repulsion, its center of gravity. And with all the differences between them, each of these possible worlds at that moment shared a vision, casual and superficial, of the island of Speranza, which caused them to act in common, and which incidentally contained a shipwrecked man called Robinson and his half-caste servant. For the present this picture occupied their minds, but for each of them it was purely temporary, destined very soon to be returned to the limbo from which it had been briefly plucked by the accident of the *Whitebird's* getting off course. And each of these possible worlds naively proclaimed itself the reality. That was what other people were: the possible obstinately passing for the real.[1]

And we can go even further in our understanding of the effects of the presence of Others. Modern psychology has elaborated a rich series of categories to account for the functioning of the perceptual field and the variations of the object within this field: form-background; depth-length; theme-potentiality; profiles-unity of the object; fringe-center; text-context; thetic-nonthetic; transitive states–substantive parts; etc. But the corresponding philosophical problem is perhaps not very well raised: one asks whether these categories belong to the perceptual field itself being immanent to it (monism), or whether they refer to subjective syntheses operating on the subject matter of perception (dualism). It would be wrong to take exception to the dualist interpretation on the pretext that perception does not occur through a judgmental intellectual synthesis; one can certainly conceive of passive sensible syntheses of an entirely different sort operating on this material (in this sense, Husserl never renounced a certain dualism). Even so, we doubt that dualism is correctly defined as long as it is established between the matter of the perceptual field and the prereflective syntheses of the ego. The true dualism lies elsewhere; it lies between the effects of the "structure-Other" of the perceptual field and the effects of its absence (what perception would be were there no Others). We must understand that the Other is not one structure among others in the field of perception (in the sense, for example, that one would recognize in it a difference of nature from objects). *It is the structure which conditions the entire field* and its functioning, by rendering possible the constitution and application of the preceding categories. It is not the ego but the Other as structure which renders perception possible. Thus, the authors who interpret dualism poorly are also the authors who cannot extricate themselves from the alternative according to which the Other would be either a particular object in the field or another subject of the field. In defining the Other, together with Tournier, as the expression of a possible world, we make of it, on the contrary, the a priori principle of the organization of every perceptual field in accordance with the categories; we make of it the structure which allows this functioning as the "categorization" of this field. Real dualism then appears with the absence of the Other. . . .

Let us return to the effects of the presence of Others, such as they follow from the definition "Other = an expression of a possible world." The fundamental effect is the distinction of my consciousness and its object. This distinction is in fact the result of the structure-Other. Filling the world with possibilities, backgrounds, fringes, and transitions; inscribing the possibility of a frightening world when I am not yet afraid, or, on the contrary, the possibility of a reassuring world when I am really frightened by the world; encompassing in different respects the world which presents itself before me developed otherwise; constituting inside the world so many blisters which contain so many possible worlds—this is the Other.[2] Henceforth, the Other causes my consciousness to tip necessarily into an "I was," into a past which no longer coincides with the object. Before the appearance of the Other, there was, for example, a reassuring world from which my consciousness could not be distinguished. The Other then makes its appearance, expressing the possibility of a frightening world which cannot be developed without the one preceding it passing away. For my part, I am nothing other than my past objects, and my self is made up of a past world, the passing away of which was brought about precisely by the Other. If the Other is a possible world, I am a past world. The mistake of theories of knowledge is that they postulate the contemporaneity of subject and object, whereas one is constituted only through the annihilation of the other.

> Then suddenly there is a click. The subject breaks away from the object, divesting it of a part of its color and substance. There is a rift in the scheme of things, and a whole range of objects crumbles in becoming *me,* each object transferring its quality to an appropriate subject. The light becomes the eye and as such no longer exists: it is simply the stimulation of the retina. The smell becomes the nostril—and the world declares itself odorless. The song of the wind in the trees is disavowed: it was nothing but a quivering of the timpani. . . . The subject is the disqualified object. My eye is the corpse of light and color. My nose is all that remains of odors when their unreality has been demonstrated. My hand refutes the thing it holds. Thus the problem of awareness is born of anachronism. It implies the simultaneous existence of the subject with the object, whose mysterious relationship to himself he seeks to define. But subject and object cannot exist apart from one another since they are one and the same thing, at first integrated into the real world and then cast out by it.[3]

The Other thus assures the distinction of consciousness and its object as a temporal distinction. The first effect of its presence concerned space and the distribution of categories; but the second effect, which is perhaps the more profound, concerns time and the distribution of its dimensions—what comes before and what comes after in time. How could there still be a past when the Other no longer functions?

In the Other's absence, consciousness and its object are one. There is no longer any possibility of error, not only because the Other is no longer there to be the tribunal of all reality—to debate, falsify, or verify that which I think I see; but also because, lacking in its structure, it allows consciousness to cling to, and to coincide with, the object in an eternal present. "And it is as though, in consequence, my days had rearranged themselves. No longer do they jostle on each other's heels. Each stands separate and upright, proudly affirming its own worth. And since they are no longer to be distinguished as the stages of a plan in process of execution, they so resemble each other as to be superimposed in my memory, so that I seem to be ceaselessly reliving the same day."[4] Consciousness ceases to be a light cast upon objects in order to become a pure phosphorescence of things in themselves. . . .

Consciousness has become not only a phosphorescence internal to things but a fire in their heads, a light over each one, and a "soaring *I.*" In this light, *something else* appears, an ethereal double of each thing. "I seemed to glimpse *another island.* . . . Now I have been transported to that other Speranza, I live perpetually in a moment of innocence."[5] It is this extraordinary birth of the erect double that the novel excels in describing. But what exactly is the difference between the thing such as it appears in the presence of Others and the double which tends to detach itself in their absence? The Other presides over the organization of the world into objects and over the transitive relations of these objects. These objects exist only through the possibilities with which Others filled up the world; each one was closed onto itself, or opened onto other objects, only in relation to possible worlds expressed by Others. In short, it is the Other who has imprisoned the elements within the limits of bodies and, further still, within the limits of the earth. For the earth itself is but a great body which retains the elements; it is earth only to the extent that it is peopled by Others. The Other fabricates bodies out of the elements and objects out of bodies, just as it fabricates its own countenance out of the worlds it expresses. Thus, the liberated double, when the Other collapses, is not a replica of things. It is, on the contrary, the new upright image in which the elements are released and renewed, having become celestial and forming a thousand capricious elemental figures. . . .

In short, the Other, as it encompasses the possible worlds, prevents the doubles from standing erect. The Other is the grand leveler, and consequently the destructuration of the Other is not a disorganization of the world, but an upright organization as opposed to the recumbent organization; it is the new uprightness, and the detachment of an image which is vertical at last and without thickness; it is the detachment of a pure element which at last is liberated. . . .

When we desire Others, are not our desires brought to bear upon this expressed small possible world which the Other wrongly envelops, instead of allowing it to float and fly above the world, developed onto a glorious double? And when we observe a butterfly pillaging a flower that exactly resembles the abdomen of the female of the species and then leaving the flower carrying on its head two horns of pollen, we are tempted to conclude that bodies are but detours to the attainment of images, and that sexuality reaches its goal much better and much more promptly to the extent that it economizes this detour and addresses itself directly to images and to the elements freed from bodies.[6] . . .

Neurosis and psychosis—this is the adventure of depth. The structure-Other organizes and pacifies depth. It renders it livable. This is why the agitations of this structure imply a disorder, a disturbance of depth, as an aggressive return of the bottomless abyss that can no longer be conjured away. Everything has lost its sense, everything becomes *simulacrum and vestige*—even the object of work, the loved one, the world in itself or the self in the world . . . ; that is, unless there be some sort of salvation for Robinson; unless he invents a new dimension or a third sense for the expression "loss of Others"; unless the absence of the Other and the dissolution of its structure do not simply disorganize the world but, on the contrary, open up a possibility of salvation. Robinson must return to the surface and discover surfaces. The pure surface is perhaps what Others were hiding from us. It is perhaps at the surface, like a mist, that an unknown image of things is detached and, from the earth, a new surface energy without possible others. For the sky does not at all signify a height which would merely be the inverse image of depth. In opposition to the deep earth, air and sky describe a pure surface, and the surveying of the field of this surface. The solipsist sky has no depth: "It is a strange prejudice which sets a higher value on depth than on breadth, and which accepts 'superficial' as meaning not 'of wide extent' but 'of little depth,' whereas 'deep,' on the other hand, signifies 'of great depth' and not 'of small surface.' Yet it seems to me that a feeling such as love is better measured, if it can be measured at all, by the extent of its surface than by its degree of depth."[7] It is at the surface that doubles and ethereal images first rise up; then the pure and free elements arise in the celestial surveying of the field. The generalized erection is the erection of surfaces, their rectification—the disappearance of the Others. At the surface of the isle and the overarching sky, simulacra ascend and become *phantasms*. Doubles without resemblance and elements without constraint—these are the two aspects of the phantasm. This restructuring of the world is Robinson's great health—the conquest of the great health, or the third sense of the "loss of Others." . . .

What is essential, however, is that Friday does not function at all like a rediscovered Other. It is too late for that, the structure has disappeared. Sometimes he functions as a bizarre object, sometimes as a strange accomplice. Robinson treats him sometimes as a slave and tries to integrate him into the economic order of the island—that is, as a poor simulacrum—and sometimes as the keeper of a new secret which threatens that order—that is, as a mysterious phantasm. Sometimes he treats him almost like an object or an animal, sometimes as if Friday were a "beyond" with respect to himself, a "beyond" Friday, his own double or image. Sometimes he treats him as if he were falling short of the Other, sometimes as if he were transcending the Other. The difference is essential. For the Other, in its normal functioning, expresses a possible world. But this possible world exists in our world and, if it is not developed or realized without changing the quality of our world, it is at least developed in accordance with laws which constitute the order of the real in general and the succession of time. But Friday functions in an entirely different way—he indicates *another*, supposedly true world, an irreducible double which alone is genuine, and in this other world, a double of the Other who no longer is and cannot be. Not an Other, but something wholly other (*un tout-autre*) than the Other; not a replica, but a double: one who reveals pure elements and dissolves objects, bodies, and the earth. "It seemed, indeed, that (Friday) belonged to an entirely different realm, wholly opposed to his master's order of earth and husbandry, on which he could have only a disruptive effect if anyone tried to imprison him within it."[8] It is for this reason that he is not even an object of desire for Robinson. Though Robinson embraces his knees and looks into his eyes, it is only in order to grasp the luminous double which now barely retains the free elements which have escaped from his body. "As to my sexuality, I may note that at no time has Friday inspired me with any sodomite desire. For one thing, he came too late, when my sexuality had already become elemental and was directed toward Speranza. . . . It was not a matter of turning me back to human loves but, while leaving me still an elemental, of causing me to change my element."[9] The Other *pulls down [rabat]*: it draws the elements into the earth, the earth into bodies, and bodies into objects. But Friday innocently makes objects and bodies stand up again. He carries the earth into the sky. He frees the elements. But to straighten up or to rectify is also to shorten. The Other is a strange detour—it brings my desires down to objects, and my love to worlds. Sexuality is linked to generation only in a detour which first channels the difference of sexes through the Other. It is initially in the Other and through the Other that the difference of the sexes is founded. To establish the world without Others, to lift the world up (as Friday does, or rather as Robinson perceives that Friday does) is to avoid the detour. It is to separate desire from its *object*, from its detour through the body, in order to relate it to a pure *cause:* the elements. ". . . So also has perished the framework of institutions and myths that permits desire to become *embodied*, in the twofold sense of the word—that is to say, to assume a positive form and to expend itself in the body of a woman."[10] . . .

Everything here is fictitious (*romanesque*), including theory, which merges with a necessary fiction—namely, a certain theory of the Other. First, we must attach a great importance to the notion of the Other as structure: not at all a particular "form" inside a perceptual field (distinct from the form "object" or the form "animal"), but rather a system which conditions the functioning of the entire perceptual field in general. We must therefore distinguish the *a priori Other*, which designates this structure, and the *concrete Other*, which designates real terms actualizing the structure in concrete fields. If this *concrete Other* is always someone—I for you and you for me—that is, in each perceptual field the subject of another field—the a priori Other, on the other hand, is no one since structure is transcendent with respect to the terms which actualize it. How then is it to be defined? The expressiveness which defines the structure-Other is constituted by the category of the possible. The a priori Other is the *existence* of the possible in general, insofar as the possible exists only as expressed—that is, in something expressing it which does not resemble what is expressed (a torsion of the expressed in that which expresses it). When Kierkegaard's hero demands "the possible, the possible or I shall suffocate," when James longs for the "oxygen of possibility," they are only invoking the a priori Other. We have tried to show in this sense how the Other conditions the entire perceptual field, the application to this field of the categories of the perceived object and the dimensions of the perceiving subject, and finally, the distribution of concrete Others in each field. In fact, perceptual laws affecting the constitution of objects (form-background, etc.), the temporal determination of the subject, and the successive development of worlds, seemed to us to depend on the possible as the structure-Other. Even desire, whether it be desire for the object or desire for Others, depends on this structure. I desire an object only as expressed by the Other in the mode of the possible; I desire in the Other only the possible worlds the Other expresses. The Other appears as that which organizes elements into earth, and earth into bodies, bodies into objects, and which regulates and measures object, perception, and desire all at once. . . .

A world without Others. Tournier assumes that Robinson, through much suffering, discovers and conquers a great health, to the extent that things end up being organized in a manner quite different than their organization in the presence of the Others. They liberate an image without resemblance, or their own double which is normally repressed. This double in turn liberates pure elements which are ordinarily held prisoner. The world is not disturbed by the absence of the Other; on the contrary, it is the glorious double of the world which is found to be hidden by its presence. This is Robinson's discovery: the discovery of the surface, of the elemental beyond, of the "otherwise-Other" [*de l'Autre qu'autrui*]. Why then do we have the impression that this great health is perverse, and that this "rectification" of the world and of desire is also a deviation and a perversion? Robinson exhibits no perverse behavior. But every study or every novel of perversion strives to manifest the existence of a "perverse structure" as the principle from which perverse behavior eventually proceeds. In this sense, the perverse structure may be specified as that which is opposed to the structure-Other and takes its place. And just as concrete Others are actual and variable terms actualizing this structure-Other, the pervert's behaviors, always presupposing a fundamental absence of the Others, are but variable terms actualizing the perverse structure.

Why does the pervert have the tendency to imagine himself as a radiant angel, an angel of helium and fire? Why does he have—against the *earth,* fertilization, and the objects of desire—the kind of hatred which is already found systematized in Sade? Tournier's novel does not intend to explain—it shows. In this manner, it rejoins, by very different ways, recent psychoanalytic studies which may renew the status of the concept of perversion and disentangle it from the moralizing uncertainty in which it was maintained by the combined forces of psychiatry and the law. Lacan and his school insist profoundly on the necessity of understanding perverse behavior on the basis of a *structure,* and of defining this structure which conditions behavior. They also insist on the manner in which desire undergoes a sort of *displacement* in this structure, and the manner by which the *cause* of desire is thus detached from the *object;* on the way in which the *difference of sexes* is disavowed by the pervert, in the interest of an androgynous world of *doubles;* on the annulment of the Other inside perversion, on the position of a "beyond the Other" [*un au-delà de l'Autre*] or of an "otherwise Other" [*un Autre qu'autrui*], as if the Other disengaged in the eyes of the pervert his own *metaphor;* finally, they insist on perverse "desubjectivation"—for it is certain that neither the victim nor the accomplice function as Others.[11] For example, it is not because he has a need or a desire to make the Other suffer that the sadist strips him of his quality of being an Other. The converse is rather the case: it is because he is lacking the structure-Other and lives within a completely different structure, as a condition for his living world, that he apprehends Others sometimes as victims and sometimes as accomplices, but in neither case does he apprehend them as Others. On the contrary, he always apprehends them as "otherwise Others" [*Autres qu'autrui*]. It is striking to see in Sade's work to what extent victims and accomplices, with their necessary reversibility, are not at all grasped as Others. Rather, they are grasped sometimes as detestable bodies and sometimes as doubles, or allied elements (certainly not as doubles of the hero, but as their own doubles, always outside of their bodies in the pursuit of atomic elements).[12]

The fundamental misinterpretation of perversion, based on a hasty phenomenology of perverse behavior and on certain legal exigencies, consists in bringing perversion to bear upon certain offenses committed against Others. Everything persuades us, from the point of view of behavior, that perversion is nothing without the presence of the Other: voyeurism, exhibitionism, etc. But from the point of view of the structure, the contrary must be asserted: it is because the structure-Other is missing, and is replaced by a completely different structure, that the real "Others" are no longer able to play the role of terms actualizing the lost primary structure. Real "Others" can only play now, in the second structure, the role of bodies-victims (in the very particular sense that the pervert attributes to bodies), or the role of accomplices-doubles, and accomplices-elements (again, in the very particular sense of the pervert). The world of the pervert is a world without Others, and thus a world without the possible. The Other is that which renders possible. The perverse world is a world in which the category of the necessary has completely replaced that of the possible. This is a strange Spinozism from which "oxygen" is lacking, to the benefit of a more elementary energy and a more rarefied air (Sky-Necessity). All perversion is an "Othercide," and an "altrucide," and therefore a murder of the possible. But altrucide is not committed through perverse behavior, it is presupposed in the perverse structure. This does not keep the pervert from being a pervert, not constitutionally, but at the end of an adventure which surely has passed through neurosis and brushed up against psychosis. This is what Tournier suggests in this extraordinary novel: we must imagine Robinson as perverse; the only Robinsonade possible is perversion itself.

7

. . .

Ethics Without Morality

No philosopher was ever more worthy, but neither was any philosopher more maligned and hated. To grasp the reason for this it is not enough to recall the great theoretical thesis of Spinozism: a single substance having an infinity of attributes, *Deus sive Natura,* all "creatures" being only modes of these attributes or modifications of this substance. It is not enough to show how pantheism and atheism are combined in this thesis, which denies the existence of a moral, transcendent, creator God. We must start rather from the practical theses that made Spinozism an object of scandal. These theses imply a triple denunciation: of "consciousness," of "values," and of "sad passions." These are the three major resemblances with Nietzsche. And already in Spinoza's lifetime, they are the reasons for his being accused of *materialism, immoralism,* and *atheism.*

I. A Devaluation of Consciousness (in Favor of Thought): Spinoza the Materialist

Spinoza offers philosophers a new model: the body. He proposes to establish the body as a model: "We do not know what the body can do." This declaration of ignorance is a provocation. We speak of consciousness and its decrees, of the will and its effects, of the thousand ways of moving the body, of dominating the body and the passions—but *we do not even know what a body can do.*[1] Lacking this knowledge, we engage in idle talk. As Nietzsche will say, we stand amazed before consciousness, but "the truly surprising thing is rather the body."

Yet, one of the most famous theoretical theses of Spinoza is known by the name of *parallelism;* it does not consist merely in denying any real causality between the mind and the body, it disallows any primacy of the one over the other. If Spinoza rejects any superiority of the mind over the body, this is not in order to establish a superiority of the body over the mind, which would be no more intelligible than the converse. The practical significance of parallelism is manifested in the reversal of the traditional principle on which morality was founded as an enterprise of domination of the passions by consciousness. It was said that when the body acted, the mind was acted upon, and the mind did not act without the body being acted upon in turn (the rule of the inverse relation, cf. Descartes, *The Passions of the Soul,* articles 1 and 2). According to the *Ethics,* on the contrary, what is an action in the mind is necessarily an action in the body as well, and what is a passion in the body is necessarily a passion in the mind.[2] There is no primacy of one series over the other.

What does Spinoza mean when he invites us to take the body as a model? It is a matter of showing that the body surpasses the knowledge that we have of it, *and that thought likewise surpasses the consciousness that we have of it.* There are no fewer things in the mind that exceed our consciousness than there are things in the body that exceed our knowledge. So it is by one and the same movement that we shall manage, if possible, to capture the power of the body beyond the given conditions of our knowledge, and to capture the power of the mind beyond the given conditions of our consciousness. One seeks to acquire a knowledge of the powers of the body in order to discover, *in a parallel fashion,* the powers of the mind that elude consciousness, and thus to be able to *compare* the powers. In short, the model of the body, according to Spinoza, does not imply any devaluation of thought in relation to extension, but much more important, a devaluation of consciousness in relation to thought: a discovery of the unconscious, of an *unconscious of thought* just as profound as *the unknown of the body.*

The fact is that consciousness is by nature the locus of an illusion. Its nature is such that it registers effects, but it knows nothing of causes. The order of causes is defined by this: each body in extension, each idea or each mind in thought are constituted by the characteristic relations that subsume the parts of that body, the parts of that idea. When a body "encounters" another body, or an idea another idea, it happens that the two relations sometimes combine to form a more powerful whole, and sometimes one decomposes the other, destroying the cohesion of its parts. And this is what is prodigious in the body and the mind alike, these sets of living parts that enter into composition with and decompose one another according to complex laws.[3] The order of causes is therefore an order of composition and decomposition of relations, which infinitely affects all of nature. But as conscious beings, we never apprehend anything but the *effects* of these compositions and decompositions: we experience *joy* when a body encounters ours and enters into composition with it, and *sadness* when, on the contrary, a body or an idea threaten our own coherence. We are in a condition such that we only take in "what happens" to our body, "what happens" to our mind, that is, the effect of a body on our body, the effect of an idea on our idea. But this is only our body in its own relation, and our mind in its own relation, and the other bodies and other minds or ideas in their respective relations, and the rules according to which all these relations compound with and decompose one another; we know nothing of all this in the given order of our knowledge and our consciousness. In short, the conditions under which we know things and are conscious of ourselves condemn us *to have only inadequate ideas,* ideas that are confused and mutilated, effects separated from their real causes.[4] That is why it is scarcely possible to think that little children are happy, or that the first man was perfect: ignorant of causes and natures, reduced to the consciousness of events, condemned to undergo effects, they are slaves of everything, anxious and unhappy, in proportion to their imperfection. (No one has been more forceful than Spinoza in opposing the theological tradition of a perfect and happy Adam.)

How does consciousness calm its anguish? How can Adam imagine himself happy and perfect? Through the operation of a triple illusion. Since it only takes in effects, consciousness will satisfy its ignorance by reversing the order of things, by taking effects for causes (*the illusion of final causes*): it will construe the effect of a body on our body as the final cause of its own actions. In this way it will take itself for the first cause, and will invoke its power over the body (*the illusion of free decrees*). And where consciousness can no longer imagine itself to be the first cause, nor the organizer of ends, it invokes a God endowed with understanding and volition, operating by means of final causes or free decrees in order to prepare for man a world commensurate with His glory and His punishments (*the theological illusion*).[5] Nor does it suffice to say that consciousness deludes itself: consciousness is inseparable from the triple illusion that *constitutes* it, the illusion of finality, the illusion of freedom, and the theological illusion. Consciousness is only a dream with one's eyes open: "The infant believes he freely wants the milk; the angry child that he freely wants vengeance; and the timid, flight. So the drunk believes that it is from a free decision of the mind that he speaks the things he later, when sober, wishes he had not said."[6]

It is still necessary for consciousness itself to have a cause. Spinoza sometimes defines desire as "appetite together with consciousness of the appetite." But he specifies that this is only a nominal definition of desire, and that consciousness adds nothing to appetite ("we neither strive for, nor will, neither want, nor desire anything because we judge it to be good; on the contrary, we judge something to be good because we strive for it, will it, want it, and desire it").[7] We need, then, to arrive at a real definition of desire, one that at the same time shows the "cause" by which consciousness is hollowed out, as it were, in the appetitive process. Now, the appetite is nothing else but the effort by which each thing strives to persevere in its being, each body in extension, each mind or each idea in thought (*conatus*). But because this effort prompts us to act differently according to the objects encountered, we should say that it is, at every moment, determined by the affections that come from the objects. *These determinative affections are necessarily the cause of the consciousness of the conatus.*[8] And since the affections are not separable from a movement by which they cause us to go to a greater or lesser perfection (joy and sadness), depending on whether the thing encountered enters into composition with us, or on the contrary tends to decompose us, consciousness appears as the continual awareness of this passage from greater to lesser, or from lesser to greater, as a witness of the variations and determinations of the *conatus* functioning in relation to other bodies or other ideas. The object that agrees with my nature determines me to form a superior totality that includes us, the object and myself. The object that does not agree with me jeopardizes my cohesion, and tends to divide me into subsets, which, in the extreme case, enter into relations that are incompatible with my constitutive relation (*death*). Consciousness is the passage, or rather the awareness of the passage from these less potent totalities to more potent ones, and vice versa. It is purely transitive. But it is not a property of the Whole or of any specific whole; it has only an informational value, and what is more, the information is necessarily confused and distorted. Here again, Nietzsche is strictly Spinozan when he writes: "The greater activity is unconscious; consciousness usually only appears when a whole wants to subordinate itself to a superior whole. It is primarily the consciousness of this superior whole, of reality external to the ego. Consciousness is born in relation to a being of which we could be a function; it is the means by which we incorporate into that being."

II. A Devaluation of All Values, and of Good and Evil in Particular (in Favor of "Good" and "Bad"): Spinoza the Immoralist

"Thou shalt not eat of the fruit . . . ": the anxious, ignorant Adam understands these words as the expression of a prohibition. And yet, what do they refer to? To a fruit that, as such, will poison Adam if he eats it. This is an instance of an encounter between two bodies whose characteristic relations are not compatible: the fruit will act as a poison; that is, *it will determine the parts of Adam's body* (and paralleling this, the idea of the fruit will determine the parts of his mind) *to enter into new relations that no longer accord with his own essence.* But because Adam is ignorant of causes, he thinks that God morally forbids him something, whereas God only reveals the natural consequence of ingesting the fruit. Spinoza is categorical on this point: all the phenomena that we group under the heading of Evil, illness, and death, are of this type: bad encounters, poisoning, intoxication, relational decomposition.[9]

In any case, there are always relations that enter into composition in their particular order, according to the eternal laws of nature. There is no Good or Evil, but there is good and bad. "Beyond Good and Evil, at least this *does not* mean: beyond good and bad."[10] The good is when a body directly compounds its relation with ours, and, with all or part of its power, increases ours. A food, for example. For us, the bad is when a body decomposes our body's relation, although it still combines with our parts, but in ways that do not correspond to our essence, as when a poison breaks down the blood. Hence good and bad have a primary, objective meaning, but one that is relative and partial: that which agrees with our nature or does not agree with it. And consequently, good and bad have a secondary meaning, which is subjective and modal, qualifying two types, two modes of man's existence. That individual will be called *good* (or free, or rational, or strong) who strives, insofar as he is capable, to organize his encounters, to join with whatever agrees with his nature, to combine his relation with relations that are compatible with his, and thereby to increase his power. For goodness is a matter of dynamism, power, and the composition of powers. That individual will be called *bad,* or servile, or weak, or foolish, who lives haphazardly, who is content to undergo the effects of his encounters, but wails and accuses every time the effect undergone does not agree with him and reveals his own impotence. For, by lending oneself in this way to whatever encounter in whatever circumstance, believing that with a lot of violence or a little guile, one will always extricate oneself, how can one fail to have more bad encounters than good? How can one keep from destroying oneself through guilt, and others through resentment, spreading one's own powerlessness and enslavement everywhere, one's own sickness, indigestions, and poisons? In the end, one is unable even to encounter oneself.[11]

In this way, ethics, which is to say, a typology of immanent modes of existence, replaces morality, which always refers existence to transcendent values. Morality is the judgment of God, the *system of Judgment.* But ethics overthrows the system of judgment. The opposition of values (Good-Evil) is supplanted by the qualitative difference of modes of existence (good-bad). The illusion of values is indistinguishable from the illusion of consciousness. Because it is content to wait for and take in effects, consciousness misapprehends all of nature. Now, all that one needs in order to moralize is to fail to understand. It is clear that we have only to misunderstand a law for it to appear to us in the form of a moral "You must." If we do not understand the rule of three, we will apply it, we will adhere to it, as a duty. Adam does not understand the rule of the relation of his body with the fruit, so he interprets God's word as a prohibition. Moreover, the confused form of moral law has so compromised the law of nature that the philosopher must not speak of natural laws, but only of eternal truths: "The application of the word 'law' to natural things seems to be metaphorical, and the ordinary meaning of law is simply a command."[12] As Nietzsche says concerning chemistry, i.e., the science of antidotes and poisons, one must be wary of the word *law*, which has a moral aftertaste.

It is easy, however, to separate the two domains—that of the eternal truths of nature and that of the moral laws of institutions—if only one considers their effects. Let us take consciousness at its word: moral law is an imperative; it has no other effect, no other finality than obedience. This obedience may be absolutely necessary, and the commands may be justified, but that is not the issue. Law, whether moral or social, does not provide us with any knowledge; it makes nothing known. At worst, it prevents the formation of knowledge (*the law of the tyrant*). At best, it prepares for knowledge and makes it possible (*the law of Abraham or of Christ*). Between these two extremes, it takes the place of knowledge in those who, because of their mode of existence, are incapable of knowledge (*the law of Moses*). But in any case, a difference of nature is constantly manifested between knowledge and morality, between the relation of command and obedience and the relation of the known and knowledge. The tragedy of theology and its harmfulness are not just speculative, according to Spinoza; they are owing to the practical confusion which theology instills in us between these two orders that differ in nature. At the least, theology considers that Scripture lays the foundation for knowledge, even if this knowledge must be developed in a rational manner, or even transposed, translated, by reason: whence the hypothesis of a moral, creating, and transcendent God. In this, as we shall see, there is a confusion that compromises the whole of ontology; the history of a *long error* whereby the command is mistaken for something to be understood, obedience for knowledge itself, and Being for a *Fiat*. Law is always the transcendent instance that determines the opposition of values (Good-Evil), but knowledge is always the immanent power that determines the qualitative difference of modes of existence (good-bad).

III. A Devaluation of All the "Sad Passions" (in Favor of Joy): Spinoza the Atheist

If ethics and morality merely interpreted the same precepts in a different way, the distinction between them would only be theoretical. This is not the case. Throughout his work, Spinoza does not cease to denounce three kinds of personages: the man with sad passions; the man who exploits these sad passions, who needs them in order to establish his power; and the man who is saddened by the human condition and by human passions in general (he may make fun of these as much as he disdains them, but this mockery is a bad laughter).[13] The slave, the tyrant, and the priest . . . , the moralist trinity. Since Epicurus and Lucretius, the deep implicit connection between tyrants and slaves has never been more clearly shown: "In despotic statecraft, the supreme and essential mystery is to hoodwink the subjects, and to mask the fear, which keeps them down, with the specious garb of religion, so that men may fight as bravely for slavery as for safety, and count it not shame but highest honor to risk their blood and lives for the vainglory of a tyrant."[14] This is possible because the sad passion is a complex that joins desire's boundlessness to the mind's confusion, cupidity to superstition. "Those who most ardently embrace every sort of superstition cannot help but be those who most immoderately desire external advantages." The tyrant needs sad spirits in order to succeed, just as sad spirits need a tyrant in order to be content and to multiply. In any case, what unites them is their hatred of life, their resentment against life. The *Ethics* draws the portrait of the *resentful man*, for whom all happiness is an offense, and who makes wretchedness or impotence his only passion:

> But those who know how to break men's minds rather than strengthen them are burdensome both to themselves and to others. That is why many, from too great an impatience of mind, and a false zeal for religion, have preferred to live among the lower animals rather than among men. They are like boys or young men who cannot bear calmly the scolding of their parents, and take refuge in the army. They choose the inconveniences of war and the discipline of an absolute commander in preference to the conveniences of home and the admonitions of a father; and while they take vengeance on their parents, they allow all sorts of burdens to be placed on them.[15]

There is, then, a philosophy of "life" in Spinoza; it consists precisely in denouncing all that separates us from life, all these transcendent values that are turned against life, these values that are tied to the conditions and illusions of consciousness. Life is poisoned by the categories of Good and Evil, of blame and merit, of sin and redemption.[16] What poisons life is hatred, including the hatred that is turned back against oneself in the form of guilt. Spinoza traces, step by step, the dreadful concatenation of sad passions; first, sadness itself, then hatred, aversion, mockery, fear, despair, *morsus conscientiae*, pity, indignation, envy, humility, repentance, self-abasement, shame, regret, anger, vengeance, cruelty. . . .[17] His analysis goes so far that even in *hatred* and *security* he is able to find that grain of sadness that suffices to make these the feelings of slaves.[18] The true city offers citizens the love of freedom instead of the hope of rewards or even the security of possessions; for "it is slaves, not free men, who are given rewards for virtue."[19] Spinoza is not among those who think that a sad passion has something good about it. Before Nietzsche, he denounces all the falsifications of life, all the values in the name of which we disparage life. We do not live, we only lead a semblance of life; we can only think of how to keep from dying, and our whole life is a death worship.

This critique of sad passions is deeply rooted in the theory of affections. An individual is first of all a singular essence, which is to say, a degree of power. A characteristic relation corresponds to this essence, and a certain capacity for being affected corresponds to this degree of power. Furthermore, this relation subsumes parts; this capacity for being affected is necessarily filled by affections. Thus, animals are defined less by the abstract notions of genus and species than by a capacity for being affected, by the affections of which they are "capable," by the excitations to which they react within the limits of their capability. Consideration of genera and species still implies a "morality," whereas the *Ethics* is an *ethology* which, with regard to men and animals, in each case only considers their capacity for being affected. Now, from the viewpoint of an ethology of man, one needs first to distinguish between two sorts of affections: *actions*, which are explained by the nature of the affected individual, and which spring from the individual's essence; and *passions*, which are explained by something else, and which originate outside the individual. Hence the capacity for being affected is manifested as a *power of acting* insofar as it is assumed to be filled by active affections, but as a *power of being acted upon* insofar as it is filled by passions. For a given individual, i.e., for a given degree of power assumed to be constant within certain limits, the capacity for being affected itself remains constant within those limits, but the power of acting and the power of being acted upon vary greatly, in inverse ratio to one another.

It is necessary to distinguish not only between actions and passions but also between two sorts of passions. The nature of the passions, in any case, is to fill our capacity for being affected while separating us from our power of acting, keeping us separated from that power. But when we encounter an external body that does not agree with our own (i.e., whose relation does not enter into composition with ours), it is as if the power of that body opposed our power, bringing about a subtraction or a fixation; when this occurs, it may be said that our power of acting is diminished or blocked, and that the corresponding passions are those of *sadness*. In the contrary case, when we encounter a body that agrees with our nature, one whose relation compounds with ours, we may say that its power is added to ours; the passions that affect us are those of *joy* and our power of acting is increased or enhanced. This joy is still a passion, since it has an external cause; we still remain separated from our power of acting, possessing it only in a formal sense. This power of acting is nonetheless increased proportionally; we "approach" the point of conversion, the point of transmutation that will establish our dominion, that will make us worthy of action, of active joys.[20]

It is this theory of the affections as a whole that defines the status of the sad passions. Whatever their justification, they represent the lowest degree of our power, the moment when we are most separated from our power of acting, when we are most alienated, delivered over to the phantoms of superstition, to the mystifications of the tyrant. The *Ethics* is necessarily an ethics of joy: only joy is worthwhile, joy remains, bringing us near to action, and to the bliss of action. The sad passions always amount to impotence. This will be the threefold practical problem of the *Ethics: How does one arrive at a maximum of joyful passions?* proceeding from there to free and active feelings (although our place in nature seems to condemn us to bad encounters and sadnesses). *How does one manage to form adequate ideas?* which are precisely the source of active feelings (although our natural condition seems to condemn us to have only inadequate ideas of our body, of our mind, and of other things). *How does one become conscious of oneself, of God, and of things?—sui et Dei et rerum aeterna quadam necessitate conscius* (although our consciousness seems inseparable from illusions).

The great theories of the *Ethics*—the oneness of substance, the univocity of the attributes, immanence, universal necessity, parallelism, etc.—cannot be treated apart from the three practical theses concerning consciousness, values, and the sad passions. The *Ethics* is a book written twice simultaneously: once in the continuous stream of definitions, propositions, demonstrations, and corollaries, which develop the great speculative themes with all the rigors of the mind; another time in the broken chain of scholia, a discontinuous volcanic line, a second version underneath the first, expressing all the angers of the heart and setting forth the practical theses of denunciation and liberation.[21] The entire *Ethics* is a voyage in immanence; but immanence is the unconscious itself, and the conquest of the unconscious. Ethical *joy* is the correlate of speculative affirmation.

8

. . .

Ethics and the Event

We are sometimes hesitant to call "Stoic" a concrete or poetic way of life, as if the name of a doctrine were too bookish or abstract to designate the most personal relation with a wound. But where do doctrines come from, if not from wounds and vital aphorisms which, with their charge of exemplary provocation, are so many speculative anecdotes? Joe Bousquet must be called Stoic. He apprehends the wound that he bears deep within his body in its eternal truth as a pure event. To the extent that events are actualized in us, they wait for us and invite us in. They signal us: "My wound existed before me, I was born to embody it."[1] It is a question of attaining this will that the event creates in us; of becoming the quasi-cause of what is produced within us, the operator; of producing surfaces and linings in which the event is reflected, finds itself again as incorporeal and manifests in us the neutral splendor which it possesses in itself in its impersonal and preindividual nature, beyond the general and the particular, the collective and the private. It is a question of becoming a citizen of the world. "Everything was in order with the events of my life before I made them mine; to live them is to find myself tempted to become their equal, as if they had to get from me only that which they have that is best and most perfect."

Either ethics makes no sense at all, or this is what it means and has nothing else to say: not to be unworthy of what happens to us. To grasp whatever happens as unjust and unwarranted (it is always someone else's fault) is, on the contrary, what renders our sores repugnant—veritable *ressentiment*, resentment of the event. There is no other ill will. What is really immoral is the use of moral notions like just or unjust, merit or fault. What does it mean then to will the event? Is it to accept war, wounds, and death when they occur? It is highly probable that resignation is only one more figure of *ressentiment*, since *ressentiment* has many figures. If willing the event is, primarily, to release its eternal truth, like the fire on which it is fed, this will would reach the point at which war is waged against war, the wound would be the living trace and the scar of all wounds, and death turned on itself would be willed against all deaths. We are faced with a volitional intuition and a transmutation. "To my inclination for death," said Bousquet, "which was a failure of the will, I will substitute a longing for death which would be the apotheosis of the will." From this inclination to this longing there is, in a certain respect, no change except a change of the will, a sort of leaping in place [*saut sur place*] of the whole body which exchanges its organic will for a spiritual will. It wills now not exactly what occurs, but something *in* that which occurs, something yet to come which would be consistent with what occurs, in accordance with the laws of an obscure, humorous conformity: the Event. It is in this sense that the *amor fati* is one with the struggle of free men. My misfortune is present in all events, but also a splendor and brightness which dry up misfortune and which bring about that the event, once willed, is actualized on its most contracted point, on the cutting edge of an operation. All this is the effect of the static genesis and of the immaculate conception. The splendor and the magnificence of the event is sense. The event is not what occurs (an accident), it is rather inside what occurs, the purely expressed. It signals and awaits us. In accordance with the three preceding determinations, it is what must be understood, willed, and represented in that which occurs. Bousquet goes on to say: "Become the man of your misfortunes; learn to embody their perfection and brilliance." Nothing more can be said, and no more has ever been said: to become worthy of what happens to us, and thus to will and release the event, to become the offspring of one's own events, and thereby to be reborn, to have one more birth, and to break with one's carnal birth—to become the offspring of one's events and not of one's actions, for the action is itself produced by the offspring of the event.

The actor is not like a god, but is rather like an "antigod" [*contre-dieu*]. God and actor are opposed in their readings of time. What men grasp as past and future, God lives it in its eternal present. The God is Chronos: the divine present is the circle in its entirety, whereas past and future are dimensions relative to a particular segment of the circle which leaves the rest out-

side. The actor's present, on the contrary, is the most narrow, the most contracted, the most instantaneous, and the most punctual. It is the point on a
straight line which divides the line endlessly, and is itself divided into past-
future. The actor belongs to the Aeon: instead of the most profound, the
most fully present, the present which spreads out and comprehends the future and the past, an unlimited past-future rises up here reflected in an
empty present which has no more thickness than the mirror. The actor or
actress represents, but what he or she represents is always still in the future
and already in the past, whereas his or her representation is impassible and
divided, unfolded without being ruptured, neither acting nor being acted
upon. It is in this sense that there is an actor's paradox; the actor maintains
himself in the instant in order to act out something perpetually anticipated
and delayed, hoped for and recalled. The role played is never that of a
character; it is a theme (the complex theme or sense) constituted by the
components of the event, that is, by the communicating singularities effectively liberated from the limits of individuals and persons. The actor strains
his entire personality in a moment which is always further divisible in order
to open himself up to the impersonal and preindividual role. The actor is
always acting out other roles when acting one role. The role has the same
relation to the actor as the future and past have to the instantaneous present
which corresponds to them on the line of the Aeon. The actor thus actualizes the event, but in a way which is entirely different from the actualization
of the event in the depth of things. Or rather, the actor redoubles this cosmic,
or physical actualization, in his own way, which is singularly superficial—
but because of it more distinct, trenchant and pure. Thus, the actor delimits
the original, disengages from it an abstract line, and keeps from the event
only its contour and its splendor, becoming thereby the actor of one's own
events—a *counteractualization.*

The physical mixture is exact only at the level of the whole, in the full
circle of the divine present. But with respect to each part, there are many
injustices and ignominies, many parasitic and cannibalistic processes
which inspire our terror at what happens to us, and our resentment at what
occurs. Humor is inseparable from a selective force: in that which occurs
(an accident), it selects the pure event. In eating, it selects speaking. Bousquet listed the characteristics of the humor-actor [*de l'humour-acteur*]: to annihilate his or her tracks whenever necessary; "to hold up among men and
works *their being before bitterness*." "to assign to plagues, tyrannies, and the
most frightful wars the comic possibility of having reigned for nothing"; in
short, to liberate for each thing "its immaculate portion," language and
will, *amor fati.*[2]

Why is every event a kind of plague, war, wound, or death? Is this simply to say that there are more unfortunate than fortunate events? No, this is not the case since the question here is about the double structure of every event. With every event, there is indeed the present moment of its actualization, the moment in which the event is embodied in a state of affairs, an individual, or a person, the moment we designate by saying "*here,* the moment has come." The future and the past of the event are evaluated only with respect to this definitive present, and from the point of view of that which embodies it. But on the other hand, there is the future and the past of the event considered in itself, sidestepping each present, being free of the limitations of a state of affairs, impersonal and preindividual, neutral, neither general nor particular, *eventum tantum.* . . . It has no other present than that of the mobile instant which represents it, always divided into past-future, and forming what must be called the counteractualization. In one case, it is my life, which seems too weak for me and slips away at a point which, in a determined relation to me, has become present. In the other case, it is I who am too weak for life, it is life which overwhelms me, scattering its singularities all about, in no relation to me, nor to a moment determinable as the present, except an impersonal instant which is divided into still-future and already-past. No one has shown better than Maurice Blanchot that this ambiguity is essentially that of the wound and of death, of the mortal wound. Death has an extreme and definite relation to me and my body and is grounded in me, but it also has no relation to me at all—it is incorporeal and infinitive, impersonal, grounded only in itself. On one side, there is the part of the event which is realized and accomplished; on the other, there is that "part of the event which cannot realize its accomplishment." There are thus two accomplishments, which are like actualization and counteractualization. It is in this way that death and its wound are not simply events among other events. Every event is like death, double and impersonal in its double. "It is the abyss of the present, the time without present with which I have no relation, toward which I am unable to project myself. For in it *I* do not die. I forfeit the power of dying. In this abyss one [*on*] dies—one never ceases to die, and one never succeeds in dying."[3]

How different this "one" is from that which we encounter in everyday banality. It is the "one" of impersonal and preindividual singularities, the "one" of the pure event wherein *it* dies in the same way that *it* rains. The splendor of the "one" is the splendor of the event itself or of the fourth person. This is why there are no private or collective events, no more than there are individuals and universals, particularities and generalities. Everything is singular, and thus both collective and private, particular and general, neither individual nor universal. Which war, for example, is not a private affair? Conversely, which wound is not inflicted by war and derived from society as a whole? Which private event does not have all its coordinates, that is, all its impersonal social singularities? There is, nevertheless, a good deal of ignominy in saying that war concerns everybody, for this is not true. It does not concern those who use it or those who serve it—creatures of *ressentiment*. And there is as much ignominy in saying that everyone has his or her own war or particular wound, for this is not true of those who scratch at their sores—the creatures of bitterness and *ressentiment*. It is true only of the free man, who grasps the event, and does not allow it to be actualized as such without enacting, the actor, its counteractualization. Only the free man, therefore, can comprehend all violence in a single act of violence, and every mortal event *in a single Event* which no longer makes room for the accident, and which denounces and removes the power of *ressentiment* within the individual as well as the power of oppression within society. Only by spreading *ressentiment* the tyrant forms allies, namely slaves and servants. The revolutionary alone is free from the *ressentiment*, by means of which one always participates in, and profits by, an oppressive order. *One and the same Event?* Mixture which extracts and purifies, or measures everything at an instant without mixture, instead of mixing everything together. All forms of violence and oppression gather together in this single event which denounces all by denouncing one (the nearest or final state of the question).

> The psychopathology which the poet makes his own is not a sinister little accident of personal destiny, or an individual, unfortunate accident. It is not the milkman's truck which has run over him and left him disabled. It is the horsemen of the Hundred Blacks carrying out their pogroms against their ancestors in the ghettos of Vilna. . . . The blows received to the head did not happen during a street brawl, but when the police charged the demonstrators. . . . If he cries out like a deaf genius, it is because the bombs of Guernica and Hanoi have deafened him.[4]

It is at this mobile and precise point, where all events gather together in one that transmutation happens: this is the point at which death turns against death; where dying is the negation of death, and the impersonality of dying no longer indicates only the moment when I disappear outside of myself, but rather the moment when death loses itself in itself, and also the figure which the most singular life takes on in order to substitute itself for me.[5]

9
. . .
The Selective Test

There is a force common to Kierkegaard and Nietzsche. (Péguy would have to be added in order to form the triptych of priest, antichrist, and catholic. Each of the three in his own way makes repetition not only a power peculiar to language and thought, a superior pathos and pathology, but also the fundamental category of the philosophy of the future. To each corresponds a testament as well as a theater, a conception of the theater, and a hero of repetition as a principal character in this theater: Job-Abraham, Dionysus-Zarathustra, Joan of Arc-Clio). What separates them is considerable, evident and well known. But nothing can hide this prodigious encounter in relation to a philosophy of repetition: *they oppose repetition to all the forms of generality.* Nor do they take the word "repetition" in a metaphorical sense: on the contrary, they have a way of taking it literally and of introducing it into their style. We can, or rather must, first of all list the principal propositions which indicate the points on which they coincide.

1. Make something new of repetition itself: connect it with a test, with a selection or selective test; make it the supreme object of the will and of freedom. Kierkegaard specifies: it is not a matter of drawing something new from repetition, of extracting something new from it. Only contemplation or the mind which contemplates from without "extracts." It is rather a matter of acting, of making repetition as such a novelty; that is,

a freedom and a task of freedom. In the case of Nietzsche: liberate the will from everything that binds it by making repetition the very object of willing. No doubt it is repetition that already binds; but if we die of repetition we are also saved and healed by it, healed above all by the other repetition. The whole mystical game of loss and salvation is therefore contained in repetition, along with the whole theatrical game of life and death, and the whole positive game of illness and health (cf. Zarathustra ill and Zarathustra convalescent by virtue of one and the same power of repetition in the eternal return).

2. In consequence, oppose repetition to the laws of nature. Kierkegaard declares that he does not speak at all of repetition in nature, of cycles and seasons, exchanges and equalities. Furthermore: if repetition concerns the most interior element of the will, this is because everything *changes* around the will in accordance with the law of nature. According to the law of nature, repetition is impossible. For this reason, Kierkegaard condemns as aesthetic repetition every attempt to obtain repetition from the laws of nature by identifying with the legislative principle, whether in the Epicurean or the Stoic manner. It will be said that the situation is not so clear with Nietzsche. Nietzsche's declarations are nevertheless explicit. If he discovers repetition in the *physis* itself, this is because he discovers in the *physis* something superior to the reign of laws: a will willing itself through all change, a power against the law, an interior of the earth opposed to the laws of its surface. Nietzsche opposes "his" hypothesis to the cyclical hypothesis. He conceives of repetition in the eternal return as Being, but he opposes this being to every legal form, to the being-similar as much as to the being-equal. How could the thinker who goes furthest in criticizing the notion of law reintroduce eternal return as a law of nature? How could such a connoisseur of the Greeks be justified in regarding his own thought as prodigious and new, if he were content to formulate that natural platitude, that generality regarding nature well known to the ancients? On two occasions, Zarathustra corrects wrong interpretations of the eternal return: with anger, directed at his demon ("Spirit of Gravity . . . do not treat this too lightly"); with kindness, directed at his animals ("O buffoons and barrel-organs . . . you have already made a refrain out of it"). The refrain is the eternal return as cycle or circulation, as being-similar and being-equal, in short as natural animal certitude and as perceptible law of nature itself.

3. Oppose repetition to moral law, to the point that it becomes the suspension of ethics, a thought beyond good and evil. Repetition appears as the logos of the solitary and the singular, the logos of the "private thinker." Both Kierkegaard and Nietzsche develop the opposition of the pri-

vate thinker, the thinker-comet, bearer of repetition, and the public professor, doctor of law, whose second-hand discourse proceeds by mediation and finds its moralising source in the generality of concepts (cf. Kierkegaard against Hegel, Nietzsche against Kant and Hegel; and from this point of view, Péguy against the Sorbonne). Job is infinite contestation and Abraham infinite resignation, but these are one and the same thing. Job challenges the law in an ironic manner, refusing all secondhand explanations and dismissing the general in order to reach the most singular as principle or as universal. Abraham submits humorously to the law, but finds in that submission precisely the singularity of his only son whom the law commanded him to sacrifice. As Kierkegaard understands it, repetition is the transcendent correlate shared by the psychical intentions of contestation and resignation. (We rediscover the two aspects in Péguy's doubling of Joan of Arc and Gervaise.) In Nietzsche's striking atheism, hatred of the law and *amor fati* (love of fate), aggression and acquiescence are the two faces of Zarathustra, gathered from the Bible and turned back against it. Further, in a certain sense one can see Zarathustra's moral test of repetition as competing with Kant. The eternal return says: whatever you will, will it in such a manner that you also will its eternal return. There is a "formalism" here which overthrows Kant on his own ground, a test which goes further since, instead of relating repetition to a supposed moral law, it seems to make repetition itself the only form of a law beyond morality. But in reality things are even more complicated. The form of repetition in the eternal return is the brutal form of the immediate, that of the universal and the singular reunited, which dethrones every general law, dissolves the mediations and annihilates the particulars subjected to the law. Just as irony and black humor are combined in Zarathustra, so there is a within-the-law and a beyond-the-law united in the eternal return.

4. Oppose repetition not only to the generalities of habit but also to the particularities of memory. For it is perhaps habit which manages to "extract" something new from a repetition contemplated from without. With habit, we only act on the condition that there is a little self within us which contemplates: it is this which extracts the new, in other words the general, from the pseudorepetition of particular cases. Memory, then, perhaps recovers the particulars dissolved in generality. These psychological movements are of little consequence: for both Nietzsche and Kierkegaard they fade away before repetition proposed as the double condemnation of habit and memory. In this way, repetition is the thought of the future: it is opposed to both the ancient category of reminiscence and the modern category of *habitus*. It is in repetition, by repeti-

tion that forgetting becomes a positive power and the unconscious a positive, superior unconscious (for example, forgetting as a force is an integral part of the lived experience of eternal return). Everything is summed up in power [*puissance*]. When Kierkegaard speaks of repetition as the second power of consciousness, "second" does not mean a second time but the infinite which belongs to a single time, the eternity which belongs to an instant, the unconscious which belongs to consciousness, the "*n*th" power. And when Nietzsche presents the eternal return as the immediate expression of the will to power, will to power does not at all mean "to want power," but on the contrary: whatever you will, carry it to the "*n*th" power; that is, separate out the superior form thanks to the selective operation of thought in the eternal return, thanks to the singularity of repetition in the eternal return itself. Here, in the superior form of everything that is, we find the immediate identity of the eternal return and the overman.[1]

We are not suggesting any resemblance whatsoever between Nietzsche's Dionysus and Kierkegaard's God. On the contrary, we suppose, we believe that the difference is insurmountable. All the more reason to ask: whence the coincidence concerning this fundamental objective, on the theme of repetition, even though they understand this objective differently? Kierkegaard and Nietzsche are among those who bring to philosophy new means of expression. In relation to them we speak readily of an overcoming of philosophy. Furthermore, in all their work *movement* is at issue. Their objection to Hegel is that he does not go beyond false movement, in other words the abstract logical movement of "mediation." They want to put metaphysics in motion, in action. They want to make it act, to carry out immediate acts. It is not enough therefore for them to propose a new representation of movement; representation is already mediation. Rather, it is a question of producing within the work a motion capable of affecting the mind outside of all representation; it is a question of making movement itself a work, without interposition; of substituting direct signs for mediate representations; of inventing vibrations, rotations, whirlings, gravitations, dances or leaps which directly touch the mind. This is the idea of a man of the theater, the idea of a director—before his time. In this sense, something completely new begins with Kierkegaard and Nietzsche. They no longer reflect on the theater in the Hegelian manner. Neither do they set up a philosophical theater. They invent an incredible equivalent of theater within philosophy, thereby founding at the same time this theater of the future and a new philosophy. It will be said that, at least from the point of view of theater, there was no production: neither the profession of priest and Copenhagan around 1840 nor the break with Wagner and Bayreuth were favorable conditions. One thing, however, is certain: when Kierkegaard speaks of ancient theater and modern drama, the environment has already changed; we are no longer in the element of reflection. We find here a thinker who lives the problem of masks, who experiences the inner emptiness of masks and who seeks to fill it, to complete it, albeit with the "absolutely different"; that is, by putting into it all the difference between the finite and the infinite, thereby creating the idea of a theater of humor and of faith. When Kierkegaard explains that the knight of faith so resembles a bourgeois in his Sunday best as to be capable of being mistaken for one, this philosophical instruction must be taken as the remark of a director showing how the knight of faith should be *played*. And when he comments on Job or Abraham, when he imagines the variations of the tale *Agnes and the Triton*, the manner in which he does so does not mislead: it is that of a scenario. Mozart's music resonates even in Abraham and Job; it is a matter of "leaping" to the tune of this music. "I only look at movements" is the language of a director who poses the highest theatrical problem, the problem of a movement which would directly touch the soul, which would be that of the soul.[2]

Even more so with Nietzsche. *The Birth of Tragedy* is not a reflection on ancient theater so much as the practical foundation of a theater of the future, the opening up of a path along which Nietzsche still thinks it possible to push Wagner. The break with Wagner is not a matter of theory, not of music; it concerns the respective roles of text, history, noise, music, light, song, dance, and decor in this theater of which Nietzsche dreams. Zarathustra incorporates the two attempts at dramatizing Empedocles. Moreover, if Bizet is better than Wagner, it is from the point of view of theater and for Zarathustra's dances. Nietzsche's reproach to Wagner is that he inverted and distorted "movement," giving us a nautical theater in which we must paddle and swim rather than one in which we can walk and dance. *Zarathustra* is conceived entirely within philosophy, but also entirely for the stage. Everything in it is scored and visualized, put in motion and made to walk or dance. How can it be read without searching for the exact sound of the cry of the higher man, how can the prologue be read without staging the episode of the tightrope walker which opens the whole story? At certain moments, it is a comic opera about terrible things; and it is not by chance that Nietzsche speaks of the comic character of the overman. Remember the song of Ariadne from the mouth of the old Sorcerer: here, two masks are superimposed—that of a young woman, almost of a Koré, which has just been laid over the mask of a repugnant old man. The actor must play the role of an old man playing the role of the Koré. And here too, for Nietzsche, it is a matter of filling the inner emptiness of the mask within a theatrical space: by multiplying the superimposed masks and inscribing the omnipresence of Dionysus in that superimposition, by inserting the infinity of real movement in the form of the absolute difference given in the repetition of the eternal return. When Nietzsche says that the overman resembles Borgia rather than Parsifal, when he suggests that the overman belongs at once to both the Jesuit order and the Prussian officer corps, we can only understand these texts by taking them for what they are: the remarks of a director indicating how the overman should be "played."

Theater is real movement, and it extracts real movement from all the arts that it employs. This is what we are told: this movement, the essence and the interiority of movement is *not opposition, not mediation* but repetition. Hegel is denounced as the one who proposes an abstract movement of concepts instead of a movement of the *physis* and the psyche. Hegel substitutes the abstract relation of the particular to the concept in general for the true relation of the singular and the universal in the Idea. He thus remains in the reflected element of "representation," within simple generality. He represents concepts instead of dramatizing Ideas: he creates a false theater, a false drama, a false movement. We must see how Hegel betrays and distorts the immediate in order to found his dialectic on that incomprehension, and to introduce mediation in a movement which is no more than that of his own thought and its generalities. When we say, on the contrary, that movement is repetition and that this is our true theater, we are not speaking of the effort of the actor who "repeats" because he has not yet learned the part. We have in mind the theatrical space, the emptiness of that space, and the manner in which it is filled and determined by signs and masks through which the actor plays a role which plays other roles; we think of how repetition is woven from one distinctive point to another, including within itself the differences. (When Marx also criticizes the abstract false movement or mediation of the Hegelians, he finds himself drawn to an idea, which he indicates rather than develops, an essentially "theatrical" idea: to the extent that history is theater, then repetition, along with the tragic and the comic within repetition, forms a condition of movement under which the "actors" or the "heros" produce something effectively new in history.) The theater of repetition is opposed to the theater of representation, just as movement is opposed to concepts and to representation which refers it back to concepts. In the theater of repetition, we experience pure forces, dynamic lines in space which act without intermediary upon the spirit, and which link it directly with nature and history, with a language which speaks before words, with gestures which develop before organized bodies, with masks before faces, with specters and phantoms before characters—the whole apparatus of repetition as a "terrible power."

It becomes easy, then, to speak of the differences between Kierkegaard and Nietzsche. But even this question must no longer be posed at the speculative level of the ultimate nature of the God of Abraham or the Dionysus of Zarathustra. It is rather a matter of knowing what it means to "produce movement," to repeat or to obtain repetition. Is it a matter of leaping, as Kierkegaard believes? Or rather is it a matter of dancing, as Nietzsche thinks; he does not like the confusion of dancing and leaping (only Zarathustra's ape, his demon, his dwarf, his buffoon, leaps).[3] Kierkegaard offers us a theater of faith; he opposes spiritual movement, the movement of faith, to logical movement. He can thus invite us to go beyond all aesthetic repetition, to go beyond irony and even humor, all the while painfully aware that he offers us only the aesthetic, ironic, and humoristic image of such a going beyond. With Nietzsche, it is a theater of unbelief, of movement as *physis,* already a theater of cruelty. Here, humor and irony are indispensable and fundamental operations of nature. And what would the eternal return be, if we forgot that it is a vertiginous movement endowed with a force: not one which causes the return of the Same in general, but one which selects, one which expels as well as creates, destroys as well as produces? Nietzsche's leading idea is to found the repetition in the eternal return at once on the death of God and the dissolution of the self. But it is a quite different alliance in the theater of faith: Kierkegaard dreams of an alliance between a God and a self rediscovered. All sorts of differences follow: is the movement in the sphere of the mind, or in the intestines of the earth which knows neither God nor self? Where will it be better protected against generalities, against mediations? Is repetition supernatural, to the extent that it is over and above the laws of nature? Or is it rather the most natural will of nature in itself and willing itself as *physis,* because nature is by itself superior to its own kingdoms and its own laws? Hasn't Kierkegaard mixed all kinds of things together in his condemnation of "aesthetic" repetition: a pseudo-repetition attributable to general laws of nature, a true repetition in nature itself; a repetition of the passions in a pathological mode, a repetition in art and the work of art? We cannot now resolve any of these problems; it has been enough for us to find theatrical confirmation of an irreducible difference between generality and repetition.

10
. . .
Eternal Recurrence

Because it is neither felt nor known, a becoming-active can only be thought as the product of a *selection*. A simultaneous double selection by the activity of force and the affirmation of the will. But what can perform the selection? What serves as the selective principle? Nietzsche replies: the eternal return. Formerly the object of disgust, the eternal return overcomes disgust and turns Zarathustra into a "convalescent," someone consoled (Z III "The Convalescent").[1] But in what sense is the eternal return selective? Firstly because, as a thought, it gives the will a practical rule (*VP* IV 229, 231/*WP* 1053, 1056 "The great selective *thought*").[2] The eternal return gives the will a rule as rigorous as the Kantian one. We have noted that the eternal return, as a physical doctrine, was the new formulation of the speculative synthesis. As an ethical thought the eternal return is the new formulation of the practical synthesis: *whatever you will, will it in such a way that you also will its eternal return.* "If, in all that you will you begin by asking yourself: is it certain that I will to do it an infinite number of times? This should be your most solid centre of gravity (*VP* IV 242). One thing in the world disheartens Nietzsche: the little compensations, the little pleasures, the little joys and everything that one is granted once, only once. Everything that can be done again the next day on the condition that it be said the day before: tomorrow I will give it up—the whole ceremonial of the obsessed. And we are like those old women who permit themselves an excess only once, we act and think like them. "Oh, that you would put from you all *half* willing, and decide upon lethargy as you do upon action. Oh that you understood my saying: 'Always do what you will—but first be such as *can* will!' "³ Laziness, stupidity, baseness, cowardice, or spitefulness that would will its own eternal return would no longer be the same laziness, stupidity, etc. How does the eternal return perform the selection here? It is the *thought* of the eternal return that selects. It makes willing something whole. The thought of the eternal return eliminates from willing everything which falls outside the eternal return, it makes willing a creation, it brings about the equation "willing = creating."

It is clear that such a selection falls short of Zarathustra's ambitions. It is content to eliminate certain reactive states, certain states of reactive forces which are among the least developed. But reactive forces which go to the limit of what they can do in their own way, and which find a powerful motor in the nihilistic will, resist the first selection. Far from falling outside the eternal return they enter into it and seem to return with it. We must therefore expect a second selection, very different from the first. But this second selection involves the most obscure parts of Nietzsche's philosophy and forms an almost esoteric element on the doctrine of the eternal return. We can therefore only summarize these Nietzschean themes, leaving a detailed conceptual explanation until later.

1. Why is the eternal return called "the most extreme form of nihilism" (*VP* III 8/*WP* 55)? And if the eternal return is the most extreme form of nihilism, nihilism itself (separated or abstracted from the eternal return) is always an "incomplete nihilism" (*VP* III 7/*WP* 28): however far it goes, however powerful it is. Only the eternal return makes the nihilistic will whole and complete.

2. The will to nothingness, as we have investigated it up to now, has always appeared in an alliance with reactive forces. Its essence was to deny active force and to lead it to deny and turn against itself. But, at the same time, it laid in this way the foundation for the conservation, triumph, and contagion of reactive forces. The will to nothingness was the universal becoming-reactive, the becoming-reactive of forces. This is the sense in which nihilism is always incomplete of its own. Even the ascetic ideal is the opposite of what we might think, "it is an expedient of the art of conserving life." Nihilism is the principle of conservation of a weak, diminished, reactive life. The depreciation and negation of life form the principle in whose shadow the reactive life conserves itself, survives, triumphs, and becomes contagious (*GM* III 13).⁴

3. What happens when the will to nothingness is related to the eternal

return? This is the only place where it breaks its alliance with reactive forces. Only the eternal return can complete nihilism *because it makes negation a negation of reactive forces themselves.* By and in the eternal return nihilism no longer expresses itself as the conservation and victory of the weak but as their destruction, their *self-destruction.* "This perishing takes the form of a self-destruction—the instinctive selection of that which must destroy. . . . The will to destruction as the will of a still deeper instinct, the instinct of self-destruction, the will for nothingness" (*VP* III 8/*WP* 55). This is why Zarathustra, as early as the Prologue, sings of the "one who wills his own downfall," "for he does not want to preserve himself," "for he will cross the bridge without hesitation" (*Z* Prologue 4). The Prologue to *Zarathustra* contains the premature secret of the eternal return.

4. Turning against oneself should not be confused with this destruction of self, this self-destruction. In the reactive process of turning against oneself active force becomes reactive. In self-destruction reactive forces are themselves denied and led to nothingness. This is why self-destruction is said to be an active operation an *"active destruction"* (*VP* III 8; *EH* III 1).[5] It and it alone expresses the becoming-active of forces: forces become active insofar as reactive forces deny and suppress themselves in the name of a principle which, a short time ago, was still assuring their conservation and triumph. Active negation or active destruction is the state of strong spirits which destroy the reactive in themselves, submitting it to the test of the eternal return and submitting themselves to this test even if it entails willing their own decline; "it is the condition of strong spirits and wills, and these do not find it possible to stop with the negative of 'judgement'; their nature demands *active negation*" (*VP* III 102/*WP* 24). This is the only way in which reactive forces *become active.* Furthermore this is why negation, by making itself the negation of reactive forces themselves, is not only active but is, as it were, *transmuted.* It expresses affirmation and becoming-active as the power of affirming. Nietzsche then speaks of the "eternal joy of becoming . . . that joy which includes even joy in destroying," "The affirmation of passing away and *destroying,* which is the decisive feature of a Dionysian philosophy" (*EH* III "The Birth of Tragedy" 3; 273);

5. The second selection in the eternal return is thus the following: the eternal return produces becoming-active. It is sufficient to relate the will to nothingness to the eternal return in order to realize that reactive forces do not return. However far they go, however deep the becoming-reactive of forces, reactive forces will not return. The small, petty, reactive man will not return. In and through the eternal return negation as a quality of the will to power transmutes itself into affirmation, it becomes an affir-

mation of negation itself, it becomes a power of affirming, an affirmative power. This is what Nietzsche presents as Zarathustra's cure and Dionysus' secret. "Nihilism vanquished by itself" thanks to the eternal return (*VP* III). This second selection is very different from the first. It is no longer a question of the simple thought of the eternal return eliminating from willing everything that falls outside this thought but rather, of the eternal return making something come into being which cannot do so without changing nature. It is no longer a question of selective thought but of selective being; for the eternal return is being and being is selection (selection = hierarchy).

All this must be taken as a simple summary of texts. These texts will only be elucidated in terms of the following points: the relation of the two qualities of the will to power (negation and affirmation), the relation of the will to power itself with the eternal return, and the possibility of transmutation as a new way of feeling, thinking, and above all being (the overman). In Nietzsche's terminology the reversal of values means the active in place of the reactive (strictly speaking it is the reversal of a reversal, since the reactive began by taking the place of action). But *transmutation* of values, or *transvaluation,* means affirmation instead of negation—negation transformed into a power of affirmation, the supreme Dionysian metamorphosis. All these as yet unanalyzed points form the summit of the doctrine of the eternal return.

From afar we can hardly see this summit. The eternal return is the being of becoming. But becoming is double: becoming-active and becoming-reactive, becoming-active of reactive forces and becoming-reactive of active forces. But only becoming-active has being; it would be contradictory for the being of becoming to be affirmed of a becoming-reactive, of a becoming that is itself nihilistic. The eternal return would become contradictory if it were the return of reactive forces. The eternal return teaches us that becoming-reactive has no being. Indeed, it also teaches us of the existence of a becoming-active. It necessarily produces becoming-active by reproducing becoming. This is why affirmation is twofold: the being of becoming cannot be fully affirmed without also affirming the existence of becoming-active. The eternal return thus has a double aspect: it is the universal being of becoming, but the universal being of becoming ought to belong to a single becoming. Only becoming-active has a being which is the being of the whole of becoming. Returning is everything but everything is affirmed in a single moment . Insofar as the eternal return is affirmed as the universal being of becoming, insofar as becoming-active is also affirmed as the symptom and product of the universal eternal return, affirmation changes nuance and becomes more and more profound. Eternal return, as a physical doctrine, affirms the being of becoming. But, as selective ontology, it affirms this being of becoming as the "self-affirming" of becoming-active. We see that, at the heart of the complicity which joins Zarathustra and his animals, a misunderstanding arises, a problem the animals neither understand nor recognize, the problem of Zarathustra's disgust and cure. "O you buffoons and barrel organs! answered Zarathustra and smiled again . . . you— have already made an old song of it" (Z III "The Convalescent" pp. 234–35). The old song is the cycle and the whole, universal being. But the complete formula of affirmation is: the whole, yes, universal being, yes, but universal being ought to belong to a single becoming, the whole ought to belong to a single moment.

11
...
Man and Overman

Foucault's general principle is that every form is a compound of relations between forces. Given these forces, our first question is with what forces from the outside they enter into a relation, and then what form is created as a result. These may be forces within man: the force to imagine, remember, conceive, wish, and so on. One might object that such forces already presuppose man: but in terms of form this is not true. The forces within man presuppose only places, points of industry, a region of the existent. In the same way forces within an animal (mobility, irritability, and so on) do not presuppose any determined form. One needs to know with what other forces the forces within man enter in a relation, in a given historical formation, and what form is created as a result from this compound of forces. We can already foresee that the forces within man do not necessarily contribute to the composition of a man-form, but may be otherwise invested in another compound or form: even over a short period of time man has not always existed, and will not exist for ever. For a man-form to appear to be delineated, the forces within man must enter into a relation with certain very special forces from the outside.

I. The "Classical" Historical Formation

Classical thought may be recognized by the way in which it thinks of the infinite. In it every reality, in a force, "equals" perfection, and so can be raised to infinity (the infinitely perfect), the rest being a limitation and nothing but a limitation. For example, the force to conceive can be raised to infinity, such that human understanding is merely the limitation placed on an infinite understanding. No doubt there are very different orders of infinity, but they are formed only on the basis of the limitation weighing down a particular force. The force to conceive can be raised to infinity directly, while that of imagining can achieve only an infinity of an inferior or derived order. The seventeenth century does not ignore the distinction between the infinite and the indefinite, but it makes the indefinite the lowest degree of infinity. The question of knowing whether or not the whole range can be attributed to God depends on the separation of whatever is reality in the range from whatever is limitation, that is to say from the order of infinity to which the range can be raised. The most typical seventeenth-century texts therefore concern the distinction between different orders of infinity: the infinity of grandeur and the infinity of smallness in Pascal; the infinite in itself, the infinite in its cause, and the infinite between limits in Spinoza; all the infinities in Leibniz, and so on. Classical thought is certainly not serene or imperious. On the contrary, it continually loses itself in infinity: as Michel Serres says, it loses all center and territory, agonizes over its attempts to fix the place of the finite in the midst of all the infinities, and tries to establish an order within infinity.[1]

In brief, the forces within man enter into a relation with those forces that raise things to infinity. The latter are indeed forces from the outside, since man is limited and cannot himself account for this more perfect power which passes through him. Thus the compound created from the confrontation between the forces within man, on the one hand, and the forces that raise to infinity, on the other, is not a man-form but the God-form. One may object that God is not a compound but an absolute and unfathomable unity. This is true, but the God-form is a compound in the eyes of every seventeenth-century author. It is a compound precisely of every force that can be directly raised to infinity (sometimes understanding and will, sometimes thought and range, etc.). As for other forces which can be raised only by their cause, or between limits, they still belong to the God-form, not in essence but in consequence, to the point where we can derive from each one of them a proof of the existence of God (proofs that are cosmological, physico-teleological, and so on). Thus, in the classical historical formation, the forces within man enter into a relation with forces from the outside in such a way that the compound is a God-form, and not at all a man-form. This is the world of infinite representation.

In the orders derived from it we must find the element that is not infinite in itself, but which nonetheless can be developed to an infinite degree and consequently enters into a scene, or unlimited series, or continuum that can be prolonged. This is the sign of the classical forms of science still prevalent in the eighteenth century: "character" for living beings, "root" for languages, money (or land) for wealth.[2] Such sciences are general, the general indicating an order of infinity. Thus there is no biology in the seventeenth century, but there is a natural history that does not form a system without organizing itself in series; there is no political economy, but there is an analysis of wealth; no philology or linguistics, but a general grammar.

Foucault will subject this triple aspect to a detailed analysis, and find it the perfect place in which to divide up statements. In accordance with this method, Foucault isolates an "archaeological ground" in classical thought which reveals unexpected affinities, but also breaks relations that are too predictable. This avoids making Lamarck into a precursor of Darwin, for example: for it is true that Lamarck's genius lay in injecting a historicity into living beings in several different ways; this is something still done from the viewpoint of the animal series, to save this idea of series which is threatened by new factors. Therefore, Lamarck differs from Darwin in belonging to the classical "ground."[3] What defines this ground and constitutes this great family of so-called classical statements, functionally, is this continual development towards infinity, formulation of continuums, and unveiling of scenes: the continual need to unfold and "explain." What is God, if not the universal explanation and supreme unveiling? The *unfold* appears here as a fundamental concept, or first aspect of an active thought that becomes embodied in the classical formation. This accounts for the frequency of the noun *unfold* in Foucault. If the clinic belongs to this formation, it is because it consists in unfolding the tissues covering "two-dimensional areas" and in developing in series the symptoms whose compositions are infinite.[4]

II. The Historical Formation of the Nineteenth Century

Mutation consists in this: the forces within man enter into a relation with new forces from the outside, which are forces of finitude. These forces are life, labor, and language—the triple root of finitude, which will give birth to biology, political economy, and linguistics. And no doubt we are used to this archaeological mutation: we often locate in Kant the source of such a revolution where the "constituent finitude" replaces the original infinity.[5] What could be more unintelligible for the classical age than that finitude should be constituent? Foucault nonetheless introduces a completely new element into this scheme: while we were once told only that man becomes aware of his own finitude, under certain historically determinable causes Foucault insists on the necessity of introducing two distinct phases. The force within man must begin by confronting and seizing hold of the forces of finitude as if they were forces from outside: it is outside oneself that force must come up against finitude. Then and only then, in a second stage, does it create from this its own finitude, where its knowledge of finitude necessarily brings it to its own finitude. All this means that when the forces within man enter into a relation with forces of finitude from outside, then and only then does the set of forces compose the man-form (and not the God-form). *Incipit Homo.*

It is here that the method for analyzing statements is shown to be a microanalysis that offers two stages where we had previously seen only one.[6] The first moment consists in this: something breaks the series and fractures the continuums, which on the surface can no longer be developed. It is like the advent of a new dimension, an irreducible depth that menaces the orders of infinite representation. With Jussieu, Vicq d'Azyr, and Lamarck, the coordination and subordination of characteristics in a plant or animal—in brief, an organizing force—imposes a division of organisms which can no longer be aligned but tend to develop each on its own (pathological anatomy accentuates this tendency by discovering an organic depth or a "pathological volume"). With Jones, a force of fluxion alters the order of roots. With Adam Smith, a force of work (abstract work, any work that is no longer evidence of a particular quality) alters the order of wealth. Not that organization, fluxion, and labor have been ignored by the classical age. But they played the role of limitations that did not prevent the corresponding qualities from being raised *to infinity,* or from being deployed to infinity, if only in law. Now, on the other hand, they disengage themselves from quality and reveal instead something that cannot be qualified or represented, death in life, pain and fatigue in work, stammering or aphasia in language. Even the land will discover its essential avarice, and get rid of its apparent order of infinity.[7]

Then everything is ready for the second stage, for a biology, a political economy, a linguistics. Things, living creatures, and words need only *fold back* on this depth as a new dimension, or *fall back* on these forces of finitude. There is no longer just a force of organization in life; there are also spatio-temporal programs of organization which are irreducible in themselves, and on the basis of which living beings are disseminated (Cuvier). There is no longer simply a force of inflection in language, but various programs on the basis of which affixive or inflected languages are distributed and where the self-sufficiency of words and letters gives way to verbal interrelations, language itself no longer being defined by what it designates or signifies, but referring back instead to "collective wills" (Bopp, Schlegel). There is no longer simply a force of productive work; instead there are conditions of production on the basis of which work itself falls back on capital (Ricardo) before the reverse takes place, in which capital falls back on the work extorted (Marx). Everywhere comparisons replace the general fact that was so dear to the seventeenth century: comparative anatomy, comparative philology, comparative economy. Everywhere it is the *fold* which dominates now, to follow Foucault's terminology, and this fold is the second aspect of the active thought that becomes incarnated in nineteenth-century development. The forces within man fall or fold back on this new dimension of in-depth finitude, which then becomes the finitude of man himself. The fold, as Foucault constantly says, is what constitutes a "thickness" as well as a "hollow."

In order to reach a better understanding of how the fold becomes the fundamental category, we need only examine the birth of biology. Everything we find proves Foucault's case (and could equally be found in any other discipline). When Cuvier outlines four great branches he does not define any generality larger than genre or class, but on the contrary concentrates on fractures that prevent any continuum of species from grouping in increasingly general terms. The branches of organizing elements set in motion certain axes, orientations, or dynamisms on the basis of which the living element is folded in a particular way. This is why the work of Cuvier extends into the comparative embryology of Baer, based on the foldings of germinal layers. And when Geoffroy Saint-Hilaire contrasts Cuvier's organizational program with a single composition or structure, he still invokes a method of folding: we pass from the vertebrate to the cephalopoid, if we bring together the two parts of the vertebrate's spine, its head towards its feet, its frame up to its neck, and so on.[8] If Geoffroy belongs to the same 'archaeological ground' as Cuvier (in accordance with Foucault's method for analysing statements), this is because both invoke the fold, one seeing it as a third dimension that brings about this move under the surface. What Cuvier, Geoffroy and Baer also have in common is that they resist evolutionism. But Darwin will found natural selection on the advantage which the living creature has, in a given environment, if it makes characteristics diverge and opens up differences. It is because they fold in different ways (the tendency to diverge) that a maximum of living creatures will be able to survive in the same place. As a result, Darwin still belongs to the same ground as Cuvier, as opposed to Lamarck, to the extent that he bases his evolutionism on the impossibility of convergence and the failure to achieve a serial continuum.[9]

If the fold and the unfold animate not only Foucault's ideas but even his style, it is because they constitute an archaeology of thought. So we are perhaps less surprised to find that Foucault encounters Heidegger precisely in this area. It is more an encounter than an influence, to the extent that in Foucault the fold and the unfold have an origin, a use, and a destination that are very different from Heidegger's. According to Foucault they reveal a relation between forces, where regional forces confront either forces that raise to infinity (the unfold) in such a way as to constitute a God-form, or forces of finitude (the fold) in such a way as to constitute a man-form. It is a Nietzschean rather than Heideggerean history, a history devoted to Nietzsche, or to *life:* "There is being only because their is life. . . . The Experience of life is thus posited as the most general law of beings . . . but this ontology discloses not so much what gives beings their foundation as what bears them for an instant towards a precarious form."[10]

III. Toward a Formation of the Future?

It is obvious that any form is precarious, since it depends on relations between forces and their mutations. We distort Nietzsche when we make him into the thinker who wrote about the death of God. It is Feuerbach who is the last thinker of the death of God: he shows that since God has never been anything but the unfold of man, man must fold and refold God. But for Nietzsche this is an old story, and as old stories tend to multiply their variants Nietzsche multiplies the versions of the death of God, all of them comic or humorous, as though they were variations on a given fact. But what interests him is the death of man. So long as God exists—that is, so long as the God-form functions—then man does not yet exist.

But when the man-form appears, it does so only by already incorporating the death of man in at least three ways. First, where can man find a guarantee of identity in the absence of God?[11] Secondly, the man-form has itself been constituted only within the folds of finitude: it places death within man (and has done so, as we have seen, less in the manner of Heidegger than in the manner of Bichat, who conceived of death in terms of a "violent death').[12] Lastly, the forces of finitude themselves mean that man exists only through the dissemination of the various methods for organizing life, such as the dispersion of languages or the divergence in modes of production, which imply that the only "critique of knowledge" is an "ontology of the annihilation of beings" (not only palaeontology, but also ethnology).[13]

What does Foucault mean when he says there is no point in crying over the death of man?[14] In fact, has this form been a good one? Has it helped to enrich or even preserve the forces within man, those of living, speaking, or

working? Has it saved living men from a violent death? The question that
continually returns is therefore the following: if the forces within man compose a form only by entering into a relation with forms from the outside,
with what new forms do they now risk entering into a relation, and what
new form will emerge that is neither God nor man? This is the correct place
for the problem that Nietzsche called "the superman."

It is a problem where we have to content ourselves with very tentative
indications if we are not to descend to the level of cartoons. Foucault, like
Nietzsche, can only sketch in something embryonic and not yet functional.[15] Nietzsche said that man imprisoned life, but the superman is what
frees life *within man himself*, to the benefit of another form, and so on.
Foucault proffers a very peculiar piece of information: if it is true that
nineteenth-century humanist linguistics was based on the dissemination of
languages, as the condition for a "demotion of language" as an object, one
repercussion was nonetheless that literature took on a completely different
function that consisted, *on the contrary*, in "regrouping" language and em-
phasizing a "being of language" beyond whatever it designates and signifies, beyond even the sounds.[16] The peculiar thing is that Foucault, in his
acute analysis of modern literature, here gives language a privilege which
he refuses to grant to life or labor: he believes that life and labor, despite a
dispersion concomitant with that of language, did not lose the regrouping of
their being.[17] It seems to us, though, that when dispersed labor and life
were each able to unify themselves only by somehow breaking free from economics or biology, just as language managed to regroup itself only when
literature broke free from linguistics.

Biology had to take a leap into molecular biology, or dispersed life regroup
in the genetic code. Dispersed work had to regroup in third-generation
machines, cybernetics, and information technology. What would be the
forces in play, with which the forces within man would then enter into a
relation? It would no longer involve raising to infinity or finitude but an
unlimited finity, thereby evoking every situation of force in which a finite
number of components yields a practically unlimited diversity of combinations. It would be neither the fold nor the unfold that would constitute the
active mechanism, but something like the *superfold*, as borne out by the foldings proper to the chains of the genetic code, and the potential of silicon in
third-generation machines, as well as by the contours of a sentence in modern literature, when literature "merely turns back on itself in an endless re-
flexivity."

This modern literature uncovers a "strange language within language"
and, through an unlimited number of superimposed grammatical construc-
tions, tends towards an atypical form of expression that marks the end of

language as such (here we may cite such examples as Mallarmé's book, Péguy's repetitions, Artaud's breaths, the agrammaticality of Cummings, Burroughs and his cut-ups and fold-ins, as well as Roussel's proliferations, Brisset's derivations, Dada collage, and so on). And is this unlimited finity or superfold not what Nietzsche had already designated with the name of eternal return?

The forces within man enter into a relation with forces from the outside, those of silicon which supersedes carbon, or genetic components which supersede the organism, or agrammaticalities which supersede the signifier. In each case we must study the operations of the superfold, of which the "double helix" is the best-known example. What is the superman? It is the formal compound of the forces within man and these new forces. It is the form that results from a new relation between forces. Man tends to free life, labor, and language *within himself.* The superman, in accordance with Rimbaud's formula, is the man who is even in charge of the animals (a code that can capture fragments from other codes, as in the new schemata of lateral or retrograde). It is man in charge of the very rocks, or inorganic matter (the domain of silicon). It is man in charge of the being of language (that formless "mute, unsignifying region where language can find its freedom" even from whatever it has to say).[18] As Foucault would say, the superman is much less than the disappearance of living men, and much more than a change of concept: it is the advent of a new form that is neither God nor man and which, it is hoped, will not prove worse than its two previous forms.

Part Three

. . .

Desire and Schizoanalysis

12
. . .
Psychoanalysis and Desire

Assemblages—in their content—are populated by becomings and intensities, by intensive circulations, by various multiplicities (packs, masses, species, races, populations, tribes . . .). And in their expression, assemblages handle indefinite articles or pronouns which are not at all indeterminate ("a" tummy, "some" people, "one" hits "a" child . . .)—verbs in the infinitive which are not undifferentiated but which mark processes (to walk, to kill, to love . . .)—proper names which are not people but events (they can be groups, animals, entities, singularities, collectives, everything that is written with a capital letter, A-HANS-BECOMING-HORSE). The collective machine assemblage is a material production of desire as well as an expressive cause of utterance: a semiotic articulation of chains of expressions whose contents are relatively the least formalized. Not representing a subject—for there is no subject of enunciation—but programming an assemblage. Not overcoding utterances but, on the contrary, preventing them from toppling under the tyranny of supposedly significant combinations. Now, it is curious that psychoanalysis—which boasts that it has so much logic—understands nothing of the logic of the indefinite article, of the infinitive of the verb and of the proper name. The psychoanalyst wants there to be, at all costs, a definite, a possessive, a personal, hidden behind the indefinite. When Melanie Klein's children say "a tummy" or ask "How do people grow up?" Melanie Klein hears "my mummy's tummy" or "Will I be big like my daddy?" When they say "a Hitler," "a Churchill." Melanie Klein sees here the possessive of the bad mother or of the good father. Military men and weathermen—more than psychoanalysts—have at least got the sense of the proper name when they use it to refer to a strategic operation or geographical process: Operation Typhoon. On one occasion Jung tells Freud about one of his dreams: he has dreamed of an ossuary. Freud wants Jung to have desired someone's death, doubtless that of his wife. "Surprised, Jung pointed out to him that there were several skulls, not just one."[1] In the same way, Freud does not want there to be six or seven wolves: there will only be one representative of the father. And again, there is what Freud does with little Hans: he takes no account of the assemblage (building-street-nextdoor-warehouse-omnibus-horse-a-horse-falls-a-horse-is-whipped!); he takes no account of the situation (the child had been forbidden to go into the street, etc); he takes no account of little Hans's endeavor (horse-becoming, because every other way out has been blocked up: the childhood bloc, the bloc of Hans's animal-becoming, the infinitive as marker of a becoming, the line of flight or the movement of deterritorialization). The only important thing for Freud is that the horse be the father—and that's the end of it. In practice, given an assemblage, extracting a segment from it, abstracting a moment from it, is sufficient to break up the ensemble of desire, to break up becoming in act [*le devenir en acte*], and to substitute for them overimaginary resemblances (a horse = my daddy) or analogies of oversymbolic relationships (to buck = to make love). All the real-desire has already disappeared: a code is put in its place, a symbolic overcoding of utterances, a fictitious subject of enunciation who doesn't give the patients a chance.

If you go to be psychoanalyzed, you believe that you will be able to talk and because of this belief you accept the need to pay. But you don't have the least chance of talking. Psychoanalysis is entirely designed to prevent people from talking and to remove from them all conditions of true enunciation. We have formed a small working group for the following task: to read reports of psychoanalysis, especially of children; to stick exclusively to these reports and make two columns, on the left what the child said, according to the account itself, and on the right what the psychoanalyst heard and retained (cf. always the card trick of the "forced choice"). It's horrifying. The two central texts in this respect are Freud's little Hans and Melanie Klein's little Richard. It's an amazing forcing,[2] like a boxing match between categories that are too unequal. At the outset there is Richard's humor, which makes fun of M. K. All these assemblages of desire on his part pass through a mapping activity during the war: a distribution of proper names, of territorialities and deterritorializing movements, thresholds and crossings. Insensitive and deaf, impervious, Mrs K. is going to break little Richard's strength. The leitmotif of the book is in the text itself: "Mrs K. interpreted, Mrs. K. *interpreted,* Mrs. K. INTERPRETED . . ." It is said that there is no longer any of this today: significance has replaced interpretation, the signifier has replaced the signified, the analyst's silence has replaced the commentaries, castration is revealed to be more certain than Oedipus, structural functions have replaced parental images, the name of the father has replaced my daddy. We see no important practical changes. A patient cannot mutter "mouths of the Rhône' [*bouches du Rhône*] without being corrected—"mother's mouth" [*bouche de la mère*]; another cannot say, "I would like to join a hippie group" [*groupe hippie*] without being asked "Why do you pronounce it big pee?" [*gros pipi*]. These two examples form part of analyses based on the highest signifier. And what could analysis consist of, if not these kind of things about which the analyst no longer even needs to talk because the person analyzed knows them as well as he does? The person analyzed has therefore become the analyzer—a particularly comic term. It's all very well to say to us: you understand nothing, Oedipus, it's not daddy-mummy, it's the symbolic, the law, the arrival at culture, it's the effect of the signifier, it's the finitude of the subject, it has the "lack-to-be which is life." And if it's not Oedipus, it will be castration, and the supposed death drives. Psychoanalysts teach infinite resignation, they are the last priests (no, there will be others after them). It cannot be said that they are very jolly; see the dead look they have, their stiff necks (only Lacan has kept a certain sense of laughter, but he admits that he is forced to laugh alone). They are right to say that they need to be "remunerated" to put up with the burden of what they hear; they have nonetheless given up supporting the thesis of a symbolic and disinterested role for money in psychoanalysis. We open by chance some article by an authoritative psychoanalyst, a two-page article: "Man's long dependence, his powerlessness to help himself . . . the human being's congenital inferiority . . . the narcissistic wound inherent in his existence . . . the painful reality of the human condition . . . which implies incompletion, conflict . . . his intrinsic misery, which it is true leads him to the most elevated creations." A priest would have been long since hounded out of his church for sustaining so insolent and obscurantist a style.

But yes, nevertheless, many things have changed in psychoanalysis. Either it has swamped, it is spread into all sorts, of techniques of therapy, of adjustment or even marketing, to which it brought its particular touch in a vast syncretism, its little line in group polyphony. Or it has hardened, in a refinement, a very lofty "return" to Freud, a solitary harmony, a triumphant specifying that wants no more pacts except with linguistics (even if the reverse is not true). But whatever their considerable difference, we believe that these two opposed directions provide evidence of the same changes, of the same evolution, which bears on several points.

1. First, psychoanalysis has displaced its center—from the family to married life. It sets itself up between spouses, lovers, or friends rather than between parents and children. Even children are guided by psychologists rather than being led along by their parents—or parent-child relations are regulated by radio consultations. The phantasm has made childhood memory redundant. This is a practical remark, which bears on the recruitment of people to be psychoanalyzed: this recruitment takes place less and less according to the genealogy of the family tree and more and more according to the circle of friends ("You ought to get analyzed as well"). As Serge Leclaire says, perhaps humorously, "there are now analyses where the circles of allegiance of couches frequented by friends and lovers take the place of relations of kinship."[3] This is of some importance to the actual form of problems: neurosis has abandoned hereditary models (even if heredity moves through a family milieu) to pursue patterns of contagion. Neurosis has acquired its most frightening power, that of propagation by contagion: "I will not let go of you until you have joined me in this condition." We admire the discretion of the earlier neurotics, of the hysterics or obsessionals, who either got on with their business alone or did it in the family: the modern depressive types are, on the contrary, particularly vampiric or poisonous. They take it on themselves to bring about Nietzsche's prophecy: they cannot bear the existence of "a" health; they will constantly draw us into their clutches. Yet to cure them would mean first destroying this will to venom in them. But how could the psychoanalyst do this—the same man who derives from it an excellent self-recruitment of his clientele? It might have been thought that May '68 would have dealt a mortal blow to psychoanalysis and would have made the style of specifically psychoanalytic utterances seem absurd. No, so many young people have returned to psychoanalysis. Precisely because it was able to abandon its discredited family model in order to take up a still more worrying direction, a "political" microcontagion instead of a "private" macrolineage. Never has psychoanalysis been so full of life, whether because it has succeeded in penetrating everything, or because it has established new foundations for its transcendent position, its specific order.

2. Historically, psychiatry does not seem to us to have been constituted around the notion of madness but, on the contrary, at the point where this notion proved difficult to apply. Psychiatry essentially ran up

against the problem of cases of delirium where the intellectual faculty was intact. On the one hand, there are people who seem to be mad, but who are not "really" so, having kept their faculties, and first and foremost the faculty of properly managing their money and their possessions (paranoid conduct, the delirium of interpretation, etc.).[4] On the other hand, there are people who are "really" mad and yet don't seem to be, suddenly committing an outrageous act which nothing led us to foresee, arson, murder, etc. (monomaniac conduct, the delirium of passion or revenge). If the psychiatrist has a bad conscience, it is because he has had one since the outset, because he is implicated in the dissolution of the notion of madness: he is accused of treating as insane certain people who are not exactly so, and of not seeing in time the madness of others who clearly are. Psychoanalysis slipped between these two poles, saying that we were at once all insane without seeming to be, but also that we seemed mad without being so. A whole "psychopathology of everyday life." In short, it is around the failure of the notion of madness that psychiatry is constituted and that psychoanalysis has been able to link up with it. It is difficult to add anything to the analyses first of Foucault, then of Robert Castel, when they show how psychoanalysis has grown in the soil of psychiatry.[5] By discovering between the two poles the world of neurotics, their intellectual faculties intact, and even absence of delirium, psychoanalysis, at its inception, succeeded in bringing off a very important maneuver: getting all sorts of people to go through the liberal contractual relationship who had until then seemed excluded from it ("madness" put all those it afflicted outside all possible contracts). The specifically psychoanalytic contract, a flux of words for a flux of money, was going to make the psychoanalyst someone able to insert himself into every pore of the society occupied by these doubtful cases. But the more psychoanalysis saw it was gaining ground, the more it turned towards the deliriums concealed behind neuroses, the less it seems to have been happy with the contractual relationship—even if, on the face of it, it was retained. Psychoanalysis had in fact achieved what was the source of Freud's anxiety at the end of his life; it had become interminable, interminable in principle. At the same time, it assumed a "mass" function. For what defines a mass function is not necessarily a collective, class or group character; it is the juridical transition from contract to statute. It seems more and more that psychoanalysis is acquiring an untransferable, inalienable, *statutory fixity*, rather than entering into a temporary *contractual relationship*. Precisely by setting itself up between the two poles where psychiatry came up against its limits, by enlarging the field between these two poles and exploring it, psychoanalysis was to invent a statute law of mental illness or psychic difficulty which constantly renewed itself and spread out into a systematic network. A new ambition was being offered to us: psychoanalysis is a lifelong affair.

The importance of the École Freudienne de Paris is perhaps particularly connected to the fact that it expressed for the first time the requirements of a new psychoanalytic order, not just in theory, but in its statutory organization, in its founding acts. For what it clearly proposes is a psychoanalytic statute, in opposition to the old contract: at a stroke it envisages a bureaucratic mutation, the transition from a bureaucracy of the eminent (the radical-socialist type, which suited the beginnings of psychoanalysis) to a mass bureaucracy; this time an ideal of giving out statutory documents like certificates of citizenship, identity cards, in contrast to limited contracts. Psychoanalysis invokes Rome, assumes a Ciceronian air and sets up its boundary between "Honestas" and "the rabble."[6] If the École Freudienne has brought so many problems to the psychoanalytic world, it is not simply as a result of its theoretical hauteur or of its practice, but because of its plan for a new explicit organization. The other psychoanalytic bodies may have judged this project to be inappropriate; but they did so because it told the truth about a change which affects the whole of psychoanalysis and which the other organizations preferred silently to leave alone, under the cover of the contractual motif. We do not regret the passing of this contractual cover-up, which was hypocritical from the start. Moreover, we are not saying that psychoanalysis is now concerned with the masses, but simply that it has assumed a mass function—whether this was phantasmal or restricted, or for an "elite." And this is the second aspect of its change: not only to have moved from family to conjugality, from kinship to match, from lineage to contagion, but also from *contract to statute*. On occasion the interminable years of psychoanalysis give social workers additional "salary increments"; psychoanalysis can be seen permeating every part of the social sector.[7] This seems to us to be more important than the practice and the theory which in general outline have stayed the same. Hence the reversal of the relations between psychoanalysis and psychiatry, hence psychoanalysis' ambition to become an official language; hence its pacts with linguistics (we do not have a contractual relationship with language).

3. Yet the theory itself has changed, seems to have changed. The transition from the signified to the signifier: if we no longer look for a signified for supposedly significant symptoms; if we look, on the contrary, for the signifier for symptoms which would be no more than its effect; if interpretation gives way to significance—then a new shift takes place. Psychoanalysis then has, in effect, its own references and has no more use for an

external "referent." Everything that happens in psychoanalysis in the analyst's consulting room is true. What happens elsewhere is derived or secondary. An excellent method for encouraging trust. Psychoanalysis has ceased to be an experimental science in order to get hold of an axiomatic system. Psychoanalysis, *index sui;* no other truth than that which emerges from the operation that presupposes it; the couch has become the bottomless well, interminable in principle. Psychoanalysis has stopped being "in search of" because it is now constitutive of truth. Once again, it is Serge Leclaire who puts it most succinctly: "The reality of the primitive scene tends to reveal itself more concretely by means of the analytic consulting room than in the surroundings of the parental bedroom. . . . From a figurative version, we move to the version of reference, a structural one, revealing the reality of a literal manoeuvre. . . . The psychoanalysts couch has become the place where the game of confronting the real properly unfolds." The psychoanalyst has become like the journalist: he creates the event. At any rate, psychoanalysis advertises its wares. So long as it interpreted or so long as it interprets (search for a signified), it returns desires and utterances to a condition which is deviant by comparison with the established order, by comparison with dominant meanings, but by the same token localizes them in the pores of this dominant, established body, like something which can be translated and exchanged by virtue of a contract. When it discovers the signifier, it appeals to a specifically psychoanalytic order (the symbolic order in opposition to the imaginary order of the signified), whose only need is itself, because it is statutory or structural: it is it which develops a body, a corpus sufficient by itself.

Once again we clearly come up against the question of power, of the apparatus of psychoanalytic power—with the same inflections as before: even if this power is narrow, localized, etc. This question can only be posed in terms of very general remarks: it is true, as Foucault says, that every formation of power needs a form of knowledge which, while not dependent on it, would itself lack all effectiveness without it. Now this usable knowledge may take two shapes: either an unofficial form, so that it can set itself up in the "pores," to seal some hole or other in the established order; or an official form, when it itself constitutes a symbolic order which gives a generalized axiomatic system to the established powers. For example, the historians of antiquity show the complementarity of Greek city and Euclidean geometry. It was not because the geometricians had power but because Euclidean geometry constituted the knowledge, or the abstract machine, that the city needed for its organization of power, space, and time. There is no State which does not need an image of thought which will serve as its axiomatic system or abstract machine, and to which it gives in return the strength to function: hence the inadequacy of the concept of ideology, which in no way takes into account this relationship. This was the unhappy role of classical philosophy—as we have seen it—that of supplying, in this way, the apparatuses of power, Church and State, with the knowledge which suited them. Could we say today that the human sciences have assumed this same role, that of providing by their own methods an abstract machine for modern apparatuses of power—receiving from them valuable endorsement in return? So psychoanalysis has submitted its tender, to become a major official language and knowledge in place of philosophy; to provide an axiomatic system of man in place of mathematics; to invoke the Honestas and a mass function. It is doubtful whether it is succeeding: the apparatuses of power have more interest in turning to physics, biology, or informatics. But psychoanalysis will have done what it could: it no longer serves the established order unofficially: it offers a specific and symbolic order, an abstract machine, an official language that it tries to weld onto linguistics in general, to assume a position of invariant. It is more and more concerned with pure "thought." Living psychoanalysis. Dead psychoanalysis, because it has little chance of succeeding in its ambition, because there are too many competitors and because, at the present time, all the forces of minority, all the forces of becoming, all the forces of language, all the forces of art, are in the process of fleeing from this particular ground—in the process of talking, thinking, acting, and becoming in other ways. Everything is happening by another route which psychoanalysis can't even intercept, or which psychoanalysis only intercepts in order to stop. And this is the very task which it sets itself: to overcode assemblages in order to subject desires to signifying chains, utterances to the status of subjective examples—all of which reconcile them with an established order. The four progressive changes that we have just seen—transition from the family to the circle of contacts, substitution of statute for contract, discovery of a specifically psychoanalytic order, a pact with linguistics—mark this ambition to take part in the regulation of assemblages of desire and of enunciation, or even to stake out a dominant position in this regulation.

We have been credited with many blunders about the *Anti-Oedipus*, about desiring machines, about what an assemblage of desire is, the forces that it mobilizes, the dangers it confronts. They did not come from us. We said that desire is in no sense connected to the "Law" and cannot be defined by any fundamental lack. For that's the real idea of the priest: the constituent law at the heart of desire, desire constituted as lack, the holy castration, the split subject, the death drive, the strange culture of death. And it is doubtless like this each time that desire is conceived as a bridge between a subject and an object: the subject of desire cannot but be split, and the object lost in advance. What we tried to show, on the contrary, was how desire was beyond these personological or objectal coordinates. It seemed to us that desire was a process and that it unrolled a *plane of consistence,* a field of immanence, a "body without organs," as Artaud put it, crisscrossed by particles and fluxes which break free from objects and subjects. . . . Desire is therefore not internal to a subject, any more than it tends towards an object: it is strictly immanent to a plane which it does not preexist, to a plane which must be constructed, where particles are emitted and fluxes combine. There is only desire insofar as there is deployment of a particular field, propagation of particular fluxes, emission of particular particles. Far from presupposing a subject, desire cannot be attained except at the point where someone is deprived of the power of saying "I." Far from directing itself toward an object, desire can only be reached at the point where someone no longer searches for or grasps an object any more than he grasps himself as subject. The objection is then made that such a desire is totally indeterminate, and that it is even more imbued with lack. But who has you believe that by losing the coordinates of object and subject you lack something? Who is pushing you into believing that indefinite articles and pronouns (a, one), third persons (he, she) and verbs in the infinitive are in the least indeterminate? The plane of consistence or of immanence, the body without organs, includes voids and deserts. But these are "fully" part of desire, far from accentuating some kind of lack in it. What a strange confusion—that of void with lack. We really do lack in general a particle of the East, a grain of Zen. Anorexia is perhaps the thing about which most wrong has been spoken—particularly under the influence of psychoanalysis. The void which is specific to the anorexic body without organs has nothing to do with a lack, and is part of the constitution of the field of desire crisscrossed by particles and fluxes. We will shortly return to this example to give more detail. But already the desert is a body without organs which has never been hostile to the groups who people it; the void has never been hostile to the particles which move about in it.

We have an image of the desert which involves the thirsty explorer, and an image of the void, as a ground which opens up. Images related to death which are only valid where the plane of consistence, which is identical to desire, is unable to establish itself and does not have the conditions to build on. But, on the plane of consistence, even the scarcity of particles and the slowing down and drying up of fluxes are part of desire, and of the pure life of desire, without indicating any lack. As Lawrence says, chastity is a flux. Is the plane of consistence something very strange? We would have to say simultaneously not only: "You've got it already, you do not feel desire without its being already there, without its being mapped out at the same time as your desire," but also: "You haven't got it, and you don't desire it if you can't manage to construct it, if you don't know how to, by finding your places, your assemblages, your particles and your fluxes." We would have to say simultaneously not only: "It is created all alone, but know how to see it," and also: "You have to create it, know how to create it, take the right directions, at your risk and peril." Desire: who, except priests, would want to call it "lack"? Nietzsche called it "will to power." There are other names for it. For example, "grace." Desiring is not at all easy, but this is precisely because it gives, instead of lacks, "virtue which gives." Those who link desire to lack, the long column of crooners of castration, clearly indicate a long resentment, like an interminable bad conscience. Is this to misunderstand the misery of those who really do lack something? But apart from the fact that psychoanalysis does not talk about these people (on the contrary, it makes the distinction, it says pompously enough that it is not concerned with real privations), those whose lack is real have no possible plane of consistence which would allow them to desire. They are prevented from doing this in a thousand ways. And as soon as they construct one, they lack nothing on this plane, and from this starting point they set off victoriously towards that which they lack outside. Lack refers to a positivity of desire, and not the desire to a negativity of lack. Even individually, the construction of the plane is a politics, it necessarily involves a "collective," collective assemblages, a set of social becoming.

13
. . .
Delirium: World-Historical, Not Familial

In the third synthesis, the conjunctive synthesis of consumption, we have seen how the body without organs was in fact an egg, crisscrossed with axes, banded with zones, localized with areas and fields, measured off by gradients, traversed by potentials, marked by thresholds. In this sense, we believe in a biochemistry of schizophrenia (in conjunction with the biochemistry of drugs), that will be progressively more capable of determining the nature of this egg and the distribution of field-gradient-threshold. It is a matter of relationships of intensities through which the subject passes on the body without organs, a process that engages him in becomings, rises and falls, migrations and displacements. R. D. Laing is entirely right in defining the schizophrenic process as a voyage of initiation, a transcendental experience of the loss of the ego, which causes a subject to remark: "I had existed since the very beginning . . . from the lowest form of life [the body without organs] to the present time, . . . I was looking . . .—not looking so much as just *feeling*—ahead of me was lying the most horrific journey."[1] When we speak here of a voyage, this is no more a metaphor than before when we spoke of an egg, and of what takes place in and on it—morphogenetic movements, displacements of cellular groups, stretchings, folds, migrations, and local variations of potentials. There is no reason to oppose an interior voyage to exterior ones: Lenz's stroll, Nijinsky's stroll, the promenades of Beckett's creatures are effective realities, but where the reality of matter has abandoned all extension, just as the interior voyage has abandoned all form and quality, henceforth causing pure intensities— coupled together, almost unbearable—to radiate within and without, intensities through which a nomadic subject passes. Here it is not a case of a hallucinatory experience nor of a delirious mode of thought, but a feeling, a series of emotions and feelings as a consummation and a consumption of intensive quantities, that form the material for subsequent hallucinations and deliriums. The intensive emotion, the affect, is both the common root and the principle of differentiation of deliriums and hallucinations.

We are also of a mind to believe that everything commingles in these intense becomings, passages, and migrations—all this drift that ascends and descends the flows of time: countries, races, families, parental appellations, divine appellations, geographical and historical designations, and even miscellaneous news items. (*I feel that*) I am becoming God, I am becoming woman, I was Joan of Arc and I am Heliogabalus and the Great Mongol, I am a Chinaman, a redskin, a Templar, I was my father and I was my son. And all the criminals, the whole list of criminals, the decent criminals and the scoundrels: Szondi rather than Freud and his Oedipus. "Perhaps it's by trying to be Worm that I'll finally succeed in being Mahood. . . . Then all I'll have to do is be Worm. Which no doubt I shall achieve by trying to be Jones. Then all I'll have to do is be Jones." But if everything commingles in this fashion it does so in intensity, with no confusion of spaces and forms, since these have indeed been undone on behalf of a new order: the intense and intensive order.

What is the nature of this order? The first things to be distributed on the body without organs are races, cultures, and their gods. The fact has often been overlooked that the schizo indeed participates in history; he hallucinates and raves universal history, and proliferates the races. All delirium is racial, which does not necessarily mean racist. It is not a matter of the regions of the body without organs "representing" races and cultures. The full body does not represent anything at all. On the contrary, the races and cultures designate regions on this body—that is, zones of intensities, fields of potentials. Phenomena of individualization and sexualization are produced within these fields. We pass from one field to another by crossing thresholds: we never stop migrating, we become other individuals as well as other sexes, and departing becomes as easy as being born or dying. Along the way we struggle against other races, we destroy civilizations, in the manner of the great migrants in whose wake nothing is left standing once they have passed through—although these destructions can be brought about, as we shall see, in two very different ways.

The crossing of a threshold entails ravages elsewhere—how could it be otherwise? The body without organs closes round the deserted places. The theater of cruelty cannot be separated from the struggle against our culture, from the confrontation of the "races," and from Artaud's great migration toward Mexico, its forces, and its religions: individuations are produced only within fields of forces expressly defined by intensive vibrations, and that animate cruel personages only in so far as they are induced organs, parts of desiring-machines (mannequins).[2] A season in hell—how could it be separated from denunciations of European families, from the call for destructions that don't come quickly enough, from the admiration for the convict, from the intense crossing of the thresholds of history, and from this prodigious migration, this becoming-woman, this becoming-Scandinavian or Mongol, this "displacement of races and continents," this feeling of raw intensity that presides over delirium as well as over hallucinations, and especially this deliberate, stubborn, material will to be "of a race inferior for all eternity": "I have known every son of good birth, I have never been of this people, I have never been Christian, . . . yes my eyes are closed to your light. I am a beast, a Negro."[3]

And can Zarathustra be separated from the "grand politics," and from the bringing to life of the races that leads Nietzsche to say, I'm not a German, I'm Polish? Here again individuations are brought about solely within complexes of forces that determine persons as so many intensive states embodied in a "criminal," ceaselessly passing beyond a threshold while destroying the factitious unity of a family and an ego: "I am Prado, I am also Prado's father. I venture to say that I am also Lesseps. . . . I wanted to give my Parisians, whom I love, a new idea—that of a decent criminal. I am also Chambige—also a decent criminal. . . . The unpleasant thing, and one that nags at my modesty, is that at root *every name in history is I*."[4] Yet it was never a question of identifying oneself with personages, as when it is erroneously maintained that a madman "takes himself for so-and-so. . . ." It is a question of something quite different: identifying races, cultures, and gods with fields of intensity on the body without organs, identifying personages with states that fill these fields, and with effects that fulgurate within and traverse these fields. Whence the role of names, with a magic all their own: there is no ego that identifies with races, peoples, and persons in a theater of representation, but proper names that identify races, peoples, and persons with regions, thresholds, or effects in a production of intensive quantities. The theory of proper names should not be conceived of in terms of representation; it refers instead to the class of "effects": effects that are not a mere dependence on causes, but the occupation of a domain, and the operation of a system of signs. This can be clearly seen in physics, where proper names designate such effects within fields of potentials: the Joule effect, the Seebeck effect, the Kelvin effect. History is like physics: a Joan of Arc effect, a Heliogabalus effect—all the *names* of history, and not the name of the father.

Everything has been said about the paucity of reality, the loss of reality, the lack of contact with life, autism and athymia. Schizophrenics themselves have said everything there is to say about this, and have been quick to slip into the expected clinical mold. Dark world, growing desert: a solitary machine hums on the beach, an atomic factory installed in the desert. But if the body without organs is indeed this desert, it is as an indivisible, non-decomposable distance over which the schizo glides in order to be everywhere, something real is produced, everywhere something real has been and will be produced. It is true that reality has ceased to be a principle. According to such a principle, the reality of the real was posed as a divisible abstract quantity, whereas the real was divided up into qualified unities, into distinct qualitative forms. But now the real is a product that envelops the distances within intensive quantities. The indivisible is enveloped, and signifies that what envelops it does not divide without changing its nature or form. The schizo has no principles: he is something only by being something else. He is Mahood only by being worm, and worm only by being Jones. He is a girl only by being an old man who is miming or simulating the girl. Or rather, by being someone who is simulating an old man simulating a girl. Or rather, by simulating someone . . . , etc. This was already true of the completely oriental art of the Roman Emperors, the twelve paranoiacs of Suetonius. In a great book by Jacques Besse, we encounter once again the double stroll of the schizo, the geographic exterior voyage following non-decomposable distances, and the interior historical voyage enveloping intensities: Christopher Columbus calms his mutinous crew and becomes admiral again only by simulating a (false) admiral who is simulating a whore who is dancing.[5]

But simulation must be understood in the same way as we spoke of identification. It expresses those nondecomposable distances always enveloped in the intensities that divide into one another while changing their form. If identification is a nomination, a designation, then simulation is the writing corresponding to it, a writing that is strangely polyvocal, flush with the real. It carries the real beyond its principle to the point where it is effectively produced by the desiring-machine. The point where the copy ceases to be a copy in order to become the real *and its artifice*. To seize an intensive real as produced in the coextension of nature and history, to ransack the Roman

Empire, the Mexican cities, the Greek gods, and the discovered continents so as to extract from them this always-surplus reality, and to form the treasure of the paranoiac tortures and the celibate glories—all the pogroms of history, that's what I am, and all the triumphs, too, as if a few simple univocal events could be extricated from this extreme polyvocity: such is the "histrionism" of the schizophrenic, according to Klossowski's formula, the true program for a theater of cruelty, the *mise-en-scène* of a machine to produce the real. Far from having lost who knows what contact with life, the schizophrenic is closest to the beating heart of reality, to an intense point identical with the production of the real, and that leads Reich to say: "What belongs specifically to the schizophrenic patient is that . . . he experiences the vital biology of the body. . . . With respect to their experiencing of life, the neurotic patient and the perverted individual are to the schizophrenic as the petty thief is to the daring safecracker."[6] So the question returns: what reduces the schizophrenic to his autistic, hospitalized profile, cut off from reality? Is it the process, or is it rather the interruption of the process, its aggravation, its continuation in the void? What forces the schizophrenic to withdraw to a body without organs that has become deaf, dumb, and blind?

We often hear it said: he thinks he's Louis XVII. Not true. In the Louis XVII affair, or rather in the finest case, that of the pretender Richemont, there is a desiring-machine or a celibate machine in the center: the horse with short, jointed paws, inside which they supposedly put the Dauphin so he could flee. And then, all around, there are agents of production and antiproduction, the organizers of the escape, the accomplices, and allied sovereigns, the revolutionary enemies, the jealous and hostile uncles, who are not persons but so many states of rising and falling through which the pretender passes. Moreover, the pretender Richemont's stroke of genius is not simply that he "takes into account" Louis XVII, or that he takes other pretenders into account by denouncing them as fake. What is so ingenious is that he takes other pretenders into account by assuming them, by authenticating them—that is to say, by making them too into states through which he passes: I am Louis XVII, but I am also Hervagault and Mathurin Bruneau, who claimed to be Louis XVII.[7] Richemont doesn't identify with Louis XVII, he lays claim to the premium due the person who traverses all the singularities of the series converging around the machine for kidnapping Louis XVII. There is no ego at the center, any more than there are persons distributed on the periphery. Nothing but a series of singularities in the disjunctive network, or intensive states in the conjunctive tissue, and a transpositional subject moving full circle, passing through all the states, triumphing over some as over his enemies, relishing others as his allies, collecting everywhere the fraudulent premium of his avatars. Partial object: a

well-situated scar—ambiguous besides—is better proof than all the memories of childhood that the pretender lacks. The conjunctive synthesis can
therefore be expressed: "So *I* am the king! So the kingdom belongs to *me!*"
But this *me* is merely the residual subject that sweeps the circle and concludes a self from its oscillations on the circle.

All delirium possesses a world-historical, political, and racial content,
mixing and sweeping along races, cultures, continents, and kingdoms; some
wonder whether this long drift merely constitutes a derivative of Oedipus.
The familial order explodes, families are challenged, son, father, mother,
sister—"I mean those families like my own, that owe all to the Declaration
of the Rights of Man!"; "When I seek out my most profound opposite, I
always encounter my mother and my sister; to see myself related to such
German rabble is, as it were, a blasphemy with respect to my doctrine of the
Eternal Return!" It is a question of knowing if the historico-political, the
racial, and the cultural are merely part of a manifest content and formally
depend on a work of elaboration, or if, on the contrary, this content should
be followed as the thread of latency that the order of families hides from us.
Should the rupture with families be taken as a sort of "familial romance"
that would indeed bring us back again to families and refer us to an event or
a structural determination inside the family itself? Or is this rather the sign
that the problem must be raised in a completely different manner, because
it is already raised elsewhere for the schizo himself, outside the family? Are
"the names of history" derivatives of the name of the father, and are the
races, cultures, and continents substitutes for daddy-mommy, dependent
on the Oedipal genealogy? Is history's signifier the dead father?

Once again let us consider Judge Schreber's delirium. To be sure, the use
of races and the mobilization or notion of history are developed there in a
manner totally different from that employed by the authors we have previously mentioned. The fact remains that Schreber's memoirs are filled with
a theory of God's chosen peoples, and with the dangers that face the currently chosen people, the Germans, who are threatened by the Jews, the
Catholics, and the Slavs. In his intense metamorphoses and passages,
Schreber becomes a pupil of the Jesuits, the burgomaster of a city where the
Germans are fighting against the Slavs, and a girl defending Alsace against
the French. At last he crosses the Aryan gradient or threshold to become a
Mongol prince. What does this becoming-pupil, burgomaster, girl, and
Mongol signify? All paranoiac deliriums stir up similar historical, geographic, and racial masses. The error would lie in concluding, for example,
that fascists are mere paranoiacs. This would be an error precisely because,
in the current state of affairs, this would still amount to leading the historical and political content of the delirium back to an internal familial deter-

mination. And what is even more disturbing to us is the fact that the entirety of this enormous content disappears completely from Freud's analysis: not one trace of it remains; everything is ground, squashed, triangulated into Oedipus; everything is reduced to the father, in such a way as to reveal in the crudest fashion the inadequacies of an Oedipal psychoanalysis.

14

· · ·

Becoming-Animal

Becoming is to emit particles that take on certain relations of movement and rest because they enter a particular zone of proximity. Or, it is to emit particles that enter that zone because they take on those relations. A haecceity is inseparable from the fog and mist that depend on a molecular zone, a corpuscular space. Proximity is a notion, at once topological and quantal, that marks a belonging to the same molecule, independently of the subjects considered and the forms determined.

Schérer and Hocquenghem made this essential point in their reconsideration of the problem of wolf-children. Of course, it is not a question of a real production, as if the child "really" became an animal; nor is it a question of a resemblance, as if the child imitated animals that really raised it; nor is it a question of a symbolic metaphor, as if the autistic child that was abandoned or lost merely became the "analogue" of an animal. Schérer and Hocquenghem are right to expose this false reasoning, which is based on a culturalism or moralism upholding the irreducibility of the human order: Because the child has not been transformed into an animal, it must only have a metaphorical relation to it, induced by the child's illness or rejection. For their own part, they appeal to an objective zone of indetermination or uncertainty, "something shared or indiscernible," a proximity "that makes it impossible to say where the boundary between the human and animal lies," not only in the case of autistic children, but for all children; it is as though, independent of the evolution carrying them toward adulthood, there were room in the child for other becomings, "other contemporaneous possibilities" that are not regressions but creative involutions bearing witness to "*an inhumanity immediately experienced in the body as such,*" unnatural nuptials "outside the programmed body." There is a reality of becoming-animal, even though one does not in reality become animal. It is useless, then, to raise the objection that the dog-child only plays dog within the limits of his formal constitution, and does nothing canine that another human being could not have done if he or she had so desired. For what needs to be explained is precisely the fact that all children, and even many adults, do it to a greater or lesser degree, and in so doing bear witness to an inhuman connivance with the animal, rather than an Oedipal symbolic community.[1] Neither should it be thought that children who graze, or eat dirt or raw flesh, are merely getting the vitamins and minerals they need. It is a question of composing a body with the animal, a body without organs defined by zones of intensity or proximity. Where does this objective indetermination or indiscernibility of which Schérer and Hocquenghem speak come from?

An example: Do not imitate a dog, but make your organism enter into composition with *something else* in such a way that the particles emitted from the aggregate thus composed will be canine as a function of the relation of movement and rest, or of molecular proximity, into which they enter. Clearly, this something else can be quite varied, and be more or less directly related to the animal in question: it can be the animal's natural food (dirt and worm), or its exterior relations with other animals (you can become-dog with cats, or become-monkey with a horse), or an apparatus or prosthesis to which a person subjects the animal (muzzle and reindeer, etc.), or something that does not even have a localizable relation to the animal in question. For this last case, we have seen how Slepian bases his attempt to become-dog on the idea of tying shoes to his hands using his mouth-muzzle. Philippe Gavi cites the performances of Lolito, an eater of bottles, earthenware, porcelains, iron, and even bicycles, who declares: "I consider myself half-animal, half-man. More animal than man. I love animals, dogs especially, I feel a bond with them. My teeth have adapted; in fact, when I don't eat glass or iron, my jaw aches like a young dog's that craves to chew a bone."[2] If we interpret the word "like" as a metaphor, or propose a structural analogy of relations (man–iron = dog–bone), we understand nothing of becoming. The word "like" is one of those words that change drastically in meaning and function when they are used in connection with haecceities, when they are made into expressions of becomings instead of signified states or signifying relations. A dog may exercise its jaw on iron, but when it does it is using its jaw as a molar organ. When Lolito eats iron, it is totally different: he makes his jaw enter into composition with the iron in such a way that he himself becomes the jaw of a molecular dog. The actor Robert De Niro walks "like" a crab in a certain film sequence; but, he says, it is not a question of his imitating a crab; it is a question of making something that has to do with the crab enter into composition with the image, with the speed of the image.[3] That is the essential point for us: you become-animal only if, by whatever means or elements, you emit corpuscles that enter the relation of movement and rest of the animal particles, or what amounts to the same thing, that enter the zone of proximity of the animal molecule. You become-animal only molecularly. You do not become a barking molar dog, but by barking, if it is done with enough feeling, with enough necessity and composition, you emit a molecular dog. Man does not become wolf, or vampire, as if he changed molar species; the vampire and werewolf are becomings of man, in other words, proximities between molecules in composition, relations of movement and rest, speed and slowness between emitted particles. Of course there are werewolves and vampires, we say this with all our heart; but do not look for a resemblance or analogy to the animal, for this is becoming-animal in action, the production of the molecular animal (whereas the "real" animal is trapped in its molar form and subjectivity). It is within us that the animal bares its teeth like Hofmannsthal's rat, or the flower opens its petals; but this is done by corpuscular emission, by molecular proximity, and not by the imitation of a subject or a proportionality of form. Albertine can always imitate a flower, but it is when she is sleeping and enters into composition with the particles of sleep that her beauty spot and the texture of her skin enter a relation of rest and movement that place her in the zone of a molecular vegetable: the becoming-plant of Albertine. And it is when she is held prisoner that she emits the particles of a bird. And it is when she flees, launches down a line of flight, that she becomes-horse, even if it is the horse of death.

Yes, all becomings are molecular: the animal, flower, or stone one becomes are molecular collectivities, haecceities, not molar subjects, objects, or form that we know from the outside and recognize from experience, through science, or by habit. If this is true, then we must say the same of things human: there is a becoming-woman, a becoming child, that do not resemble the woman or the child as clearly distinct molar entities (although it is possible—only possible—for the woman or child to occupy privileged positions in relation to these becomings). What we term a molar entity is, for example, the woman as defined by her form, endowed with organs and functions and assigned as a subject. Becoming-woman is not imitating this entity or even transforming oneself into it. We are not, however, overlooking the importance of imitation, or moments of imitation, among certain homosexual males, much less the prodigious attempt at a real transformation on the part of certain transvestites. All we are saying is that these indissociable aspects of becoming-woman must first be understood as a function of something else: not imitating or assuming the female form, but emitting particles that enter the relation of movement and rest, or the zone of proximity, of a microfemininity, in other words, that produce in us a molecular woman, create the molecular woman. We do not mean to say that a creation of this kind is the prerogative of the man, but on the contrary that the woman as a molar entity *has to become-woman* in order that the man also becomes- or can become-woman. It is, of course, indispensable for women to conduct a molar politics, with a view to winning back their own organism, their own history, their own subjectivity: "we as women . . ." makes its appearance as a subject of enunciation. But it is dangerous to confine oneself to such a subject, which does not function without drying up a spring or stopping a flow. The song of life is often intoned by the driest of women, moved by *ressentiment,* the will to power and cold mothering. Just as a desiccated child makes a much better child, there being no childhood flow emanating from it any longer. It is no more adequate to say that each sex contains the other and must develop the opposite pole in itself. Bisexuality is no better a concept than the separateness of the sexes. It is as deplorable to miniaturize, internalize the binary machine as it is to exacerbate it; it does not extricate us from it. It is thus necessary to conceive of a molecular women's politics that slips into molar confrontations, and passes under or through them.

When Virginia Woolf was questioned about a specifically women's writing, she was appalled at the idea of writing "as a woman." Rather, writing should produce a becoming-woman as atoms of womanhood capable of crossing and impregnating an entire social field, and of contaminating men, of sweeping them up in that becoming. Very soft particles—but also very hard and obstinate, irreducible, indomitable. The rise of women in English novel writing has spared no man: even those who pass for the most virile, the most phallocratic, such as Lawrence and Miller, in their turn continually tap into and emit particles that enter the proximity or zone of indiscernibility of women. In writing, they become-women. The question is not, or not only, that of the organism, history, and subject of enunciation that oppose masculine to feminine in the great dualism machines. The question is fundamentally that of the body—the body they *steal* from us in order to fabricate opposable organisms. This body is stolen first from a girl: Stop behaving like that, you're not a little girl anymore, you're not a tomboy, etc. The girl's becoming is stolen first, in order to impose a history, or prehistory, upon her. The boys's turn comes next, but it is by using the girl as an example, by pointing to the girl as the object of his desire, that an opposed organism, a dominant history is fabricated for him too. The girl is the first victim, but she must also serve as an example and a trap. That is why, conversely, the reconstruction of the body as a "body without organs," the anorganism of the body, is inseparable from a becoming-woman, or the production of a molecular woman. Doubtless, the girl becomes a woman in the molar or organic sense. But conversely, becoming-woman or the molecular woman is the girl herself. The girl is certainly not defined by virginity; she is defined by a relation of movement and rest, speed and slowness, by a combination of atoms, an emission of particles: haecceity. She never ceases to roam upon a body without organs. She is an abstract line, or a line of flight. Thus girls do not belong to an age group, sex, order, or kingdom: they slip in everywhere, between orders, acts, ages, sexes; they produce *n* molecular sexes on the line of flight in relation to the dualism machines they cross right through. The only way to get outside the dualisms is to be-between, to pass between, the intermezzo—that is what Virginia Woolf lived with all her energies, in all of her work, never ceasing to become. The girl is like the block of becoming that remains contemporaneous to each opposable term, man, woman, child, adult. It is not the girl who becomes a woman; it is becoming-woman that produces the universal girl. Trost, a mysterious author, painted a portrait of the girl, to whom he linked the fate of the revolution: her speed, her freely machinic body, her intensities, her abstract line or line of flight, her molecular production, her indifference to memory, her non-figurative character—"the nonfigurative of desire."[4] Joan of Arc? The special role of the girl in Russian terrorism: the girl with the bomb, guardian of dynamite? It is certain that molecular politics proceeds via the girl and the child. But it is also certain that girls and children draw their strength neither from the molar status that subdues them nor from the organism and subjectivity they receive; they draw their strength from the becoming-molecular they cause to pass between sexes and ages, the becoming-child of the adult as well as of the child, the becoming-woman of the man as well as of the woman. The girl and the child do not become; it is becoming itself that is a child or a girl. The child does not become an adult any more than the girl becomes a woman; the girl is the becoming-woman of each sex, just as the child is the becoming-young of every age. Knowing how to age does not mean remaining young; it means extracting from one's age the particles, the speeds and slownesses, the flows that constitute the youth of *that* age. Knowing how to love does not mean remaining a man or a woman; it means extracting from one's sex the particles, the speeds and slownesses, the flows, the *n* sexes that constitute the girl of *that* sexuality. It is age itself that is a becoming-child, just as sexuality, any sexuality, is a becoming-woman, in other words, a girl. This by way of response to the stupid question, "why did Proust make Albert Albertine?"

15
. . .
The Signs of Madness: Proust

In this essay, we do not intend to raise the problem of the relation between art and madness in Proust's work. Such an approach makes little sense. Even less do we want to raise the question of whether or not Proust himself was mad. This question too would be utterly pointless. The question of this essay, rather, concerns the presence of madness in Proust's work, and the distribution, the use, and the function of this presence.

In at least two of the main characters of *Remembrance of Things Past*, Charlus and Albertine, madness is manifest, although it operates differently in each case. Ever since his initial appearance, Charlus' strange expression and his eyes are described as those of a spy, of a thief, a merchant, a policeman, a *madman*.[1] Later, toward the conclusion, Morel is terrified, and with good reason, by the thought that Charlus' disposition toward him is based on criminal madness.[2] Charlus is constantly under suspicion for a madness which makes him infinitely more frightening than if he were immoral, perverted, wicked, or guilty. Bad manners

> scare . . . one by making one feel that that way madness lies, far more than by its immorality. Mme de Surgis le Duc could not be said to have highly developed moral sense, and would have tolerated in her sons any-

thing, however base, that could be explained by material interest, which is comprehensible to all mankind. But she forbade them to go on visiting M. de Charlus when she learned that, by a sort of internal clockwork, he was inevitably drawn upon each of their visits to pinch their chins and to make each of them pinch his brother's. She felt that uneasy sense of a physical mystery which makes us wonder whether the neighbour with whom we have been on friendly terms is not tainted with cannibalism, and to the Baron's repeated inquiry: "When am I going to see the young men?" She would reply, conscious of the wrath she was bringing down on herself, that they were very busy working for examinations, preparing to go abroad, and so forth. Irresponsibility aggravates faults, and even crimes, whatever may be said. Landru (assuming that he really did kill his women) may be pardoned. If he did so from financial motives, which it is possible to resist, but not if it was from irresistible sadism.[3]

Past the responsibility of error, one finds madness as the innocence of the crime.

In the beginning, that Charlus is mad is a mere probability; by the end, his madness is almost a certainty. As for Albertine, her madness is a posthumous eventuality, casting retrospectively upon her gestures, her words, her entire life a new and troubling light in which Morel is always held. "She felt in her heart that her obsession was a sort of criminal lunacy, and I've often wondered whether it wasn't after an incident of that sort, which had led to a suicide in a family, that she killed herself on purpose."[4] What is this combination of madness, crime, irresponsibility, and sexuality? Clearly, it blends with the theme of patricide, so dear to Proust, but it cannot be reduced to the familiar Oedipal scheme. Could it be that a kind of innocence exists in the crime caused by madness—the kind of innocence that such prevenance would make even more difficult to bear, to the point of suicide?

Let us examine first the case of Charlus. His initial presence is that of a strong personality with an imperial individuality. The point is, however, that his individuality is an empire and a constellation, concealing and holding many unknown things. But what is Charlus' secret? The constellation is, in fact, built around two shiny, singular points: the eyes and the voice. Sometimes, imperious gleams emanate from the eyes, while at other times, prying agitations. Sometimes they betray a kind of feverish activity, while at other times, a doleful indifference. As for the voice, it brings about the coexistence of a virile content of speech and an effeminate mannerism of expression. Charlus is presented as both an enormous, flickering sign and as a large, optical, voice box. Whosoever hears him, or meets his eyes, is confronted with a secret to uncover, and a mystery to penetrate and interpret.

One senses early on that the secret and the mystery could go as far as madness. The need to interpret Charlus is grounded upon the fact that Charlus himself interprets endlessly; it is as if endless interpretation is already his madness and as if his delirium is the delirium of interpretation.

From the constellation named "Charlus," there emerges a series of speeches, which follow the rhythm of the shifting eyes. In fact, three long narrated speeches find their source in the signs interpreted by Charlus, the prophet and seer; these speeches find their destination in the signs that Charlus proposes to the narrator. The latter has by now been reduced to the status of the disciple and the pupil. However, that which is essential to the speeches is found elsewhere: in the freely organized words, in the independently arranged sentences, and in the *Logos* that calculates and transcends the signs it uses. Charlus emerges as the master of *Logos*. From this perspective, it seems that the three long speeches, despite their differences in rhythm and intensity, share a common structure. First, a period of denegation, when Charlus says to the narrator: "You do not interest me, don't you believe you interest me, yet . . ."; then comes a second period, the time of distanciation: "The distance between you and me is infinite, but we can complement each other, I offer you a contract. . . ." There is also an unexpected, third period and, in it, one might say that *Logos* suddenly begins to skid as it is run through by something which refuses to be organized. It is inspired by a force of a different order—anger, insult, provocation, profanity, sadic phantasm, mad gesture, irruption of madness. This is already evident in the first speech which, despite the fact that it is made entirely of noble tenderness, reaches nonetheless its aberrant conclusion the next day on the beach in Charlus' coarse but prophetic remark: "But he doesn't give a damn for his old grandmother, does he, eh? Little rascal!"[5] The second speech imparts a fantasy of Charlus, depicting a comical scene in which Bloch has a contest with his father and gives a good thrashing to his hag of a mother. "As he poured out these terrible, almost insane words, M. de Charlus squeezed my arm until it hurt."[6] Finally, the third speech moves swiftly to the violent trail of the trampled and ruined hat. Actually, this time it is not Charlus who steps on the hat; it is the narrator. But as we all see, the narrator has at his disposal enough madness for everyone; his madness communicates with Charlus and Albertine's madness, and can set out to anticipate their madness or even to bring about its consequences.[7]

Regardless of how much Charlus appears to be the master of *Logos,* his speeches are agitated by involuntary signs resisting the sovereign organization of language, preventing their being mastered by words and sentences, and causing, just the same, the flight of *Logos* as well as our departure to another domain.

Whatever the fine words with which he embellished all his hatreds, one felt that, whether he was moved by offended pride or disappointed love, whether his motivating force was rancour, sadism, teasing or obsession, this man was capable of committing murder.[8]

We find signs of violence and madness that constitute an entire pathos against and beneath the voluntary signs concocted through "logic and noble language." This pathos will be revealed for what it is in the various appearances of Charlus, as he speaks less and less from the heights of his sovereign constitution, but also betrays himself more and more in the course of his physical and social decomposition. No longer are we faced with the world of speeches whose vertical communications once expressed a hierarchy of rules and positions; we are now faced with a world of anarchic encounters, violent chance-happenings that communicate among themselves in an aberrant and transversal way. We are left with the meeting between Charlus and Jupien, and with the long-awaited unveiling of the secret of Charlus' homosexuality. But is this really the secret? What is unveiled is not so much the homosexuality that was, at any rate, foreseeable and suspected for a long time, but rather a general condition in view of which the homosexuality is a particular case of a deeper and growing universal madness, with innocence and crime intertwined in so many ways. What is unveiled is the world, where no one speaks any longer, the silent vegetal universe and the madness of flowers, the fragmented theme of which gives a certain rhythm to the encounter with Jupien.

Logos is a large animal whose parts are assembled into a whole and unified under a principle or a directing idea. *Pathos,* on the other hand, is a plant composed of separate parts; the parts communicate only indirectly with one another and by means of a part which is itself separate, and so on ad infinitum, to the point where there can be no further unification of this world; its ultimate pieces no longer lack anything. We now face the schizoid world of sealed boxes, of separate parts, where even contiguity is distance: the world of sex. This is what Charlus teaches us, past his speeches. Given that every individual consists of both sexes, albeit "separated by a partition," we must be prepared to admit an abstract set of eight elements, so that the masculine or feminine "aspect" of a man or a woman could strike a relation with the feminine and masculine "aspect" of another woman or man: *there are ten possible combinations of the eight elements.*[9] We are then left with aberrant relations between sealed vases; a bumblebee that makes flowers communicate, while losing its own carnality, because in relation to them, it is no longer anything but a separate part and a disparate element in the apparatus of plant reproduction.

Here, perhaps, we face the same situation that we can find everywhere in *Remembrance:* from an initial constellation representing an apparently circumscribed, unifiable, and totalizable whole, one or more series are being released. These series, in turn, run into a new constellation, this time decentred or eccentric, made of spinning sealed boxes and mobile disparate parts that follow transversal lines of flight. Charlus' situation is precisely this: the initial constellation with the shine of his eyes and his voice; in the sequence, the series of speeches; finally, the past, disquieting world of signs and boxes, of signs composing Charlus, which are located inside one another and then separated, allowing themselves to be opened midway and interpreted according to the line of flight of a star aging together with its satellites. "M. de Charlus, steering towards us the Bulk of his huge body, drawing unwillingly in his wake one of those ruffians or beggars who nowadays, when he passed, sprang out without fail from even the most apparently deserted corners."[10]

It is the same situation which permeates Albertine's story: the constellation of the young girls from which Albertine gradually is extracted; the long series of the two consecutive jealousies affecting Albertine; finally, the coexistence of all boxes wherein Albertine imprisons herself in her own lies, and where the narrator also imprisons her. This is a new constellation, compensating in a way for the initial one, because the end of love is like a return to the indivisibility of the young girls. A comparison between the lines of flight of Albertine and Charlus is inevitable. Notice the beautiful passage in which Albertine is kissed. The narrator, hiding, begins with the face of Albertine as with a mobile whole wherein her beauty spot shines as a singular point. In the sequence, as the lips of the narrator near the cheek, the desired face moves through a succession of frames, each of which corresponds to another Albertine, with the beauty spot leaping from one frame to another. Finally, we come to the last blur, with Albertine's face distorted and done in, where the narrator, having lost the use of his lips, eyes and nose, recognizes in "these detestable signs" that he is in the act of embracing the loved one.

This great law of composition and decomposition applies to both Albertine and Charlus because it is the law of love and sexuality. Heterosexual love affairs, and especially the love of the narrator for Albertine, are not merely appearances behind which Proust would hide his homosexuality. On the contrary, these love affairs form the initial background from which, eventually, the two series of homosexuality represented by Albertine and Charlus will be derived. "The two sexes shall die, each in a place apart." These series, however, extend to a transsexual world wherein the compartmentalized and interlocking sexes are regrouped in each series in order to communicate with the sexes of another, as they follow aberrant and trans-versal ways. A kind of superficial normalcy marks the first level or the first set; on the contrary, all the sufferings, anxieties and culpabilities of what we call "neurosis" mark the liberated series at the second level: the curse of Oedipus and the prophecy of Samson. As for the third level, in the midst of decomposition it restores a vegetal innocence by offering an absolving func-tion to madness in a world of exploding and later sealed boxes, of crimes and illegal confinements which form the Proustian "human comedy." As a result, a new and final power develops that overthrows all others. This power is stark mad—the power of *Remembrance* itself—and it ranks together, policeman with insane, spy with merchant, interpreter with redress-seeker.

Although the stories of Albertine and Charlus follow the same general law, the fact remains that in these two situations, madness has very diverse forms and functions, and it is distributed differently. Between madness-Charlus and madness-Albertine, there are three major differences. First, Charlus has a superior individuation in the guise of an imperial individu-ality. His disorder is in communication: the queries, "What is Charlus hid-ing?" "Which secret boxes does he conceal in his individuality?" refer us to yet undiscovered communications and to the aberrancies of these com-munications. Consequently, madness-Charlus can neither interpret itself nor be manifested and interpreted, except through accidental and violent encounters, in view of the new surroundings into which Charlus is thrust. These encounters function as revealing points, inductors and communica-tors: encounters with the narrator, encounter with Jupien, encounter with the Verdurins, encounter in the brothel.

Albertine's situation is different because her disorder affects individua-tion: which of the young girls is she? How can we pick her out of the indivis-ible group of young girls? In this case, one might say that Albertine's com-munications are evident from the beginning, while whatever is hidden is precisely the mystery of her individuation. The only way to pierce this mys-tery is to have the communications interrupted and forcefully stopped, and for Albertine to be imprisoned, immured and confined. A second difference follows. Charlus is the master of discourse; everything happens by means of words, yet, on the other hand, nothing happens in these words. Charlus' investments are primarily verbal, to the extent that things or objects present themselves as involuntary signs; as such, they turn against discourse, some-times causing it to derail, and other times, forming a counterlanguage which develops within the silence and the muteness of encounters. As for Albertine's relation to language, it is a poor lie, not a majestic deviance. Her investment is in things or objects expressed in language, but only on the condition that its voluntary signs fragment and submit to the rules of the lie that the involuntary inserts in it: in such a case, everything, including silence, can happen in language, precisely because nothing moves through language.

Finally, there is a third difference. At the turn of the twentieth century, psychiatry established a very interesting distinction between two kinds of sign-delirium: the delirium of interpretation, present in paranoia, and the delirium of redress-seeking, present in erotomania or jealousy. The former, with an insidious beginning and a gradual development essentially depending upon endogenous forces, expands over a general network which mobilizes all verbal investments. The latter has a much more abrupt beginning and is tied to external factors that may be real or imaginary. It depends on a kind of "postulate" regarding a specific object, and enters limited constellations. It is less a delirium of ideas running through the extended system of verbal investments, and more a delirium of acts, animated by an intensive object-investment. Erotomania, for example, presents itself as a delirious pursuit of the loved object rather than as the delirious illusion of being loved. *The delirium of redress-seeking forms a sequence of finite linear processes, while the delirium of interpretation forms radiant, circular wholes.* We do not content that Proust attributed to his characters a psychiatric distinction which was being elaborated during his time. Yet Charlus and Albertine, in *Remembrance,* follow pathways that correspond accurately to this distinction. We tried to show this with Charlus: the early appearances of this grand paranoiac are insidious; the onset and development of delirium, in his case, testify to the presence of fearful, endogenous forces; with his entire interpretive dementia, he conceals the most mysterious, verbal signs of a nonlanguage that gives him form. Such is the vast Charlus-network. We also tried to show this with Albertine: being an object, or in pursuit of objects, she issues postulates that are familiar to her, or rather, she is trapped by the narrator inside a postulate with no escape, which leaves her victimized. (*Albertine is presented as necessarily and a priori guilty; she loves without being loved; she is hard, cruel, and treacherous toward the object of one's love.*) Albertine is both erotomaniac and jealous, although it is rather the narrator who reveals himself to her in these colors. The series of jealousies that have Albertine as their object are in each case inseparable from an external occasion and constitute sequential processes. Finally, the signs of language and nonlanguage intertwine and form the limited constellations of the lie. We are left with a delirium of action and redress-seeking, different from the delirium of ideas and interpretations that characterizes Charlus.

But why should we confuse Albertine with the narrator's behavior toward Albertine, as if they were one and the same? It is obvious that the narrator's jealousy is directed toward an Albertine who, in turn, is extremely jealous of her own "objects." As for the narrator's erotomania toward Albertine, that is, the delirious pursuit of the loved one, without the illusion of being loved in return, it is conveyed by the erotomania of Albertine, which was for a long time suspected to be, and then confirmed as, the secret behind the narrator's jealousy. Again, the narrator's redress-seeking for the imprisonment and confinement of Albertine conceals Albertine's redress-seeking, which falls under suspicion too late. Charlus' situation is similar: we are unable to distinguish the labor of Charlus' interpretive delirium from the long labor over the interpretation of Charlus' delirium, through which the narrator suffers. But we were searching precisely for the provenance of the necessity of these partial identifications and for their function in *Remembrance*.

Jealous of Albertine and the interpreter of Charlus, who, really, is the narrator himself? We do not consider it to be at all compelling to distinguish between the narrator and the hero as subject of the utterance and subject of the statement, respectively, because this would result in referring *Remembrance* to an alien system of subjectivity (with a double and cloven subject).[11] This is not so much a question of a narrator, as it is of a machine for *Remembrance;* it is less a question of a hero, and more of arrangements in the middle of which the machine functions under certain configurations or articulations, for the sake of certain uses or productions. Only in this sense, do we have the right to inquire about the narrator-hero who does not behave as subject. The reader is struck by Proust's persistent portrayal of the narrator as one incapable of seeing, perceiving, remembering, or understanding. This is the grand opposition to the Goncourt and the Saint-Beuve method, and the constant theme of *Remembrance,* which reaches its apex in the country at the house of the Verdurins. ("I see you like draughts.")[12] In fact, the narrator has no organs, or rather, he does not have the organs that he needs and hopes for. He himself makes this point in the scene of Albertine's first kiss, as he complains that we are lacking adequate organs for an activity that fills our lips, plugs our noses, and blocks our eyes. In other words, the narrator is an enormous body without organs.

But what is a body without organs? The spider, too, does not see, perceive, or remember. Only at the tip of its web does it register the smallest vibration, which gradually spreads over its body in a wave of intensity, making it pounce on the precise point of agitation. Without eyes, nose, or mouth, it responds to signs only; the smallest sign penetrates and then waves through the spider's body, causing the spider to pounce on its prey. *Remembrance* is not structured like a cathedral or a garment: it is built like a web. The narrator-spider has *Remembrance* as his web, in the course of being shaped and woven, as each of its threads is stirred by an unusual sign: the web and the spider, the web and the body are one and the same machine. The narrator might very well be endowed with extreme sensibility and a prodigious memory; nevertheless, he has no organs so long as he is deprived of all voluntary and organized use of his faculties. But, on the other hand, a certain faculty functions within him whenever it is constrained and forced to do so; the organ, corresponding to this faculty, is given to him as an *intensive sketch* only, stirred by the waves that set off its involuntary practice. Involuntary sensibility, involuntary memory, and involuntary thought, are each the global, intense reactions of the body without organs to the different signs. It is this body-web-spider that is agitated in order to halfway open and then quickly close again the small boxes which bump against the sticky thread of *Remembrance*. Strange plasticity of the narrator. This body-spider-narrator—spy, policeman, jealous, interpreter, redress-seeker, *madman*, universal schizophrenic—will pay out one thread to the paranoid Charlus and another to the erotomaniac Albertine in order to transform them into marionettes of its own delirium, into intensive powers of its own body without organs, and into profiles of its own madness.

Trans. Constantin Boundas

16

. . .

What Is Desire?

Do you realize how simple a desire is? Sleeping is a desire. Walking is a desire. Listening to music, or making music, or writing, are desires. A spring, a winter, are desires. Old age also is a desire. Even death. Desire never needs interpreting, it is it which experiments. Then we run up against very exasperating objections. They say to us that we are returning to an old cult of pleasure, to a pleasure principle, or to a notion of the festival (the revolution will be a festival. . .). By way of objection they hold up those who are stopped from sleeping, whether for internal or external reasons, and who have neither the means nor the time for a festival; or who have neither the time nor the culture to listen to music; nor the ability to walk, nor to go into a catatonic state except in hospital; or who are suddenly struck by a horrible old age or death, in short all those who suffer: don't they "lack" something? And above all, it is objected that by releasing desire from lack and law, the only thing we have left to refer to is a state of nature, a desire that would be natural and spontaneous reality. We say quite the opposite: *desire only exists when assembled or machined.* You cannot grasp or conceive of a desire outside a determinate assemblage, on a plane which is not preexistent but which must itself be constructed. All that is important is that each group or individual should construct the plane of immanence on which they lead their life and carry on their business. Without these conditions you obviously do lack something, but you lack precisely the conditions which make a desire possible. Organizations of forms, formations of subjects (the other plane), "incapacitate" desire: they subjugate it to law and introduce lack into it. If you tie someone up and say to him "Express yourself, friend," the most he will be able to say is that he doesn't want to be tied up. The only spontaneity in desire is doubtless of that kind: to not want to be oppressed, exploited, enslaved, subjugated. But no desire has ever been created with nonwishes. Not to want to be enslaved is a nonproposition. In retrospect every assemblage expresses and creates a desire by constructing the plane which makes it possible and, by making it possible, brings it about. Desire is not restricted to the privileged; neither is it restricted to the success of a revolution once it has occurred. It is in itself an immanent revolutionary process. *It is constructivist, not at all spontaneist.* Since every assemblage is collective, is itself a collective, it is indeed true that every desire is the affair of the people, or an affair of the masses, a molecular affair.

We don't even believe in internal drives which would prompt desire. The plane of immanence has nothing to do with an interiority; it is like the outside where all desires come from. When we hear of a thing as stupid as the supposed death drive, it is like seeing a shadow theater. Eros and Thanatos. We have to ask: could there be an assemblage so warped, so hideous, that the utterance "Long live death" would be an actual part of it and death itself be desired in it? Or isn't this the opposite of an assemblage, its downfall, its failure? We must describe the assemblage in which such a desire becomes possible, gets moving and declares itself. But never will we point to drives which would refer to structural invariants, or to genetic variables. Oral, anal, genital, etc.: we ask each time into which assemblages these components enter, not to which drives they correspond, nor to which memories or fixations they owe their importance, nor to which incidents they refer, but with which extrinsic elements they combine to create a desire, to create desire. This is already the case with children who fabricate their desire with the outside, with the conquest of the outside, not in internal stages or by transcendent structures. Once again little Hans: there is the street, the horse, the omnibus, the parents, Professor Freud himself, the "has a pee" [*fait-pipi*] which is neither an organ nor a function, but a machine function, one of the parts of the machine. There are speeds and slownesses, affects and haecceities: a horse a day the street. There are only different politics of assemblages, even with children: in this sense everything is political. There are only programs, or rather diagrams or planes, not memories or even phantasms. There are only becomings and blocs, childhood blocs, blocs of femininity, of animality, blocs of present becoming, and nothing of the memorial, the imaginary or the symbolic. Desire is no more symbolic than figurative, no more signified than signifier: it is made up of different lines which cross, articulate, or impede each other and which constitute a particular assemblage on a plane of immanence. But the plane does not preexist these assemblages which comprise it, these abstract lines which map it out. We can always call it plane of nature, in order to underline its immanence. But the nature-artifice distinction is not at all relevant here. There is no desire that does not result in the coexistence of several levels, some of which can be called natural in contrast to others; but this is a nature that must be constructed with all the fabrications of the plane of immanence. The assemblage of feudalism includes among its elements "horse-stirrup-lance." The natural position of the knight, the natural way of holding the lance, depends on a new symbiosis of man-animal which makes the stirrup the most natural thing in the world and the horse the most artificial one. The figures of desire do not derive from this, but were already mapping out the assemblage, the set of elements, retained or created by the assemblage, the lady no less than the horse, the sleeping knight no less than the wandering quest for the grail.

We say that there is assemblage of desire each time that there are produced, in a field of immanence, or on a plane of consistence, *continuums of intensities, combinations of fluxes, emissions of particles* at variable speeds. Guattari speaks of a Schumann-assemblage. What is a musical assemblage like this, designated by a proper name? What are the dimensions of such an assemblage? There is the relationship with Clara, woman-child-virtuoso, the Clara line. There is the little manual machine that Schumann puts together to hold the middle finger tight and secure the independence of the fourth finger. There is the ritornello, the little ritornellos that haunt Schumann and run through all his work like so many childhood blocs, a whole concerted enterprise of involution, restraint, and exhaustion of the theme and form. And there is also the use of the piano, this movement of deterriorialization that carries away the ritornello ("wings have sprouted on the child") on a melodic line, in an original polyphonic assemblage capable of producing dynamic and affective relations of speed or slowness, of delay or anticipation which are very complex, on the basis of an intrinsically simple or simplified form. There is the intermezzo, or rather there are nothing but intermezzi in Schumann, making the music pass *to the middle* preventing the sound plane from toppling under a law of organization or development.[1] All of this is articulated in the constitutive assemblage of desire. It is desire itself which passes and moves. There is no need to be Schumann. Listen to Schumann. Conversely, there is what happens to make the whole assemblage waver: the little manual machine leads to paralysis of the finger, and

then to Schumann's mad-becoming. . . . We simply say that desire is inseparable from a plane of consistence which must be constructed every time
piece by piece and from assemblages on this plane, continuums, combinations, emissions. Without lack, but definitely not without risk or peril. Desire, says Félix: a ritornello. But this is already very complicated: for the
ritornello is a kind of sound territoriality, the child reassuring himself when
he is afraid of the dark, "Rockabye baby on the tree-top." . . .[2] (Psychoanalysis seriously misunderstood the famous "Fort-Da" when it saw in it an
opposition of a phonological kind instead of recognizing a ritornello.) But it
is also the whole movement of deterriorialization which takes hold of a form
and a subject to extract from them variable speeds and floating affects; then
the music begins. What counts in desire is not the false alternative of law-
spontaneity, nature-artifice; it is the respective play of territorialities, reterritorializations, and movements of deterritorialization.

In speaking of desire we were no longer thinking of pleasure and its fes-
tivals. Certainly pleasure is agreeable; certainly we move toward it with all
our might. But in its most attractive and indispensable forms, it comes
rather as an interruption in the process of desire as constitution of a field of
immanence. There is nothing more revealing than the idea of a pleasure-
discharge; once pleasure is attained, one would have a little calm before desire is rekindled: there is a lot of hatred, or fear, of desire, in the cult of pleasure. Pleasure is the attribution of the affect, the affection for a person or
subject, it is the only means for a person to "find himself again" in the process of desire that overwhelms him. Pleasures, even the most artificial, or
the dizziest, can only be reterriorialization. Desire does not have pleasure as
its norm, but this is not in the name of an internal lack which could not be
filled, but on the contrary by virtue of its positivity; that is, of the plane of
consistence that it traces in the course of its process. It is the same error
which relates desire to the law of the lack and to the norm of pleasure. It is
when you keep relating desire to pleasure, to the attainment of pleasure,
that you also notice that something fundamental is missing. To the point
where, to break these preformed alliances between desire-pleasure-lack, we
are obliged to make detours through bizarre fabrications, with much ambiguity. Take, as an example, courtly love, which is an assemblage of desire
connected to feudalism as end. Dating an assemblage is not doing history, it
is giving the assemblage its coordinates of expression and content, proper
names, infinitive-becomings, articles, haecceities. (So that's what doing history is?) Now, it is well known that courtly love implies tests which postpone
pleasure, or at least postpone the ending of coitus. This is certainly not a
method of deprivation. It is the constitution of a field of immanence, where

desire constructs its own plane and lacks nothing, any more than it allows itself to be interrupted by a discharge which would indicate that it is too heavy for it to bear. Courtly love has two enemies which merge into one: a religious transcendence of lack and a hedonistic interruption which introduces pleasure as discharge. It is the immanent process of desire which fills itself up, the continuum of intensities, the combination of fluxes, which replace both the law-authority and the pleasure-interruption. The process of desire is called "joy," not lack or demand. Everything is permitted, except what would come and break up the integral process of desire, the assemblage. This is not something to do with nature: on the contrary, it requires a great deal of artifice to exorcise the internal lack, the higher transcendent element and the apparent exterior. Ascesis, why not? Ascesis has always been the condition of desire, not its disciplining or prohibition. You will always find an ascesis if you think of desire. Now, it has been "historically" necessary that a certain field of immanence should be possible at a particular moment, at a particular place. Chivalrous love properly speaking was not possible until the two fluxes had combined, the warrior flux and the erotic flux, in the sense that valor gave the right to love. But courtly love required a new demarcation in which valor became itself internal to love, and where love included the test.[3] One can say as much, in other conditions, of the masochist assemblage: the organization of humiliations and suffering in it appear less as a means of exorcizing anguish and so attaining a supposedly forbidden pleasure, than as a procedure, a particularly convoluted one, to constitute a body without organs and develop a continuous process of desire which pleasure, on the contrary, would come and interrupt.

We do not believe in general that sexuality has the role of an infrastructure in the assemblages of desire, nor that it constitutes an energy capable of transformation or of neutralization and sublimation. Sexuality can only be thought of as one flux among others, entering into conjunction with other fluxes, emitting particles which themselves enter into particular relationships of speed and slowness in the *vicinity* of certain other particles. No assemblage can be characterized by one flux exclusively. What a depressing idea of love, to make it a relation between two people, whose monotony must be vanquished as required by adding extra people. And it is not improved by the idea of leaving aside people altogether by bringing sexuality down to the construction of perverse or sadistic little machines which enclose sexuality in a theater of phantasms: something dirty or stale is given off by all this, something which is too sentimental in any case, too narcissistic, as when a flux begins to revolve around itself and grow stale. So Félix's fine phrase "desiring machines" ought to be given up for these reasons. The question about sexuality is: into the vicinity of what else does it enter to form such and such a haecceity, particular relations of movement and rest? The more it is articulated with other fluxes, the more it will remain sexuality, pure and simple sexuality, far from all idealizing sublimation. It will be all the more sexuality for itself, inventive, amazed, with neither phantasm which turns round and round nor idealization which leaps into the air: the masturbator is the only one who makes phantasms. Psychoanalysis is exactly a masturbation, a generalized, organized, and coded narcissism. Sexuality does not allow itself to be sublimated, or phantasmed, because its concern is elsewhere, in the real vicinity of and in real combination with other fluxes, which exhaust or precipitate it—all depends on the moment and the assemblage. And it is not simply from one to the other of the two "subjects" that this vicinity or combination takes place; it is in each of the two that several fluxes combine to form a bloc of becoming which makes demands on them both, music-becoming of Clara, woman- or child-becoming of Schumann. Not the man and woman as sexual entities, caught in a binary apparatus, but a molecular becoming, birth of a molecular woman in music, birth of molecular sonority in a woman. "The relations between the two spouses profoundly change over the years, often without them realizing anything; while each change is a cause of suffering, even if it causes a certain joy. . . . With each change a new being appears, a new rhythm is established. . . . Sex is a changing thing, sometimes lively, sometimes resting, sometimes inflamed and sometimes dead."[4] At each moment we are made up of lines which are variable at each instant, which may be combined in different ways, packets of lines, longitudes and latitudes, tropics and meridians, etc. There are no monofluxes. The analysis of the unconscious should be a geography rather than a history. Which lines appear blocked, moribund, closed in, dead-ended, falling to a black hole or exhausted, which others are active or lively, which allow something to escape and draw us along? Little Hans again: how was the line of the building and of the neighbors cut off from him; how was the Oedipal tree developed, what role did Professor Freud's branching-off play, why did the child seek refuge on the line of a horse-becoming, etc.? Psychoanalysis has always haunted parental and familial pathways, we should not reproach it for having chosen a particular way of branching off rather than another, but for having made a dead end out of this one, for having invented conditions of enunciation which crushed in advance the new utterances that it nevertheless gave rise to. We should get to the point of being able to say: your father, your mother, your grandmother, everything is fine, even the name of the father, every entry is fine from the moment that there are multiple exits. But psychoanalysis has produced everything—except exits. "Anywhere the rails lead us, anywhere at all, and if we come to an old offshoot rail line we don't know anything about, what the hell, we'll just take it, go down it, to see where it goes. And some year, by God, we'll boat down the Mississippi, always wanted to do that. Enough to last us a lifetime. And that's just how long I want to take to do it all."[5]

Part Four

· · ·

Minor Languages and Nomad Art

17

Language: Major and Minor

Since everybody knows that language is a heterogeneous, variable reality, what is the meaning of the linguists' insistence on carving out a homogeneous system in order to make a scientific study possible? It is a question of extracting a set of constants from the variables, or of determining constant relations between variables (this is already evident in the phonologists' concept of commutativity). But the scientific model taking language as an object of study is one with the political model by which language is homogenized, centralized, standardized, becoming a language of power, a major or dominant language. Linguistics can claim all it wants to be science, nothing but pure science—it wouldn't be the first time that the order of pure science was used to secure the requirements of another order. What is grammaticality, and the sign *S*, the categorical symbol that dominates statements? It is a power marker before it is a syntactical marker, and Chomsky's trees establish constant relations between power variables. Forming grammatically correct sentences is for the normal individual the prerequisite for any submission to social laws. No one is supposed to be ignorant of grammaticality; those who are belong in special institutions. The unity of language is fundamentally political. There is no mother tongue, only a power takeover by a dominant language that at times advances along a broad front, and at times swoops down on diverse centers simultaneously. We can conceive of several ways for a language to homogenize, centralize: the republican way is not necessarily the same as the royal way, and is not the least harsh.[1] The scientific enterprise of extracting constants and constant relations is always coupled with the political enterprise of imposing them on speakers and transmitting order-words.

> Speak white and loud
> yes what a wonderful language
> for hiring
> giving orders
> appointing the hour of death in the works
> and of the break that refreshes . . .

Must a distinction then be made between two kinds of languages, "high" and "low," major and minor? The first would be defined precisely by the power [*pouvoir*] of constants, the second by the power [*puissance*] of variation. We do not simply wish to make an opposition between the unity of a major language and the multiplicity of dialects. Rather, each dialect has a zone of transition and variation; or better, each minor language has a properly dialectical zone of variation. According to Malmberg, it is rare to find clear boundaries on dialect maps; instead, there are transitional and limitrophe zones, zones of indiscernibility. It is also said that "the Québecois language is so rich in modulations and variations of regional accents and in games with tonic accents that it sometimes seems, with no exaggeration, that it would be better preserved by musical notation than by any system of spelling."[2] The very notion of dialect is quite questionable. Moreover, it is relative because one needs to know in relation to what major language it exercises its function: for example, the Québecois language must be evaluated not only in relation to standard French but also in relation to major English, from which it borrows all kinds of phonetic and syntactical elements, in order to set them in variation. The Bantu dialects must be evaluated not only in relation to the mother tongue but also in relation to Afrikaans as a major language, and English as a counter–major language preferred by blacks.[3] In short, the notion of dialect does not elucidate that of minor language, but the other way around; it is the minor language that defines dialects through its own possibilities for variation. Should we identify major and minor language on the basis of regional situations of bilingualism or multilingualism including at least one dominant language and one dominated language, or a world situation giving certain languages an imperialist power over others (for example, the role of American English today)?

At least two things prevent us from adopting this point of view. As Chomsky notes, a dialect, ghetto language, or minor language is not immune to the kind of treatment that draws a homogeneous system from it and extracts constants: Black English has its own grammar, which is not defined by a sum of mistakes or infractions against standard English; but that grammar can be studied only by applying to it the same rules of study that are applied to standard English. In this sense, the notions of major and minor seem to have no linguistic relevance. When French lost its worldwide major function it lost nothing of its constancy and homogeneity, its centralization. Conversely, Afrikaans attained homogeneity when it was a locally minor language struggling against English. Even politically, especially politically, it is difficult to see how the upholders of a minor language can operate if not by giving it (if only by writing in it) a constancy and homogeneity making it a locally major language capable of forcing official recognition (hence the political role of writers who assert the rights of a minor language). But the opposite argument seems more compelling: the more a language has or acquires the characteristics of a major language, the more it is affected by continuous variations that transpose it into a "minor" language. It is futile to criticize the worldwide imperialism of a language by denouncing the corruptions it introduces into other languages (for example, the purists' criticisms of English influences in French, the petit-bourgeois or academic denunciation of "Franglais"). For if a language such as British English or American English is major on a world scale, it is necessarily worked upon by all the minorities of the world, using very diverse procedures of variation. Take the way Gaelic and Irish English set English in variation. Or the way Black English and any number of "ghetto languages" set American English in variation, to the point that New York is virtually a city without a language. (Furthermore, American English could not have *constituted* itself without this linguistic labor of the minorities.) Or the linguistic situation in the old Austrian empire: German was a major language in relation to the minorities, but as such it could not avoid being treated by those minorities in a way that made it a minor language in relation to the German of the Germans. There is no language that does not have intralinguistic, endogenous, internal minorities. So at the most general level of linguistics, Chomsky's and Labov's positions are constantly passing and converting into each other. Chomsky can say that even a minor, dialectical, or ghetto language cannot be studied unless invariants are extracted from it and "extrinsic or mixed" variables are eliminated; and Labov can respond that even a standard or major language cannot be studied independently of "inherent" variations, which are precisely neither mixed nor extrinsic. *You will never find a homogeneous system that is not still or already affected by a regulated, continuous, immanent process of variation* (why does Chomsky pretend not to understand this?).

There are not, therefore, two kinds of languages but two possible treatments of the same language. Either the variables are treated in such a way as to extract from them constants and constant relations or in such a way as to place them in continuous variation. We were wrong to give the impression at times that constants existed alongside variables, linguistic constants alongside variables of enunciation: that was only for convenience of presentation. For it is obvious that the constants are drawn from the variables themselves; universals in linguistics have no more existence in themselves than they do in economics and are always concluded from a universalization or a rendering-uniform involving variables. *Constant is not opposed to variable;* it is a treatment of the variable opposed to the other kind of treatment, or continuous variation. So-called obligatory rules correspond to the first kind of treatment, whereas optional rules concern the construction of a continuum of variation. Moreover, there are a certain number of categories or distinctions that cannot be invoked, that are inapplicable and useless as a basis for objections because they presuppose the first treatment and are entirely subordinated to the quest for constants: for example, language as opposed to speech; synchrony as opposed to diachrony; competence as opposed to performance; distinctive features as opposed to nondistinctive (or secondarily distinctive) features. For nondistinctive features, whether prosodic, stylistic, or pragmatic, are not only omnipresent variables, in contrast to the presence or absence of a constant; they are not only superlinear and "suprasegmental" elements, in contrast to linear segmental elements; their very characteristics give them the power to place all the elements of language in a state of continuous variation—for example, the impact of tone on phonemes, accent on morphemes, or intonation on syntax. These are not secondary features but another treatment of language that no longer operates according to the preceding categories.

"Major" and "minor" do not qualify two different languages but rather two usages or functions of language. Bilingualism, of course, provides a good example, but once again we use it simply for the sake of convenience. Doubtless, in the Austrian empire Czech was a minor language in relation to German; but the German of Prague already functioned as a potentially minor language in relation to the German of Vienna or Berlin; and Kafka, a Czechoslovakian Jew writing in German, submits German to creative treatment as a minor language, constructing a continuum of variation, negotiating all of the variables both to constrict the constants and to expand the variables: make language stammer, or make it "wail," stretch tensors through all of language, even written language, and draw from it cries, shouts, pitches, durations, timbres, accents, intensities. Two conjoined tendencies in so-called minor languages have often been noted: an impoverishment, a shedding of syntactical and lexical forms; but simultaneously a strange proliferation of shifting effects, a taste for overload and paraphrase. This applies to the German of Prague, Black English, and Québecois. But with rare exceptions, the interpretation of the linguists has been rather malevolent, invoking a consubstantial poverty and preciosity. The alleged poverty is in fact a restriction of constants and the overload an extension of variations functioning to deploy a continuum sweeping up all components. The poverty is not a lack but a void or ellipsis allowing one to sidestep a constant instead of tackling it head on, or to approach it from above or below instead of positioning oneself within it. And the overload is not a rhetorical figure, a metaphor, or symbolic structure; it is a mobile paraphrase bearing witness to the unlocalized presence of an indirect discourse at the heart of every statement. From both sides we see a rejection of reference points a dissolution of constant form in favor of differences in dynamic. The closer a language gets to this state, the closer it comes not only to a system of musical notation, but also to music itself.[4]

Subtract and place in variation, remove and place in variation: a single operation. Minor languages are characterized not by overload and poverty in relation to a standard or major language, but by a sobriety and variation that are like a minor treatment of the standard language, a becoming-minor and the major language. The problem is not the distinction between major and minor language; it is one of a becoming. It is a question not of reterritorializing oneself on a dialect or a patois but of deterritorializing the major language. Black Americans do not oppose Black to English, they transform the American English that is their own language into Black English. Minor languages do not exist in themselves: they exist only in relation to a major language and are also investments of that language for the purpose of making it minor. One must find the minor language, the dialect or rather idiolect, on the basis of which one can make one's own major language minor. That is the strength of authors termed "minor," who are in fact the greatest, the only greats: having to conquer one's own language, in other words, to attain that sobriety in the use of a major language, in order to place it in a state of continuous variation (the opposite of regionalism). It is in one's own language that one is bilingual or multilingual. Conquer the major language in order to delineate in it as yet unknown minor languages. Use the minor language to *send the major language racing*. Minor authors are foreigners in their own tongue. If they are bastards, if they experience themselves as bastards, it is due not to a mixing or intermingling of languages but rather to a subtraction and variation of their own language achieved by stretching tensors through it.

The notion of *minority* is very complex, with musical, literary, linguistic, as well as juridical and political, references. The opposition between minority and majority is not simply quantitative. Majority implies a constant, of expression or content, serving as a standard measure by which to evaluate it. Let us suppose that the constant or standard is the average adult-white-heterosexual-European-male speaking a standard language (Joyce's or Ezra Pound's Ulysses). It is obvious that "man" holds the majority, even if he is less numerous than mosquitoes, children, women, blacks, peasants, homosexuals, etc. That is because he appears twice, once in the constant and again in the variable from which the constant is extracted. Majority assumes a state of power and domination, not the other way around. It assumes the standard measure, not the other way around. Even Marxism "has almost always translated hegemony from the point of view of the national worker, qualified, male and over thirty-five."[5] A determination different from that of the constant will therefore be considered minoritarian, by nature and regardless of number, in other words, a subsystem or an outsystem. This is evident in all the operations, electoral or otherwise, where you are given a choice, but on the condition that your choice conform to the limits of the constant ("you mustn't choose to change society. . ."). But at this point, everything is reversed. For the majority, insofar as it is analytically included in the abstract standard, is never anybody, it is always Nobody—Ulysses—whereas the minority is the becoming of everybody, one's potential becoming to the extent that one deviates from the model. There is a majoritarian "fact," but it is the analytic fact of Nobody, as opposed to the becoming-minoritarian of everybody. That is why we must distinguish between: the majoritarian as a constant and homogeneous system; minorities as subsystems; and the minoritarian as a potential, creative and created, becoming. The problem is never to acquire the majority, even in order to install a new constant. There is no becoming-majoritarian; majority is never becoming. All becoming is minoritarian. Women, regardless of their numbers, are a minority, definable as a state or subset; but they create only by making possible a becoming over which they do not have ownership, into which they themselves must enter; this is a becoming-woman affecting all of humankind, men and women both. The same goes for minor languages: they are not simply sublanguages, idiolects or dialects, but potential agents of the major language's entering into a becoming-minoritarian of all of its dimensions and elements. We should distinguish between minor languages, the major language, and the becoming-minor of the major language. Minorities, of course, are objectively definable states, states of language, ethnicity, or sex with their own ghetto terriorialities, but they must also be thought of as seeds, crystals of becoming whose value is to trigger uncontrollable movements and deterritorializations of the mean or majority. That is why Pasolini demonstrated that the essential thing, precisely in free indirect discourse, is to be found neither in language A, nor in language B, but "in language X, which is none other than language A in the actual process of becoming language B."[6] There is a universal figure of minoritarian consciousness as the becoming of everybody, and that becoming is creation. One does not attain it by acquiring the majority. The figure to which we are referring is continuous variation, as an amplitude that continually oversteps the representative threshold of the majoritarian standard, by excess or default. In erecting the figure of a universal minoritarian consciousness, one addresses powers [*puissances*] of becoming that belong to a different realm from that of Power [*Pouvoir*] and Domination. Continuous variation constitutes the becoming-minoritarian of everybody, as opposed to the majoritarian Fact of Nobody. Becoming-minoritarian as the universal figure of consciousness is called autonomy. It is certainly not by using a minor language as a dialect, by regionalizing or ghettoizing, that one becomes revolutionary; rather, by using a number of minority elements, by connecting, conjugating them, one invents a specific, unforeseen, autonomous becoming.[7]

18
· · ·
Minor Literature: Kafka

So far we have dealt with little more than contents and their forms: bent head–straightened head, triangles–lines of escape. And it is true that in the realm of expression, the bent head connects to the photo, and the erect head to sound. But as long as the form and the deformation or expression are not considered for themselves, there can be no real way out, even at the level of contents. Only expression gives us the *method*. The problem of expression is staked out by Kafka not in an abstract and universal fashion but in relation to those literatures that are considered minor, for example, the Jewish literature of Warsaw and Prague. A minor literature doesn't come from a minor language; it is rather that which a minority constructs within a major language. But the first characteristic of minor literature in any case is that in it language is affected with a high coefficient of deterritorialization. In this sense, Kafka marks the impasse that bars access to writing for the Jews of Prague and turns their literature into something impossible—the impossibility of not writing, the impossibility of writing in German, the impossibility of writing otherwise.[1] The impossibility of not writing because national consciousness, uncertain or oppressed, necessarily exists by means of literature ("The literary struggle has its real justification at the highest possible levels"). The impossibility of writing other than in German is for the Prague Jews the feeling of an irreducible distance from their primitive territoriality. And the impossibility of writing in German is the deterritorialization of the German population itself, an oppressive minority that speaks a language cut off from the masses, like a "paper language" or an artificial language: this is all the more true for the Jews who are simultaneously a part of this minority and excluded from it, like "gypsies who have stolen a German child from its crib." In short, Prague German is a deterritorialized language, appropriate for strange and minor uses. (This can be compared in another context to what blacks in America today are able to do with the English language.)

The second characteristic of minor literatures is that everything in them is political. In major literatures, in contrast, the individual concern (familial, marital, and so on) joins with other no less individual concerns, the social milieu serving as a mere environment or a background; this is so much the case that none of these Oedipal intrigues are specifically indispensable or absolutely necessary but all become as one in a large space. Minor literature is completely different; its cramped space forces each individual intrigue to connect immediately to politics. The individual concern thus becomes all the more necessary, indispensable, magnified, because a whole other story is vibrating within it. In this way, the family triangle connects to other triangles—commercial, economic, bureaucratic, juridical—that determine its values. When Kafka indicates that one of the goals of a minor literature is the "purification of the conflict that opposes father and son and the possibility of discussing that conflict," it isn't a question of an Oedipal phantasm but of a political program. "Even though something is often thought through calmly, one still does not reach the boundary where it connects up with similar things, one reaches the boundary soonest in politics, indeed, one even strives to see it before it is there, and often sees this limiting boundary everywhere. . . . What in great literature goes on down below, constituting a not indispensable cellar of the structure, here takes place in the full light of day, what is there a matter of passing interest for a few, here absorbs everyone no less than as a matter of life and death."[2]

The third characteristic of minor literature is that in it everything takes on a collective value. Indeed, precisely because talent isn't abundant in a minor literature, there are no possibilities for an individuated enunciation that would belong to this or that "master" and that could be separated from a collective enunciation. Indeed, scarcity of talent is in fact beneficial and allows the conception of something other than a literature of masters; what each author says individually already constitutes a common action, and what he or she says or does is necessarily political, even if others aren't in agreement. The political domain has contaminated every statement [énoncé]. But above all else, because collective or national consciousness is "of-

ten inactive in external life and always in the process of break-down," literature finds itself positively charged with the role and function of collective,
and even revolutionary, enunciation. It is literature that produces an active
solidarity in spite of skepticism; and if the writer is in the margins or completely outside his or her fragile community, this situation allows the writer
all the more the possibility to express another possible community and to
forge the means for another consciousness and another sensibility; just as
the dog of "Investigations" calls out in his solitude to *another science*. The
literary machine thus becomes the relay for a revolutionary machine-to-
come, not at all for ideological reasons but because the literary machine
alone is determined to fill the conditions of a collective enunciation that is
lacking elsewhere in this milieu: *literature is the people's concern.*[3] It is certainly
in these terms that Kafka sees the problem. The message doesn't refer back
to an enunciating subject who would be its cause, no more than to a subject
of the statement [*sujet d'énoncé*] who would be its effect. Undoubtedly, for a
while, Kafka thought according to these traditional categories of the two
subjects, the author and the hero, the narrator and the character, the
dreamer and the one dreamed of.[4] But he will quickly reject the role of the
narrator, just as he will refuse an author's or master's literature, despite his
admiration for Goethe. Josephine the mouse renounces the individual act of
singing in order to melt into the collective enunciation of "the immense
crowd of the heros of [her] people." A movement from the individuated animal to the pack or to a collective multiplicity—seven canine musicians. In
"The Investigations of a Dog," the expressions of the solitary researcher
tend toward the assemblage [*agencement*] of a collective enunciation of the
canine species even if this collectivity is no longer or not yet given. There
isn't a subject; *there are only collective assemblages of enunciation,* and literature
expresses these acts insofar as they're not imposed from without and insofar as they exist only as diabolical powers to come or revolutionary forces
to be constructed. Kafka's solitude opens him up to everything going on in
history today. The letter K no longer designates a narrator or a character
but an assemblage that becomes all the more machine-like, an agent that
becomes all the more collective because an individual is locked into it in
his or her solitude (it is only in connection to a subject that something individual would be separable from the collective and would lead its own
life).

The three characteristics of minor literature are the deterritorialization
of language, the connection of the individual to a political immediacy, and
the collective assemblage of enunciation. We might as well say that minor
no longer designates specific literatures but the revolutionary conditions for
every literature within the heart of what is called great (or established) literature. Even he who has the misfortune of being born in the country of a

great literature must write in its language, just as a Czech Jew writes in German, or an Ouzbekian writes in Russian. Writing like a dog digging a hole, a rat digging its burrow. And to do that, finding his own point of under-development, his own patois, his own third world, his own desert. There has been much discussion of the questions "What is a marginal literature?" and "What is a popular literature, a proletarian literature?" The criteria are ob-viously difficult to establish if one doesn't start with a more objective concept—that of minor literature. Only the possibility of setting up a minor practice of major language from within allows one to define popular litera-ture, marginal literature, and so on.[5] Only in this way can literature really become a collective machine of expression and really be able to treat and develop its contents. Kafka emphatically declares that a minor literature is much more able to work over its material.[6] Why this machine of expression, and what is it? We know that it is in a relation of multiple deterritorializa-tions with language; it is the situation of the Jews who have dropped the Czech language at the same time as the rural environment, but it is also the situation of the German language as a "paper language." Well, one can go even farther; one can push this movement of deterritorialization of expres-sion even farther. But there are only two ways to do this. One way is to ar-tificially enrich this German, to swell it up through all the resources of sym-bolism, of oneirism, of esoteric sense, of a hidden signifier. This is the approach of the Prague school, Gustav Meyrink and many others, includ-ing Max Brod.[7] But this attempt implies a desperate attempt at symbolic reterritorilization, based in archetypes, Kabbala, and alchemy, that accen-tuates its break from the people and will find its political result only in Zion-ism and such things as the "dream of Zion." Kafka will quickly choose the other way, or, rather, he will invent another way. He will opt for the German language of Prague as it is and in its very poverty. Go always farther in the direction of deterritorialization, to the point of sobriety. Since the language is arid, make it vibrate with a new intensity. Oppose a purely intensive usage of language to all symbolic or even significant or simply signifying usages of it. Arrive at a perfect and unformed expression, a materially in-tense expression. (For these two possible paths, couldn't we find the same alternatives, under other conditions, in Joyce and Beckett? As Irishmen, both of them live within the genial conditions of a minor literature. That is the glory of this sort of minor literature—to be the revolutionary force for all literature. The utilization of English and of every language in Joyce. The utilization of English and French in Beckett. But the former never stops op-erating by exhilaration and overdetermination and brings about all sorts of worldwide reterritorializations. The other proceeds by dryness and so-briety, a willed poverty, pushing deterritorialization to such an extreme that nothing remains but intensities.)

How many people today live in a language that is not their own? Or no longer, or not yet, even know their own and know poorly the major language that they are forced to serve? This is the problem of immigrants, and especially of their children, the problem of minorities, the problem of a minor literature, but also a problem for all of us: how to tear a minor literature away from its own language, allowing it to challenge the language and making it follow a sober revolutionary path? How to become a nomad and an immigrant and a gypsy in relation to one's own language? Kafka answers: steal the baby from its crib, walk the tightrope.

Rich or poor, each language always implies a deterritorialization of the mouth, the tongue, and the teeth. The mouth, tongue, and teeth find their primitive territoriality in food. In giving themselves over to the articulation of sounds, the mouth, tongue, and teeth deterritorialize. Thus, there is a certain disjunction between eating and speaking, and even more, despite all appearances, between eating and writing. Undoubtedly, one can write while eating more easily than one can speak while eating, but writing goes further in transforming words into things capable of competing with food. Disjunction between content and expression. To speak, and above all to write, is to fast. Kafka manifests a permanent obsession with food, and with that form of food par excellence, in other words, the animal or meat—an obsession with the mouth and with teeth and with large, unhealthy, or gold-capped teeth.[8] This is one of Kafka's main problems with Felice. Fasting is also a constant theme in Kafka's writings. His writings are a long history of fasts. The Hunger Artist, surveyed by butchers, ends his career next to beasts who eat their meat raw, placing the visitors before an irritating alternative. The dogs try to take over the mouth of the investigating hound by filling it with food so that he'll stop asking questions, and there too there is an irritating alternative: "They would have done better to drive me away and refuse to listen to my questions. No, they did not want to do that; they did not indeed want to listen to my questions, but it was because I asked these questions that they did not want to drive me away." The investigating hound oscillates between two sciences, that of food—a science of the Earth and of the bent head ("Whence does the Earth procure this food?")—and that of music which is a science of the air and of the straightened head, as the seven musical dogs of the beginning and the singing dog of the end well demonstrate. But between the two there is something in common, since food can come from high up and the science of food can only develop through fasting, just as the music is strangely silent.

Ordinarily, in fact, language compensates for its deterritorialization by a reterritorialization in sense. Ceasing to be the organ of one of the senses, it becomes an instrument of sense. And it is sense, as a correct sense, that presides over the designation of sounds (the thing or the state of things that the word designates) and, as figurative sense, over the affection of images and metaphors (those other things that words designate under certain situations or conditions). Thus, there is not only a spiritual reterritorialization of sense, but also a physical one. Similarly, language exists only through the distinction and the complementarity of a subject of enunciation, who is in connection with sense, and a subject of the statement, who is in connection, directly or metaphorically, with the designated thing. This sort of ordinary use of language can be called extensive or representative—the reterritorializing function of language (thus, the singing dog at the end of the "Investigations" forces the hero to abandon his fast, a sort of re-Oedipalization).

Now something happens: the situation of the German language in Czechoslovakia, as a fluid language intermixed with Czech and Yiddish, will allow Kafka the possibility of invention. Since things are as they are ("it is as it is, it is as it is," a formula dear to Kafka, marker of a state of facts), he will abandon sense, render it no more than implicit; he will retain only the skeleton of sense, or a paper cutout.

Since articulated sound was a deterritorialized noise but one that will be reterritorialized in sense, it is now sound itself that will be deterritorialized irrevocably, absolutely. The sound or the word that traverses this new deterritorialization no longer belongs to a language of sense, even though it derives from it, nor is it an organized music or song, even though it might appear to be. We noted Gregor's warbling and the ways it blurred words, the whistling of the mouse, the cough of the ape, the pianist who doesn't play, the singer who doesn't sing and gives birth to her song out of her nonsinging, the musical dogs who are musicians in the very depths of their bodies since they don't emit any music. Everywhere, organized music is traversed by a line of abolition—just as a language of sense is traversed by a line of escape—in order to liberate a living and expressive material that speaks for itself and has no need of being put into a form.[9] This language torn from sense, conquering sense, bringing about an active neutralization of sense, no longer finds its value in anything but an accenting of the word, an inflection: "I live only here or there in a small word in whose vowel. . . . I lose my useless head for a moment. The first and last letters are the beginning and end of my fishlike emotion."[10] Children are well skilled in the exercise of repeating a word, the sense of which is only vaguely felt, in order to make it vibrate around itself (at the beginning of *The Castle*, the schoolchildren are speaking so fast that one cannot understand what they are saying). Kafka tells how, as a child, he repeated one of his father's expressions in order to make it take flight on a line of non-sense: "end of the month, end of the month."[11] The proper name, which has no sense in itself, is particularly propitious for this sort of exercise. *Milena,* with an accent on the *i,* begins by evoking "a Greek or a Roman gone astray in Bohemia, violated by Czech, cheated of its accent," and then, by a more delicate approximation, it evokes "a woman whom one carries in one's arms out of the world, out of the fire," the accent marking here an always possible fall or, on the contrary, "the lucky leap which you yourself make with your burden."[12]

It seems to us that there is a certain difference, even if relative and highly nuanced, between the two evocations of the name Milena: one still attaches itself to an extensive, figurative scene of the fantasmatic sort; the second is already much more intensive, marking a fall or a leap as a threshold of intensity contained within the name itself. In fact, we have here what happens when sense is actively neutralized. As Wagenbach says, "The word is master; it directly gives birth to the image." But how can we define this procedure? Of sense there remains only enough to direct the lines of escape. There is no longer a destination of something by means of a proper name, nor an assignation of metaphors by means of a figurative sense. But *like* images, the thing no longer forms anything but a sequence of intensive states, a ladder or a circuit for intensities that one can make race around in one sense or another, from high to low, or from low to high. The image is this very race itself; it has become becoming—the becoming-dog of the man and the becoming-man of the dog, the becoming-ape or the becoming-beetle of the man and vice versa. We are no longer in the situation of an ordinary, rich language where the word dog, for example, would directly designate an animal and would apply metaphorically to other things (so that one could say "like a dog").[13] *Diaries,* 1921: "Metaphors are one of the things that makes me despair of literature." Kafka deliberately kills all metaphor, all symbolism, all signification, no less than all designation. Metamorphosis is the contrary of metaphor. There is no longer any proper sense or figurative sense, but only a distribution of states that is part of the range of the word. The thing and other things are no longer anything but intensities overrun by deterritorialized sound or words that are following their line of escape. It is no longer a question of a resemblance between the comportment of an animal and that of a man; it is even less a question of a simple wordplay. There is no longer man or animal, since each deterritorializes the other, in a conjunction of flux, in a continuum of reversible intensities. Instead, it is now a question of a becoming that includes the maximum of difference as a difference of intensity, the crossing of a barrier, a rising or a falling, a bending or an erecting, an accent on the word. The animal does not speak "like" a man but pulls from the language tonalities lacking in signification; the words themselves are not "like" the animals but in their own way climb about, bark and roam around, being properly linguistic dogs, insects, or mice.[14] To make the sequences vibrate, to open the word onto unexpected internal intensities—in short, an asignifying *intensive utilization* of language. Furthermore, there is no longer a subject of the enunciation, nor a subject of the statement. It is no longer the subject of the statement who is a dog, with the subject of the enunciation remaining "like" a man; it is no longer the subject of enunciation who is "like" a beetle, the subject of the statement remaining a man. Rather, there is a circuit of states that forms a mutual becoming in the heart of a necessarily multiple or collective assemblage.

How does the situation of the German language in Prague—a withered vocabulary, an incorrect syntax—contribute to such a utilization? Generally, we might call the linguistic elements, however varied they may be, that express the "internal tensions of a language" *intensives* or *tensors*. It is in this sense that the linguist Vidal Sephiha terms intensive "any linguistic tool that allows a move toward the limit of a notion or a surpassing of it," marking a movement of language toward its extremes, toward a reversible beyond or before.[15] Sephiha well shows the variety of such elements which can be all sorts of master-words, verbs, or prepositions that assume all sorts of senses; prenominal or purely intensive verbs as in Hebrew; conjunctions, exclamations, adverbs; and *terms that connote pain*.[16] One could equally cite the accents that are interior to words, their discordant function. And it would seem that the language of a minor literature particularly develops these tensors or these intensives. In the lovely pages where he analyzes the Prague German that was influenced by Czech, Wagenbach cites as the characteristics of this form of German the incorrect use of prepositions; the abuse of the pronominal; the employment of malleable verbs (such as *Giben,* which is used for the series "put, sit, place, take away" and which thereby becomes intensive); the multiplication and succession of adverbs; the use of pain-filled connotations; the importance of the accent as a tension internal to the word; and the distribution of consonants and vowels as part of an internal discordance. Wagenbach insists on this point: all these marks of the poverty of a language show up in Kafka but have been taken over by a creative utilization for the purposes of a new sobriety, a new expressivity, a new flexibility, a new intensity.[17] "Almost every word I write jars up against the next, I hear the consonants rub leadenly against each other and the vowels sing an accompaniment like Negroes in a minstrel show."[18] *Language stops being representative in order to now move toward its extremities or its limits.* The connotation of pain accompanies this metamorphosis, as in the words that become a painful warbling with Gregor, or in Franz's cry "single and irrevocable." Think about the utilization of French as a spoken language in the films of Godard. There too is an accumulation of stereotypical adverbs and conjunctions that form the base of all the phrases—a strange poverty that makes French a minor language within French; a creative process that directly links the word to the image; a technique that surges up at the end of sequences in connection with the intensity of the limit "that's enough, enough, he's had enough," and a generalized intensification, coinciding with a panning shot where the camera pivots and sweeps around without leaving the spot, making the image vibrate.

Perhaps the comparative study of images would be less interesting than the study of the functions of language that can work in the same group across different languages—bilingualism or even multilingualism. Because the study of the functions in distinct languages alone can account for social factors, relations of force, diverse centers of power, it escapes from the "informational" myth in order to evaluate the hierarchic and imperative system of language as a transmission of orders, an exercise of power or of resistance to this exercise. Using the research of Ferguson and Gumperz, Henri Gobard has proposed a tetralinguistic model: vernacular, maternal, or territorial language, used in rural communities or rural in its origins; a vehicular, urban, governmental, even worldwide language, a language of businesses, commercial exchange, bureaucratic transmission, and so on, a language of the first sort of deterritorialization; referential language, language of sense and of culture, entailing a cultural reterritorialization; mythic language, on the horizon of cultures, caught up in a spiritual or religious reterritorialization. The spatiotemporal categories of these languages differ sharply: vernacular language is *here;* vehicular language is *everywhere;* referential language is *over there;* mythic language is *beyond.* But above all else, the distribution of these languages varies from one group to the next and, in a single group, from one epoch to the next (for a long time in Europe, Latin was a vehicular language before becoming referential, then mythic; English has become the worldwide vehicular language for today's world).[19] What can be said in one language cannot be said in another, and the totality of what can and can't be said varies necessarily with each language and with the connections between these languages.[20] Moreover, all these factors can have ambiguous edges, changing borders, that differ for this or that material. One language can fill a certain function for one material and another function for another material. Each function of a language divides up in turn and carries with it multiple centers of power. A blur of languages, and not at all a system of languages. We can understand the indignation of integrationists who cry when Mass is said in French, since Latin is being robbed of its mythic function. But the classicists are even more behind the times and cry because Latin has even been robbed of its referential cultural function. They express regret in this way for the religious or educational forms of powers that this language exercised and that have now been replaced by other forms. There are even more serious examples that cross over between groups. The revival of regionalisms, with a reterritorialization through dialect or patois, a vernacular language—how does that serve a worldwide or transnational technocracy? How can that contribute to revolutionary movements, since they are also filled with archaisms that they are trying to impart a contemporary sense to? From Servan-Schreiber to the Breton bard to the Canadian singer. And that's not really how the borders divide up, since the Canadian singer can also bring about the most reactionary, the most Oedipal of reterritorializations, oh mama, oh my native land, my cabin, olé, olé. We would call this a blur, a mixed-up history, a political situation, but linguists don't know about this, don't want to know about this, since, as linguists, they are "apolitical," pure scientists. Even Chomsky compensated for his scientific apoliticism only by his courageous struggle against the war in Vietnam.

Let's return to the situation in the Hapsburg empire. The breakdown and fall of the empire increases the crisis, accentuates everywhere movements of deterritorialization, and invites all sorts of complex reterritorializations—archaic, mythic, or symbolist. At random, we can cite the following among Kafka's contemporaries: Einstein and his deterritorialization of the representation of the universe (Einstein teaches in Prague, and the physicist Philipp Frank gives conferences there with Kafka in attendance); the Austrian dodecaphonists and their deterritorialization of musical representation (the cry that is Marie's death in *Wozzeck*, or Lulu's, or the echoed *si* that seems to us to follow a musical path similar in certain ways to what Kafka is doing); the expressionist cinema and its double movement of deterritorialization and reterritorialization of the image (Robert Wiene, who has Czech background; Fritz Lang, born in Vienna; Paul Wegener and his utilization of Prague themes). Of course, we should mention Viennese psychoanalysis and Prague school linguistics.[21] What is the specific situation of the Prague Jews in relation to the "four languages"? The vernacular language for these Jews who have come from a rural milieu is Czech, but the Czech language tends to be forgotten and repressed; as for Yiddish, it is often disdained or viewed with suspicion—it *frightens*, as Kafka tells us. German is the vehicular language of the towns, a bureaucratic language of the state, a commercial language of exchange (but English has already started to become indispensable for this purpose). The German language—but this time, Goethe's German—has a cultural and referential function (as does French to a lesser degree). As a mythic language, Hebrew is connected with the start of Zionism and still possesses the quality of an active dream. For each of these languages, we need to evaluate the degrees of territoriality, deterritorialization, and reterritorialization. Kafka's own situation: he is one of the few Jewish writers in Prague to understand and speak Czech (and this language will have a great importance in his relationship with Milena). German plays precisely the double role of vehicular and cultural language, with Goethe always on the horizon (Kafka also knows French, Italian, and probably a bit of English). He will not learn Hebrew until later. What is complicated is Kafka's relation to Yiddish; he sees it less as a sort of linguistic territoriality for the Jews than as a nomadic movement of deterritorialization that reworks German language. What fascinates him in Yiddish is less a language of a religious community than that of a popular theater (he will become patron and impresario for the traveling theater of Isak Lowy).[22] The manner in which Kafka, in a public meeting, presented Yiddish to a rather hostile Jewish bourgeois audience is completely remarkable: Yiddish is a language that frightens more than it invites disdain, "dread mingled with a certain fundamental distaste"; it is a language that is lacking a grammar and that is filled with vocables that are fleeting, mobilized, emigrating, and turned into nomads that interiorize "relations of force." It is a language that is grafted onto Middle-High German and that so reworks the German language from within that one cannot translate it into German without destroying it; one can understand Yiddish only by "feeling it" in the heart. In short, it is a language where minor utilizations will carry you away: "Then you will come to feel the true unity of Yiddish and so strongly that it will frighten you, yet it will no longer be fear of Yiddish but of yourselves. Enjoy this self-confidence as much as you can!"[23]

Kafka does not opt for a reterritorialization through the Czech language. Nor toward a hypercultural usage of German with all sorts of oneiric or symbolic or mythic flights (even Hebrew-ifying ones), as was the case with the Prague school. Nor toward an oral, popular Yiddish. Instead, using the path that Yiddish opens up to him, he takes it in such a way as to convert it into a unique and solitary form of writing. Since Prague German is deterritorialized to several degrees, he will always take it farther, to a greater degree of intensity, but in the direction of a new sobriety, a new and unexpected modification, a pitiless rectification, a straightening of the head. Schizo politeness, a drunkenness caused by water.[24] He will make the German language take flight on a line of escape. He will feed himself on abstinence; he will tear out of Prague German all the qualities of underdevelopment that it has tried to hide; he will make it cry with an extremely sober and rigorous cry. He will pull from it the barking of the dog, the cough of the ape, and the bustling of the beetle. He will turn syntax into a cry that will embrace the rigid syntax of this dried-up German. He will push it toward a deterritorialization that will no longer be saved by culture or by myth, that will be an absolute deterritorialization, even if it is slow, sticky, coagulated.

To bring language slowly and progressively to the desert. To use syntax in order to cry, to give a syntax to the cry.

There is nothing that is major or revolutionary exept the minor. To hate all languages of masters. Kafka's fascination for servants and employees (the same thing in Proust in relation to servants, to their language). What interests him even more is the possibility of making of his own language— assuming that it is unique, that it is a major language or has been—a minor utilization. To be a sort of stranger *within* his own language; this is the situation of Kafka's Great Swimmer.[25] Even when it is unique, a language remains a mixture, a schizophrenic mélange, a Harlequin costume in which very different functions of language and distinct centers of power are played out, blurring what can be said and what can't be said; one function will be played off against the other, all the degrees of territoriality and relative deterritorialization will be played out. Even when major, a language is open to an intensive utilization that makes it take flight along creative lines of escape which, no matter how slowly, no matter how cautiously, can now form an absolute deterritorialization. All this inventiveness, not only lexically, since the lexical matters little, but sober syntactical invention, simply to write like a dog (but a dog can't write—exactly, exactly). It's what Artaud did with French—cries, gasps; what Celine did with French, following another line, one that was exclamatory to the highest degree. Celine's syntactic evolution went from *Voyage* to *Death on the Credit Plan*, then from *Death on the Credit Plan* to *Guignol's Band*. (After that, Celine had nothing more to talk about except his own misfortunes; in other words, he had no longer any desire to write, only the need to make money. And it always ends like that, language's lines of escape: silence, the interrupted, the interminable, or even worse. But until that point, what a crazy creation, what a writing machine! Celine was so applauded for *Voyage* that he went even further in *Death on the Credit Plan* and then in the prodigious *Guignol's Band* where language is nothing more than intensities. He spoke with a kind of "minor music." Kafka, too, is a minor music, a different one, but always made up of deterritorialized sounds, a language that moves head over heels and away.) These are the true minor authors. An escape for language, for music, for writing. What we call "pop"—pop music, pop philosophy, pop writing— *Worterflucht*. To make use of the polylingualism of one's own language, to make a minor or intensive use of it, to oppose the oppressed quality of this language to its oppressive quality, to find points of nonculture or underdevelopment, linguistic Third-World zones by which a language can escape, an animal enters into things, an assemblage comes into play. How many styles or genres or literary movements, even very small ones, have only one single dream: to assume a major function in language, to offer themselves as a sort of state language, an official language (for example, psychoanalysis today, which would like to be a master of the signifier, of metaphor, or wordplay). Create the opposite dream: know how to create a becoming-minor. (Is there a hope for philosophy, which for a long time has been an official, referential genre? Let us profit from this moment in which antiphilosophy is trying to be a language of power.)

19
. . .
Nomad Art: Space

The Aesthetic Model: Nomad Art

Several notions, both practical and theoretical, are suitable for defining nomad art and its successors (barbarian, Gothic, and modern). First, "close-range" vision, as distinguished from long-distance vision; second, "tactile," or rather "haptic" space, as distinguished from optical space. *Haptic* is a better word than *tactile* since it does not establish an opposition between two sense organs but rather invites the assumption that the eye itself may fulfill this nonoptical function. It was Aloïs Riegl who, in some marvelous pages, gave fundamental aesthetic status to the couple, *close vision–haptic space*. But for the moment we should set aside the criteria proposed by Riegl (then by Wilhelm Worringer, and more recently by Henri Maldiney), and take some risks ourselves, making free use of these notions.[1] It seems to us that the smooth is both the object of a close vision par excellence and the element of a haptic space (which may be as much visual or auditory as tactile). The striated, on the contrary, relates to a more distant vision, and a more optical space—although the eye in turn is not the only organ to have this capacity. Once again, as always, this analysis must be corrected by a coefficient of transformation according to which passages between the striated and the smooth are at once necessary and uncertain, and all the more disruptive. The law of the painting is that it be done at close range, even if it is viewed from relatively far away. One can back away from a thing, but it is a bad painter who backs away from the painting he or she is working on. Or from the "thing" for that matter. Cézanne spoke of the need to *no longer see* the wheat field, to be too close to it, to lose oneself without landmarks in smooth space. Afterward, striation can emerge: drawing, strata, the earth, "stubborn geometry," the "measure of the world," "geological foundations," "everything falls straight down." . . . The striated itself may in turn disappear in a "catastrophe," opening the way for a new smooth space, and another striated space. . . .

A painting is done at close range, even if it is seen from a distance. Similarly, it is said that composers do not hear: they have close-range hearing, whereas listeners hear from a distance. Even writers write with short-term memory, whereas readers are assumed to be endowed with long-term memory. The first aspect of the haptic, smooth space of close vision is that its orientations, landmarks, and linkages are in continuous variation; it operates step by step. Examples are the desert, steppe, ice, and sea, local spaces of pure connection. Contrary to what is sometimes said, one never sees from a distance in a space of this kind, nor does one see it from a distance; one is never "in front of," any more than one is "in" (one is "on." . .). Orientations are not constant but change according to temporary vegetation, occupations, and precipitation. There is no visual model for points of reference that would make them interchangeable and unite them in an inertial class assignable to an immobile outside observer. On the contrary, they are tied to any number of observers, who may be qualified as "monads" but are instead *nomads* entertaining tactile relations among themselves. The interlinkages do not imply an ambient space in which the multiplicity would be immersed and which would make distances invariant; rather, they are constituted according to ordered differences that give rise to intrinsic variations in the division of a single distance.[2] These questions of orientation, location, and linkage enter into play in the most famous works of nomad art: the twisted animals have no land beneath them; the ground constantly changes direction, as in aerial acrobatics; the paws point in the opposite direction from the head, the hind part of the body is turned upside down; the "monadological" points of view can be interlinked only on a nomad space; the whole and the parts give the eye that beholds them a function that is haptic rather than optical. This is an animality that can be seen only by touching it with one's mind, but without the mind becoming a finger, not even by way of the eye. (In a much cruder fashion, the kaleidoscope has exactly the same function: to give the eye a digital function.) Striated space, on the contrary, is defined by the requirements of long-distance vision: constancy of orientation, invariance of distance through an interchange of inertial points of reference, interlinkage by immersion in an ambient milieu, constitution of a central perspective. It is less easy to evaluate the creative potentialities of striated space, and how it can simultaneously emerge from the smooth and give everything a whole new impetus.

The opposition between the striated and the smooth is not simply that of the global and the local. For in one case, the global is still relative, whereas in the other the local is already absolute. Where there is close vision, space is not visual, or rather the eye itself has a haptic, nonoptical function: no line separates earth from sky, which are of the same substance; there is neither horizon nor background nor perspective nor limit nor outline or form nor center; there is no intermediary distance, or all distance is intermediary. Like Eskimo space.[3] In a totally different way, in a totally different context, Arab architecture constitutes a space that begins very near and low, placing the light and the airy below and the solid and heavy above. This reversal of the laws of gravity turns *lack of direction* and negation of volume into constructive forces. There exists a nomadic absolute, as a local integration moving from part to part and constituting smooth space in an infinite succession of linkages and changes in direction. It is an absolute that is one with becoming itself, with process. It is the absolute of passage, which in nomad art merges with its manifestation. Here the absolute is local, precisely because place is not delimited. If we now turn to the striated and optical space of long-distance vision, we see that the relative global that characterizes that space also requires the absolute, but in an entirely different way. The absolute is now the horizon or background, in other words, the Encompassing Element without which nothing would be global or englobed. It is against this background that the relative outline or form appears. The absolute itself can appear in the Encompassed, but only in a privileged place well delimited as a center, which then functions to repel beyond the limits anything that menaces the global integration. We can see clearly here how smooth space subsists, but only to give rise to the striated. The desert, sky, or sea, the Ocean, the Unlimited, first plays the role of an encompassing element, and tends to become a horizon: the earth is thus surrounded, globalized, "grounded" by this element, which holds it in immobile equilibrium and makes Form possible. Then to the extent that the encompassing element itself appears at the center of the earth, it assumes a second role, that of casting into the loathesome deep, the abode of the dead, anything smooth or nonmeasured that may have remained.[4] The striation of the earth implies as its necessary condition this double treatment of the smooth: on the one hand, it is carried or reduced to the absolute state of an encompassing horizon, and on the other it is expelled from the relative encom-

168 MINOR LANGUAGES AND NOMAD ART

passed element. Thus the great imperial religions need a smooth space like the desert, but only in order to give it a law that is opposed to the *nomos* in every way, and converts the absolute.

This perhaps explains for us the ambiguity of the excellent analyses by Riegl, Worringer, and Maldiney. They approach haptic space under the imperial conditions of Egyptian art. They define it as the presence of a horizon-background; the reduction of space to the plane (vertical and horizontal, height and width); and the rectilinear outline enclosing individuality and withdrawing it from change. Like the pyramid-form, every side a plane surface, against the background of the immobile desert. On the other hand, they show how in Greek art (then in Byzantine art, and up to the Renaissance), an optical space was differentiated from haptic space, one merging background with form, setting up an interference between the planes, conquering depth, working with cubic or voluminous extension, organizing perspective, and playing on relief and shadow, light and color. Thus at the very beginning they encounter the haptic at a point of mutation, in conditions under which it already serves to striate space. The optical makes that striation tighter and more perfect, or rather tight and perfect in a different way (it is not associated with the same "artistic will"). Everything occurs in a striated space that goes from empires to city-states, or evolved empires. It is not by chance that Riegl tends to eliminate the specific factors of nomad or even barbarian art; or that Worringer, when he introduces the idea of Gothic art in the broadest sense, relates it on the one hand to the Germanic and Celtic migrations of the North, and on the other to the empires of the East. But between the two were the nomads, who are reducible neither to empires they confronted nor the migrations they triggered. The Goths themselves were nomads of the steppe, and with the Sarmatians and Huns were an essential vector of communication between the East and the North, a factor irreducible to either of these two dimensions.[5] On one side, Egypt had its Hyksos, Asia Minor its Hittites, China its Turco-Mongols; and on the other, the Hebrews had their Habiru, the Germans, Celts, and Romans their Goths, the Arabs their Bedouins. The nomads have a specificity that is too hastily reduced to its consequences, by including them in the empires or counting them among the migrants, assimilating them to one or the other, denying them their own "will" to art. Again, there is a refusal to accept that the intermediary between the East and the North had its own absolute specificity, that the intermediary, the interval, played exactly this substantial role. Moreover, it does not have that role in the guise of a "will"; it only has a becoming, it invents a "becoming-artist."

When we invoke a primordial duality between the smooth and the striated, it is in order to subordinate the differences between "haptic" and "optic," "close vision" and "distant vision" to this distinction. Hence we will not define the haptic by the immobile background, by the plane and the contour, because these have to do with an already mixed state in which the haptic serves to striate, and uses its smooth components only in order to convert them to another kind of space. The haptic function and close vision presuppose the smooth, which has no background, plane, or contour, but rather changes in direction and local linkages between parts. Conversely, the developed optical function is not content to take striation to a new level of perfection, endowing it with an imaginary universal value and scope; it is also capable of reinstating the smooth, liberating light and modulating color, restoring a kind of aerial haptic space that constitutes the unlimited site of intersection of the planes.[6] In short, the smooth and the striated must be defined in themselves before the relative distinctions between haptic and optical, near and distant, can be derived.

This is where a third couple enters in: "abstract line–concrete line" (in addition to "haptic-optical," "close-distant"). It is Worringer who accorded fundamental importance to the abstract line, seeing it as the very beginning of art or the first expression of an artistic will. Art as abstract machine. Once again, it will doubtless be our inclination to voice in advance the same objections: for Worringer, the abstract line seems to make its first appearance in the crystalline or geometrical imperial Egyptian form, the most rectilinear of forms possible. It is only afterward that it assumes a particular avatar, constituting the "Gothic or Northern line" understood very broadly.[7] For us, on the other hand, the abstract line is fundamentally "Gothic," or rather, nomadic, not rectilinear. Consequently, we do not understand the aesthetic motivation for the abstract line in the same way, or its identity with the beginning of art. Whereas the rectilinear (or "regularly" rounded) Egyptian line is negatively motivated by anxiety in the face of all that passes, flows, or varies, and erects the constancy and eternity of an In-Itself, the nomad line is abstract in an entirely different sense, precisely because it has a multiple orientation and passes *between* points, figures, and contours: it is positively motivated by the smooth space it draws, not by any striation it might perform to ward off anxiety and subordinate the smooth. The abstract line is the affect of smooth spaces, not a feeling of anxiety that calls forth striation. Furthermore, although it is true that art begins only with the abstract line, the reason is not, as Worringer says, that the rectilinear is the first means of breaking with the nonaesthetic imitation of nature upon which the prehistoric, savage, and childish supposedly depend, lacking, as he thinks they do, a "will to art." On the contrary, if prehistoric art is fully art it is precisely because it manipulates the abstract, though nonrectilinear, line: "Primitive art begins with the abstract, and even the prefigurative. . . . Art is abstract from the outset, and at its origin could not have been otherwise."⁸ In effect, the line is all the more abstract when writing is absent, either because it has yet to develop or only exists outside or alongside. When writing takes charge of abstraction, as it does in empires, the line, already downgraded, necessarily tends to become concrete, even figurative. Children forget how to draw. But in the absence of writing, or when peoples have no need for a writing system of their own because theirs is borrowed from more or less nearby empires (as was the case for the nomads), the line is necessarily abstract; it is necessarily invested with all the power of abstraction, which finds no other outlet. That is why we believe that the different major types of imperial lines—the Egyptian rectilinear line, the Assyrian (or Greek) organic line, the supraphenomenal, encompassing Chinese line—convert the abstract line, rend it from its smooth space, and accord it concrete values. Still, it can be argued that these imperial lines are contemporaneous with the abstract line; the abstract line is no less at the "beginning," inasmuch as it is a pole always presupposed by any line capable of constituting another pole. The abstract line is at the beginning as much because of its historical abstraction as its prehistoric dating. It is therefore a part of the originality or irreducibility of nomad art, even when there is reciprocal interaction, influence, and confrontation with the imperial lines of sedentary art.

The abstract is not directly opposed to the figurative. The figurative as such is not inherent to any "will to art." In fact, we may oppose a figurative line in art to one that is not. The figurative, or imitation and representation, is a consequence, a result of certain characteristics of the line when it assumes a given form. We must therefore define those characteristics first. Take a system in which transversals are subordinated to diagonals, diagonals to horizontals and verticals, and horizontals and verticals to points (even when there are virtual). A system of this kind, which is rectilinear or unilinear regardless of the number of lines, expresses the formal conditions under which a space is striated and the line describes a contour. Such a line is inherently, formally, representative in itself, even if it does not represent anything. On the other hand, *a line that delimits nothing, that describes no contour,* that no longer goes from one point to another but instead passes between points, that is always declining from the horizontal and the vertical and deviating from the diagonal, that is constantly changing direction, a mutant line of this kind that is without outside or inside, form or background, beginning or end and that is as alive as a continuous variation—such a line is truly an abstract line, and describes a smooth space. It is not inexpressive. Yet is true that it does not constitute a stable and symmetrical *form of expression* grounded in a resonance of points and a conjunction of lines. It is nevertheless accompanied by *material traits of expression,* the effects of which multiply step by step. This is what Worringer means when he says that the Gothic line (for us, the nomadic line invested with abstraction) has the power of expression and not of form, that it has repetition as a power, not symmetry as form. Indeed, it is through symmetry that rectilinear systems limit repetition, preventing infinite progression and maintaining the *organic* domination of a central point with radiating lines, as in reflected or star-shaped figures. It is free action, however, which by its essence unleashes the power of repetition as a *machinic* force that multiplies its effect and pursues an infinite movement. Free action proceeds by disjunction and decentering, or at least by peripheral movement: disjointed polythetism instead of symmetrical antithetism.[9] Traits of expression describing a smooth space and connecting with a matter-flow thus should not be confused with striae that convert space and make it a form of expression that grids and organizes matter.

Worringer's finest pages are those in which he contrasts the abstract with the organic. The organic does not designate something represented, but above all the form of representation, and even the feeling that unites representation with a subject (*Einfühlung,* "empathy"). "Formal processes occur within the work of art which correspond to the natural organic tendencies in man."[10] But the rectilinear, the geometrical, cannot be opposed to the organic in this sense. The Greek organic line, which subordinates volume and spatiality, takes over from the Egyptian geometrical line, which reduced them to the plane. The organic, with its symmetry and contours inside and outside, still refers to the rectilinear coordinates of a striated space. The organic body is prolonged by straight lines that attach it to what lies in the distance. Hence the primacy of human beings, or of the face: We are this form of expression itself, simultaneously the supreme organism and the relation of all organisms to metric space in general. The abstract, on the contrary, begins only with what Worringer presents as the "Gothic" avatar. It is this nomadic line that he says is mechanical, but in free action and swirling; it is inorganic, yet alive, and all the more alive for being inorganic. It is distinguished both from the geometrical and the organic. It raises "mechanical" relations to the level of *intuition.* Heads (even a human being's when it is not a face) unravel and coil into ribbons in a continuous process; mouths curl in spirals. Hair, clothes . . . This streaming, spiraling, zigzagging, snaking, feverish line of variation liberates a power of life that human beings had rectified and organisms had confined, and which matter now expresses as the trait, flow, or impulse traversing it. If everything is alive, it is not because everything is organic or organized but, on the contrary, because the organism is a diversion of life. In short, the life in question is inorganic, germinal, and intensive, a powerful life without organs, a body that is all the more alive for having no organs, everything that passes *between* organisms ("once the natural barriers of organic movement have been overthrown, there are no more limits").[11] Many authors have wished to establish a kind of duality in nomad art between the ornamental abstract line and animal motifs, or more subtly, between the speed with which the line integrates and carries expressive traits, and the slowness or fixity of the animal matter traversed, between a line of flight without beginning or end and an almost immobile swirling. But in the end everyone agrees that it is a question of a single will, or a single becoming.[12] This is not because the abstract engenders organic motifs, by chance or by association. Rather, it is precisely because pure animality is experienced as inorganic, or supraorganic, that it can combine so well with abstraction, and even combine the slowness or heaviness of a matter with the extreme speed of a line that has become entirely spiritual. The slowness belongs to the same world as the extreme speed: relations of speed and slowness between elements, which surpass in every way the movement of an organic form and the determination of organs. The line escapes geometry by a fugitive mobility at the same time as life tears itself free from the organic by a permutating, stationary whirlwind. This vital force specific to the abstraction is what draws smooth space. The abstract line is the affect of smooth space, just as organic representation was the feeling presiding over striated space. The haptic-optical, near-distant distinctions must be subordinated to the distinction between the abstract line and the organic line; they must find their principle in a general confrontation of spaces. The abstract line cannot be defined as geometrical and rectilinear. What then should be termed *abstract* in modern art? A line of variable direction that describes no contour and delimits no form. . . .[13]

20
. . .
Cinema and Space: The Frame

We will start with very simple definitions, even though they may have to be corrected later. We will call *the determination of a closed system, a relatively closed system which includes everything which is present in the image*—sets, characters and props—*framing*. The frame therefore forms a set which has a great number of parts, that is of elements, which themselves form subsets. It can be broken down. Obviously these parts are themselves in image [*en image*]. This is why Jakobson calls them object-signs, and Pasolini "cinemes." However this terminology suggests comparisons with language (cinemes would be very like phonemes, and the shot would be like a moneme) which do not seem necessary.[1] For, if the frame has an analogue, it is to be found in an information system rather than a linguistic one. The elements are the data [*données*], which are sometimes very numerous, sometimes of limited number. The frame is therefore inseparable from two tendencies: toward saturation or toward rarefaction. The big screen and depth of field in particular have allowed the multiplication of independent data, to the point where a secondary scene appears in the foreground while the main one happens in the background (Wyler), or where you can no longer even distinguish between the principal and the secondary (Altman). On the other hand, rarefied images are produced, either when the whole accent is placed on a single object (in Hitchcock, the glass of milk lit from the inside, in *Suspicion;* the glowing cigarette end in the black rectangle of the window in *Rear Window*) or when the set is emptied of certain subsets (Antonioni's deserted landscapes; Ozu's vacant interiors). The highest degree of rarefaction seems to be attained with the empty set, when the screen becomes completely black or completely white. Hitchcock gives an example of this in *Spellbound,* when another glass of milk invades the screen, leaving only an empty white image. But, from either side—whether rarefaction or saturation—the frame teaches us that the image is not just given to be seen. It is legible as well as visible. The frame has the implicit function of recording not merely sound information, but also visual information. If we see very few things in an image, this is because we do not know how to read it properly; we evaluate its rarefaction as badly as its saturation. There is a pedagogy of the image, especially with Godard, when this function is made explicit, when the frame serves as an opaque surface of information, sometimes blurred by saturation, sometimes reduced to the empty set, to the white or black screen.[2]

In the second place, the frame has always been geometrical *or* physical, depending on whether it constitutes the closed system in relation to chosen coordinates or in relation to selected variables. The frame is therefore sometimes conceived of as a spatial composition of parallels and diagonals, the constitution of a receptacle such that the blocs [*masses*] and the lines of the image which come to occupy it will find an equilibrium and their movements will find an invariant. It is often like this in Dreyer; Antonioni seems to go to the limit of this geometric conception of the frame which preexists that which is going to be inserted within it (*Eclipse*).[3] Sometimes the frame is conceived as a dynamic construction in act [*en acte*], which is closely linked to the scene, the image, the characters and the objects which fill it. The iris method in Griffith, which isolates a face first of all, then opens and shows the surroundings; Eisenstein's researches inspired by Japanese drawing, which adapt the frame to the theme; Gance's variable screen which opens and closes "according to the dramatic necessities," and like a "visual accordion"—from the very beginning attempts were made to test dynamic variations of the frame. In any case framing is limitation.[4] But, depending on the concept itself the limits can be conceived in two ways, mathematically or dynamically: either as preliminary to the existence of the bodies whose essence they fix, or going as far as the power of existing bodies goes. For ancient philosophy, this was one of the principal features of the opposition between the Platonists and the Stoics.

The frame is also geometric or physical in another way—in relation to the parts of the system that it both separates and brings together. In the first case, the frame is inseparable from rigid geometric distinctions. A very fine image in Griffith's *Intolerance* cuts the screen along a vertical which corresponds to a wall of the ramparts of Babylon; whilst on the right one sees the king advancing on a higher horizontal, a high walk on the ramparts; on the left the chariots enter and leave, on a lower horizontal, through the gates of the city. Eisenstein studied the effects of the golden section on cinematographic imagery; Dreyer explored horizontals and verticals, symmetries, the high and the low, alternations of black and white; the expressionists developed diagonals and counterdiagonals, pyramidal or triangular figures which agglomerate bodies, crowds, places, the collision of these masses, a whole paving of the frame "which takes on a form like the black and white squares of a chess-board" (Lang's *The Nibelungen* and *Metropolis*).[5] Even light is the subject of a geometrical optic, when it is organized with shadows into two halves, or into alternating rays, as is done by one expressionist tendency (Wiene, Lang). The lines separating the great elements of nature obviously play a fundamental role, as in Ford's skies: the separation of earth and sky, the earth pushed down to the base of the screen. But it also involves water and earth, or the slender line which separates air and water, when water hides an escapee in its depths, or drowns a victim at the limit of the surface (Le Roy's *I am a Fugitive from a Chain Gang* and Newman's *Sometimes a Great Notion*). As a general rule, the powers of nature are not framed in the same way as people or things, and individuals are not framed in the same way as crowds, and subelements are not framed in the same way as terms, so that there are many different frames in the frame. Doors, windows, box office windows, skylights, car windows, mirrors, are all frames in frames. The great directors have particular affinities with particular secondary, tertiary, etc. frames. And it is by this dovetailing of frames that the parts of the set or of the closed system are separated, but also converge and are reunited.

On the other hand, the physical or dynamic conception of the frame produces imprecise sets which are now only divided into zones or bands. The frame is no longer the object of geometric divisions, but of physical gradations. The parts of the set are now intensive parts, and the set itself is a mixture which is transmitted through all the parts, through all the degrees of shadow and of light, through the whole light-darkness scale (Wegener, Murnau). This was the expressionist optic's other tendency, although some directors, both inside and outside expressionism, participate in both. It is the hour when it is no longer possible to distinguish between sunrise and sunset, air and water, water and earth, in the great mixture of a marsh or a tempest.[6] Here, it is by degrees of mixing that the parts become distinct or confused in a continual transformation of values. The set cannot divide into parts without qualitatively changing each time: it is neither divisible nor indivisible, but "dividual" [*dividuel*]. Admittedly this was already the case in the geometric conception—there the dovetailing of frames indicated the qualitative changes. The cinematographic image is always dividual. This is because, in the final analysis, the screen, as the frame of frames, gives a common standard of measurement to things which do not have one—long shots of countryside and close-ups of the face, an astronomical system and a single drop of water—parts which do not have the same denominator of distance, relief, or light. In all these senses the frame insures a deterritorialization of the image.

In the fourth place, the frame is related to an angle of framing. This is because the closed set is itself an optical system which refers to a point of view on the set of parts. Of course, the point of view can be—or appear to be—bizarre or paradoxical: the cinema shows extraordinary points of view—at ground level, or from high to low, from low to high, etc. But they seem to be subject to a pragmatic rule which is not just valid for the narrative cinema: to avoid falling into an empty aestheticism they must be explained, they must be revealed as normal and regular—either from the point of view of a more comprehensive set which includes the first, or from the point of view of an initially unseen, not given, element of the first set. In Jean Mitry we find a description of a sequence which is exemplary here (Lubitsch's *The Man I Killed*); the camera, in a lateral midheight traveling shot, shows a row of spectators seen from behind and tries to glide to the front, then stops at a one-legged man whose missing leg provides a vista on the scene—a passing military parade. It thus frames the good leg, the crutch, and, under the stump, the parade. Here we have an eminently bizarre angle of framing. But another shot shows another cripple behind the first, one with no legs at all, who sees the parade in precisely this way, and who actualizes or accomplishes the preceding point of view.[7] It can therefore be said that the angle of framing was justified. However, this pragmatic rule is not always valid, or even when it is valid, it is not the whole story. Bonitzer has constructed the interesting concept of "deframing" (*décadrage*] in order to designate these abnormal points of view which are not the same as an oblique perspective or a paradoxical angle, and refer to another dimension of the image.[8] We find examples of this in Dreyer's cutting frames; faces cut by the edge of the screen in *The Passion of Joan of Arc*. But, we see it even more in empty spaces like those of Ozu, which frame a dead zone, or in disconnected spaces as in Bresson, whose parts are not connected and are beyond all narrative or more generally pragmatic justification, perhaps tending to confirm that the visual image has a legible function beyond its visible function.

There remains the out-of-field [*hors-champ*]. This is not a negation; neither is it sufficient to define it by the noncoincidence between two frames, one visual and the other sound (for example, in Bresson, when the sound testifies to what is not seen, and "relays" the visual instead of duplicating it).[9] The out-of-field refers to what is neither seen nor understood, but is nevertheless perfectly present. This presence is indeed a problem and itself refers to two new conceptions of framing. If we return to Bazin's alternative of mask or frame, we see that sometimes the frame works like a mobile mask according to which every set is extended into a larger homogeneous set with which it communicates, and sometimes it works as a pictorial frame which isolates a system and neutralizes its environment. This duality is most clearly expressed in Renoir and Hitchcock; in the former space and action always go beyond the limits of the frame which only takes elements from an area; in the latter the frame "confines all the components," and acts as a frame for a tapestry rather than one for a picture or a play. But, if a partial set only communicates formally with its out-of-field through the positive characteristics of the frame and the reframing, it is nonetheless true that a system which is closed—even one which is very closed up—only apparently suppresses the out-of-field, and in its own way gives it an even more decisive importance.[10] All framing determines an out-of-field. There are not two types of frame only one of which would refer to the out-of-field; there are rather two very different aspects of the out-of-field, each of which refers to a mode of framing.

The divisibility of content means that the parts belong to various sets, which constantly subdivide into subsets or are themselves the subset of a larger set, on to infinity. This is why content is defined both by the tendency to constitute closed systems and by the fact that this tendency never reaches completion. Every closed system also communicates. There is always a thread to link the glass of sugared water to the solar system, and any set whatever to a larger set. This is the first sense of what we call the out-of-field: when a set is framed, therefore seen, there is always a larger set, or another set with which the first forms a larger one, and which can in turn be seen, on condition that it gives rise to a new out-of-field, etc. The set of all these sets forms a homogeneous continuity, a universe or a plane [*plan*] of genuinely unlimited content. But it is certainly not a "whole," although this plane or these larger and larger sets necessarily have an indirect relationship with the whole. We know the insoluble contradictions we fall into when we treat the set of all sets as a whole. It is not because the notion of the whole is devoid of sense; but it is not a set and does not have parts. It is rather that which prevents each set, however big it is, from closing in on itself, and that which forces it to extend itself into a larger set. The whole is therefore like thread that traverses set and gives each one the possibility, which is necessarily realized, of communicating with another, to infinity. Thus the whole is the open, and relates back to time or even to spirit rather than to content and to space. Whatever their relationship, one should therefore not confuse the extension of sets into each other with the opening of the whole which passes into each one. A closed system is never absolutely closed; but on the one hand it is connected in space to other systems by a more or less "fine" thread, and on the other hand it is integrated or reintegrated into a whole which transmits a duration to it along this thread.[11] Hence, it is perhaps not sufficient to distinguish, with Burch, a concrete space from an imaginary space in the out-of-field, the imaginary becomes concrete when it in turn passes into a field, when it thus ceases to be out-of-field. In itself, or as such, the out-of-field already has two qualitatively different aspects: a relative aspect by means of which a closed system refers in space to a set which is not seen, and which can in turn be seen, even if this gives rise to a new unseen set, on to infinity; and an absolute aspect by which the closed system opens onto a duration which is immanent to the whole universe, which is no longer a set and does not belong to the order of the visible.[12] *Deframings [décadrages] which are not "pragmatically" justified refer to precisely this second aspect as their raison d'être.*

In one case, the out-of-field designates that which exists elsewhere, to one side or around; in the other case, the out-of-field testifies to a more disturbing presence, one which cannot even be said to exist, but rather to "insist" or "subsist," a more radical elsewhere, outside homogeneous space and time. Undoubtedly these two aspects of the out-of-field intermingle constantly. But, when we consider a framed image as a closed system, we can say that one aspect prevails over the other, depending on the nature of the "thread." The thicker the thread which links the seen set to other unseen sets, the better the out-of-field fulfills its first function, which is the adding of space to space. But, when the thread is very fine, it is not content to reinforce the closure of the frame or to eliminate the relation with the outside. It certainly does not bring about a complete isolation of the relatively closed system, which would be impossible. But, the finer it is—the further duration descends into the system like a spider—the more effectively the out-of-field fulfills its other function, which is that of introducing the transspatial and the spiritual into the system which is never perfectly closed. Dreyer made this into an ascetic method: the more the image is spatially closed, even reduced to two dimensions, the greater is its capacity to *open itself* on to a fourth dimension which is time, and on to a fifth which is spirit, the spiritual decision of Jeanne or Gertrud.[13] When Claude Ollier defines Antonioni's geometric frame, he not only says that the awaited character is not yet visible (the first function of the out-of-field) but also that he is momentarily in a zone of emptiness, "white on white which is impossible to film," and truly invisible (the second function). And, in another way, Hitchcock's frames are not content to neutralize the environment, to push the closed system as far as possible and to enclose the maximum number of components in the image; at the same time they make the image into a *mental image*, open (as we will see) on to a play of relations which are purely thought and which weave a whole. This is why we said that there is always out-of-field, even in the most closed image. And that there are always simultaneously the two aspects of the out-of-field: the actualizable relation with other sets, and the virtual relation with the whole. But in the one case the second relation—the most mysterious—is reached indirectly, on to infinity, through the intermediary and the extension of the first, in the succession of images; in the other case it is reached more directly, in the image itself, and by limitation and neutralization of the first.

Let us summarize the results of this analysis of the frame. Framing is the art of choosing the parts of all kinds which became part of a set. This set is a closed system, relatively and artificially closed. The closed system determined by the frame can be considered in relation to the data that it communicates to the spectators: it is "informatic," and saturated or rarefied. Considered in itself and as limitation, it is geometric or dynamic-physical. Considered in the nature of its parts, it is still geometric or physical and dynamic. It is an optical system when it is considered in relation to the point of view, to the angle of framing: it is then pragmatically justified, or lays claim to a higher justification. Finally, it determines an out-of-field, sometimes in the form of a larger set which extends it, sometimes in the form of a whole into which it is integrated.

21
· · ·
Cinema and Time

A purely optical and sound situation does not extend into action, any more than it is induced by an action. It makes us grasp, it is supposed to make us grasp, something intolerable and unbearable. Not a brutality as nervous aggression, an exaggerated violence that can always be extracted from the sensory-motor relations in the action-image. Nor is it a matter of scenes of terror, although there are sometimes corpses and blood. It is matter of something too powerful, or too unjust, but sometimes also too beautiful, and which henceforth outstrips our sensory-motor capacities. *Stromboli:* a beauty which is too great for us, like too strong a pain. It can be a limit-situation, the irruption of the volcano, but also the most banal, a plain factory, a wasteland. In Godard's *Les carabiniers* the girl militant recites a few revolutionary slogans, so many clichés; but she is so beautiful, of a beauty which is unbearable for her torturers who have to cover up her face with a handkerchief. And this handkerchief, lifted again by breath and whisper ("Brothers, brothers, brothers . . ."), itself becomes unbearable for us the viewers. In any event something has become too strong in the image. Romanticism had already set out this aim for itself: grasping the intolerable or the unbearable, the empire of poverty, and thereby becoming visionary, to produce a means of knowledge and action out of pure vision.[1]

Nevertheless, are there not equal amounts of fantasy and dreaming in what we claim to see as there are of objective apprehending? Moreover, do we not have a subjective sympathy for the unbearable, an empathy which permeates what we see? But this means that the unbearable itself is inseparable from a revelation or an illumination, as from a third eye. Fellini has strong sympathies with decadence, only insofar as he prolongs it, extends its range, "to the intolerable," and reveals beneath the movements, faces, and gestures a subterranean or extraterrestrial world, "the tracking shot becoming a means of peeling away, proof of the unreality of movement," and the cinema becoming, no longer an undertaking of recognition [*reconnaisance*], but of knowledge [*connaisance*], "a science of visual impressions, forcing us to forget our own logic and retinal habits."[2] Ozu himself is not the guardian of traditional or reactionary values, he is the greatest critic of daily life. He picks out the intolerable from the insignificant itself, provided that he can extend the force of a contemplation that is full of sympathy or pity across daily life. The important thing is always that the character or the viewer, and the two together, become visionaries. The purely optical and sound situation gives rise to a seeing function, at once fantasy and report, criticism and compassion, whilst sensory-motor situations, no matter how violent, are directed to a pragmatic visual function which "tolerates" or "puts up with" practically anything, from the moment it becomes involved in a system of actions and reactions.

In Japan and Europe, Marxist critics have attacked these films and their characters for being too passive and negative, in turn bourgeois, neurotic or marginal, and for having replaced modifying action with a "confused" vision.[3] And it is true that, in cinema, characters of the trip/ballad are unconcerned, even by what happens to them: whether in the style of Rossellini, the foreign woman who discovers the island, the bourgeoise woman who discovers the factory; or in the style of Godard, the Pierrot-le-fou generation. But it is precisely the weakness of the motor-linkages, the weak connections, that are capable of releasing huge forces of disintegration. These are the characters with a strange vibrance in Rossellini, strangely well informed in Godard and Rivette. In the West as in Japan, they are in the grip of a mutation, they are themselves mutants. On the subject of *Two or Three Things* . . . , Godard says that *to describe* is to observe mutations.[4] Mutation of Europe after the war, mutation of an Americanized Japan, mutation of France in 1968: it is not the cinema that turns away from politics, it becomes completely political, but in another way. One of the two women strollers in Rivettes's *Pont du Nord* has all the characteristics of an unforeseeable mutant: she has at first the capacity of detecting the Maxes, the members of the organization for enslaving the world, before going through a metamorphosis inside a cocoon, then being drafted into their ranks. Similarly with the ambiguity of the *Petit soldat.* A new type of character for a new cinema. It is because what happens to them does not belong to them and only half concerns them, because they know how to extract from the event the part that cannot be reduced to what happens: that part of inexhaustible possibility that constitutes the unbearable, the intolerable, the visionary's part. A new type of actor was needed: not simply the nonprofessional actors that neo-realism had revived at the beginning, but what might be called professional nonactors, or, better, "actor-mediums," capable of seeing and showing rather than acting, and either remaining dumb or undertaking some never-ending conversation, rather than of replying or following a dialogue (such as, in France, Bulle Ogier or Jean-Pierre Léaud).[5]

Neither everyday nor limit-situations are marked by anything rare or extraordinary. It is just a volcanic island of poor fishermen. It is just a factory, a school. . . . We mix with all that, even death, even accidents, in our normal life or on holidays. We see, and we more or less experience, a powerful organization of poverty and oppression. And we are precisely not without sensory-motor schemata for recognizing such things, for putting up with and approving of them and for behaving ourselves subsequently, taking into account our situation, our capabilities and our tastes. We have schemata for turning away when it is too unpleasant, for prompting resignation when it is terrible and for assimilating when it is too beautiful. It should be pointed out here that even metaphors are sensory-motor evasions, and furnish us with something to say when we no longer know what do to: they are specific schemata of an affective nature. Now this is what a cliché is. A cliché is a sensory-motor image of the thing. As Bergson says, we do not perceive the thing or the image in its entirety, we always perceive less of it, we perceive only what we are interested in perceiving, or rather what it is in our interest to perceive, by virtue of our economic interests, ideological beliefs, and psychological demands. We therefore normally perceive only clichés. But, if our sensory-motor schemata jam or break, then a different type of image can appear: a pure optical-sound image, the whole image without metaphor, brings out the thing in itself, literally, in its excess of horror or beauty, in its radical or unjustifiable character, because it no longer has to be "justified," for better or for worse. . . . The factory creature gets up, and we can no longer say "Well, people have to work. . . ." *I thought I was seeing convicts:* the factory is a prison, school is a prison, literally, not metaphorically. You do not have the image of a prison following one of a school: that would simply be pointing out a resemblance, a confused relation between two clear images. On the contrary, it is necessary to discover the separate elements and relations that elude us at the heart of an unclear image: to show *how and in what sense* school is a prison, housing estates are examples of prostitution, bankers killers, photographs tricks—literally, without metaphor.[6] This is the method of Godard's *Comment ça va:* not being content to enquire if "things are OK" or if "things are not OK" between two photos, but "how are things" [*comment ça va*] for each one and for the two together. This was the problem with which volume 1 ended: tearing a real image from clichés.

On the one hand, the image constantly sinks to the state of cliché: because it is introduced into sensory-motor linkages, because it itself organizes or induces these linkages, because we never perceive everything that is in the image, because it is made for that purpose (so that we do not perceive everything, so that the cliché hides the image from us. . .). Civilization of the image? In fact, it is a civilization of the cliché where all the powers have an interest in hiding images from us, not necessarily in hiding the same thing from us, but in hiding something in the image. On the other hand, at the same time, the image constantly attempts to break through the cliché, to get out of the cliché. There is no knowing how far a real image may lead: the importance of becoming visionary or seer. A change of conscience or of heart is not enough (although there is some of this, as in the heroine's heart in *Europe 51*, but, if there were nothing more, everything would quickly return to the state of cliché, other clichés would simply have been added on). Sometimes it is necessary to restore the lost parts, to rediscover everything that cannot be seen in the image, everything that has been removed to make it "interesting." But sometimes, on the contrary, it is necessary to make holes, to introduce voids and white spaces, to rarify the image, by suppressing many things that have been added to make us believe that we are seeing everything. It is necessary to make a division or make emptiness in order to find the whole again.

What is difficult is to know in what respect an optical and sound image is not itself a cliché, at best a photo. We are not thinking simply of the way in which these images provide more cliché as soon as they are repeated by authors who use them as formulas. But is it not the case that the creators themselves sometimes have the idea that the new image has to stand up against the cliché on its own ground, make a higher bid than the postcard, add to it and parody it, as a better way of getting over the problem (Robbe-Grillet, Daniel Schmid)? The creators invent obsessive framings, empty or disconnected spaces, even still lifes: in a certain sense they stop movement and rediscover the power of the fixed shot, but is this not to resuscitate the cliché that they aim to challenge? Enough, for victory, to parody the cliché, not to make holes in it and empty it. It is not enough to disturb the sensory-motor connections. It is necessary to *combine* the optical-sound image with the enormous forces that are not those of a simply intellectual consciousness, nor of the social one, but of a profound, vital intution.[7]

Pure optical and sound images, the fixed shot and the montage-cut, do define and imply a beyond of movement. But they do not strictly stop it, neither in the characters nor even in the camera. They mean that movement should not be perceived in a sensory-motor image, but grasped and thought in another type of image. The movement-image has not disappeared, but now exists only as the first dimension of an image that never stops growing in dimensions. We are not talking about dimensions of space, since the image may be flat, without depth, and through this very fact assumes all the more dimensions or powers which go beyond space. Three of these growing powers can be briefly summarized. First, while the movement-image and its sensory-motor signs were in a relationship only with an indirect image *of* time (dependent on montage), the pure optical and sound image, its op-signs and sonsigns, are directly connected to a time-image which has subordinated movement. It is this reversal which means that time is no longer the measure of movement but movement is the perspective of time: it constitutes a whole cinema of time, with a new conception and new forms of montage (Welles, Resnais). In the second place, at the same time as the eye takes up a clairvoyant function, the sound as well as visual elements of the image enter into internal relations which means that the whole image has to be "read," no less than seen, readable as well as visible. For the eye of the seer as of the soothsayer, it is the "literalness" of the perceptible world which constitutes it like a book. Here again all reference of the image of description to an object assumed to be independent does not disappear, but is now subordinated to the internal elements and relations which tend to replace the object and to delete it where it does appear, continually displacing it. Godard's formula, "it isn't blood, it's some red," stops being only pictural and takes on a sense specific to the cinema. The cinema is going to become an analytic of the image, implying a new conception of cutting, a whole "pedagogy" which will operate in different ways; for instance, in Ozu's work, in Rossellini's late period, in Godard's middle period, or in the Straubs. Finally, the fixity of the camera does not represent the only alternative to movement. Even when it is mobile, the camera is no longer content sometimes to follow the characters' movement, sometimes itself to undertake movements of which they are merely the object, but in every case it subordinates description of a space to the functions of thought. This is not the simple distinction between the subjective and the objective, the real and the imaginary, it is on the contrary their indiscernibility which will endow the camera with a rich array of functions, and entail a new conception of the frame and reframings. Hitchcock's premonition will come true: a camera-consciousness which would no longer be defined by the movements it is able to follow or make, but by the mental connections it is able to enter into. And it becomes questioning, responding, objecting, provoking, theorematizing, hypothesizing, experimenting, in accordance with the open list of logical conjunctions ("or," "therefore," "if," "because," "actually," "although," . . .), or in accordance with the functions of thought in a *cinéma-vérité*, which, as Rouch says, means rather truth of cinema [*vérité du cinéma*].

This is the triple reversal which defines a beyond of movement. The image had to free itself from sensory-motor links; it had to stop being action-image in order to become a pure optical, sound (and tactile) image. But the latter was not enough: it had to enter into relations with yet other forces, so that it could itself escape from a world of clichés. It had to open up to powerful and direct revelations, those of the time-image, of the readable image and the thinking image. It is in this way that opsigns and sonsigns refer back to "chronosigns," "lectosigns," and "noosigns."[8]

Antonioni, considering the evolution of neorealism in relation to *Outcry,* said that he was tending to do without a bicycle—De Sica's bicycle, naturally. Bicycleless neorealism replaces the last quest involving movement (the trip) with a specific weight of time operating inside characters and excavating them from within (the chronicle).[9] Antonioni's art is like the intertwining of consequences, of temporal sequences and effects which flow from events out-of-field. Already in *Story of a Love Affair* the investigation has the result, of itself, of provoking the outcome of a first love affair, and the effect of making two oaths of murder ring out in the future and in the past. It is a whole world of chronosigns, which would be enough to cast doubt on the false evidence according to which the cinematographic image is necessarily in the present. If we are sick with Eros, Antonioni said, it is because Eros is himself sick; and he is sick not just because he is old and worn out in his content, but because he is caught in the pure form of a time which is torn between an already determined past and a deadend future. For Antonioni, there is no other sickness than the chronic. Chronos is sickness itself. This is why chronosigns are inseparable from lectosigns, which force us to read so many symptoms in the image, that is, to treat the optical and sound image like something that is also readable. Not only the optical and the sound, but the present and the past, and the here and the elsewhere, constitute internal elements and relations which must be deciphered, and can be understood only in a progression analogous to that of a reading: from *Story of a Love Affair,* indeterminate spaces are given a scale only later on, in which Burch calls a "continuity grasped through discrepancy" [*raccord à appréhension décalée*], closer to a reading than to a perception.[10] And later, Antonioni the colorist would be able to treat variations of colors as symptoms, and monochrome as the chronic sign which wins a world, thanks to a whole play of deliberate modifications. But *Story of a Love Affair* already exhibits a "camera autonomy" when it stops following the movement of the characters or directing its own movement at them, to carry out constant reframings as functions of thought, noosigns expressing the logical conjunctions of sequel, consequence, or even intention.

22
. . .
Painting and Sensation

There are two ways of transcending figuration (whether illustrative or narrative): toward abstract form or toward figure. Cézanne alluded to the way toward figure by the term *sensation*. Figure is the sensible form related to sensation; it acts immediately on the nervous system which is of the flesh. Abstract form on the other hand is directed to the brain, and acts through the brain, closer to the bone. Certainly Cézanne did not invent the path of sensation in painting, but he gave it an unprecedented status. Sensation is the opposite of the facile, the ready-made, and the cliché, but also of the "sensational," the spontaneous, etc. One face of sensation is turned toward the subject (the nervous system, vital movement, "instinct," "temperament," an entire vocabulary which is common to both naturalism and Cézanne); the other face is turned toward the object ("the fact," the place, the event). Or rather, sensation has no faces at all, it is indissolubly both things, it is being-in-the-world, in the phenomenological sense. At the same time, I *become* in sensation, and something *happens* through sensation, one through the other and one in the other.[1] And, in the last analysis, it is the same body which, being both subject and object, gives and receives sensation. As a spectator, I experience sensation only by entering the painting and by having access to the unity of the sensing and the sensed. This is Cézanne's lesson that goes beyond impressionism: sensation is not the "free" or disembodied play of light and color (impressions), rather sensation is in the body, even if this is the body of an apple. Color and sensation are in the body, and not in the sky. Sensation is that which is painted. That which is painted in the painting is the body, not insofar as it is represented as object but insofar as it is lived as experiencing a particular sensation (what Lawrence, in discussing Cézanne, called "the being-apple [*l'être pommesque*] of the apple").[2]

This is the general thread that links Bacon to Cézanne: *to paint sensation* or, as Bacon says, using words that closely resemble Cézanne's, to record the fact. "It's a very, very close and difficult thing to know why some paint comes across directly onto the nervous system."[3] We might say that there are only obvious differences between these two painters: Cézanne's world as landscape and still lives, even before the portraits that are treated as landscapes; and the inverse hierarchy in Bacon, which gives up still lives and landscapes.[4] The world of nature for Cézanne and the world as artifact for Bacon. But precisely, should not these very obvious differences be ascribed to "sensation" and "temperament," in other words, should they not be inscribed within that which links Bacon to Cézanne, or within that which is common to both? When Bacon speaks of sensation, he means two things that are very close to what Cézanne meant. Negatively, he says that form as it relates to sensation (figure) is the opposite of form as it relates to an object that the form is supposed to represent (figuration). According to Valéry's words, sensation is that which is directly transmitted and which avoids the detour and the boredom of a story to be told.[5] And positively, Bacon continually says that sensation is that which passes from one "order" to another, from one "level" to another, or from one "domain" to another. This is why sensation is the master of deformations or rather the agent of bodily deformations. In this respect, we can make the same criticism of figurative and of abstract painting: they pass through the brain, they do not act directly upon the nervous system, they do not have access to sensation, they do not liberate the figure—all of this as a result of the fact that they remain at *one and the same level*.[6] They can bring about transformations or form but they do not achieve bodily deformations. We will have the opportunity to see exactly how much Cézannian Bacon is, even more so than if he were a disciple of Cézanne.

What does Bacon mean in his interviews when he speaks of "orders of sensation," "sensitive levels," "sensible domains," or "moving sequences"? We might initially believe that a specified sensation corresponds to each order, level, or domain: each sensation would thus be one term in a sequence or in a series. For example, Rembrandt's series of self-portraits carries us along into different sensible domains.[7] And it is true that painting, and especially Bacon's painting, proceeds through series: series of crucifixions, series of the pope, series of portraits, series of self-portraits, series of the mouth, of the mouth which screams or smiles. . . . Moreover, the series can be one of simultaneity, as in the case of the triptychs that make at least three orders or levels coexist. The series can be closed when it has a contrasting composition, but it can be open when it is continued or continuable beyond three.[8] All of this is true. But the point is that it would not be true if there were not something else as well which already applies to each painting, figure, or sensation.

Each painting or figure is a moving sequence or a series (and not only one term within a series). Each sensation is at diverse levels, of different orders or in several domains. Therefore, there are not sensations of different orders but, rather, different orders of one and the same sensation. It is characteristic of sensation to encompass a constitutive difference of level and a plurality of constituting domains. Every sensation and every figure is already an "accumulated" or "coagulated" sensation like a figure in limestone.[9] Hence the irreducibly synthetic character of sensation. We can ask henceforth where this synthetic character comes from, by virtue of which each material sensation has several levels, orders, or domains. What are these levels and what makes up their sensing and sensed unity?

A first response must obviously be rejected. That which would make up the material and synthetic unity of sensation would be the represented object, or the thing which is figured. This is theoretically impossible since figure is opposed to figuration. But even if we observe practically, as Bacon does, that something is nevertheless figured (for example, a screaming pope), this secondary figuration rests on the neutralization of every primary figuration. Bacon himself formulates this problem, which concerns the inevitable retention of a practical figuration at the moment when figure affirms its intention to break away from the figurative. We will see how he resolves this problem. In any case, Bacon has always wanted to eliminate the "sensational," that is, the primary figuration of that which provokes a violent sensation. This is what the following expression means: "I wanted to paint the scream more than the horror." When he paints the screaming pope, there is nothing that causes horror, and the curtain in front of the pope is not only a way of isolating and shielding him from view; it is rather the way in which the pope himself sees nothing and screams *in the presence of the invisible*. Being neutralized, the horror is multiplied because it is induced from the scream, and not vice versa. Certainly, it is not easy to renounce the horror, or the primary figuration. It is sometimes necessary to turn against our own instincts and to renounce our experience. Bacon carries all the violence of Ireland with him, as well as the violence of Nazism and the violence of war. He goes through the horror of the crucifixions, and especially of the fragment of crucifixion, of the head-meat or of the bleeding suitcase. But when he judges his own paintings, he turns away from all those that are too "sensational," because the figuration that subsists in them reconstitutes, albeit secondarily, a scene of horror, and from then on reintroduces a story to be told: even bullfights are too dramatic. As soon as horror is present, a story is reintroduced, and we botched the scream. In the last analysis, the maximum of violence will be in the sitting or crouching figures which are not undergoing any torture or brutality, to whom nothing visible is happening and which realize even better the power of the painting. The reason for this is that violence has two very different meanings: "When talking about the violence of paint, it's nothing to do with the violence of war."[10] To the violence of that which is represented (the sensational, the cliché) the violence of sensation is opposed. The latter is identical with its direct action upon the nervous system, the levels through which it passes and the domains which it traverses: being itself figure, it owes nothing to the nature of the object which is figured. It is as in Artaud: cruelty is not what we believe, and it depends less and less on that which is represented.

A second interpretation must also be rejected, which would confuse the levels of sensation, that is, the valencies of sensation, with an ambivalence of feeling. Sylvester suggests at one moment that "since you talk about recording different levels of feeling in one image . . . you may be expressing at one and the same time a love and a hostility towards them . . . both a caress and an assault." To which, Bacon responds that this is "too logical. I don't think that's the way things work. I think it goes to a deeper thing: how do I feel I can make this image more immediately real to myself? That's all."[11] In fact, the psychoanalytic hypothesis of ambivalence has not only the disadvantage of localizing sensation in the spectator who looks at the painting; even if we presuppose an ambivalence of figure itself, it would involve feelings that the figure would experience in relation to the represented things or in relation to a story being told. Now there are no feelings in Bacon's work. There is nothing but affects, that is, "sensations" and "instincts" according to the formula of naturalism. And sensation is that which determines the instinct at a particular moment, just as the instinct is the passage from one sensation to another, the search for the "best" sensation (not the most agreeable, but the one that fills the flesh at a particular moment of its descent, contraction, or dilation).

There is a third, more interesting hypothesis. This is the motor hypothesis. The levels of sensation would be like arrests or snapshots of motion synthetically recomposing the movement in its continuity, speed, and violence: for example, synthetic cubism, futurism, or Duchamp's *Nude*. And it is true that Bacon is fascinated by the decompositions of movement in Muybridge and makes use of them as his material. It is also true that he obtains in his work violent movements of great intensity, such as the 180 degree turn of George Dyer's head towards Lucian Freud. And more generally, Bacon's figures are often frozen in the middle of a strange stroll: for example, *Man carrying a child* or the *Van Gogh*. The insulation of the figure, the circle and the parallelepiped, themselves become motors, and Bacon does not renounce the project that a mobile sculpture would achieve more easily: in this case, the contour or base can be moved along the armature so that the figure goes for a daily "stroll."[12] But it is precisely the nature of this stroll that can inform us of the status of movement in Bacon's work. Never have Beckett and Bacon been closer to each other, and this is a stroll after the fashion of the strolls of Beckett's characters, who also trundle along without departing from their circle or parallelepiped. It is the stroll of the paralytic child and his mother clinging onto the edge of the balustrade in a curious race for the handicapped. It is the about-face of *The Turning Figure*. It is George Dyer's bicycle ride, which resembles closely that of Moritz's hero: "the vision was limited to the small piece of ground that he could see around him . . . the end of all things seemed to him to be at the end of his race *toward a certain point*." Therefore, even when the contour is displaced, movement is less this displacement than the amoebian exploration through which figure surrenders itself to the contour. Movement does not explain sensation; it is rather explained by the elasticity of sensation, by its *vis elastica*. According to Beckett's or Kafka's law, there is immobility beyond movement: beyond standing up, there is sitting down, and beyond sitting down, lying down in order to be finally dissipated. The true acrobat is the one who is immobile within the circle. The large feet of the figures often do not lend themselves to walking; they are almost clubfeet (and armchairs sometimes seem to resemble shoes for clubfeet). In short, it is not movement that explains the levels of sensation; rather levels of sensation explain that which subsists of movement. And, in fact, Bacon is not exactly interested in movement, although his painting makes movement very intense and violent. But, in the last analysis, it is a movement in one place or a spasm that reveals an entirely different problem characteristic of Bacon: *the action of invisible forces on the body* (hence, the bodily deformations for which this more profound cause is responsible). In the 1973 triptych the movement of translation occurs between two spasms, between two movements of contraction in one place.

There may still be another, "phenomenological," hypothesis. The levels of sensation would really be sensible domains referring to different sensory organs; but precisely each level, each domain would have a way of referring

192 MINOR LANGUAGES AND NOMAD ART

to others, independently of their common represented object. Between a color, a taste, a touch, a smell, a noise, a weight, there would be an existential communication that would constitute the (nonrepresentative) moment of "pathos" of *the* sensation. For example, in Bacon's *Bullfights* we hear the hoofbeats of the animal; in the 1976 triptych we touch the quivering of the bird that plunges into the place where the head should be, and each time that meat is represented, we touch it, smell it, eat it, weigh it, just like in Soutine's work; and the portrait of Isabel Rawthorne causes a head to emerge to which ovals and features are added in order to widen the eyes, enlarge the nostrils, lengthen the mouth, and mobilize the skin in a joint exercise of all organs at once. It is thus the painter's task to *make us see* a kind of original unity of the senses and to make a multisensible figure appear visibly. But this operation is only possible if the sensation of a particular domain (here, visual sensation) directly seizes a vital power that overflows all domains and traverses them. This power is rhythm, which is deeper than vision, hearing, etc. And rhythm appears as music when it invests the auditory level, and as painting when it invests the visual level.

This is the "logic of the senses" as Cézanne said, which is neither rational, nor cerebral. The ultimate then is the relation between rhythm and sensation, which places in each sensation the levels and domains through which it passes. And this rhythm runs through a painting as it runs through music. It is diastole-systole: the world that captures me by closing in on me, the "ego" that opens to the world and opens the world to itself.[13] It is said of Cézanne that he placed a precisely vital rhythm in visual sensation. Must we say the same thing about Bacon, with his coexistence of movements when the flat tint closes on figure and when figure contracts or rather expands in order to rejoin the flat tint, to the point of merging with it? Could it be that Bacon's artificial and closed world reveals the same vital movement as Cézanne's nature? These are not empty words, when Bacon declares that he is cerebrally pessimistic, but nervously optimistic, with an optimism that only believes in life.[14] Is this the same temperament as Cézanne's? Bacon's formula would then be figuratively pessimistic, yet figurally optimistic.

Trans. Constantin Boundas and Jacqueline Code

23
...
The Diagram

We do not listen enough to what painters say. They say that the painter is *already* in the canvas. Here, he encounters all the figurative and probabilistic data that occupy and preoccupy the canvas. An entire battle occurs in the canvas between the painter and his data. There is thus preparatory work that fully belongs to painting and that nevertheless precedes the act of painting. This preparatory work may take the form of sketches, but not necessarily, and even sketches do not replace it (Bacon, like many contemporary painters, does not make sketches). This preparatory work is invisible and silent, but nevertheless very intense. Therefore, the act of painting emerges as an *après-coup* (hysteresis) in relation to this work.

What is this act of painting? Bacon defines it as follows: making marks at random (brushstrokes-lines); cleaning, sweeping, or wiping places or areas (daubs-color); throwing paint at varied angles and speeds. Now this act (or acts) presuppose that there are already figurative data on the canvas (and also within the painter's head) that are more or less virtual or more or less actual. These data will be precisely demarcated, cleaned, swept, and wiped, or covered over, by the act of painting. For example, we lengthen a mouth, we make it go from one side of the head to the other; we clean part of a head with a brush, a scrubbing brush, a sweeping brush, or a rag. This is what Bacon calls a *Diagram;* it is as if, all of a sudden, we introduced a Sahara, a

Sahara region in the head; it is as if we stretched over it a rhinoceros skin seen through a microscope; it is as if we tore apart two parts of the head by means of an ocean; it is as if we changed the unit of measurement and replaced figurative units with micrometric or even cosmic units.[1] A Sahara, a rhinoceros skin, this is the diagram suddenly stretched out. It is like a *catastrophe* happening unexpectedly to the canvas, inside figurative or probabilistic data.

It is like the emergence of another world. For these marks or brushstrokes are irrational, involuntary, accidental, free, and random. They are nonrepresentative, nonillustrative, and nonnarrative. No longer are they significative or signifying: they are asignifying features. They are features of sensation, but of confused sensations (the confused sensations we bring with us when we are born, as Cézanne said). And above all, they are manual features. It is here that the painter works with a rag, brushes, scrubbing brush, or sweeping brush: it is here that he throws paint with his hands.[2] It is as if the hand assumed an independence and passed into the service of other forces, tracing marks that no longer depend on our will or on our vision. These almost blind, manual marks reveal the intrusion of another world into the visual world of figuration. To some extent, they remove the painting from the optical organization that already governed it, and made it figurative in advance. The painter's hand is interposed in order to shake its own dependence and to break up the sovereign, optical organization: we can no longer see anything, as in a catastrophe or chaos.

This is the act of painting or the turning point of the painting. There are indeed two ways in which the painting can fail, once visually and once manually. We can remain entangled in figurative data and in the optical organization of representation, but we can also fail with the diagram, spoil it, overload it to such an extent that it is rendered inoperative (this is another way of remaining within the figurative: we will have mutilated or mistreated the cliché).[3] The diagram is thus the operative set of lines and areas, of asignifying and nonrepresentative brushstrokes and daubs of color. And the operation of the diagram, its function, as Bacon says, is to "suggest." Or, more rigorously, it is the introduction of "possibilities of fact": an expression that resembles Wittgenstein's language.[4] Brushstrokes and daubs of color must break away from figuration all the more since they are destined to give us figure. This is why they themselves are not sufficient; they must be "utilized": they outline possibilities of fact, but do not yet constitute a fact (pictorial fact). In order to be converted into fact, in order to evolve into figure, they must be reinjected into the visual whole; but thus, precisely, under the influence of these marks, the visual whole is no longer that of an optical organization; it would give the eye a different power, as well as an object which would no longer be figurative.

The diagram is the operative set of brushstrokes and daubs of color, lines, and areas. For example, the diagram of Van Gogh: it is the set of straight and curved cross-hatchings that raises and lowers the ground, twists the trees, makes the sky palpitate and that assumes a particular intensity from 1888 onward. We cannot only differentiate diagrams but also date the diagram of a painter, because there is always a moment when the painter confronts it more directly. The diagram is indeed a chaos, a catastophe, but also a seed of order and of rhythm. It is a violent chaos in relation to the figurative data, but it is a seed of rhythm in relation to the new order of painting: as Bacon says, it "unlock[s] areas of sensation."[5] The diagram completes the preparatory work and begins the act of painting. There is no painter who does not make this experiment of the chaos-seed where she no longer sees anything and risks floundering: the breakdown of visual coordinates. This is not a psychological experiment but a properly pictorial experiment, although it can have a great influence on the psychic life of a painter. Here, the painter faces the greatest dangers for her work and for herself. It is a kind of experiment always recommended by different painters: Cézanne's "abyss" or "catastrophe" and the possibility that this abyss will make room for rhythm; Paul Klee's "chaos," the vanishing "gray point," and the possibility that this gray point will "leap over itself" and open up dimensions of sensation.[6] Of all the arts, painting is undoubtedly the only one that necessarily and "hysterically" integrates its own catastrophe and is constituted therefore as a flight forward. In the other arts, the catastrophe is only associated. But the painter moves through catastrophe, he embraces chaos and attempts to leave it behind. Where painters differ is in their manner of embracing this nonfigurative chaos, in their evaluation of the pictorial order to come, and of the relation of this order with this chaos. In this respect, we could perhaps distinguish three great paths: each one groups very different painters together but also designates a "modern" function of painting or states what painting claims to bring to "modern man" (why is there still painting today?).

Abstraction would be one of these paths, but a path that reduces the abyss or chaos, as well as the manual, to a minimum: it proposes an asceticism or spiritual salvation. By means of an intense spiritual effort, it is elevated above figurative data, but it also makes chaos a mere stream we must cross in order to discover the abstract and signifying forms. Mondrian's square emerges from the figurative (landscape) and leaps over chaos. From this leap, it retains a kind of oscillation. Such an abstraction is essentially seen. We would like to say, about abstract painting, the same thing that Péguy said about Kantian morality: it has pure hands, but it does not have hands. Abstract forms belong to a new, purely optical space that no longer even needs to be subordinate to manual or tactile elements. They are distinguished, in fact, from uniquely geometric forms by "tension": tension is that which internalizes in the visual the manual movement that describes the form and the invisible forces that determine it. It is that which makes form a purely visual transformation. Thus, the abstract optical space no longer requires the tactile connotations that were still being organized by classical representation. But then it follows that abstract painting, on the basis of great formal oppositions, develops a symbolic *code* rather than a diagram. It replaces the diagram with a code. This code is "digital," not in the sense of manual but in the sense of a finger that counts. "Digits" are indeed units that visually group together terms in opposition. For example, according to Kandinsky, vertical-white-activity, horizontal-black-inertia, etc. Hence, there emerges a conception of binary choice that is opposed to random choice. Abstract painting has pursued extensively the development of such a properly pictorial code (Herbin's "plastic alphabet," where the distribution of forms and colors can be carried out according to the letters of a word). The code is responsible for answering the question of painting today: what is it that can save man from the abyss, that is, the external tumult and the manual chaos? This amounts to opening a spiritual state for the man of the future without hands and to giving him a pure, internal, optical space made up perhaps exclusively of the horizontal and the vertical. "Modern man seeks tranquility because he is deafened by the outside."[7] The hand is reduced to the finger that presses on an internal optical keyboard.

A second path, which has often been called abstract expressionism or informal art, proposes an entirely different response in the antipodes. This time, the abyss or chaos is deployed to a maximum degree. Being a bit like a map that is as big as the country, the diagram merges with the entire painting, and the entire painting is the diagram. Optical geometry breaks down in favor of a line that is exclusively manual. The eye finds it difficult to follow. In fact, the incomparable discovery of this kind of painting is one of a line (and a daub of color) that does not form a contour, which demarcates nothing, either internal or external, either concave or convex: Pollock's line, Morris Louis's daub of color. It is the northern daub of color, the "gothic line": the line does not run from one point to another, but rather passes *between* the points, continually changes direction, and attains a power superior to *1*, becoming adequate to the entire surface. We understand that, from this point of view, abstraction remains figurative since its line still demarcates a contour. If we seek the forerunners of this new path and of this radical way of escaping the figurative, we will find them each time that an old great painter ceases painting things in order "to paint between things."[8] Turner's last watercolors already conquer not only the forces of impressionism but also the power of an explosive line without contour that makes painting itself become an unequaled catastrophe (instead of illustrating catastrophe romantically). Is it not also one of the most phenomenal constants of painting that is isolated and selected here? For Kandinsky, there were nomadic lines without contour next to abstract geometric lines; and for Mondrian, the unequal thickness of the two sides of the square opened up a virtual diagonal without contour. But with Pollock, this brushstroke-line and color-daub reach the limit of their function: no longer the transformation of the form but rather a decomposition of the matter that yields to us its lineaments and granulations. Thus, painting becomes a catastrophe-painting and a diagram-painting at the same time. This time, it is at the closest point to catastrophe, and in absolute proximity, that modern man finds rhythm: we can easily see to what extent the response to the question of a "modern" function of painting is different from that of abstraction. Now internal vision no longer provides infinity but rather the extension of an *all-over* manual power from one edge of the painting to the other.

In the unity of the catastrophe and the diagram, man discovers rhythm as matter and material. The painter no longer has as his instruments the paintbrush and the easel, which used to translate the subordination of the hand to the demands of an optical organization. The hand is liberated, using sticks, sponges, rags, and syringes: such is action painting, the "frenetic dance" of the painter around the painting, or rather in the painting, which is not stretched onto the easel but rather nailed unstretched onto the floor. A conversion of the horizon to the ground has taken place: the optical horizon has entirely reverted to a tactile ground. The diagram expresses all painting at once, that is, the optical catastrophe and the manual rhythm. And the current evolution of abstract expressionism completes this process by actualizing what was still only a metaphor in Pollock's work: (1) the extension of the diagram to the spatial and temporal totality of the painting (displacement of the "*avant-coup*" and the "*après-coup*"); (2) the abandonment of any visual sovereignty, and even of any visual control, over the painting in the process of being created (blindness of the painter); (3) development of lines that are "more" than lines, surfaces that are "more" than surfaces or, conversely, volumes that are "less" than volumes (Carl André's plane sculptures, Ryman's fibers, Barré's laminated works, Bonnefoi's strata).[9]

It is even more curious that the American critics, who have analyzed so extensively this abstract expressionism, have defined it by the creation of a purely and exclusively optical space, characteristic of "modern man." It seems that this is a quarrel over words, an ambiguity of words. What is meant, in fact, is that the pictorial space has lost all its imaginary, tactile referents that allowed us, in classical three-dimensional representation, to see depths and contours, forms and grounds. But these tactile referents in classical representation expressed a relative subordination of the hand to the eye, of the manual to the visual. In liberating a space that is taken (wrongly) to be purely optical, the abstract expressionists, in fact, only reveal an exclusively manual space, defined by the plane surface of the canvas, the "impenetrability" of the scene, the "gesturality" of the color. This space is imposed upon the eye as a completely foreign power in which the eye finds no peace.[10] We are no longer confronted with tactile referents of vision, but, since it is the manual space of that which is seen, we are faced with a violent act upon the eye. We could almost say it is abstract painting that produces a purely optical space and suppresses tactile referents in favor of an eye of the mind: it suppresses the task of directing the hand that the eye retained in classical representation. But action painting does something entirely different: it overturns this classical subordination, it subordinates the eye to the hand, it imposes the hand upon the eye, and it replaces the horizon with a ground.

One of the most profound tendencies of modern painting is the tendency to abandon the easel. For the easel was a decisive element not only in the retention of a figurative appearance, not only in the relation of the painter with nature (the quest for motif), but also in the demarcation (frame and edges) and in the internal organization of the scene (depth, perspective . . .). Now what counts today is less the fact—does the painter still have an easel?—than the tendency and the diverse ways in which the tendency is realized. In the abstractions of Mondrian, the painting ceases to be an organism or an isolated organization, in order to become a division of its own surface that must create relations with the divisions of the "room" where it will be placed. It is in this sense that Mondrian's painting is by no means decorative, but rather architechtonic, and that it abandons the easel in order to become mural painting. Pollock and others explicitly impugn the easel in an entirely different manner: this time, they create "all-over" paintings by rediscovering the secret of the Gothic line (in Worringer's sense), by restoring an entire world of equal probabilities, by tracing lines that go from one edge of the painting to the other and that begin and continue outside the frame, and by opposing the power of a mechanical repetition elevated to intuition, to organic symmetry and center. The result is no longer an easel painting; it is rather a ground painting (real horses have the ground as their only horizon).[11] But in truth, there are many ways of breaking away from the easel: Bacon's triptych form is one of these ways, which is very different from the two previous ones; in his work, what is true of the triptychs is also true for each independent painting, which is always in some sense composed like a triptych. In the triptych, as we have seen, the edges of the three scenes no longer isolate, although they continue to separate and divide: there is a union-separation, which is Bacon's technical solution and which, in fact, affects the totality of his procedures in their difference from those of abstraction and the unformed. Are these three ways of becoming "Gothic" again?

The importance lies, in fact, in the reason Bacon did not become involved in either one of the previous paths. The severity of his reactions does not pretend to be judgmental, but rather to state what does not suit Bacon; this explains why Bacon does not take either of these paths. On one hand, he is not attracted by a kind of painting that tends to substitute a spiritual, visual code for the involuntary diagram (even if this is an exemplary attitude of the artist). The code is necessarily cerebral and misses sensation, the essential reality of the fall, that is, the direct action on the nervous system. Kandinsky defined abstract painting by "tension," but, according to Bacon, tension is that which is most lacking in abstract painting: by internalizing it in the optical form, abstract painting neutralized it. And finally, by virtue of being abstract, the code risks being a simple symbolic coding of the figurative.[12] On the other hand, Bacon is no more attracted by abstract expressionism or by the power and the mystery of the line without contour. This is because, he says, the diagram has taken over the entire painting, and its proliferation creates a veritable "mess." All the violent means of action painting—stick, brush, broom, rag, and even pastry syringe—explode in a painting-catastrophe: this time, sensation is indeed attained, but it remains in an irredeemably confused state. Bacon continually discusses the absolute necessity of preventing the diagram from proliferating, the necessity of keeping it in certain areas of the painting and in certain moments of the act of painting. He thinks that, in the domain of the irrational stroke and the line without contour, Michaux goes further than Pollock, precisely because he maintains his mastery of the diagram.[13]

There is nothing more important for Bacon than saving contour. A line that demarcates nothing still has a contour. Blake at least knew this.[14] The diagram should not, therefore, engulf the entire painting; it should remain limited in space and time. It should remain operative and controlled. Violent means should not be unleashed, and the necessary catastrophe should not submerge everything. The diagram is a possibility of fact—it is not the fact itself. Not all figurative data should disappear, and especially, a new figuration, that of figure, should emerge from the diagram and carry sensation to the clear and the precise. Emerge from the catastrophe. . . . Even if we finish with a stream of paint afterward, it is like a localized "crack of the whip," which makes us emerge rather than sink.[15] Could we say that the *"malerisch"* period at least extended the diagram to the entire painting? Is it not the entire surface of the painting that is lined with brushstrokes or with variations of a somber color-daub functioning as a curtain? But even so, the precision of sensation, the clarity of figure, and the rigor of contour continued to act upon the blob of color or beneath the strokes that did not erase them; it rather gave them a power of vibration and illocalization (the smiling or screaming mouth). Bacon's subsequent period returns to a random localization of strokes and cleaned areas. Thus, Bacon follows a third path, neither optical as in abstract painting, nor manual as in action painting.

Trans. Constantin Boundas and Jacqueline Code

24
. . .
Music and Ritornello

1. A child in the dark, gripped with fear, comforts himself by singing under his breath. He walks and halts to his song. Lost, he takes shelter, or orients himself with his little song as best he can. The song is like a rough sketch of a calming and stabilizing, calm and stable, center in the heart of chaos. Perhaps the child skips as he sings, hastens or slows his pace. But the song itself is already a skip: it jumps from chaos to the beginnings of order in chaos and is in danger of breaking apart at any moment. There is always sonority in Ariadne's thread. Or the song of Orpheus.

2. Now we are at home. But home does not preexist: it was necessary to draw a circle around that uncertain and fragile center, to organize a limited space. Many, very diverse, components have a part in this, landmarks and marks of all kinds. This was already true of the previous case. But now the components are used for organizing a space, not for the momentary determination of a center. The forces of chaos are kept outside as much as possible, and the interior space protects the germinal forces of a task to fulfill or a deed to do. This involves an activity of selection, elimination and extraction, in order to prevent the interior forces of the earth from being submerged, to enable them to resist, or even to take something from chaos across the filter or sieve of the space that has been drawn. Sonorous or vocal components are very important: a wall of

sound, or at least a wall with some sonic bricks in it. A child hums to summon the strength for the schoolwork she has to hand in. A housewife sings to herself, or listens to the radio, as she marshals the antichaos forces of her work. Radios and television sets are like sound walls around every household and mark territories (the neighbor complains when it gets too loud). For sublime deeds like the foundation of a city or the fabrication of a golem, one draws a circle, or better yet walks in a circle as in a children's dance, combining rhythmic vowels and consonants that correspond to the interior forces of creation as to the differentiated parts of an organism. A mistake in speed, rhythm, or harmony would be catastrophic because it would bring back the forces of chaos, destroying both creator and creation.

3. Finally, one opens the circle a crack, opens it all the way, lets someone in, calls someone, or else goes out oneself, launches forth. One opens the circle not on the side where the old forces of chaos press against it but in another region, one created by the circle itself. As though the circle tended on its own to open onto a future, as a function of the working forces it shelters. This time, it is in order to join with the forces of the future, cosmic forces. One launches forth, hazards an improvisation. But to improvise is to join with the world, or meld with it. One ventures from home on the thread of a tune. Along sonorous, gestural, motor lines that mark the customary path of a child and graft themselves onto or begin to bud "lines of drift" with different loops, knots, speeds, movements, gestures, and sonorities.[1]

These are not three successive moments in an evolution. They are three aspects of a single thing, the refrain (*ritournelle*). They are found in tales (both horror stories and fairy tales), and in lieder as well. The refrain has all three aspects, it makes them simultaneous or mixes them: sometimes, sometimes, sometimes. Sometimes chaos is an immense black hole in which one endeavors to fix a fragile point as a center. Sometimes one organizes around that point a calm and stable "pace" (rather than a form): the black hole has become a home. Sometimes one grafts onto that pace a breakaway from the black hole. Paul Klee presented these three aspects, and their interlinkage, in a most profound way. He calls the black hole a "gray point" for pictorial reasons. The gray point starts out as nonlocalizable, nondimensional chaos, the force of chaos, a tangled bundle of aberrant lines. Then the point "jumps over itself" and radiates a dimensional space with horizontal layers, vertical cross sections, unwritten customary lines, a whole terrestrial interior force (this force also appears, at a more relaxed pace, in the atmosphere and in water). The gray point (black hole) has thus jumped from one state to another, and no longer represents chaos but the abode or home. Finally, the point launches out of itself, impelled by wandering centrifugal forces that fan out to the sphere of the cosmos: one "tries convulsively to fly from the earth, but at the following level one actually rises above it . . . powered by centrifugal forces that triumph over gravity."[2]

The role of the refrain has often been emphasized: it is territorial, a territorial assemblage. Bird songs: the bird sings to mark its territory. The Greek modes and Hindu rhythms are themselves territorial, provincial, regional. The refrain may assume other functions, amorous, professional or social, liturgical or cosmic: it always carries earth with it; it has a land (sometimes a spiritual land) as its concomitant; it has an essential relation to a Natal, a Native. A musical "nome" is a little tune, a melodic formula that seeks recognition and remains the bedrock or ground of polyphony (*cantus firmus*). The *nomos* as customary, unwritten law is inseparable from a distribution of space, a distribution in space. By that token, it is *ethos*, but the ethos is also the Abode.[3] Sometimes one goes from chaos to the threshold of a territorial assemblage: directional components, infra-assemblage. Sometimes one organizes the assemblage: dimensional components, intra-assemblage. Sometimes one leaves the territorial assemblage for other assemblages, or for somewhere else entirely; inter-assemblage, components of passage or even escape. And all three at once. Forces of chaos, terrestrial forces, cosmic forces: all of these confront each other and converge in the territorial refrain.

25
. . .
One Manifesto Less

I. The Theater and Its Critique

With regard to his play *Romeo and Juliet,* Carmelo Bene says: "It is a critical essay on Shakespeare." But the fact is that CB is not writing on Shakespeare; his critical essay is itself a piece of theater. How are we to understand this relationship between theater and its critique, between the original play and the one derived from it? CB's theater has a critical function— but of what?

It is not a question of "criticizing" Shakespeare, nor of a play within a play, nor of a parody, nor of a new version of a play, etc. CB proceeds in a more original manner. Suppose that he amputates one of the component parts of the original play. He subtracts something from the original. To be precise, he does not call his play on Hamlet one more *Hamlet* but, like Laforgue, "one less *Hamlet*." He does not proceed by addition, but by subtraction, by amputation. How he chooses the component for amputation is another question, as we shall see shortly. But, for example, he amputates Romeo, he neutralizes Romeo in the original play. So the whole play, because it now lacks a part chosen nonarbitrarily, will perhaps tip over, turn around on itself, land on another side. If you amputate Romeo, you will witness an astonishing development, that of Mercutio, who was no more than a potentiality in Shakespeare's play. Mercutio dies quickly in Shakespeare, but in CB he does not want to die, cannot die, does not succeed in dying, since he will constitute the new play.

It is a matter then, in the first place, of the very constitution of a character on stage. Even the objects, the props, await their destiny, that is to say, the necessity that the *caprice* of the character is going to give them. The play consists first of all in the making up of the character, his preparation, his birth, his babblings, his changes, his developments. This critical theater is a constituting theater, the critique is a constitution. The man of the theater is no longer an author, actor, or director. He is an operator. By operation, one must understand the activity of subtraction, of amputation, but already masked by another activity which gives birth to and multiplies the unexpected, as in a prosthesis: amputation of Romeo *and* immense development of Mercutio, the one within the other. This is a theater of surgical precision. Consequently, if CB often has need of an original play, it is not in order to make a fashionable parody of it, nor to add literature to literature. On the contrary it is in order to subtract the literature, for example to subtract the text, a part of the text, and to see what happens. *Let the words stop making up a "text."* . . . This is a theater-experimentation that involves more love for Shakespeare than all the commentaries.

Take the case of *S.A.D.E.* Against the background of a frozen recitation of texts by De Sade, it is the sadistic image of the master which finds itself amputated, paralyzed, reduced to a masturbatory tic, at the same time that the masochistic slave searches for his identity, develops, metamorphizes, tests himself, constitutes himself on the stage according to the inadequacies and impotencies of the master. The slave is not at all the reverse image of the master, nor his replica nor his contradictory identity: he constitutes himself piece by piece, morsel by morsel, through the neutralization of the master; he gains his autonomy through the master's amputation.

Finally, consider *Richard the Third*, where CB goes perhaps furthest in his theatrical construction. What is amputated here, what is subtracted, is the whole royal and princely system. Only Richard III and the women are retained. But as a result that which existed only potentially in the tragedy appears under a new light. *Richard the Third* is perhaps the only Shakespeare tragedy in which the women do battle for themselves. And as for Richard III, it is not so much that he covets power as that he wants to reintroduce or reinvent a war-machine, even if it means destroying the apparent equilibrium or the peace of the State (Shakespeare calls this Richard's secret, the "secret goal"). In operating the subtraction of the characters of State power, CB will give free rein to the constitution of the man of war on the state, with his prostheses, his deformities, his outgrowths, his defects, his variations. The man of war has always been considered in mythology as of another origin from that of the statesman or the king: deformed and twisted, he always comes from somewhere else. CB makes him come to pass on the stage: while the women at war enter and exit, worried about their whining infants, Richard III must make himself deformed to amuse the infants and keep the attention of the mothers. He makes prostheses for himself of objects he takes out of drawers at random. He constitutes himself a little like Mr. Hyde—of colors, of sounds, of things. He forms himself, or rather deforms himself, following a line of continuous variation. CB's play begins with a very nice "note on the feminine" (is there not already in Kleist's *Penthesilea* a similar relationship between a man of war, Achilles, and the feminine, the transvestite?).

CB's plays are short; no one knows better than he how to end. He detests every principle of constancy or eternity, of the permanence of the text: "The spectacle starts and finishes at the moment one makes it." And the play ends with the constitution of the character, it has no other aim but the process of this constitution and does not extend beyond it. It ends with birth, whereas customarily one ends with death. One should not conclude from this that these characters have an "ego." On the contrary, they have nothing of the sort. Richard III, the slave, Mercutio, only come to life in a continuous series of metamorphoses and variations. The character is nothing more than the totality of the scenic assemblages, colors, lights, gestures, words. It is odd that one often says of CB: he is a great actor—a compliment mixed with reproach, an accusation of narcissism. It is rather CB's pride to launch a process of which he is the controller, the mechanic, or the operator (he himself says: the protagonist) rather than the actor. To give birth to a monster or to a giant. . . .

This is neither a theater of the author, nor a critique of the author. But if this theater is inseparably creative and critical, what is it critical of? It is not CB criticizing Shakespeare.

At the very most one could say that, if an Englishman at the end of the sixteenth century constructs a certain image of Italy, an Italian of the twentieth century can return an image of the England where Shakespeare is present: the admirable, gigantic decor of *Romeo and Juliet* with its huge glasses and flasks, and Juliet who falls asleep in a cake, makes us see Shakespeare by way of Lewis Carroll, but Lewis Carroll by way of Italian comedy (Carroll already suggested a whole system of subtractions on Shakespeare in order to develop unexpected potentialities). It is no longer a question of criticizing countries or societies. One asks what the initial subtractions operated by CB concern. In the three preceding cases it is the elements of power, the elements that make up or represent a system of power, which are subtracted, amputated, or neutralized: Romeo as representative of the power of families, the master as representative of sexual power, the kings and princes as representatives of the power of the State. Now the elements of power in the theater are those which assure at once the coherence of the subject dealt with and the coherence of the representation on stage. It is at the same time the power of that which is represented and the power of theater itself. In this sense the traditional actor has an ancient complicity with princes and kings—the theater, with power: thus Napoleon and Talma. Theater's own power is not separable from the representation of power in the theater, even if it is a critical representation. Now CB has another conception of critique. When he chooses to *amputate* the components of power, it is not only the theatrical material that he changes, it is also the form of theater, which ceases to be "representation" at the same time that the actor ceases to be an actor. He gives free rein to other theatrical material and another theatrical form, which would not have been possible without this subtraction. One will say that CB is not the first to make a theater of nonrepresentation. One will cite at random Artaud, Bob Wilson, Grotowski, the living theater. . . . But we do not believe in the usefulness of filiations. Alliances are more important than filiations. CB has very diverse degrees of alliance with those whom we have just cited. He belongs to a movement that is stirring the theater profoundly today. But he belongs to this movement only by virtue of what he himself is inventing and not the reverse.

And the originality of his approach, the ensemble of his procedures, seems to us to consist first of all in this: the subtraction of stable components of power, which releases a new potentiality of theater, a nonrepresentational force always in disequilibrium.

II. The Theater and Its Minorities

CB is very interested in the notions of major and minor. He gives them a lived content. What is a "minor" character? What is a "minor" author? CB begins by pointing out that it is stupid to be interested in the beginning or end of something, the points of origin and termination. What is interesting is never the way someone starts or finishes. The interesting thing is the middle, what happens on the way. It is not by chance that the greatest speed is at the halfway point. People often dream of commencing or recommencing at zero; and they are also afraid of where they are going to arrive, their landing point. They think in terms of future or of past, but the past and even the future are *history*. What counts, on the contrary, is the becoming: becoming-revolutionary, and not the future or the past of the revolution. "I shall not arrive anywhere, I will not arrive anywhere. There are no arrivals.

It does not interest me where someone ends up. A man may also end up mad. What does that mean?" It is in the middle where one finds the becoming, the movement, the velocity, the vortex. The middle is not the mean, but on the contrary an excess. It is by the middle that things push. That was Virginia Woolf's idea. Now the middle does not at all imply to be in one's time, to be of one's time, to be historical—on the contrary. It is that by which the most diverse times communicate. It is neither the historical nor the eternal, but the untimely. A minor author is just that: without future or past, she has only a becoming, a middle, by which she communicates with other times, other spaces. Goethe gave Kleist stern lessons, explaining that a great author, a major author must devote himself to being of his time. But Kleist was incurably minor. "Antihistoricism," says CB: do you know who those men are who must be seen in their century? Those whom one calls the greatest, Goethe for example (one cannot see him outside the Germany of his time, or if he leaves his time it is immediately to join the eternal). But the true great authors are the minor ones, the untimely ones. It is the minor author who provides the true masterpieces; the minor author does not interpret his time, the man does not have a determinate time, the time depends on the man: François Villon, Kleist, or Laforgue. Is there not therefore great interest in submitting authors considered major to treatment as minor authors, in order to rediscover their potential for becoming? Shakespeare, for example?

It is as if there are two opposing operations. On the one side one raises to the "major": from a thought one makes a doctrine, from a way of living one makes a culture, from an event one makes history. One claims in this way to acknowledge and admire, but in fact one normalizes. As with the peasants of Apuglia, according to CB: one can give them theater and cinema and even television. It is not a question of regretting the old times, but of being alarmed in the face of the operation to which one is submitting them, the graft, the transplant which one has made in their backs to normalize them. They have become major. So, operation for operation, surgery for surgery, one can conceive of the reverse: how to reduce or *minorize* (*minorer*—a term used by mathematicians), how to impose a minor or minimizing treatment in order to extricate becomings from history, lives from culture, thoughts from doctrine, grace or disgrace from dogma. When one sees what Shakespeare is subjected to in the traditional theater, his magnification-normalization, one clamors for another treatment that would rediscover in him this active minoritarian force. Theologians are major, but certain Italian saints are minor. "The saints who have made it by grace: Saint Joseph of Copertino, the imbeciles, the saintly fools, Saint Francis of Assisi dancing before the Pope. . . . I say there is already culture from the moment we are in the process of examining an idea, not living that idea. If we are the idea, then we can dance the dance of Saint-Guy and we are in a state of grace. We begin to be wise precisely when we are dis-graced." We do not save ourselves, we do not become minor, save by the constitution of a disgrace or deformity. That is the operation of grace itself. As in the story of Lourdes: make my hand come back like the other. . . . But God always chooses the bad hand. How are we to understand this operation? Kleist stammering and grinding his teeth?

"Major" and "minor" are also said of languages. Can one distinguish in each epoch major common languages—international or national—and minor vernaculars? English, American—is that a major language today? Would Italian be a minor one? One distinguishes a high language and a low one in societies that express themselves in two languages or more. But is this not true even for unilingual societies? One could define some languages as major, even though they have little international standing: these would be languages with strongly homogeneous structure (standardization), and centered on invariants, constants, or universals of a phonological, syntactic, or semantic nature. CB sketches a linguistics, just for fun: thus French seems to be a major language, even though it has lost its international reach, because it retains a strong homogeneity and strong phonological and syntactic constants. This is not without consequences for the theater: "French theatres are museums of the everyday, a disconcerting and wearisome repetition, because in the name of a spoken and written language one goes in the evening to see and hear that which one has heard and seen during the day. Theatrically, between Marivaux and the stationmaster of Paris there is really no difference, except that at the Odeon one cannot catch the train." English bases itself on other invariants—for example, on constants that are rather semantic; it is always by dint of constants and homogeneity that a language is major: "England is a history of kings. . . . The Gielguds and the Oliviers are living copies of bygone Kembles and Keans. The monarchy of *once upon a time*—that is the English tradition." In short, however different they may be, the major languages are languages of power. To them one will oppose the minor languages: Italian, for example ("Our country is young, it does not yet have a language. . ."). And already one has no further choice; one must define the minor languages as *languages with continuous variability*—whichever dimension one is considering: phonological, syntactic, semantic, or even stylistic. A minor language is made up of only a minimum of structural constants and homogeneities. It is not, however, a porridge, a mixture of patois, since it finds its *rules* in the construction of a continuum. In effect, continuous variation applies to all the components, vocal and linguistic, in a kind of generalized chromaticism. This is theater itself, or "spectacle."

But, at the same time, it is hard to oppose languages that are major by nature to others that are minor. People protest, notably in France, against the imperialism of English or American. But this imperialism has precisely for its counterpart that English and American are worked on to the greatest extent from within by the minorities that use them. Observe how Anglo-Irish works on English in Synge, and imposes on it a line of flight or continuous variation: "the way. . .". No doubt this is not the same way by the minorities work on American, with black English and all the Americans of the ghetto. But in any case there is no imperial language that is not tunneled through, dragged along by these inherent and continuous lines of variation, by these minor uses. That being the case, major and minor do not so much qualify different languages as different uses of the same language. Kafka, a Czech Jew writing in German, makes a minor use of German and thereby produces a decisive linguistic masterpiece (more generally, the work of minorities on German in the Austrian Empire). At the most, one could say that a language is more or less endowed for these minor uses.

Linguists often have a debatable conception of their object of study. They say that each language is, assuredly, a heterogeneous mixture but that one can only study it scientifically if one extracts from it a homogeneous and constant subsystem: a dialect, a patois, a ghetto language would thus be submitted to the same condition as a standard language (Chomsky). From this point of view, the variations that affect a language will be considered either as extrinsic or extrasystemic or as bearing witness to a mixture between two systems of which each is homogeneous. But perhaps this condition of constancy and homogeneity already presupposes a certain use of the language upon consideration: a major use that treats the language as a condition of power, a marker of power. A small number of linguists (notably William Labov) have isolated in each language the existence of lines of variation, bearing on all the components, and constituting immanent rules of a new type. You will not arrive at a homogeneous system that is not still worked on by immanent, continuous, and regulated variation: this is what defines every language by its minor use; a broadened chromaticism, a black English for each language. The continuous variability is not to be explained by a bilingualism, nor by a mixture of dialects, but by the creative property most inherent in the language when it is in the grips of a minor use. And, in a certain way, this is the "theater" of the language.

III. The Theater and Its Language

It is not a question of an antitheater, of a theater within the theater, or which denies the theater, etc.: CB feels disgust for the pat phrases of the avant-garde. It is a question of a more precise operation: you begin by subtracting, taking away everything that comprises an element of power, in language and in gestures, in representation and in the represented. You cannot even say that it is a negative operation inasmuch as it already engages and sets in motion positive processes. You will thus take away or amputate history, because history is the temporal marker of power. You will take away structure because it is the synchronic marker, the ensemble of relations among variants. You will subtract the constants, the stable or stabilized elements, because they belong to the major use. You will amputate the text, because the text is like the domination of language over speech and bears witness, too, to an invariance or homogeneity. You cut back on the dialogue because the dialogue transmits to speech the elements of power and makes them circulate: it is your turn to speak, in such-and-such codified conditions (the linguists are trying to determine the "universals of dialogue"), etc., etc. As Franco Quadri says, you deduct even the diction, even the action: the play-back is, first of all, a subtraction. But what remains? Everything remains, but under a new light, with new sounds, new gestures.

For example, you say "I swear it." But it is not at all the same statement according to whether you make it before a tribunal, in a love scene, or as a child. And this variation affects not only the external situation, not only the physical intonation but also from within the sense, the syntax, and the phonemes. You will thus make a statement pass by way of all the variables that can affect it in the shortest space of time. The statement will be no more than the sum of its own variations, which make it escape every apparatus of power capable of fixing it and which enable it to dodge every constancy. You will construct the continuum of *I swear it*. Let us suppose that Lady Anne says to Richard III: "I loathe you!" In no respect is this the same statement according to whether it is the cry of a woman at war, a child confronting a toad, a young girl who feels an already consenting and amorous pity. . . . Lady Anne must pass by way of all these variables, she must rise up as a soldier, regress to infancy, come to life again as a young girl, along a line of continuous variation and as fast as possible. CB never ceases tracing these lines along which are strung positions, regressions, rebirths, as he puts language and speech in continuous variation. Whence the very original use of lip-sync ("play-back") by CB, since lip-sync assures the amplitude of the variations and gives them rules. This is odd, as if there is no dialogue in CB's theater, for the voices, simultaneous or successive, superimposed or transposed, are engaged in this spatiotemporal continuity of variation. It is a kind of *Sprechgesang*. In song it is a matter of maintaining the pitch, but in *Sprechgesang* one keeps abandoning it by a rise or fall. Hence it is not the text that counts, since it is simply material for the variation. It is even necessary

212 MINOR LANGUAGES AND NOMAD ART

to weigh down the text with nontextual—yet internal—indications, *which are not merely stage directions*, which function as operators, expressing each time the scale of the variables by which the statement passes, exactly as in a musical score. Now this is just how CB himself writes, with a writing that is neither literary nor theatrical but really operative, and whose effect on the reader is very strong, very strange. Look at those operators which, in *Richard III*, take up much more room than the text itself. CB's whole theater must be seen but also read, even though the text properly speaking is not the essential. This is not a contradiction. It is rather like sight-reading a score. This explains CB's reserved attitude towards Brecht: Brecht has carried out the greatest "critical operation," but he has effected this operation "on the written word and not on stage." The complete critical operation is that which consists in (1) deducting the stable elements, (2) putting everything in continuous variation, and also, consequently, (3) transposing everything into the *minor* (that is the role of the operators, corresponding to the idea of the "minimal" interval).

What is this use of language according to variation? One could express it in several ways: being bilingual, *but* in a single tongue. . . . Being a foreigner, *but* in one's own tongue. . . . Stammering, *but* as a stammerer of language itself and not simply of speech. . . . CB adds: talking to oneself, in one's own ear, *but* in the middle of the marketplace, in the public square. . . . We might take each one of these formulas in itself to define the work of CB, and see not which dependencies but which alliances, which engagements it makes with other attempts, past or present. Bilingualism puts us on the path, but only on the path. For the bilingual person leaps from one language to another; the one may have a minor use, the other a major. One can even make a heterogeneous mixture of several languages or of several dialects. But here it is in one and the same language that one must succeed in being bilingual, it is on my own language that I must impose the heterogeneity of variation, it is in it that I must carve out a minor use and cut away the elements of power or of majority. One can always start off from an external situation: for example Kafka, a Czech Jew writing in German; Beckett, an Irishman, writing simultaneously in English and in French; Pasolini using dialectal varieties of Italian. But it is within German itself that Kafka traces a line of flight or of continuous variation. It is French itself that Beckett makes stammer, as does Jean-Luc Godard in another way and Gherasim Luca in yet another way. And it is English that Bob Wilson causes to whisper, to murmur (for whispering does not imply a weak intensity, but, on the contrary, an intensity that has no definite pitch). Now the formula of stammering is as approximate as that of bilingualism. Stammering, in general, is a disorder of speech. But to make a language stammer is another affair. It is to impose on the language, on all the inner elements of the language—phonological, syntactic, semantic—the work of continuous variation. I believe that Gherasim Luca is one of the greatest French poets, and of all time. He certainly does not owe this to his Romanian origin, but he makes use of this origin to make French stammer in itself, with itself, to carry the stammering into the language itself, not simply the speaking of it. Read or listen to the poem "Passionément," which has been recorded as well as published in the collection *Le Chant de la Carpe*. One has never achieved such an intensity in the language, such an intensive use of language. A public recitation of poems by Gherasim Luca is a marvelous and complete theatrical event. So, to be a foreigner in one's own language. . . . This is not to talk "like" an Irishman or a Romanian talking French. That is not the case with either Beckett or Luca. It is to impose on the language, insofar as one speaks it perfectly and soberly, that line of variation that will make of you a foreigner in *your own* tongue, or of the foreign tongue, yours, or of your tongue, an immanent bilingualism for your foreignness. One always comes back to Proust's formulation: "Beautiful books are written in a sort of foreign language." Or, conversely, Kafka's short story "The Great Swimmer" (who never knew how to swim): "I must remark that I am here in my own country and that, despite all my efforts, I do not understand a word of the language which you are speaking." So much for the alliances or the encounters of CB, involuntary or not, with those whom we have just cited. They have value only by the way CB constructs his own methods to make his own language stammer, whisper, and vary, and to make it intensive at the level of each of its elements.

All the linguistic and acoustic components, indissolubly language *and* speech, are thus put into a state of continuous variation. But this is not without effect on the other, nonlinguistic, components: actions, passions, gestures, attitudes, objects, etc. For one cannot deal with the elements of language and speech as so many internal variables without placing them in reciprocal relation with the external variables, in the same continuity, in the same flux of continuity. It is in the same movement that language will tend to escape the system of power that structures it and action the system of mastery or domination that organizes it. In a fine article, Corrado Augias has shown how CB combines a work of "aphasia" on language (diction whispered, stammering, or deformed; sounds scarcely perceptible or quite deafening) with a work of "impediment" on things and gestures (costumes that hinder movement instead of assisting it, props that are awkward to shift, gestures that are too stiff or "limp"). Thus, the apple in *Salome* continually swallowed and spat out again; and the costumes that keep falling off and having to be put on again; always the useful object that deserts instead of serving, the table that interposes itself instead of supporting—one is always obliged to get clear of the objects rather than handle them; or once more in *S.A.D.E.*, the copulation perpetually postponed, and above all the slave who entangles himself, ties himself up in knots in the continuous series of his metamorphoses, for he must not *master* his role of *slave;* and at the beginning of *Richard III*, Richard who never stops losing his balance, wobbling, slipping off the chest of drawers on which he is leaning. . . .

IV. The Theater and Its Gestures

Is it necessary to point out, nonetheless, that this double principle, of aphasia and impediment, reveals relations of force by which each body makes itself an obstacle to the body of the other, as each will shackles that of others? It is something other than a play of oppositions that will lead us back to the system of power and domination. It is that by continual impediment gestures and movements are put in a state of continuous variation, the former in relation to the latter as well as each in itself, exactly as voices and linguistic elements are brought into this milieu of variation. Richard III's gesture keeps abandoning its proper level, its proper height, by a fall, a rise, a slide: the gesture in positive disequilibrium. The piece of clothing one takes off and puts back on, which falls off and is donned again, is like the variation of clothing. Or consider the variation of flowers that occupies such a place in CB's practice. In effect there are very few collisions and oppositions in CB's theater. We can conceive of procedures that would produce stammering by causing words to collide, phonemes to oppose each other, or even dialectal varieties to confront one another. But these are not the means that CB himself employs. On the contrary the beauty of his *style* is to achieve the stammering by instituting melodic lines which pull the language outside a system of dominating oppositions. And the same goes for the *grace* of gestures on stage. It is curious in this regard that angry women, and even critics, have reproached CB for his direction of the female body and have accused him of sexism or phallocracy.

The female-object of *S.A.D.E.*, the naked girl, passes through all the metamorphoses the sadistic master imposes on her, transforming her into a successive series of objects of use: but she just traverses these metamorphoses, she never adopts a degrading posture, she strings together her gestures following the line of a variation which allows her to escape the domination of the master and come to life outside his grasp, maintaining her dignity throughout the whole series. Hats off to the actress who played the part in Paris! It is never in relations of force and opposition that CB's theater is deployed, although this theater is "tough" and "cruel." Much more, the relations of force and opposition belong to that which is shown only for the purpose of being subtracted, cut away, neutralized. Conflicts do not much interest CB. They are simply a medium for variation. CB's theater is deployed only in relations of variation that eliminate "masters."

In variation, what count are relations of speed or slowness, the modification of these relations insofar as they involve gestures and statements, following variable coefficients along a line of transformation. It is in this way that the writing and gestures of CB are musical: it is because every form is deformed by modifications of speed, with the result that one does not use the same gesture or the same word twice without obtaining different temporal characteristics. This is the musical formula of continuity, or of transformable form. The "operators" that function in CB's style and direction are precisely indicators of speed, which no more belong to the theater than they are external to it. CB has in fact found the way to articulate them fully in the "text" of his pieces, even though they do not belong to the text. The physicists of the Middle Ages spoke of *deformed* movements and qualities according to the distribution of velocities among the different points of a moving body or the distribution of intensities among the different points of a subject. The subordination of form to speed, to variation in speed, the subordination of the subject to intensity or affect, to the intensive variation of affects: these are, it seems to us, two essential goals to achieve in the arts. CB is a full participant in this movement that is bringing criticism to bear on the form as well as on the subject (in the double sense of "theme" and of "ego"). Affects and no subject, velocities and no form. But once again what count are CB's own means for realizing this goal: the continuity of variation. When he identifies the grace in the movement of disgrace (the "idiot saints" whom he loves), he wishes only to subordinate the designated forms to the deformity of movement or of quality themselves. There is a whole geometry in CB's theater, but a geometry in the manner of Nicolas Oresme, a geometry of speeds and intensities, of affects.

CB's films are not filmed theater. Perhaps this is so because the cinema does not employ the same velocities of variation as the theater, and above all because the two variations, that of language and that of gestures, do not stand in the same relation in cinema. In particular, is it possible that the cinema may directly constitute a sort of visual music, as if it is the eyes that grasp the sound first, while the theater, where even the actions are first of all heard, has a hard time disabusing itself of the primacy of the ear? (Already in his theatrical version of *Notre-Dame of the Turks* CB was seeking ways for the theater to get beyond this domination by words and to attain to a direct perception of the action: "The public had to follow the action through panes of glass, and heard nothing except when the actor deigned to open a little window.") But at all events the important thing, in the theater as in the cinema, is that the two variations must not remain parallel. One way or another they must be *placed one within the other.* The continuous variation of gesture and things, the continuous variation of language and sounds can interrupt, intersect, cut each other off; they must nevertheless both continue, *forming one and the same continuum,* which will be—according to the case—filmic, theatrical, musical, etc. Someone should do a special study of CB's films. But remaining within the theater, we should like to find out how CB proceeds in *Richard III,* his most recent piece, in which he goes furthest.

The whole beginning of *Richard III* is based on two lines of variation, which intermix and take turns but have not yet merged. Richard's gestures never cease to slip, change level, fall only to rise again; the gestures of the servant, cross-dressed as Buckingham, accord with his own. But also the voice of the duchess never stops changing tone, passing by way of all the variations of the mother, at the same time that Richard's voice babbles and reduces itself to the "articulations of a cave-dweller." If the two variations still remain relatively separate, as two continuities that intersect, it is because Richard is not yet constituted on stage. In this beginning, there are still to be sought, in his head and in things, the elements of his impending constitution. He is not yet an object of fear, of love, and of pity. He has not yet made his "political choice," not yet raised up his war-machine. He has not yet attained the disgrace of "his" grace, the deformity of his form. But now, in the great scene with Lady Anne, Richard will constitute himself before our very eyes. Shakespeare's sublime scene, with respect to which he has sometimes been taxed for extravagance or implausibility, is not parodied by CB but multiplied according to the velocities or variable developments that will unite in a single continuity of constitution (not a unity of representation). (1) Richard, or rather the actor who plays Richard, begins to "comprehend." He begins to comprehend his own idea and the means of this idea. First he goes through the drawers of the commode, which contain plaster casts and prostheses, all the monstrosities of the human body. He takes them out, drops them, picks up another, tests them, hides them from Anne, then adorns himself with them in triumph. He achieves the *miracle* whereby the good hand becomes as contorted, as crooked as the other. He wins his political choice; he constitutes his deformities and his war-machine. (2) Lady Anne, from her side, enters into a strange complicity with Richard: she wounds and hates him while he is in his "form," but distraught before each deformation and already amorous and consenting. It is as if a new personality were constituting itself in her too, matching her own variation with that of Richard. She begins by helping him vaguely in his search for the prostheses. And, better and better, faster and faster, she starts to seek herself for the amorous deformation. She will wed a war-machine, instead of remaining in the dependency and power of a State apparatus. She enters herself into a variation that weds that of Richard, never ceasing to undress and redress herself continually, to a rhythm of regression-progression that corresponds to the subtractions-constructions of Richard. (3) The vocal variations of the one and the other, phonemes and tonalities, form a line drawn tighter and tighter, which slips between the gestures and vice versa. The spectator must not only understand but hear and see the goal that the mutterings and stumblings of the beginning were already pursuing without knowing it: the Idea becomes visible, sensible, politics become erotic. At that moment, there will no longer be two continuities that intersect but one and the same continuum where words and gestures play the role of variables in transformation . . . (one would have to analyze the whole rest of the play and the admirable constitution of the ending—where one sees clearly that it was not a question for Richard of conquering a State apparatus but of constructing a war-machine inseparably political *and* erotic).

V. The Theater and Its Politics

Let us suppose that those who admire CB are more or less in accord on these functions of theater, as we have tried to define them: elimination of constants or invariants not only in the language and the gestures, but also in the theatrical representation and in that which is represented on stage; thus the elimination of everything which "makes" power, the power of what the theater represents (the king, the princes, the masters, the system), but also the power of the theater itself (the text, the dialogue, the actor, the director, the structure). Hence the passage of everything through continuous variation, as if on a creative line of flight, which constitutes a minor tongue within the language, a minor character on stage, a minor transformational group across the dominant forms and subjects. Suppose one is in accord on these points. It will be all the more necessary to get to the following simple, practical questions: (1) What is the external use of all this, since it is still theater, nothing but theater? (2) And in what respect, precisely, does CB place in question the power of theater or the theater as power? In what respect is he less narcissistic than an actor, less authoritarian than a director, less despotic than a text? Is he not all the more so—he that claims to be at once the text, the actor, and the director (I am a mass; "see how politics becomes mass, the mass of *my* atoms.")?

One has not accomplished anything until one has reached that which merges with someone's genius: his extreme modesty, the point where he is humble. All CB's declarations of pride are made to express something very humble. And first of all that the theater, even the one he dreams of, is no big thing; that the theater obviously does not change the world and does not make the revolution. CB does not believe in the avant-garde. No more does he believe in a popular theater, a theater for everyone, a communication between the man of the theater and the people. For when one speaks of a popular theater, one tends always toward a certain *representation of conflicts*, conflicts of individual and of society, of life and of history, contradictions and oppositions of all sorts that traverse a society, but also individuals. Now that which is truly narcissistic—and which everyone finds acceptable—is this representation of conflicts, be it naturalistic or hyperrealistic or whatever. There is a popular theater that is like the narcissism of the worker. No doubt there is Brecht's attempt to ensure that the contradictions, the oppositions are something other than represented, but Brecht himself desires only that they be "comprehended" and that the spectator have the elements of a "possible" solution. This is not to exit from the domain of representation—it is only to pass from a dramatic pole of bourgeois representation to an epic pole of popular representation. Brecht does not push the "critique" far enough. For the representation of conflicts, CB claims to substitute the presence of variation as a more active, more aggressive element.

But why are conflicts generally subordinated to representation, why does the theater remain representational each time it takes as its object conflicts, contradictions, oppositions? It is because the conflicts are already normalized, codified, institutionalized. They are "products." They are already a representation—all the more fit to be represented on stage. When a conflict is not yet normalized, that is because it depends on something else more profound, because it is like the lightning flash that announces something else and that comes from something else, a sudden emergence of a creative variation, unexpected, subrepresentational. Institutions are the organs of representation of recognized conflicts, and the theater is an institution, the theater—even the avant-garde, even the popular—is "official." By what destiny have the Brechtians taken power over an important part of the theater? The critic Giuseppi Bertolucci described the situation of theater in Italy (and elsewhere) when CB was starting his endeavors: because social reality escapes it "the theater has become for everyone an ideological snare and an objective factor of immobility." And the same thing goes for the Italian cinema, with its pseudopolitical ambitions: as Marco Montesano remarks, "It is a cinema of institution, despite the conflictual appearances, for the conflict filmed ("mis en scene") is the conflict which the institution foresees and controls." It is a theater and a cinema that are narcissistic, historicist, and moralizing. The same for the rich as for the poor: CB describes them as belonging to the same system of power and domination that divides them into "poor slaves" and "rich slaves," and where the artist has the function of an intellectual slave, on one side or the other. But just how is one to exit from this situation of conflictual, official, institutionalized representation? How is one to turn to good account the subterranean work of a free and present variation, which insinuates itself among the chains of slavery and bursts them apart?

Then there are the other directions: the living theater, where the conflicts are lived rather than represented, as in a psychodrama. The aesthetic theater, where the formalized conflicts become abstract, geometrical, ornamental. The mystical theater, which tends to abandon representation in order to become communal and ascetic life "beyond the spectacle." None of these directions suits CB; he still prefers representation pure and simple. . . . Like Hamlet, he is seeking a simpler, more humble formula.

The whole question turns around the *majoritarian fact*. For the theater for all, the popular theater, is a little like democracy; it appeals to a majoritarian fact. But this fact is very ambiguous. It assumes a state of power or domination and not the opposite. Obviously there may be more flies and mosquitoes than men, but man nevertheless constitutes the meterstick in relation to which men necessarily have the majority. "The majority" does not designate a larger quantity, but first and foremost that meterstick in relation to which the other quantities, whatever they may be, will be said to be smaller. For example, women and children, blacks and Indians, etc., will be minoritarian relative to the meterstick constituted by man—the white Christian ordinary-male-adult-inhabitant of today's American or European cities (Ulysses). But at this point everything is turned upside down. For if "the majority" refers to a model of power, historical or structural or both at once, one must also say that *everyone* is minoritarian, potentially minoritarian to the extent that they deviate from this model. Now is not continuous variation precisely that which keeps overflowing—by excess or by defect—the representational threshold of the majoritarian standard? Is not continuous variation the becoming-minoritarian of everyone, in opposition to the majoritarian fact of Someone? May the theater not therefore find for itself a function modest enough, and yet effective? This antirepresentational function would be to trace, to constitute a sort of diagram of minoritarian consciousness, as a potentiality of every person. To render a potentiality present, actual, is quite another thing from representing a conflict. One could no longer say that art has a power, that it still belongs to power, even when it criticizes power. For in drawing up the form of a minoritarian consciousness, it would be addressing itself to the powers of becoming, which are of another domain from that of power and of the representation-standard. "Art is not a form of power, it is that when it ceases to be art and begins to become demagogy." Art submits to many powers, but it is not a form of power. It matters little that the actor-author-director exercises an ascendancy and behaves when need be in an authoritarian—very authoritarian—manner. This is the authority of a perpetual variation, in opposition to the power or despotism of the invariant. This is the authority, the autonomy of the stammerer, of him who has conquered the right to stammer, in opposition to the "well-spoken" major. Of course the risk is always great that the form of minority will restore a majority, refashion a standard (when art begins to become demagogy. . .). The variation itself must keep varying, that is, passing in effect along new and always unexpected paths.

What are these paths from the point of view of a politics of the theater? Who is this man of the minority? Even the word *man* is no longer appropriate, so much is it affected by the majoritarian sign. Why not *woman* or *transvestite*? But they too are already codified. One can see a politics being sketched out through CB's declarations or positions. The frontier, that is to say, the line of variation, does not pass between the masters and the slaves, nor between the rich and the poor. For between them a whole regime of relations and oppositions is woven that makes of the master a rich slave and of the slave a poor master, *within the same majoritarian system.* The frontier does not pass through history, nor even through the interior of an established structure, nor even through "the people." Everyone calls on the spirit of the people, in the name of the majoritarian language, but who is the people? "It is the people that is missing." In truth, the frontier passes between history and antihistoricism, that is to say, concretely, "those of whom History does not take account." It passes between the structure and the lines of flight that traverse it. It passes between the people and the *ethnic group.* The ethnic group is the minoritarian, the line of flight in the structure, the antihistorical element in history. CB lives his own minority in relation to the folk of Apuglia: his South or his Third World, in the sense in which everyone has a South and a Third World. Now when he speaks of the folk of Apuglia to which he belongs, he senses that the word *poor* is not at all suitable. How can one term people poor who would rather die of hunger than work? How can one term people slaves who do not enter into the game of master and slave? How can one speak of a "conflict" where there was something quite different, a blazing variation, an antihistorical variant—the mad riot of Campi Salentina, as CB describes it. But see how one has performed a strange graft on them, a strange operation: they have been planned, represented, normalized, historicized, integrated to the majoritarian fact, and yes, one has turned them into the poor, into slaves, into the people, into history—they have been rendered major.

A final danger, before we can believe that we have understood what CB is saying. He is not especially interested—not at all—in becoming the head of a regionalist troupe. On the contrary, he demands and clamors for State theaters, he fights for them, there is no cult of poverty in his work. One requires a lot of political bad faith to see a "contradiction" there or a recuperation. CB has never claimed to be creating a regionalist theater, and a minority begins already to be normalized when one closes it in on itself and when one circumscribes it with the dance of the good old times (thus one makes of it a subcomponent of the majority). CB never belongs more to Apuglia, to the South, than when he is making a universal theater with English, French, and American alliances. What he extracts from Apuglia is a line of variation, air, soil, sun, colors, lights, and sounds, which he himself will cause to vary in quite another way, on other lines—for example, *Notre-Dame of the Turks,* in which there is more of Apuglia than if he had represented it in poetry.

To conclude, *minority has two senses,* undoubtedly related, but quite distinct. *Minority* designates first a factual condition, that is, the situation of a group that, whatever its number, is excluded from the majority, or even included, but as a subordinate fraction in relation to a standard of measure that makes the law and fixes the majority. One may say in this sense that women, children, the South, the Third World, etc., are still minorities, however numerous they may be. But then let us take this first sense "at its word." Immediately there is a second sense: minority no longer designates a factual condition, but a becoming in which one is engaged. Becoming-minoritarian is a goal, but a goal that concerns everyone, since everyone enters into this goal and this becoming to the extent that each person constructs his/her variation around the despotic unity of measure, and escapes, one way or another, the system of power that made him/her a part of the majority. According to this second sense, it is evident that the minority is much more numerous than the majority. For example, according to the first sense women are a minority, but in the second sense there is a becoming-woman of all, a becoming-woman that is a potentiality for all, and women have to become-woman no less than men themselves. This is a universal becoming-minoritarian. Here *minority* designates the capacity for becoming, while *majority* designates the power or incapacity of a state, of a situation. It is here that theater or art can spring up with a specific political function, on condition that minority does not represent anything regionalist, but also nothing aristocratic, aesthetic, or mystical.

Theater will spring up as that which represents nothing, but which presents and constitutes a consciousness of minority, as becoming-universal, operating alliances here or there as the case may be, following lines of transformation that leap outside the theater and take another form or that reconvert themselves into theater in order to prepare a new leap. It is very much a question of awareness, although it has nothing to do with a psychoanalytic consciousness, nor with a Marxist or even a Brechtian political consciousness. Consciousness, awareness, is a great capacity, but it is not made for solutions or for interpretations. It is when consciousness has abandoned solutions and interpretations that it conquers its light, its gestures, its sounds, and its decisive transformation. Henry James writes: "She had finished by coming to know the extent to which she could no longer interpret anything; there were no more darknesses that would enable her to see clearly, there remained nothing but a cruel light." The more one achieves this form of minority consciousness, the less one feels alone. Light. One is a mass all to oneself, "the mass of my atoms." And beneath the ambition of formulas, there is the more modest appreciation of what could be a revolutionary theater, a simple, loving potentiality, a component for a new becoming of consciousness.

Trans. Alan Orenstein

Part Five

. . .

Politics

26
· · ·
On the Line

Whether we are individuals or groups, we are made up of lines and these lines are very varied in nature. The first kind of line which forms us is segmentary—of rigid segmentarity (or rather there are already many lines of this sort): family—profession; job—holiday; family—and then school— and then the army—and then the factory—and then retirement. And each time, from one segment to the next, they speak to us, saying: "Now you're not a baby any more"; and at school, "You're not at home now"; and in the army, "You're not at school now." . . . In short, all kinds of clearly defined segments, in all kinds of directions, which cut us up in all sense, packets of segmentarized lines. At the same time, we have lines of segmentarity which are much more supple, as it were molecular. It's not that they are more inti- mate or personal—they run through societies and groups as much as indi- viduals. They trace out little modifications, they make detours, they sketch out rises and falls: but they are no less precise for all this, they even direct irreversible processes. But rather than molar lines with segments, they are molecular fluxes with thresholds or quanta. *A threshold is crossed, which does not necessarily coincide with a segment of more visible lines*. Many things happen on this second kind of line—becomings, micro-becomings, which don't even have the same rhythm as our "history." This is why family histories, regis- trations, commemorations, are so unpleasant, whilst our true changes take place elsewhere—another politics, another time, another individuation. A profession is a rigid segment, but also what happens beneath it, the connections, the attractions and repulsions, which do not coincide with the segments, the forms of madness which are secret but which nevertheless relate to the public authorities: for example, being a teacher, or a judge, a barrister, an accountant, a cleaning lady? At the same time, again, there is a third kind of line, which is even more strange: as if something carried us away, across our segments, but also across our thresholds, toward a destination which is unknown, not foreseeable, not preexistent. This line is simple, abstract, and yet is the most complex of all, the most tortuous: it is the line of gravity or velocity, the line of flight and of the greatest gradient ("the line that the center of gravity must describe is certainly very simple, and, so he believed, straight in the majority of cases. . . but, from another point of view, this line has something exceedingly mysterious, for, according to him, it is nothing other than the progression of the soul of the dancer. . ."[1]). This line appears to arise [surgir] afterwards, to become detached from the two others, if indeed it succeeds in detaching itself. For perhaps there are people who do not have this line, who have only the two others, or who have only one, who live on only one. Nevertheless, in another sense, this line has always been there, although it is the opposite of a destiny: it does not have to detach itself from the others, rather it is the first, the others are derived from it. In any case, the three lines are immanent, caught up in one another. We have as many tangled lines as a hand. We are complicated in a different way from a hand. What we call by different names—schizoanalysis, micropolitics, pragmatics, diagrammatism, rhizomatics, cartography—has no other object than the study of these lines, in groups or as individuals.

Fitzgerald explains, in a wonderful short story, that a life always goes at several rhythms, at several speeds.[2] Though Fitzgerald is a living drama—defining life as a demolition process—his text is somber, but no less exemplary for that, each sentence inspiring love. His genius is never so great as when he speaks of his loss of genius. Thus, he says that for him there were at first great segments—rich-poor, young-old, success–loss of success, health-sickness, love–love's drying up, creativity-sterility—which were related to social events (economic crisis, stock market crash, rise of the cinema which replaced the novel, formation of fascism, all sorts of things which could be said to be heterogeneous, but whose segments respond to and precipitate each other). Fitzgerald calls these "cuts" [coupures]; each segment marks or can mark a cut. This is a type of line, the segmented line, which concerns us all at a particular time, at a particular place. Whether it heads towards degradation or success does not alter much (on this model a successful life is not the best, the American Dream is as much in the street sweeper starting out to become a multimillionaire as in the multimillionaire himself, the opposite; the same segments). And Fitzgerald says something else, at the same time: there are lines of crack [*fêlure*], which do not coincide with the lines of great segmentary cuts. This time we might say that a plate cracks. But it is rather when everything is going well, or everything goes better on the other line, that the crack happens on this new line—secret, imperceptible, marking a threshold of lowered resistance, or the rise of a threshold of exigency: you can no longer stand what you put up with before, even yesterday; the distribution of desires has changed in us, our relationships of speed and slowness have been modified, a new type of anxiety comes upon us, but also a new serenity. Fluxes have moved, it is when your health is at its best, your riches most assured, your talent most manifest, that the little cracking which will move the line obliquely starts to happen. Or the opposite: things go better for you when everything cracks on the other line, producing immense relief. Not being able to bear something any longer can be a progression, but it can also be an old man's fear, or the development of a paranoia. It can be a political or affective appraisal that is perfectly correct. We do not change, we do not age, in the same way—from one line to the other. Nevertheless, the supple line is not more personal, more intimate. Microcracks are also collective, no less than macrocuts are personal. And then, Fitzgerald speaks of yet another line, a third, which he calls *rupture*. It might be thought that nothing has changed, and nevertheless everything has changed. Certainly it is not the great segments, changes, or even journeys that produce this line; but neither is it the most secret mutations, the mobile and fluent thresholds, although these approximate more closely to it. It might be said rather than an "absolute" threshold has been reached. There are no longer secrets. You have become like everyone, but in fact you have turned the "everyone" into a *becoming*. You have become imperceptible, clandestine. You have undergone a curious stationary journey. Despite the different tones, it is a little like the way in which Kierkegaard describes the knight of the faith, ONLY MOVEMENTS CONCERN ME:[3] the knight no longer has segments of resignation, but neither does he have the suppleness of a poet or of a dancer, he does not make himself obvious, he resembles rather a bourgeois, a taxcollector, a tradesman, he dances with so much precision that they say that he is only walking or even staying still, he blends into the wall but the wall has become alive, he is painted gray on gray, or like the Pink Panther he has painted the world in his own color, he has acquired something invulnerable, and he knows that by loving, even by loving and for loving, one must be self-contained, abandon love and the ego. . . (it is curious that Lawrence has written similar passages). There is now only an abstract line, a pure movement which is difficult to discover, he never begins, he takes things by the middle, he is always in the middle—in the middle of two other lines? "Only movements concern me."

A cartography is suggested today by Deligny when he follows the course of autistic children: the lines of custom, and also the supple lines where the child produces a loop, finds something, claps his hands, hums a ritornello, retraces his steps, and then the "lines of wandering" mixed up in the two others.[4] All these lines are tangled. Deligny produces a geoanalysis, an analysis of lines which takes his path far from psychoanalysis, and which relates not only to autistic children, but to all children, to all adults (watch someone walking down the street and see what little inventions he introduces into it, if he is not too caught up in his rigid segmentarity, what little inventions he puts there), and not only their walk, but their gestures, their affects, their language, their style. First of all, we should give a more precise status to the three lines. For the molar lines of rigid segmentarity, we can indicate a certain number of characteristics which explain their assemblage, or rather their functioning in the assemblages of which they form part (and there is no assemblage which does not include them). Here therefore are the approximate characteristics of the first kind of line.

1. Segments depend on binary machines which can be very varied if need be. Binary machines of social classes; of sexes, man-woman; of ages, child-adult; of races, black-white; of sectors, public-private; of subjectivations, ours–not ours. These binary machines are all the more complex for cutting across each other, or colliding against each other, confronting each other, and they cut us up in all sorts of directions. And they are not roughly dualistic, they are rather dichotomic: they can operate diachronically (if you are neither a nor b, then you are c: dualism has shifted, and no longer relates to simultaneous elements to choose between, but successive choices; if you are neither black nor white, you are a half-breed; if you are neither man nor woman, you are a transvestite: each time the machine with binary elements will produce binary choices between elements which are not present at the first cutting-up).

2. Segments also imply devices of power, which vary greatly among themselves, each fixing the code and the territory of the corresponding segment. These are the devices which have been analyzed so profoundly by Foucault, who refused to see in them the simple emanations of a pre-existing State apparatus. Each device of power is a code-territory complex (do not approach my territory, it is I who give the orders here. . .). M. de Charlus collapses at Mme Verdurin's, because he has ventured beyond his own territory and his code no longer works. The segmentarity of adjacent offices in Kafka. It is by discovering this segmentarity and this heterogeneity of modern powers that Foucault was able to break

with the hollow abstractions of the State and of "the" law and renew all the assumptions of political analysis. It is not that the apparatus of the State has no meaning: it has itself a very special function, inasmuch as it overcodes all the segments, both those that it takes on itself at a given moment and those that it leaves outside itself. Or rather the apparatus of the State is a concrete assemblage which realizes the machine of over-coding of a society. This machine in its turn is thus not the State itself, it is the abstract machine which organizes the dominant utterances and the established order of a society, the dominant languages and knowledge, conformist actions and feelings, the segments which prevail over the others. The abstract machine of overcoding ensures the homogenization of different segments, their convertibility, their translatability, it regulates the passages from one side to the other, and the prevailing force under which this takes place. It does not depend on the State, but its effectiveness depends on the State as the assemblage which realizes it in a social field (for example, different monetary segments, different kinds of money have rules of convertibility, between themselves and with goods, which refer to a central bank as State apparatus). Greek geometry functioned as an abstract machine which organized the social space, in the conditions of the concrete assemblage of power of the city. We should ask today which are the abstract machines of overcoding, which are exercised as a result of the forms of the modern State. One can even conceive of "forms of knowledge" which make their offers of service to the State, proposing themselves for its realization, claiming to provide the best machines for the tasks or the aims of the State: today informatics? But also the human sciences? There are no sciences of the State but there are abstract machines which have relationships of interdependence with the State. This is why, on the line of rigid segmentarity, one must distinguish the *devices of power* which code the diverse segments, the *abstract machine* which overcodes them and regulates their relationships and the *apparatus of the State* which realizes this machine.

3. Finally, all rigid segmentarity, all the lines of rigid segmentarity, enclose a certain plane, which concerns both forms and their development, subjects and their formation. *A plane of organization* which always has at its disposal a supplementary dimension (overcoding). The education of the subject and the harmonization of the form have constantly haunted our culture, inspired the segmentations, the planifications, the binary machines which cut them and the abstract machines which cut them again. As Pierre Fleutiaux says, when an outline begins to tremble, when a segment wavers, we call the terrible Lunette to cut things up, the laser which puts forms in order and subjects in their place.[5]

The status of the other type of lines seems to be completely different. The segments here are not the same, proceeding by thresholds, constituting becomings, blocs of becoming, marking continuums of intensity, combinations of fluxes. The abstract machines here are not the same, they are mutating and not overcoding, marking their mutations at each threshold and each combination. The plane is not the same *plane of consistence or of immanence*, which tears from forms particles between which there are now only relationships of speed and slowness, and tears from subjects affects which now only carry out individuations by "haecceity." The binary machines no longer engage with this real, not because the dominant segment would change (a particular class, a particular sex . . .), nor because mixtures like bisexuality or class-mixing would be imposed: on the contrary, because the molecular lines make fluxes of deterritorialization shoot between the segments, fluxes which no longer belong to one or to the other, but which constitute an asymmetrical becoming of the two, molecular sexuality which is no longer that of a man or of a woman, molecular masses which no longer have the outline of a class, molecular races like little lines which no longer respond to the great molar oppositions. It is certainly no longer a matter of a synthesis of the two, of a synthesis of 1 and 2, but of a third which always comes from elsewhere and disturbs the binarity of the two, not so much inserting itself in their opposition as in their complementarity. It is not a matter of adding a new segment onto the preceding segments on the line (a third sex, a third class, a third age), but of tracing another line in the middle of the segmentary line, in the middle of the segments, which carries them off according to the variable speeds and slownesses in a movement of flight or of flux. To continue the use of geographical terms: imagine that between *the West and the East* a certain segmentarity is introduced, opposed in a binary machine, arranged in the State apparatuses, overcoded by an abstract machine as the sketch of a world order. It is then from *North to South* that the destabilization takes place, as Giscard d'Estaing said gloomily, and a stream erodes a path, even if it is a shallow stream, which brings everything into play and diverts the plane of organization. A Corsican here, elsewhere a Palestinian, a plane hijacker, a tribal upsurge, a feminist movement, a Green ecologist, a Russian dissident—there will always be someone to rise up to the South. Imagine the Greeks and the Trojans as two opposed segments, face to face: but look, the Amazons arrive, they begin by overthrowing the Trojans, so that the Greeks cry, "The Amazons are with us," but they turn against the Greeks, attacking them from behind with the violence of a torrent. This is how Kleist's *Penthesilea* begins. The great ruptures, the great oppositions, are always negotiable; but not the little crack, the imperceptible ruptures which come from the South. We say *South* without attaching any importance to this. We talk of the South in order to mark a direction different from that of the line of segments. But everyone has his South—it doesn't matter where it is—that is, his line of slope or flight. Nations, classes, sexes have their South. Godard: what counts is not merely the two opposed camps on the great line where they confront each other, but also the frontier, through which everything passes and shoots on a broken molecular line of a different orientation. May 1968 was an explosion of such a molecular line, an irruption of the Amazons, a frontier which traced its unexpected line, drawing along the segments like torn-off blocs which have lost their bearings.

We may be criticized for not escaping from dualism, with two kinds of lines, which are cut up, planified, machined, differently. But what defines dualism is not the number of terms, any more than one escapes from dualism by adding other terms ($\times$ 2). You only escape dualisms effectively by shifting them like a load, and when you find between the terms, whether they are two or more, a narrow gorge like a border or a frontier which will turn the set into a multiplicity, independently of the number of parts. What we call an assemblage is, precisely, a multiplicity. Now, any assemblage necessarily includes lines of rigid and binary segmentarity, no less than molecular lines, or lines of border, of flight or slope. The devices of power do not seem to us to be exactly constitutive of assemblages, but to form part of them in one dimension on which the whole assemblage can topple over or turn back on itself. But, in fact, insofar as dualisms belong to this dimension, there is another dimension of the assemblage which does not form a dualism with this latter. There is no dualism between abstract overcoding machines and abstract machines of mutation: the latter find themselves segmentarized, organized, overcoded by the others, at the same time as they undermine them; both work within each other at the heart of the assemblage. In the same way there is no dualism between the two planes of transcendent organization and immanent consistence: indeed it is from the forms and subjects of the first plane that the second constantly tears the particles between which there are no longer relationships of speed and slowness, and it is also on the plane of immanence that the other arises, working in it to block movements, fix affects, organize forms and subjects. The speed indicators presuppose forms that they dissolve, no less than the organizations presuppose the material in fusion which they put in order. We do not therefore speak of a dualism between two kinds of "things," but of a multiplicity of dimensions, of lines and directions in the heart of an assemblage. To the question "How can desire desire its own repression, how can it desire its slavery?" we reply that the powers which crush desire, or which subjugate it, themselves already form part of assemblages of desire: it is sufficient for desire to follow this particular line, for it to find itself caught, like a boat, under this particular wind. There is no desire *for* revolution, as there is no desire *for* power, desire *to* oppress or *to* be oppressed; but revolution, oppression, power, etc., are the actual component lines of a given assemblage. It is not that these lines are preexistent; they are traced out, they are formed, immanent to each other, mixed up in each other, at the same time as the assemblage of desire is formed, with its machines tangled up and its planes intersecting. We don't know in advance which one will function as line of gradient, or in what form it will be barred. This is true of a musical assemblage, for example: with its codes and territorialities, its constraints and its apparatuses of power, its dichotomized measures, its melodic and harmonic forms which are developed, its transcendent plane of organization, but also with its transformers of speed between sound molecules, its "nonpulsed time," its proliferations and dissolutions, its child-becomings, woman-becomings, animal-becomings, its immanent plane of consistence. The long-term role of the power of the Church, in musical assemblages, and what the musicians succeed in making pass into this, or into the middle. This is true of all assemblages.

What must be compared in each case are the movements of deterritorialization and the processes of reterritorialization which appear in an assemblage. But what do they mean, these words which Félix invents to make them into variable coefficients? We could go back to the commonplaces of the evolution of humanity: man, *deterritorialized animal*. When they say to us that the hominoid removed its front paws from the earth and that the hand is at first locomotor, then prehensile, these are thresholds or the quanta of deterritorialization, but each time with a complementary reterritorialization: the locomotor hand as the deterritorialized paw is reterritorialized on the branches which it uses to pass from tree to tree; the prehensile hand as deterritorialized locomotion is reterritorialized on the torn-off, borrowed elements called tools that it will brandish or propel. But the "stick" tool is itself a deterritorialized branch; and the great inventions of man imply a passage to the steppe as deterritorialized forest; at the same time man is reterritorialized on the steppe. The breast is said to be a mammary gland deterritorialized by vertical stature; and the mouth a deterritorialized animal mouth, by the turning-up of the mucous membranes to the exterior: but a correlative reterritorialization is carried out of the lips onto the breast and conversely, so that the bodies and the environments are traversed by very different speeds of deterritorialization, by differential speeds, whose complementarities form continuums of intensity, but also give rise to processes of reterritorialization. At the limit, it is the earth itself, the deterritorialized ("the desert grows . . ."), and it is the nomad, the man of earth, the man of deterritorialization—although he is also the one who does not move, who remains attached to the environment, desert, or steppe. But it is in concrete social fields, at specific moments, that the comparative movements of deterritorialization, the continuums of intensity and the combinations of flux that they form must be studied. We take some examples from around the eleventh century: the movement of flight of monetary masses; the great deterritorialization of peasant masses under the pressure of the latest invasions and the increased demands of the lords; the deterritorialization of the masses of the nobility, which takes forms as varied as the Crusades, settlement in towns, the new types of exploitation of the earth (renting or wage labor); the new forms of towns, whose installations become less and less territorial; the deterritorialization of the Church, with the dispossession of its lands, its "peace of God," its organization of Crusades; the deterritorialization of woman with chivalric love and then courtly love. The Crusades (including the Children's Crusade) may appear as a threshold of combination of all these movements. One might say in a certain sense that what is primary in a society are the lines, the movements of flight. For, far from being a flight from the social, far from being utopian or even ideological, these constitute the social field, trace out its gradation and its boundaries, the whole of its becoming. A Marxist can be quickly recognized when he says that a society contradicts itself, is defined by its contradictions, and in particular by its class contradictions. We would rather say that, in a society, everything flees and that a society is defined by its lines of flight which affect masses of all kinds (here again, "mass" is a molecular notion). A society, but also a collective assemblage, is defined first by its points of deterritorialization, its fluxes of deterritorialization. The great geographical adventures of history are lines of flight, that is, long expeditions on foot, on horseback or by boat: that of the Hebrews in the desert, that of Genseric the Vandal crossing the Mediterranean, that of the nomads across the steppe, the long march of the Chinese—it is always on a line of flight that we create, not, indeed, because we imagine that we are dreaming but, on the contrary, because we trace out the real on it, we compose there a plane of consistency. To flee, but in fleeing to seek a weapon.

This primacy of lines of flight must not be understood chronologically, or in the sense of an eternal generality. It is rather the fact and the right of the untimely: a time which is not pulsed, a haecceity like a wind which blows up, a midnight, a midday. For reterritorializations happen at the same time: monetary ones on new circuits; rural ones on new modes of exploitation; urban ones on new functions, etc. To the extent that an accumulation of all these reterritorializations takes place, a "class" then emerges which benefits particularly from it, capable of homogenizing it and overcoding all its segments. At the limit it would be necessary to distinguish the movements of masses of all kinds, with their respective coefficients of speed, and the stabilizations of classes, with their segments distributed in the reterritorialization of the whole—the same thing acting as mass and as class, but on two different lines which are entangled, with contours which do not coincide. One is then better able to understand why we sometimes say that there are at least three different lines, sometimes only two, sometimes only one which is very muddled. Sometimes three lines because the line of flight or rupture combines all the movements of deterritorialization, precipitates their quanta, tears from them the accelerated particles which come into contact with one another, carries them onto a plane of consistence or a mutating machine; and then a second, molecular line where the deterritorializations are merely relative, always compensated by reterritorializations which impose on them so many loops, detours, of equilibrium and stabilization; finally the molar line with clearly determined segments, where the reterritorializations accumulate to form a plane of organization and pass into an overcoding machine. Three lines, one of which would be like the nomadic line, another migrant and the third sedentary (the migrant is not at all the same as the nomadic). Or else there would be only two lines, because the molecular line would appear only to be oscillating between the two extremes, sometimes carried along by the combination of fluxes of deterritorialization, sometimes brought back to the accumulation of reterritorializations (the migrant sometimes allies with the nomad, sometimes is a mercenary or the federate of an empire: the Ostrogoths and Visigoths). Or else there is only one line, the primary line of flight, of border or frontier, which is relativized in the second line, which allows itself to be stopped or cut in the third. But even then it may be convenient to present THE line as being born from the explosion of the two others. Nothing is more complicated than the line or the lines—it is that which Melville speaks of, uniting the boats in their organized segmentarity, Captain Ahab in his animal-and-molecular-becoming, the white whale in its crazy flight. Let us go back to the regimes of signs about which we spoke earlier: how the line of flight is barred under a despotic regime, affected by a negative sign; how it finds in the Hebrews' regime a positive but relative value, cut up into successive processes. . . . These were two cases only, briefly outlined, and there are many others: each time it is the essential element of politics. Politics is active experimentation, since we do not know in advance which way a line is going to turn. Draw the line, says the accountant: but one can in fact draw it *anywhere*.

27
. . .
Capitalism

The subjectifications, conjunctions, and appropriations do not prevent the decoded flows from continuing to flow, and from ceaselessly engendering new flows that escape (we saw this, for example, at the level of a micropolitics of the Middle Ages). This is where there is an ambiguity in these apparatuses: they can only function with decoded flows, and yet they do not let them stream together; they perform topical conjunctions that stand as so many knots or recodings. This accounts for the historians' impression that capitalism "could have" developed beginning at a certain moment, in China, in Rome, in Byzantium, in the Middle Ages, that the conditions for it existed but were not effectuated or even capable of being effectuated. The situation is that the pressure of the flows draws capitalism in negative outline, but for it to be realized there must be a whole *integral of decoded flows*, a whole *generalized conjunction* that overspills and overturns the preceding apparatuses. And in fact when Marx sets about defining capitalism, he begins by invoking the advent of a single unqualified and global subjectivity, which capitalizes all of the processes of subjectification, "all activities without distinction": "productive activity in general," "the sole subjective essence of wealth. . . ." And this single subject now expresses itself in an object in general, no longer in this or that qualitative state: "Along with the abstract universality of wealth-creating activity we have now the universality of the object defined as wealth, viz. the product in general, or labor in general, but as past, materialized labor."[1] Circulation constitutes capital as a subjectivity commensurate with society in its entirety. But this new social subjectivity can form only to the extent that the decoded flows overspill their conjunctions and attain a level of decoding that the State apparatuses are no longer able to reclaim: *on the one hand,* the flow of labor must no longer be determined as slavery or serfdom but must become naked and free labor; and *on the other hand,* wealth must no longer be determined as money dealing, merchant's or landed wealth, but must become pure homogeneous and independent capital. And doubtless, these two becomings at least (for other flows also converge) introduce many contingencies and many different factors on each of the lines. But it is their abstract conjunction in a single stroke that constitutes capitalism, providing a universal subject and object in general for one another. Capitalism forms when the flow of unqualified wealth encounters the flow of unqualified labor and conjugates with it.[2] This is what the preceding conjunctions, which were still topical or qualitative, had always inhibited (the two principal inhibitors were the feudal organization of the countryside and the corporative organization of the towns). This amounts to saying that capitalism forms with *a general axiomatic of decoded flows.* "Capital is a right, or, to be more precise, a relation of production that is manifested as a right, and as such it is independent of the concrete form that it cloaks at each moment of its productive function."[3] Private property no longer expresses the bond of personal dependence but the independence of a subject that now constitutes the sole bond. This makes for an important difference in the evolution of private property: private property in itself relates to rights, instead of the law relating it to the land, things, or people (this raises in particular the famous question of the elimination of ground rent in capitalism). *A new threshold of deterritorialization.* And when capital becomes an active right in this way, the entire historical figure of the law changes. The law ceases to be the overcoding of customs, as it was in the archaic empire; it is no longer a set of topics, as it was in the evolved States, the autonomous cities, and the feudal systems; it increasingly assumes the direct form and immediate characteristics of an axiomatic, as evidenced in our civil "code."[4]

When the flows reach this capitalist threshold of decoding and deterritorialization (naked labor, independent capital), it seems that there is no longer a need for a State, for distinct juridical and political domination, in order to ensure appropriation, which has become directly economic. The economy constitutes a worldwide axiomatic, a "universal cosmopolitan energy which overflows every restriction and bond,"[5] a mobile and convertible substance "such as the total value of annual production." Today we can depict an enormous, so-called stateless, monetary mass that circulates through foreign exchange and across borders, eluding control by the States, forming a multinational ecumenical organization, constituting a de facto supranational power untouched by governmental decisions.[6] But whatever dimensions or quantities this may have assumed today, capitalism has from the beginning mobilized a force of deterritorialization infinitely surpassing the deterritorialization proper to the State. For since Paleolithic and Neolithic times, the State has been deterritorializing to the extent that it makes the earth an *object* of its higher unity, a forced aggregate of coexistence, instead of the free play of territories among themselves and with the lineages. But this is precisely the sense in which the State is termed "territorial." Capitalism, on the other hand, is not at all territorial, even in its beginnings: its power of deterritorialization consists in taking as its object, not the earth, but "materialized labor," the commodity. And private property is no longer ownership of the land or the soil, nor even of the means of production as such, but of convertible abstract rights.[7] That is why capitalism marks a mutation in worldwide or ecumenical organizations, which now take on a consistency of their own: the worldwide axiomatic, instead of resulting from heterogeneous social formations and their relations, for the most part distributes these formations, determines their relations, while organizing an international division of labor. From all these standpoints, it could be said that capitalism develops an economic order that could do without the State. And in fact capitalism is not short on war cries against the State, not only in the name of the market, but by virtue of its superior deterritorialization.

This however, is only one very partial aspect of capital. If it is true that we are not using the word *axiomatic* as a simple metaphor, we must review what distinguishes an axiomatic from all manner of codes, overcodings, and recordings: the axiomatic deals directly with purely functional elements and relations whose nature is not specified, and which are immediately realized in highly varied domains simultaneously; codes, on the other hand, are relative to those domains and express specific relations between qualified elements that cannot be subsumed by a higher formal unity (overcoding) except by transcendence and in an indirect fashion. The *immanent axiomatic* finds in the domains it moves through so many models, termed *models of realization*. It could similarly be said that capital as right, as a "qualitatively homogeneous and quantitatively commensurable element," is realized in sectors and means of production (or that "unified capital" is realized in "differentiated capital"). However, the different sectors are not alone in serving as models of realization—*the States* do too. Each of them groups together and combines several sectors, according to its resources, population, wealth, industrial capacity, etc. Thus the States, in capitalism, are not canceled out but change form and take on a new meaning: models of realization for a worldwide axiomatic that exceeds them. But to exceed is not at all the same thing as doing without. We have already seen that capitalism proceeds by way of the State-form rather than the town-form; the basis for the fundamental mechanisms described by Marx (the colonial regime, the public debt, the modern tax system and indirect taxation, industrial protectionism, trade wars) may be laid in the towns, but the towns function as mechanisms of accumulation, acceleration, and concentration only to the extent they are appropriated by States. Recent events tend to confirm this principle from another angle. For example, NASA appeared ready to mobilize considerable capital for interplanetary exploration, as though capitalism were riding a vector taking it to the moon; but following the USSR, which conceived of extraterrestrial space as a belt that should circle the earth taken as the "object," the American government cut off funds for exploration and returned capital in this case to a more centered model. It is thus proper to State deterritorialization to moderate the superior deterritorialization of capital and to provide the latter with compensatory reterritorializations. More generally, this extreme example aside, we must take into account a "materialist" determination of the modern State or nation-state: a group of producers in which labor and capital circulate freely, in other words, in which the homogeneity and competition of capital is effectuated, in principle without external obstacles. In order to be effectuated, capitalism has always required there to be a new force and a new law of States, on the level of the flow of labor as on the level of the flow of independent capital.

So States are not at all transcendent paradigms of an overcoding but immanent models of realization for an axiomatic of decoded flows. Once again, our use of the word *axiomatic* is far from a metaphor; we find literally the same theoretical problems that are posed by the models in an axiomatic repeated in relation to the State. For models of realization, though varied, are supposed to be *isomorphic* with regard to the axiomatic they effectuate; however, this isomorphy, concrete variations considered, accommodates itself to the greatest of formal differences. Moreover, a single axiomatic seems capable of encompassing polymorphic models, not only when it is not yet "saturated," but with those models as integral elements of its saturation.[8] These "problems become singularly political when we think of modern States.

1. Are not all modern States isomorphic in relation to the capitalist axiomatic, to the point that the difference between democratic, totalitarian, liberal, and tyrannical States depends only on concrete vari-

ables, and on the worldwide distribution of those variables, which always undergo eventual readjustments? Even the so-called socialist States are isomorphic, to the extent that there is *only one world market,* the capitalist one.

2. Conversely, does not the world capitalist axiomatic tolerate a real polymorphy, or even a heteromorphy, of models, and for two reasons? On the one hand, capital as a general relation of production can very easily integrate concrete sectors or modes of production that are noncapitalist. But on the other hand, and this is the main point, the bureaucratic socialist States can themselves develop different modes of production that only conjugate with capitalism to form a set whose "power" exceeds that of the axiomatic itself (it will be necessary to try to determine the nature of this power, why we so often think of it in apocalyptic terms, what conflicts it spawns, what slim chances it leaves us. . .).

3. A typology of modern States is thus coupled with a metaeconomics: it would be inaccurate to treat all States as "interchangeable" (even isomorphy does not have that consequence), but it would be no less inaccurate to privilege a certain form of the State (forgetting that polymorphy establishes strict complementarities between the Western democracies and the colonial or neocolonial tyrannies that they install or support in other regions), or to equate the bureaucratic socialist States with the totalitarian capitalist States (neglecting the fact that the axiomatic can encompass a real heteromorphy from which the higher power of the aggregate derives, even if it is for the worse).

What is called a nation-state, in the most diverse forms, is precisely the State as a model of realization. And the birth of nations implies many artifices: Not only are they constituted in an active struggle against the imperial or evolved systems, the feudal systems, and the autonomous cities, but they crush their own "minorities," in other words, minoritarian phenomena that could be termed "nationalitarian," which work from within and if need be turn to the old codes to find a greater degree of freedom. The constituents of the nation are a land and a people: the "natal," which is not necessarily innate, and the "popular," which is not necessarily pregiven. The problem of the nation is aggravated in the two extreme cases of a land without a people and a people without a land. How can a people and a land be made, in other words, a nation—a refrain? The coldest and bloodiest means vie with upsurges of romanticism. The axiomatic is complex, and is not without passions. The natal or the land, as we have seen elsewhere, implies a certain deterritorialization of the territories (community land, imperial provinces, seigneurial domains, etc.), and the people, a decoding of the population. The nation is constituted on the basis of these flows and is inseparable from the modern State that gives consistency to the corresponding land and people. It is the flow of naked labor that makes the people, just as it is the flow of capital that makes the land and its industrial base. In short, the nation is the very operation of a collective subjectification, to which the modern State corresponds as a process of subjection. It is in the form of the nation-state, with all its possible variations, that the State becomes the model of realization for the capitalist axiomatic. This is not at all to say that nations are appearances or ideological phenomena; on the contrary, they are the passional and living forms in which the qualitative homogeneity and the quantitative competition of abstract capital are first realized.

We distinguish *machinic enslavement* and *social subjection* as two separate concepts. There is enslavement when human beings themselves are constituent pieces of a machine that they compose among themselves and with other things (animals, tools), under the control and direction of a higher unity. But there is subjection when the higher unity constitutes the human being as a subject linked to a now exterior object, which can be an animal, a tool, or even a machine. The human being is no longer a component of the machine but a worker, a user. He or she is subjected *to* the machine and no longer enslaved *by* the machine. This is not to say that the second regime is more human. But the first regime does seem to have a special relation to the archaic imperial formation: human beings are not subjects but pieces of a machine that overcodes the aggregate (this has been called "generalized slavery," as opposed to the private slavery of antiquity, or feudal serfdom). We believe that Lewis Mumford is right in designating the archaic empires megamachines, and in pointing out that, once again, it is not a question of a metaphor: "If a machine can be defined more or less in accord with the classic definition of Reuleaux, as a combination of resistant parts, each specialized in function, operating under human control to transmit motion and to perform work, then the *human machine* was a real machine."[9] Of course, it was the modern State and capitalism that brought the triumph of machines, in particular of motorized machines (whereas the archaic State had simple machines at best); but what we are referring to now are *technical machines*, which are definable extrinsically. One is not enslaved by the technical machine but rather subjected to it. It would appear, then, that the modern State, through technological development, has substituted an increasingly powerful social subjection for machinic enslavement. Ancient slavery and feudal serfdom were already procedures of subjection. But the naked or "free" worker of capitalism takes subjection to its most radical expression, since the process of subjectification no longer even enter into partial conjunctions that interrupt the flow. In effect, capital acts as the point of subjectification that constitutes all human beings as subjects; but some, the "capitalists," are subjects of enunciation that form the private subjectivity of capital, while the others, the "proletarians," are subjects of the statement, subjected to the technical machines in which constant capital is effectuated. The wage regime can therefore take the subjection of human beings to an unprecedented point, and exhibit a singular cruelty, yet still be justified in its humanist cry: No, human beings are not machines, we don't treat them like machines, we certainly don't confuse variable capital and constant capital. . . .

Capitalism arises as a worldwide enterprise of subjectification by constituting an axiomatic of decoded flows. Social subjection, as the correlate of subjectification, appears much more in the axiomatic's models of realization than in the axiomatic itself. It is within the framework of the nation-state, or of national subjectivities, that processes of subjectification and the corresponding subjections are manifested. The axiomatic itself, of which the States are models of realization, restores or reinvents, in new and now technical forms, an entire system of machinic enslavement. This is no way represents a return to the imperial machine since we are now in the immanence of an axiomatic, and not under the transcendence of a formal unity. But it is the reinvention of a machine of which human beings are constituent parts, instead of subjected workers or users. If motorized machines constituted the second age of the technical machine, cybernetic and informational machines form a third age that reconstructs a generalized regime of subjection: recurrent and reversible "humans-machines systems" replace the old nonrecurrent and nonreversible relations of subjection between the two elements; the relation between human and machine is based on internal, mutual communication, and no longer on usage or action.[10] In the organic composition of capital, variable capital defines a regime of subjection of the worker (human surplus value), the principal framework of which is the business or factory. But with automation comes a progressive increase in the proportion of constant capital; we then see a new kind of enslavement: at the same time the work regime changes, surplus value becomes machinic, and the framework expands to all of society. It could also be said that a small amount of subjectification took us away from machinic enslavement, but a large amount brings us back to it. Attention has recently been focused on the fact that modern power is not at all reducible to the classical alternative "repression or ideology" but implies processes of normalization, modulation, modeling, and information that bear on language, perception, desire, movement, etc., and which proceed by way of microassemblages. This aggregate includes both subjection and enslavement taken to extremes, as two simultaneous parts that constantly reinforce and nourish each other. For example, one is subjected to TV insofar as one uses and consumes it, in the very particular situation of a subject of the statement that more or less mistakes itself for a subject of enunciation ("you, dear television viewers, who make TV what it is . . ."); the technical machine is the medium between two subjects. But one is enslaved by TV as a human machine insofar as the television viewers are no longer consumers or users, nor even subjects who supposedly "make" it, but intrinsic component pieces, "input" and "output," feedback or recurrences that are no longer connected to the machine in such a way as to produce or use it. In machinic enslavement, there is nothing but transformations and exchanges of information, some of which are mechanical, others human.[11] The term "subjection," of course, should not be confined to the national aspect, with enslavement seen as international or worldwide. For information technology is also the property of the States that set themselves up as humans-machines systems. But this is so precisely to the extent that the two aspects, the axiomatic and the models of realization, constantly cross over into each other and are themselves in communication. Social subjection proportions itself to the model of realization, just as machinic enslavement expands to meet the dimensions of the axiomatic that is effectuated in the model. We have the privilege of undergoing the two operations simultaneously, in relation to the same things and the same events. Rather than stages, subjection and enslavement constitute two coexistent poles.

We may return to the different forms of the State, from the standpoint of a universal history. We distinguish three major forms: (1) imperial archaic States, which are paradigms and constitute a machine of enslavement by overcoding already-coded flows (these States have little diversity, due to a certain formal immutability that applies to all of them); (2) extremely diverse States—evolved empires, autonomous cities, feudal systems, monarchies—which proceed instead by subjectification and subjection, and constitute qualified or topical conjunctions of decoded flows; (3) the modern nation-states, which take decoding even further and are models of realization for an axiomatic or a general conjugation of flows (these States combine social subjection and the new machinic enslavement, and their very diversity is a function of isomorphy, of the eventual heteromorphy or polymorphy of the models in relation to the axiomatic).

There are, of course, all kinds of external circumstances that mark profound breaks between these types of States, and above all submit the archaic empires to utter oblivion, a shrouding lifted only by archaeology. The empires disappeared suddenly, as though in an instantaneous catastrophe. As in the Dorian invasion, a war-machine looms up and bears down from without, killing memory. Yet things proceed quite differently on the inside, where all the States resonate together, appropriate armies for themselves, and exhibit a unity of composition in spite of their differences in organization and development. It is evident that all decoded flows, of whatever kind, are prone to forming a war-machine directed against the State. But everything changes depending on whether these flows connect up with a war-machine or, on the contrary, enter into conjunctions or a general conjugation that appropriates them for the State. From this standpoint, the modern States have a kind of transspatiotemporal unity with the archaic State. The internal correlation between (1) and (2) appears most clearly in the fact that the fragmented forms of the Aegean world presuppose the great imperial form of the Orient and find in it a stock or agricultural surplus, which they consequently have no need to produce or accumulate for themselves. And to the extent that the States of the second age are nevertheless obliged to reconstitute a stock, if only because of external circumstances—what State can do without one?—in so doing they always reactivate an evolved imperial form. We find the revival of this form in the Greek, Roman, and feudal worlds: there is always an empire on the horizon, which for the subjective States plays the role of signifier and encompassing element. And the correlation between (2) and (3) is no less pronounced, for industrial revolutions are not wanting, and the difference between topical conjunctions and the great conjugation of decoded flows is so thin that one is left with the impression that capitalism was continually being born, disappearing and reviving at every crossroads of history. And the correlation between (3) and (1) is also a necessary one: the modern States of the third age do indeed restore the most absolute of empires, a new "megamachine," whatever the novelty or timeliness of its now immanent form; they do this by realizing an axiomatic that functions as much by machinic enslavement as by social subjection. Capitalism has reawakened the *Urstaat*, and given it new strength.[12]

Not only, as Hegel said, does every State imply "the essential moments of its existence as a State," but there is a unique moment, in the sense of a coupling of forces, and this moment of the State is capture, bond, knot, *nexum*, magical capture. Must we speak of a second pole, which would operate instead by pact and contract? Is this not instead that other force, with capture as the unique moment of coupling? For the two forces are the overcoding of coded flows, and the treatment of decoded flows. The contract is a juridical expression of the second aspect: it appears as the proceeding of subjectification, the outcome of which is subjection. And the contract must be pushed to the extreme; in other words, it is no longer concluded between two people but between self and self, within the same person—*Ich = Ich*—as subjected and sovereign. The extreme perversion of the contract, reinstating the purest of knots. The knot, bond, capture, thus travel a long history: first, the objective, imperial collective bond; then all of the forms of subjective personal bonds; finally, the subject that binds itself, and in so doing renews the most magical operation, "a cosmopolitan, universal energy which overflows every restriction and bond so as to establish itself instead as the sole bond."[13] Even subjection is only a relay for the fundamental moment of the State, namely, civil capture or machinic enslavement. The State is assuredly not the locus of liberty, nor the agent of a forced servitude or war capture. Should we then speak of "voluntary servitude"? This is like the expression "magical capture": its only merit is to underline the apparent mystery. There is a machinic enslavement, about which it could be said in each case that it presupposes itself, that it appears as preaccomplished; this machinic enslavement is no more "voluntary" than it is "forced."

28
. . .
The Three Aspects of Culture

Culture means training and selection. Nietzsche calls the movement of culture the "morality of customs" (*D* 9);[1] this latter is inseparable from iron collars, from torture, from the atrocious means which are used to train man. But the genealogist's eye distinguishes two elements in this violent training (*BGE* 188)[2]: (1) That which is obeyed, in a people, race or class, is always historical, arbitrary, grotesque, stupid, and limited; this usually represents the worst *reactive* forces. (2) But in the fact that something, no matter what it is, is obeyed, appears a principle which goes beyond peoples, races, and classes. To obey the law because it is the law: the form of the law means that a certain *activity*, a certain active force, is exercised on man and is given the task of training him. *Even if they are historically inseparable* these two aspects must not be confused: on the one hand, the historical pressure of a State, a Church etc., on the individuals that it aims to assimilate; on the other hand, the activity of man as generic being, the activity of the human species as such. Hence Nietzsche's use of the words *primitive, prehistoric:* the morality of customs *precedes* universal history (*D* 18); culture is generic activity; "the labor performed by man upon himself during the greater part of the existence of the human race, his entire *prehistoric* labor . . . notwithstanding the severity, tyranny, stupidity and idiocy involved in it" (*GM* II 2, p. 59).[3] Every historical law is arbitrary, but what is not arbitrary, what is pre-

historic and generic, is the law of obeying laws. (Bergson will rediscover this
thesis when he shows, in *Les Deux Sources,* that all habits are arbitrary but
that the habit of taking on habits is natural.)

Prehistoric means generic. Culture is man's prehistoric activity. But
what does this activity consist in? It is always a matter of giving man habits,
of making him obey laws, of training him. Training man means forming him
in such a way that he can act his reactive forces. The activity of culture is, in
principle, exercised on reactive forces, it gives them habits and imposes
models on them in order to make them suitable for being acted. Culture as
such is exercised in many directions. It even attacks the reactive forces of
the unconscious and the most subterranean digestive and intestinal forces
(the diet and something analogous to what Freud will call the education
of the sphincters—*EH* II "Why I am so Clever").[4] But its principal object is
to reinforce consciousness. This consciousness which is defined by the fugitive
character of excitations, this consciousness which is itself based on the faculty of forgetting must be given a consistency and a firmness which it does
not have on its own. Culture endows consciousness with a new faculty which
is apparently opposed to the faculty of forgetting: memory. But the memory
with which we are concerned here is not the memory of traces. This original
memory is no longer a function of the past, but a function of the future. It is
not the memory of the sensibility but of the will. It is not the memory of
traces but of words.[5] It is the faculty of promising, commitment to the future, memory of the future itself. Remembering the promise that has been
made is not recalling that it was made at a particular past moment, but that
one must hold to it at a future moment. This is precisely the selective object
of culture: forming a man capable of promising and thus of making use of
the future, a free and powerful man. Only such a man is active; he acts his
reactions, everything in him is active or acted. The faculty of promising is
the effect of culture as the activity of man on man; the man who can promise
is the product of culture as species activity.

We understand why culture does not, in principle, recoil from any kind of
violence: "perhaps indeed there was nothing more fearful and uncanny in
the whole prehistory of man than mnemotechnics. . . . Man could never do
without blood, torture and sacrifices when he felt the need to create a memory for himself" (*GM* II 3, p. 61). How many tortures are necessary in order
to train reactive forces, to constrain them to be acted, before culture reaches
its goal (the free, active, and powerful man). Culture has always used the
following means: it made pain a medium of exchange, a currency, an equivalent; precisely the exact equivalent of a forgetting, of an inquiry caused a
promise not kept (*GM* II 4). Culture, when related to this means, is called
justice; the means itself is called *punishment.* "Inquiry caused = pain

undergone"—this is the equation of punishment that determines a relationship of man to man. This relationship between men is determined, following the equation, as a *relationship of a creditor and a debtor:* justice makes man *responsible for a debt.* The debtor-creditor relationship expresses the activity of culture during the process of training or formation. Corresponding to prehistoric activity this relationship itself is the relationship of man to man, "the most primitive of individuals" preceding even "the origins of any social organization."[6] It also serves as a model "for the crudest and most primitive social constitutions." Nietzsche sees the archetype of social organization in credit rather than exchange. The man who pays for the injury he causes by his pain, the man held responsible for a debt, the man treated as responsible for his reactive forces: these are the means used by culture to reach its goal. Nietzsche therefore offers us the following genetic lineage: (1) Culture as prehistoric or generic activity, an enterprise of training and selection; (2) The means used by this activity, the equation of punishment, the relationship of debt, the responsible man; (3) The product of this activity: the active man, free and powerful, the man who can promise.

Culture Considered from the Posthistoric Point of View

We have posed the problem of bad conscience. The genetic lineage of culture does not seem to get us any nearer a solution. On the contrary: the most obvious conclusion is that neither bad conscience nor *ressentiment* intervene in the process of culture and justice. "The 'bad conscience,' this most uncanny and most interesting plant of all our earthly vegetation, did *not* grow on this soil" (*GM* II 14, p. 82). On the one hand, revenge and *ressentiment* are not the origin of justice. Moralists, even socialist ones, make justice derive from a reactive feeling, from deeply felt offense, a spirit of revenge or justiciary reaction. But such a derivation explains nothing; it would have to show how the pain of others can be a satisfaction of revenge, a reparation for revenge. We will never understand the cruel equation "injury caused = pain undergone" if a third term is not introduced—the pleasure which is felt in inflicting pain or in contemplating it.[7] But this third term, the external meaning of pain, has an origin which is completely different from revenge or reaction: it reflects an active standpoint, active forces, which are given the training of reactive forces as their task and for their pleasure. Justice is the generic activity that trains man's reactive forces, that makes them suitable for being acted and holds man responsible for this suitability itself. To justice we can oppose the way in which *ressentiment* and then bad conscience are formed: by the triumph of reactive forces, through their unsuitability for being acted, through their hatred for everything that is active, through their resistance, through their fundamental injustice. Thus *ressentiment,* far from being at the origin of justice, is "the last sphere to be conquered by the spirit of justice. . . . The active, aggressive, arrogant man is still a hundred steps closer to justice than the reactive man."[8]

Just as *ressentiment* is not the origin of justice so bad conscience is not the product of punishment. However many meanings punishment can have there is always one meaning which it *does not have.* Punishment cannot awaken a feeling of guilt in the culprit.

> It is precisely among criminals and convicts that the sting of conscience is extremely rare; prisons and penitentiaries are *not* the kind of hotbed in which this species of gnawing worm is likely to flourish. . . . Generally speaking, punishment makes men hard and cold; it concentrates; it sharpens the feeling of alienation; it strengthens the power of resistance. If it happens that punishment destroys the vital energy and brings about a miserable prostration and self-abasement, such a result is certainly even less pleasant than the usual effects of punishment—characterized by dry and gloomy seriousness. If we consider those millenia *before* the history of man, we may unhesitantly assert that it was precisely through punishment that the development of the feeling of guilt was most powerfully *hindered*—at least in the victims upon whom the punitive force was vented. (*GM* II 14, pp. 81–82)

We can oppose point by point the state of culture in which man, at the cost of his pain, feels himself responsible for his reactive forces and the state of bad conscience where man, on the contrary, feels himself to blame for his active forces and experiences them as culpable. However we consider culture or justice we always see in them the exercise of a formative activity, the opposite of *ressentiment* and bad conscience.

This impression is further reinforced if we consider the product of cultural activity: the free and active man, the man who can promise. Just as culture is the prehistoric element of man the product of culture is his posthistoric element.

> If we place ourselves at the end of this tremendous process, where the tree at last brings forth fruit, where society and the morality of customs at last reveal *what* they have simply been the means to: then we discover that the ripest fruit is the *sovereign individual,* like only to himself, liberated again from morality of customs, autonomous and supramoral (for "autonomous" and "moral" are mutually exclusive), in short, the man who has his own independent, protracted will and the *right to make promises.* (*GM* II 2, p. 59).

Nietzsche's point is that we must not confuse the product of culture with its means. Man's species activity constitutes him as responsible for his reactive forces: *responsibility-debt*. But this responsibility is only a means of training and selection: it progressively measures the suitability of reactive forces for being acted. The finished product of species activity is *not* the responsible man himself or the moral man, but the autonomous and supramoral man, that is to say, the one who actually acts his reactive forces and in whom all reactive forces are acted. He alone "is able to" promise, precisely because he is no longer responsible to any tribunal. The product of culture is not the man who obeys the law, but the sovereign and legislative individual who defines himself by power over himself, over destiny, over the law: the free, the light, the *irresponsible*. In Nietzsche the notion of responsibility, even in its higher form, has the limited value of a simple means: the autonomous individual is no longer responsible to justice for his reactive forces, he is its master, the sovereign, the legislator, the author, and the actor. It is he who speaks, he no longer has to *answer*. The only active sense of responsibility-debt is its disappearing in the movement by which man is liberated: the creditor is liberated because he participates in the right of the masters, the debtor liberates himself, even at the price of his flesh and his pain: both of them liberate themselves from the process which trained them (*GM* II 5, 13, 21). This is the general movement of culture: the means disappearing in the product. Responsibility as responsibility before the law, law as the law of justice, justice as the means of culture—all this disappears in the product of culture itself. The morality of customs, the spirit of the laws, produces the man emancipated from the law. This is why Nietzsche speaks of a self-destruction of justice.[9] Culture is man's species activity; but, since this activity is selective, it produces the individual as its final goal, where species is itself suppressed.

We have proceeded as if culture goes straight from prehistory to posthistory. We have seen it as a species activity which, through the long labor of prehistory, arrives at the individual as its posthistoric product. And indeed, this is its essence, in conformity to the superiority of active forces over reactive forces. But we have neglected an important point: the triumph, in fact, of inferior and reactive forces. We have neglected *history*. We must say of culture both that it disappeared long ago and that it has not yet begun. Species activity disappears into the night of the past as its product does into the night of the future. In history culture takes on a sense which is very different from its own essence, having been seized by strange forces of a completely different nature. Species activity in history is inseparable from a movement which perverts it and its product. Furthermore, history is this very perversion, it is identical to the "degeneration of culture." Instead of species activity, history presents us with races, peoples, classes, Churches, and States. Onto species activity are grafted social organizations, associations, communities of a *reactive* character, parasites which cover it over and absorb it. By means of species activity—the movement of which they falsify—reactive forces form collectivities, what Nietzsche calls "herds" (*GM* III 18). Instead of justice and its process of self-destruction, history presents us with societies which have no wish to perish and which cannot imagine anything superior to their own laws. What State would listen to Zarathustra's advice: "Let yourself, therefore be overthrown" (*Z* II "Of Great Events")?[10] In history the law becomes confused with the content which determines it, reactive content which provides its ballast and prevents it from disappearing, unless this is to benefit other, even heavier and more stupid, contents. Instead of the sovereign individual as the product of culture, history presents us with its own product, the domesticated man in whom it finds the famous meaning of history: "the sublime abortion," "the gregarious animal, docile, sickly, mediocre being, the European today" (*BGE* 62; *GM* I 11). History presents all the violence of culture as the legitimate property of peoples, States, and Churches, as the manifestation of *their* force. And in fact, all the procedures of training are employed, but inside-out, twisted, inverted. A morality, a Church, a State are still enterprises of selection, theories of hierarchy. The most stupid laws, the most limited communities, still want to train man and make use of his reactive forces. But to make use of them for what? To carry out what training, what selection? Training procedures are used but in order to turn man into a gregarious, docile, and domesticated animal. Training procedures are used but in order to break the strong, to sort out the weak, the suffering or the slaves. Selection and hierarchy are put the wrong way round. Selection becomes the opposite of what is was from the standpoint of activity, it is now only a means of preserving, organising and propagating the reactive life (*GM* III 13–20; *BGE* 62).

History thus appears as the act by which reactive forces take possession of culture or divert its course in their favor. The triumph of reactive forces is not an accident in history but the principle and meaning of "universal history." This idea of a historical degeneration of culture occupies a prominent place in Nietzsche's work: it is an argument in Nietzsche's struggle against the philosophy of history and the dialectic. It is the source of Nietzsche's disappointment: culture begins "Greek" but becomes "German." . . . From the *Untimely Mediations* onward Nietzsche tries to explain how and why culture comes to serve reactive forces which pervert it.[11] More profoundly, Zarathustra develops an obscure symbol: the fire-dog (*Z* II "Of Great Events"). The fire-dog is the image of species activity, it expresses man's relation to the earth. But, in fact, the earth has two sicknesses, man and the fire-dog itself. For man is domesticated man; species activity is deformed, unnatural activity which serves reactive forces, which becomes mixed up with the Church and the State: "'The church?' I answered, 'The church is a kind of State and indeed the most mendacious kind. But keep quiet, you hypocrite dog! You surely know your own kind best! Like you, the state is a hypocrite dog; like you, it likes to speak with smoke and bellowing—to make believe, like you, that it speaks out of the belly of things. For the state wants to be absolutely the most important beast on earth; and it is believed to be so, too!'" (*Z* II "Of Great Events," p. 154). Zarathustra appeals to another fire-dog, "This one really speaks from the heart of the earth." Is this still species activity? But, this time, species activity seized in the element of prehistory, to which man corresponds insofar as he is produced in the element of posthistory? This interpretation must be taken into consideration, even if it is insufficient. In the *Untimely Meditations* Nietzsche was already putting his trust in "the non-historical and suprahistorical element of culture" (what he called the Greek sense of culture (*UM* II 10, 8).[12]

In fact there are a certain number of questions that we cannot yet answer. What is the status of this double element of culture? Is it real? Is it anything but one of Zarathustra's "visions"? Culture is inseparable from the history of the movement that perverts it and puts it at the service of reactive forces; but culture is also inseparable from history itself. The activity of culture, man's species activity: is this not a simple idea? If man is essentially (that is to say generically) a *reactive* being, how could he have, or even have had in prehistory, a species *activity*? How could an active man appear, even in a posthistory? If man is essentially reactive it seems that activity must concern a being different from man. If man, on the contrary, has a species activity, it seems that it can only be deformed in an accidental way. For the moment we can only list Nietzsche's theses, their precise significance must be considered later: man is essentially reactive; there is nevertheless a species activity of man, but one that is necessarily deformed, necessarily missing its goal, leading to the domesticated man; this activity must be taken up again on another plane, the plane on which it produces, but produces something other than man. . . .

It is, however, already possible to explain why species activity necessarily falls in history and turns to the advantage of reactive forces. If the schema of the *Untimely Meditations* is insufficient, Nietzsche's work presents other directions in which a solution can be found. The aim of the activity of culture is to train man, that is to say, to make reactive forces suitable for service, for being acted. But throughout the training this suitability for service remains profoundly ambiguous. For at the same time it allows reactive forces to put themselves at the service of other reactive forces, to give these latter forces an appearance of activity, an appearance of justice, to form with them a fiction that gets the better of active forces. It will be recalled that, in *ressentiment*, certain reactive forces prevent other reactive forces from being acted. Bad conscience reaches the same end by almost opposite means: *in bad conscience some reactive forces make use of their suitability for being acted to give other reactive forces an appearance of acting.* There is no less fiction in this procedure than in the procedure of *ressentiment*. *In this way associations of reactive forces are formed under the cover of species activity.* These associations are grafted onto species activity and necessarily divert it from its real sense. Training provides reactive forces with a marvelous opportunity to go into partnership, to form a collective reaction usurping species activity.

29
. . .
Toward Freedom

The differences do not pass between the individual and the collective, for we see no duality between these two types of problem: there is no subject of enunciation, but every proper name is collective, every assemblage is already collective. Neither do the differences pass between the natural and the artificial since they both belong to the machine and interchange there. Nor between the spontaneous and the organized, since the only question is one of modes of organization. Nor between the segmentary and the centralized, since centralization is itself an organization which rests on a form of rigid segmentarity. The effective differences pass between the lines, even though they are all immanent to one another, all entangled in one another. This is why the question of schizoanalysis or pragmatics, micropolitics itself, never consists in interpreting, but merely in asking what are your lines, individual or group, and what are the dangers on each.

  1. What are your rigid segments, your binary and overcoding machines? For even these are not given to you ready-made, we are not simply divided up by binary machines of class, sex, or age: there are others which we constantly shift, invent without realizing it. And what are the dangers if we blow up these segments too quickly? Wouldn't this kill the organism itself, the organism which possesses its own binary machines, even in its nerves and its brain?

2. What are your supple lines, what are your fluxes and thresholds? Which is your set of relative deterritorializations and correlative reterritorializations? And the distribution of black holes: which are the black holes of each one of us, where a beast lurks or a microfascism thrives?

3. What are your lines of flight, where the fluxes are combined, where the thresholds reach a point of adjacence and rupture? Are they still tolerable, or are they already caught up in a machine of destruction and self-destruction which would reconstitute a molar fascism? It may happen that an assemblage of desire and of enunciation is reduced to its most rigid lines, its devices of power. There are assemblages which have only these sorts of lines. But other dangers stalk each of them, more supple and viscous dangers, of which each of us alone is judge, as long as there is still time. The question "How is it that desire can desire its own repression?" does not give rise to real theoretical difficulty, but to many practical difficulties each time. There is desire as soon as there is a machine or "body without organs." But there are bodies without organs like hardened empty envelopes, because their organic components have been blown up too quickly and too violently, an "overdose." There are bodies without organs which are cancerous and fascist, in black holes or machines of abolition. How can desire outmaneuver all that by managing its plane of immanence and of consistence which each time runs up against these dangers?

There is no general prescription. We have done with all globalizing concepts. Even concepts are haecceities, events. What is interesting about concepts like desire, or machine, or assemblage is that they only have value in their variables, and in the maximum of variables which they allow. We are not for concepts as big as hollow teeth, THE law, THE master, THE rebel. We are not here to keep the tally of the dead and the victims of history, the martyrdom of the Gulags, and to draw the conclusion that "The revolution is impossible, but we thinkers must think the impossible since the impossible only exists through our thought!" It seems to us that there would never have been the tiniest Gulag if the victims had kept up the same discourse as those who weep over them today. The victims would have had to think and live in a quite different way to give substance to those who weep in their name, and who think in their name, and who give lessons in their name. It was their life force which impelled them, not their bitterness; their sobriety, not their ambition; their anorexia, not their huge appetites, as Zola would have said. We have set out to write a book of life, not of accounts, or of the tribunal even of the people or of pure thought. The question of a revolution has never been utopian spontaneity versus State organization. When we challenge the model of the State apparatus or of the party organization that is modeled on the conquest of that apparatus, we do not, however, fall into the grotesque alternatives: either that of appealing to a state of nature, to a spontaneous dynamic, or that of becoming the self-styled lucid thinker of an impossible revolution, whose very impossibility is such a source of pleasure. The question has always been organizational, not at all ideological: is an organization possible which is not modelled on the apparatus of the State, even to prefigure the State to come? Perhaps a war-machine with its lines of flight? In order to oppose the war-machine to the State apparatus in every assemblage—even a musical or literary one—it would be necessary to evaluate the degree of proximity to this or that pole. But how would a war-machine, in any domain whatever, become modern, and how would it ward off its own fascist dangers, when confronted by the totalitarian dangers of the State, its own dangers of destruction in comparison with the conservation of the State? In a certain way it is very simple, this happens on its own and every day. The mistake would be to say: there is a globalizing State, the master of its plans and extending its traps; and then, a force of resistance which will adopt the form of the State even if it entails betraying us, or else which will fall into local spontaneous or partial struggles, even if it entails being suffocated and beaten every time. The most centralized State is not at all the master of its plans, it is also an experimenter, it performs injections, it is unable to look into the future: the economists of the State declare themselves incapable of predicting the increase in a monetary mass. American politics is forced to proceed by empirical injections, not at all by apodictic programs. What a sad and sham game is played by those who speak of a supremely cunning master, in order to present the image of themselves as rigorous, incorruptible, and "pessimist" thinkers. It is along the different lines of complex assemblages that the powers that be carry out their experiments, but along them also arise experimenters of another kind, thwarting predictions, tracing out active lines of flight, looking for the combination of these lines, increasing their speed or slowing it down, creating the plane of consistence fragment by fragment, with a war-machine which would weigh the dangers that it encountered at each step.

What characterizes our situation is both beyond and on this side of the State. *Beyond* national States, the development of a world market, the power of multinational companies, the outline of a "planetary" organization, the extension of capitalism to the whole social body, clearly forms a great abstract machine which overcodes the monetary, industrial, and technological fluxes. At the same time the means of exploitation, control, and surveillance become more and more subtle and diffuse, in a certain sense molecular (the workers of the rich countries necessarily take part in the plundering of the third world, men take part in the overexploitation of women, etc.). But the abstract machine, with its dysfunctions, is no more infallible than the national States which are not able to regulate them on their own territory and from one territory to another. The State no longer has at its disposal the political, institutional, or even financial means which would enable it to fend off the social repercussions of the machine; it is doubtful whether it can eternally rely on the old forms like the police, armies, bureaucracies, even trade union bureaucracies, collective installations, schools, families. Enormous land slides are happening *on this side of* the state, following lines of gradient or of flight, affecting principally: (1) the marking out of territories; (2) the mechanisms of economic subjugation (new characteristics of unemployment, of inflation); (3) the basic regulatory frameworks (crisis of the school, of trade unions, of the army, of women . . .); (4) the nature of the demands which become qualitative as much as quantitative ("quality of life" rather than the "standard of living").

All this constitutes what can be called a *right to desire*. It is not surprising that all kinds of minority questions—linguistic, ethnic, regional, about sex, or youth—resurge not only as archaisms, but in up-to-date revolutionary forms which call once more into question in an entirely immanent manner both the global economy of the machine and the assemblages of national States. Instead of gambling on the eternal impossibility of the revolution and on the fascist return of a war-machine in general, why not think that *a new type of revolution is in the course of becoming possible*, and that all kinds of mutating, living machines conduct wars, are combined and trace out a plane of consistence which undermines the plane of organization of the world and the States? For, once again, the world and its States are no more masters of their plan than revolutionaries are condemned to the deformation of theirs. Everything is played in uncertain games, "front to front, back to back, back to front. . . ." The question of the future of the revolution is a bad question because, insofar as it is asked, there are so many people who do not *become* revolutionaries, and this is exactly why it is done, to impede the question of the revolutionary-becoming of people, at every level, in every place.

Notes

Editor's Introduction

1. François Châtelet, *Chronique des idées perdues* (Paris: Stock, 1977).
2. Gilles Deleuze and Claire Parnet, *Dialogues*, trans. Hugh Tomlinson and Barbara Habberjam (New York: Columbia University Press, 1987), p. 12.
3. Gilles Deleuze, "Il a été mon maître," *Arts* (28 October–3 November 1964): 8–9.
4. Deleuze and Parnet, *Dialogues*, p. 13.
5. Ibid., pp. 14–15.
6. Gilles Deleuze, *Empiricism and Subjectivity. An Essay on Hume's Theory of Human Nature*, trans. with an introduction by Constantin V. Boundas (New York: Columbia University Press, 1991).
7. Gilles Deleuze, *Expressionism in Philosophy: Spinoza*, trans. Martin Joughin (New York: Zone Books, 1990).
8. Gilles Deleuze, *Spinoza: Practical Philosophy*, trans. Robert Hurley (San Francisco: City Lights, 1988).
9. Gilles Deleuze, *Bergsonism*, trans. Hugh Tomlinson and Barbara Habberjam (New York: Zone Books, 1988).
10. Gilles Deleuze, *Difference and repetition*, trans. Paul Patton (London: Athlone, Forthcoming).
11. Gilles Deleuze, *Cinema 1: The Movement-Image*, trans. Hugh Tomlinson and Barbara Habberjam (Minneapolis: University of Minnesota Press, 1986).

12. Gilles Deleuze, *Nietzsche and Philosophy*, trans. Hugh Tomlinson (New York: Columbia University Press, 1983).

13. Gilles Deleuze, *Nietzsche* (Paris: Presses Universitaires de France, 1965).

14. See *Nietzsche and Philosophy*, pp. 47–49, 68–72; see also *Différence et répétition*, (Paris: Presses Universitaires de France: 1968) pp. 96–168, 365–89, and "Conclusions sur la volonté de puissance et l'éternel retour," *Nietzsche: Cahiers de Royaumont* (Paris: Editions de Minuit, 1967), pp. 275–87. I have argued these points, in a more elaborate way, in "Minoritarian Deconstruction of the Rhetoric of Nihilism," in *Nietzsche and the Rhetoric of Nihilism: Essays on Interpretation, Language, and Politics*, ed. Tom Darby, Bela Egyed, and Ben Jones (Ottawa: Carleton University Press, 1989), pp. 81–92.

15. Gilles Deleuze, *The Logic of Sense*, trans. Mark Lester with Charles Stivale, ed. Constantin V. Boundas (New York: Columbia University Press, 1990), p. 1.

16. Ibid., pp. 148–53.

17. Gilles Deleuze, *Le Pli. Leibniz et le baroque* (Paris: Editions de Minuit, 1988); translation forthcoming from the University of Minnesota Press.

18. Deleuze, *Différence et répétition*, p. 136.

19. Deleuze, *The Logic of Sense*, pp. 42–47.

20. Gilles Deleuze, *Foucault*, trans. Sean Hand (Minneapolis: University of Minnesota Press, 1988), pp. 94–123.

21. Deleuze and Parnet, *Dialogues*, pp. 124ff.

22. Gilles Deleuze and Félix Guattari, *A Thousand Plateaus: Capitalism and Schizophrenia*, trans. Brian Massumi (Minneapolis: University of Minnesota Press, 1987), pp. 195–200.

23. Bruno Paradis, "Leibniz: un monde unique et relatif," *Magazine Littéraire*, 257 (September 1988): 26.

24. Gilles Deleuze, "Klossowski or Bodies-Language," in *The Logic of Sense*, p. 296.

25. Gilles Deleuze, *Kant's Critical Philosophy: The Doctrine of the Faculties*, trans. Hugh Tomlinson and Barbara Habberjam (Minneapolis: University of Minnesota Press, 1984). See also Gilles Deleuze, "L'Idée de genèse dans l'esthétique de Kant," *Revue d'Esthétique*, 16 (1963): 113–36.

26. This *idée mère* structures his discussion of intensity-extension, paranoia-schizophrenia, sense-nonsense, nomads-sedentaries, etc.

27. For Deleuze's theory of intensity, see *Différence et répétition*, pp. 286–335.

28. Gilles Deleuze and Félix Guattari, *Anti-Oedipus: Capitalism and Schizophrenia*, trans. R. Hurley, M. Seem, and H. R. Lane (New York: Viking, 1977), passim; *A Thousand Plateaus*, passim.

29. Deleuze and Parnet, *Dialogues*, pp. 77–123.

30. See Herbert Marcuse, *Eros and Civilization: A Philosophical Inquiry into Freud* (Boston: Beacon, 1955); Paul Ricoeur, *Freud and Philosophy: An Essay on Interpretation*, trans. Denis Savage (New Haven: Yale University Press, 1970); Jürgen Habermas, *Knowledge and Human Interests*, trans. Jeremy Shapiro (Boston: Beacon, 1971), chs. 10, 11, 12.

31. Deleuze and Guattari's approach to Lacan is guarded. They praise him for rendering schizophrenic the psychoanalytic field instead of Oedipalizing the psychotic field, but they are critical of Lacan's distinction between imaginary and symbolic, that is, between inclusive and exclusive disjunctions. See Deleuze and Parnet, *Dialogues*, pp. 81–89.

32. Schizoanalytic theory and practice are discussed at length in Deleuze and Guattari's *Anti-Oedipus*, pp. 325–457; see also Gilles Deleuze and Félix Guattari, *Politique et Psychanalyse* (Alençon: Des mots perdus, 1977).

33. Deleuze and Guattari's criticism of the "death drive" is developed in *Anti-Oedipus*, pp. 329–38.

34. For a detailed discussion of the body without organs, see "November 28, 1947: How Do You Make Yourself A Body Without Organs?" in *A Thousand Plateaus*, pp. 149–66.

35. Deleuze calls "molecular" the partial objects of desire between which there is a difference of nature, not only a difference of degree; the distinctions between them are qualitative, not merely quantitative—as it is with the molar objects. Partial objects are the molecular functions of the unconscious.

36. See "1227: Treatise on Nomadology—The War Machine" and "7000 B.C.: Apparatus of Capture," in *A Thousand Plateaus*, pp. 351–423, 424–73.

37. "Signes et événements," Raymond Bellour and François Ewald interview Gilles Deleuze, *Magazine Littéraire*, 257 (September 1988): 24.

38. François Ewald, "La schizo-analyse," *Magazine Littéraire*, 257 (September 1988): 53.

39. Monique Scheepers, "Subjektivität und Politik," *Lendemains*, 53 (1989): pp. 30–34.

40. P. Levôyer and P. Encrenaz, "Politique de Deleuze," *Lendemains*, 53 (1989): 38.

41. Deleuze, *Foucault*, p. 103.

42. See pp. 69–77; 245–52.

43. The expression *minor deconstruction* is not Deleuze's. François Laruelle uses it frequently in *Le déclin de l'écriture* (Paris: Aubier-Flammarion, 1977) and *Au-delà du principe de pouvoir* (Paris: Payot, 1978). For Deleuze's discussion of the issues that Laruelle labeled "minor deconstruction," see *A Thousand Plateaus*, pp. 3–25, 111–48.

44. Gilles Deleuze and Félix Guattari, *Kafka: Toward a Minor Literature* (Minneapolis: University of Minnesota Press, 1986).

45. Gilles Deleuze and Carmelo Bene, *Superpositions* (Paris: Editions de Minuit, 1979).

46. See *A Thousand Plateaus*, pp. 75–85. *Order-word* and *password* translate the French *mot d'ordre* and *mot de passe*.

47. For an overview of the Russian formalists, see Tzvetan Todorov, *Théorie de la littérature* (Paris: Editions du Seuil, 1965).

48. On the tensions between two models of science—the nomadic and the royal—see *A Thousand Plateaus*, pp. 361–74.

49. Deleuze, *Différence et répétition*, p. 251.

50. Gilles Deleuze, *Francis Bacon: Logique de la sensation*, 2 vols. (Paris: Editions de la Différence, 1987); translation forthcoming.

51. Cited by Deleuze in *A Thousand Plateaus*, p. 342.

52. Patrick Vauday, "Écrit à vue: Deleuze-Bacon," *Critique*, 38 (1982): 959.

53. Deleuze, *Francis Bacon*, 1: 27.

54. Deleuze and Guattari, *A Thousand Plateaus*, pp. 310–50.

55. The term was coined by Ronald Bogue as the title of an essay published in *Substance*, 66 (1991). See Marcuse, *Eros and Civilization*, esp. part II. "It concerns alliance. If evolution includes any veritable becomings, it is in the domain of *symbioses* that bring into play beings of totally different scales and kingdoms." *A Thousand Plateaus*, p. 238.

56. On this distinction, see *A Thousand Plateaus*, pp. 43–45 and Deleuze's indebtedness to Hjelmslev.

57. Gilles Deleuze, *Cinema 2: Time-Image*, trans. Hugh Tomlinson and Robert Galeta (London: Athlone, 1989).

58. Gilles Deleuze and Félix Guattari, *Qu'est-ce que la philosophie?* (Paris: Editions de Minuit, 1991).

59. Deleuze and Parnet, *Dialogues*, pp. 16, 17.

1. Rhizome Versus Trees

1. Translator's note: U. Weinreich, W. Labov, and M. Herzog, "Empirical Foundations for a Theory of Language," in W. Lehmann and Y. Malkeiel, eds., *Directions for Historical Linguistics* (1968), p. 125; cited by Françoise Robert, "Aspects sociaux de changement dans une grammaire générative," *Languages*, 32 (December 1973): 90.

2. Bertil Malmberg, *New Trends in Linguistics*, trans. Edward Carners (Stockholm: Lund, 1964), pp. 65–67 (the example of the Castilian dialect).

3. Ernst Jünger, *Approches; drogues et ivresse* (Paris: Table Ronde, 1974), p. 304, sec. 218.

4. Rémy Chauvin, in *Entretiens sur la sexualité*, ed. Max Aron, Robert Courrier, and Etienne Wolff (Paris: Plon, 1969), p. 205.

5. On the work of R. E. Benveniste and G. J. Todaro, see Yves Christen, "Le rôle des virus dans l'évolution," *La Recherche*, 54 (March 1975): "After integration-extraction in a cell, viruses may, due to an error in excision, carry off fragments of their host's DNA and transmit them to new cells: this in fact is the basis for what we call ''genetic engineering.' As a result, the genetic information of one organism may be transferred to another by means of viruses. We could even imagine an extreme case where this transfer of information would go from a more highly evolved species to one that is less evolved or was the progenitor of the more evolved species. This mechanism, then, would run in the opposite direction to evolution in the classical sense. If it turns out that this kind of transferral of information has played a major role, we would in certain cases have to *substitute reticular schemas (with communications between branches after they have become differentiated) for the bush or tree schemas currently used to represent evolution*" (p. 271).

6. François Jacob, *The Logic of Life*, trans. Betty E. Spillmann (New York: Pantheon, 1973), pp. 291–92, 311 (quote).

7. Carlos Castaneda, *The Teachings of Don Juan* (Berkeley: University of California Press, 1971), p. 88.

8. Pierre Boulez, *Conversations with Célestine Deliège* (London: Eulenberg Books, 1976): "a seed which you plant in compost, and suddenly it begins to proliferate like a weed" (p. 15); and on musical proliferation: "a music that floats and in which the writing itself makes it impossible for the performer to keep in with a pulsed time" (p. 69 [translation modified]).

2. What Is Becoming?

1. Plato, *Philebus*, 24d., trans. R. Hackforth; *Parmenides*, 154–55, trans. F. M. Cornforth; in E. Hamilton and H. Cairns, eds. *Plato: The Collected Dialogues* (Princeton: Princeton University Press, 1961).

2. Plato, *Cratylus*, 437ff.

3. What Is an Event?

1. Emile Bréhier, *La Theorie des incorporels dans l'ancien stoicisme* (Paris: Vrin, 1928), pp. 11–13.

2. On this example, see the commentary of Bréhier, p. 20.

3. On the distinction between real internal causes and external causes entering into limited relations of "confatality," see Cicero, *De Fato*, 9, 13, 15, and 16.

4. The Epicurean notion of the event is very similar to that of the Stoics: see Epicurus, *To Herodotus*, 39–40, 68–73, and Lucretius, *De Rerum Natura*, 1:449ff. As he analyzes the event, "the rape of Tyndareus' daughter," Lucretius contrasts *eventa* (servitude-liberty, poverty-wealth, war-peace) with *conjuncta* (real qualities which are inseparable from bodies). Events are not exactly incorporeal entities. They are presented nevertheless as not existing by themselves—impassible, pure results of the movements of matter, or actions and passions of bodies. It does not seem likely though that the Epicureans developed this theory of the event—perhaps because they bent it to the demands of a homogeneous causality and subsumed it under their own conception of the *simulacrum*.

5. On the account of Stoic categories, see Plotinus, 6:1.25. See also Bréhier, p. 43.

6. This description of the purse comprises some of Carroll's best writing: see *Sylvie and Bruno Concluded* (New York: Dover, 1988), ch. 7.

7. This discovery of the surface and this critique of depth represent a constant in modern literature. They inspire the work of Robbe-Grillet. In another form, we find them again in Klossowski, in the relation between Roberte's epidermis and her glove: see Klossowski's remarks to this effect in the postface to *Les Lois de l'hospitalité* (Paris: Gallimard, 1965), pp. 135, 344; see also Michel Tournier's *Friday*, trans. Norman Denny (New York: Pantheon Books, 1985, by arrangement with Doubleday), p. 67: "It is a strange prejudice which sets a higher value on depth than on breadth,

and which accepts 'superficial' as meaning not 'of wide extent' but 'of little depth,' whereas 'deep,' on the other hand, signifies 'of great depth,' and not 'of small surface.' Yet it seems to me that a feeling such as love is better measured, if it can be measured at all, by the extent of its surface than by its degree of depth."

4. What Is a Multiplicity?

1. For example, in the system of memory, the formation of a memory implies a diagonal that turns present A into representation A' in relation to the new present B,

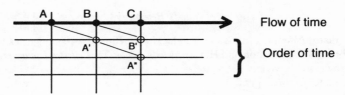

and into A'' in relation to C, etc.: see Edmund Husserl, *The Phenomenology of Internal Time-Consciousness*, ed. Martin Heidegger, trans. James S. Churchill, intro. Calvin O. Schrag (Bloomington: Indiana University Press, 1964), pp. 48–50.

2. Friedrich Nietzsche, *Untimely Meditations*, trans. R. J. Hollingdale (New York: Cambridge University Press, 1983), "On the Uses and Disadvantages of History for Life," sec. 1, pp. 63–64.

3. On all of these themes, see Pierre Boulez. (1) On how transversals always tend to escape horizontal and vertical coordinates of music, sometimes even drawing "virtual lines," see *Notes of an Apprenticeship*, ed. Paule Thevenin, trans. Robert Weinstock (New York: Knopf, 1968), pp. 231–32, 295–301, 382–83. (2) On the idea of the sound block or "block of duration," in relation to this transversal, see *Boulez on Music Today*, trans. Susan Bradshaw and Richard Bennett (Cambridge, Mass.: Harvard University Press, 1971), pp. 55–59. (3) On the distinction between points and blocks, "punctual sets," and "aggregative sets" with varying individuality, see "Sonate que me veux-tu?" *Médiations*, 7 (1964). The hatred of memory appears frequently in Boulez; see "Éloge de l'amnésie," *Musique en jeu*, 4 (1971), pp. 5–14, and "J'ai horreur du souvenir," in *Roger Desormière et son temps*, ed. Denise Mayer and Pierre Souvtchinsky (Monaco: Ed. du Rocher, 1966). Confining ourselves to contemporary examples, one finds analogous declarations in Stravinsky, Cage, and Berio. Of course, there is a musical memory that is tied to coordinates and is exercised in social settings (getting up, going to bed, beating a retreat). But the perception of a musical "phrase" appeals less to memory, even of the reminiscence type, than to an extension or contraction of perception of the encounter type. It should be studied how each musician sets in motion veritable *blocks of forgetting:* for example, what Jean Barraque calls "slices of forgetting" and "absent developments" in the work of Debussy; *Debussy* (Paris: Seuil, 1977), pp. 169–71. One can refer to a general study by Daniel Charles, "La musique et l'oubli," *Traverses*, 4 (1977), pp. 14–23.

4. Roland Barthes, "Rasch," in *The Responsibility of Forms,* trans. Richard Howard (New York: Hill and Wang, 1985), pp. 300–302, 308–9.

5. There are many differences among painters, in all respects, but also a common movement: see Wassily Kandinsky, *Point and Line to Plane* in *Complete Writings on Art,* vol. 2, ed. Kenneth C. Lindsay and Peter Vergo (Boston: G. K. Hall, 1982), pp. 524–700, and Paul Klee, *On Modern Art,* trans. Paul Findlay, intro. Herbert Reed (London: Faber, 1966). The aim of statements like those of Mondrian on the exclusive value of the vertical and the horizontal is to show the conditions under which the vertical and horizontal are sufficient to create a transversal, which does not even have to be drawn; for example, coordinates of unequal thickness intersect inside the frame and extend outside the frame, opening a "dynamic axis" running transversally (see Michel Butor's comments in *Repertoire* [Paris: Minuit, 1960–61], vol. 3, "Le carre et son habitant"). One can also consult Michel Fried's article on Pollock's line, *Three American Painters* (Cambridge, Mass.: Fogg Art Museum, 1965), and Henry Miller's discussion of Nash's line, *On Turning Eighty* (London: Village Press, 1973).

5. Individuation

1. This is sometimes written "ecceity," deriving the word from *ecce,* "here is." This is an error, since Duns Scotus created the word and the concept from *haec,* "this thing." But it is a fruitful error because it suggests a mode of individuation that is distinct from that of a thing or a subject.

2. Michel Tournier, *Les Météores* (Paris: Gallimard, 1975), ch. 23, "L'âme déployé."

3. Translator's note: On *Aeon* versus *chronos,* Deleuze, *Logique du sense* (Paris: Minuit, 1969), especially series 23, pp. 190–97.

4. Pierre Boulez, *Conversations with Célestin Deliège* (London: Eulenberg Books, 1976), pp. 68–71: "It is not possible to introduce phenomena of tempo into music that has been calculated only electronically, in . . . lengths expressed in seconds or microseconds" (p. 70).

5. Ray Bradbury, *The Machineries of Joy* (New York: Simon and Schuster, 1964), p. 53.

6. Translator's note: Virginia Wolff, *Mrs. Dalloway* (New York: Harcourt Brace and World, 1925), p. 11.

7. Gustave Guillaume has proposed a very interesting conception of the verb. He distinguishes between an interior time, enveloped in the "process," and an exterior time, pertaining to the distinction between epochs (*Epoques et niveaux temporels dans le systeme de la conjugaison française, Cahiers de linguistique structurale* [Universite de Laval, Quebec], 4 [1955]). It seems to us that these two poles correspond respectively to the infinitive-becoming, Aeon, and the present-being, Chronos. Each verb leans more or less in the direction of one pole or the other, not only according to its nature, but also according to the nuances of its modes and tenses, with the exception of "becoming" and "being," which correspond to both poles. Proust, in his study of

Flaubert's style, shows how the imperfect tense in Flaubert takes on the value of an infinitive-becoming: *Chroniques* (Paris: Gallimard, 1927), pp. 197–99.

8. On the problem of proper names (in what sense is the proper name outside the limits of classification and of another nature, and in what sense is it at the limit and still a part of classification?), see Alan Henderson Gardiner, *The Theory of Proper Names*, 2d ed. (New York: Oxford University Press, 1957), and Levi-Strauss, *The Savage Mind*, ch. 7 ("Time Regained"), pp. 217–44.

9. We have already encountered this problem of the indifference of psycho-analysis to the use of the indefinite article or pronoun among children; as early as Freud, but more especially in Melanie Klein (the children she analyzes, in particular, Little Richard, speak in terms of "a," "one," "people," but Klein exerts incredible pressure to turn them into personal and possessive family locutions). It seems to us that Laplanche and Pontalis are the only ones in psychoanalysis to have had any inkling that indefinites play a specific role; they protested against any overrapid interpretive reduction: see "Fantasme originaire," *Les temps modernes*, 215, April 1964, pp. 1861, 1868.

10. See the subjectivist or personalist conception of language in Emile Benveniste, *Problems in General Linguistics*, trans. Mary Elizabeth Meek (Coral Gables, Fla.: University of Miami Press, 1971), chs. 20 ("Subjectivity in Language," pp. 223–30) and 21 ("Analytical Philosophy and Language," pp. 231–38), especially pp. 220–21 and 225–26.

11. The essential texts of Maurice Blanchot serve to refute the theory of the "shifter" and of personology in linguistics. See *L'entretien infini* (Paris: Gallimard, 1969), pp. 556–67. And on the difference between the two propositions, "I am unfortunate" and "he is unfortunate," or between "I die" and "one dies," see *La part du feu* (Paris: Gallimard, 1949), pp. 29–30, and *The Space of Literature*, trans. Ann Smock (Lincoln: University of Nebraska Press, 1982), pp. 90, 122, 126. Blanchot demonstrates that in all of these cases the indefinite has nothing to do with "the banality of daily life," which on the contrary would be on the side of the personal pronoun.

12. Translator's note: These quotes, the first from Nietzsche, the second from Kafka, are quoted more fully in ch. 12 of *A Thousand Plateaus*, "1227: Treatise on Nomadology," p. 353.

13. For example, see François Cheng, *Chinese Poetic Writing*, trans. Donald A. Riggs and Jerome P. Seaton (Bloomington: Indiana University Press, 1982), especially his analysis of what he calls "the passive procedures," pp. 23–42.

6. A Theory of the Other

1. Michel Tournier, *Vendredi ou les limbes du Pacifique* (Paris: Gallimard, 1967). English translation, *Friday*, trans. Norman Denny (New York: Pantheon Books, 1985, by arrangement), pp. 186–87.

2. Tournier's conception clearly contains Leibnizian echoes (the monad as expression of the world); it also contains Sartrean echoes. Sartre's theory in *Being and Nothingness* is the first great theory of the Other, because it transcends the alternative: is the Other an object (even if it is a particular object inside the perceptual

field), or rather a subject (even if it is another subject for another perceptual field)? Sartre is here the precursor of structuralism, for he is the first to have considered the Other as a real structure or a specificity irreducible to the object and the subject. But, since he defined this structure by means of the "look," he fell back into the categories of object and subject, making of the Other the one who constitutes me as an object when he looks at me, even if this means that the Other would himself become an object when I, in turn, look at him. It seems that the structure-Other precedes the look; the latter, rather, marks the moment at which *someone* happens to fill the structure. The look brings about only the effectuation or the actualization of a structure which must nonetheless be independently defined.

3. Tournier, *Friday* pp. 94–96.

4. Ibid., p. 204.

5. Ibid., p. 205.

6. Ibid., p. 115–16.

7. Ibid., p. 67.

8. Ibid., p. 180.

9. Ibid., pp. 211–12.

10. Ibid., p. 113.

11. See the collection *Le Désir et la perversion* (Paris: Seuil, 1967). Guy Rosolato's article, "Étude des perversions sexuelles a partir du fétishisme," contains some very interesting, though too brief, remarks on "sexual difference" and "the double" (pp. 25–26). Jean Clavreul's article, "Le couple pervers," shows that neither the victim nor the accomplice takes the place of an Other; (on "desubjectivization," see p. 110, and on the distinction between the cause and the object of desire, see the same author's "Remarques sur la question de la realité dans les perversions," *La Psychanalyse,* 8, pp. 290ff.). It seems that these studies, founded on Lacan's structuralism and on his analysis of the *Verleugnung,* are in the course of development.

12. In Sade there is the ever-present theme of molecular combination.

7. *Ethics Without Morality*

1. Benedict de Spinoza, *The Ethics and Selected Letters,* trans. Samuel Shirley, ed. with introduction by Seymour Feldman (Indianapolis: Hackett, 1982). *Ethics,* III, 2, schol.

2. *Ethics,* III, 2, schol. (and II, 13, schol.).

3. Even the mind has a very large number of parts: cf. *Ethics,* II, 15.

4. *Ethics,* II, 28, 29.

5. *Ethics,* I, appendix.

6. *Ethics,* III, 2, schol.

7. *Ethics,* III, 9, schol.

8. *Ethics,* III, definition of Desire ("in order to involve the cause of this consciousness in my definition. . .").

9. *Spinoza: The Political Works,* ed. A. G. Wernham (Oxford: Oxford University Press, 1958). Spinoza, *Theological-Political Treatise,* ch. 4. And *Letter XIX,* to Blyenbergh, *The Ethics and Selected Letters.*

10. Friedrich Nietzsche, *On the Genealogy of Morals*, ed. with commentary by Walter Kaufmann (New York: Random House, 1967) first essay, sec. 17.

11. Cf. the text on suicide, *Ethics*, IV, 20, schol.

12. *Theological-Political Treatise*, ch. 4.

13. Cf. Spinoza's denunciation of "satire": *Political Treatise, Spinoza: The Political Works*, ed. A. G. Wernham, ch. I, sec. 1, and *Ethics*, III, preface.

14. *Theological-Political Treatise*, preface.

15. *Ethics*, IV, appendix, ch. 13.

16. *Ethics*, I, appendix.

17. *Ethics*, III.

18. *Ethics*, IV, 47, schol.

19. *Political Treatise*, ch. 10, sec. 8.

20. On the two sorts of passion, cf. *Ethics*, III, general definition of the affects.

21. This was a common procedure that consisted in concealing the boldest or least orthodox arguments in appendices or notes (Bayle's dictionary is a later example). Spinoza renewed the procedure with his systematic method of scholia, which refer to each other and are themselves connected to the prefaces and appendices, thus forming a second subterranean *Ethics*.

8. Ethics and the Event

1. With respect to Joe Bousquet's work, which is in its entirety a meditation on the wound, the event, and language, see two essential articles in *Cahiers du Sud*, 303 (1950): René Nelli, "Joe Bousquet et son double;" and Ferdinand Alquié, "Joe Bousquet et la morale du language."

2. See Joe Bousquet, *Les capitales* (Paris: Le Cercle du Livre, 1955), p. 103.

3. Maurice Blanchot, *L'Espace littéraire* (Paris: Gallimard, 1955), p. 160.

4. Essay by Claude Roy on Ginsbert, *Nouvel Observateur*, 1968.

5. See Blanchot, *L'Espace*, p. 155: "This attempt to elevate death to itself, to bring about the coincidence of the point at which it disappears in itself and that at which I disappear outside of myself, is not a simple internal affair, but implies an immense responsibility with regard to things and is possible only through their mediation."

9. The Selective Test

1. In the preceding comparison, we are referring to some of the best-known texts of Nietzsche and Kierkegaard. In the case of Kierkegaard, these include *Fear and Trembling* and *Repetition*, ed. and trans. H. V. and E. H. Hong, published as two volumes in one (Princeton University Press, 1983); the very important note in *The Concept of Anxiety*, trans. R. Thomte, ed. H. V. and E. H. Hong (Princeton University Press, 1980); and passages from the *Journals and Papers*, ed. H. V. and E. H. Hong (Indiana University Press, 1967–78). On the critique of memory, cf. *Philosophical Fragments* or *A Fragment of Philosophy*, rev. trans. H. V. Hong (Princeton University

Press, 1962), and *Stages on Life's Way: Studies by Various Persons*, ed. and trans. H. V. and E. H. Hong (Princeton University Press, 1988).

In the case of Nietzsche, see *Thus Spoke Zarathustra* (especially part II, "Of Redemption"; and the two main passages in part III, "Of the Vision and the Riddle" and "The Convalescent," one concerning Zarathustra ill, talking to his demon, and the other concerning Zarathustra convalescent, conversing with his animals), trans. R. J. Hollingdale (Penguin, 1961); but also the Notes of 1881–1882 (in which Nietzsche explicitly opposes "his" hypothesis to the cyclical hypothesis and criticizes all notions of resemblance, equilibrium, and identity. Cf. *La Volonté de Puissance*, trans. Bianquis (Paris: Gallimard, S.d.), pp. 295–301). Finally, for Péguy, see essentially *Clio* (Paris: Gallimard, 1931) and *Le mystère de la charité de Jeanne d'Arc* (Paris, Gallimard, 1955/ New York, Pantheon Books, 1943).

2. See Kierkegaard, *Fear and Trembling* (*Crainte et Tremblement*, trans. Tisseau, (Paris: Aubier, 1984), pp. 52–67) on the nature of the real movement which is not mediation but "repetition" and which stands opposed to the abstract logical, false movement described by Hegel. See the remarks from the *Journal* published as an appendix to *La Répétition*, trans. and ed. Tisseau. One also finds in Péguy a profound critique of "logical movement": Péguy denounces this as a conservative, accumulative, and capitalistic pseudomovement. See *Clio*, pp. 45 et seq. This is close to the Kierkegaardian critique.

3. See Nietzsche, *Thus Spoke Zarathustra*, part III, "Of Old and New Law-Tables," sec. 4: "But only a buffoon thinks: 'Man can also be jumped over.'"

10. Eternal Recurrence

1. Friedrich Nietzsche, *Thus Spoke Zarathustra*, trans. by R. J. Hollingdale (New York: Penguin Books, 1961); hereafter *Z*.

2. Friedrich Nietzsche, *La volonté de puissance*, trans. by G. Bianquis (Paris: Gallimard, 1935); hereafter *VP*. Friedrich Nietzsche, *The Will to Power*, trans. by Walter Kaufmann and R. J. Hollingdale (New York: Random House, 1968); hereafter *WP*.

3. *Z* III, "Of the Virtue That Makes Small," p. 191; *Z* II, "Of the Compassionate," p. 113: "But worst of all are petty thoughts. Truly, better even to have done wickedly than to have thought pettily! To be sure, you will say: 'Delight in petty wickedness spares us many a great evil deed.' But here one should not wish to be spared."

4. Friedrich Nietzsche, *On the Genealogy of Morals*, trans. by Walter Kaufmann (New York: Random House, 1967).

5. Friedrich Nietzsche, *Ecce Home*, trans. by W. Kaufmann (New York: Random House, 1967); hereafter *EH*.

11. Man and Overman

1. M. Serres, *Le système de Leibniz* (Paris: Presses Universitaires de France, 1982), pp. 648–57.

268 11. MAN AND OVERMAN

2. See *The Order of Things*, trans. A. Sheridan (New York: Pantheon 1970), chs. 4, 5, 6; hereafter *OT.*

3. *Les Mots et les choses* (Paris: Gallimard, 1966), p. 243 (hereafter *MC*), (*OT*, pp. 320–31). Daudin's exemplary study, *Les classes zoologiques et l'idée de série animale* (Paris: Éditions des Archives contemporaraines, 1983), had shown how classification in the classical age developed according to series.

4. *Naissance de la clinique* (Paris: Presses Universitaires de France, 1963), pp. 119, 138 (*The Birth of the Clinic*, trans. A. Sheridan (New York: Pantheon, 1973), pp. 118, 136).

5. This theme has found its fullest expression in J. Vuillemin's book *L'héritage kantien et la révolution copernicienne* (Paris: Presses Universitaires de France, 1954).

6. In *OT* Foucault constantly recalls the necessity of recognizing two stages, but these are not always defined in the same way: either, in a narrow sense, they are things which first receive a particular historicity, and then man appropriates this historicity for himself in the second stage (*MC*, pp. 380–81 [*OT*, pp. 370–71]); or else, in a larger sense, it is "the configurations" which change first, followed by their "mode of being" (*MC*, p. 233 [*OT*, p. 221]).

7. *MC*, p. 268 (*OT*, p. 258).

8. See Etienne Geoffroy Saint-Hilaire, *Principes de phillosophie zoologique* (Paris: Pichon et Didiet, 1830), which contains the polemic with Cuvier on folding.

9. On the great "break" brought about by Cuvier, whereby Lamarck still belongs to classical natural history while Cuvier makes possible a history of the living creature that will manifest itself in Darwin, see *MC*, pp. 287–89 (*OT*, pp. 174–76) and *MC*, p. 307 (*OT*, p. 294): "evolutionism is a biological theory, of which the condition of possibility was a biology without evolution—that of Cuvier."

10. *MC*, p. 291 (*OT*, p. 278). We feel that this text, which deals with nineteenth-century biology, has much wider implications and expresses a fundamental aspect of Foucault's thought.

11. This is the point emphasized by P. Klossowski in his *Nietzsche et le cercle vicieux* (Paris: Mercure de France, 1978).

12. As we have seen, it is Bichat who breaks with the classical conception of death, as being a decisive indivisible instant (Marraux's formula, taken up again by Sartre, whereby death is that which "transforms life into a destiny," still belongs to the classical conception). Bichat's three great innovations are to have seen death as being coextensive with life, to have made it the global result of partial deaths, and above all to have taken "violent death" rather than "natural death" as the model (on the reasons for this last point, see *Recherches physiologiques sur la vie et la mort* [Paris: Fortin, Masson et Cie., ca. 1800], pp. 116–19). Bichat's book is the first act of a modern conception of death.

13. See *MC*, p. 291 (*OT*, p. 278).

14. See "What Is an Author?" in *Language, Counter-Memory, Practice*, ed. D. F. Bouchard (Ithaca: Cornell University Press, 1977), pp. 136–39.

15. *MC*, pp. 397–98 (*OT*, pp. 385–87).

16. See *MC*, pp. 309, 313, 316–18, 395–97 (*OT*, pp. 296, 300, 305–6, 384–85), on

the characteristics of modern literature as being "the experience of death . . . , unthinkable thought . . . , repetition . . . , finitude."

17. On the reasons given by Foucault for this special situation in language, see *MC*, pp. 306–7 (*OT*, pp. 293–94) and *MC*, pp. 315–16 (*OT*, pp. 304–5).

18. *MC*, p. 395 (*OT*, p. 383). Rimbaud's letter not only invokes language or literature, but the two other aspects: the future man is in charge not only of the new language, but also of animals and whatever is unformed (in the "Letter to Paul Demeny" [Paris: Pleiade, 1972], p. 255).

12. Psychoanalysis and Desire

1. E. A. Bennett, *Ce que Jung a vraiment dit* (Paris: Gérard, 1973), p. 80.
2. Translators' note: in English in the original.
3. Serge Leclaire, *Démasquer le réel* (Paris: Seuil, 1971), p. 35.
4. Cf. the famous case of President Schreber and the verdict which grants him his rights. (Translators' note: the reference is to Freud's essay, "Psychoanalytic Notes on an Autobiographical Account of a Case of Paranoia [Dementia Paranoides]," in vol. 9 of the Pelican Freud Library, *Case Histories II* [Harmondsworth: Penguin, 1979]).
5. Cf. Robert Castel, *Le Psychoanalysme* (Paris: François Maspero, 1973).
6. Cf. a curious text of J. A. Miller in *Ornicar*, 1.
7. Jacques Donzelot, in *The Policing of Families*, trans. R. Hurley (London: Hutchinson, 1980), shows that psychoanalysis has evolved from the private relationship and that it perhaps entered the "social" sector very much earlier than has been thought.

13. Delirium: World-Historical, Not Familial

1. R. D. Laing, *The Politics of Experience* (New York: Ballantine, 1967), pp. 154–55.
2. On the interplay of races and intensities in the theater of cruelty, see Antonin Artaud, *Oeuvres complètes* (Paris: Gallimard), vols. 4 and 5: for example, the project of "La conquête du Mexique," vol. 4, p. 151; and the role of intensive vibrations and rotations in "Les Cenci," vol. 5, pp. 46ff. (Translators' note: for the English text of the latter, see Antonin Artaud, *The Cenci*, trans. Simon Watson Taylor [New York: Grove Press, 1970], pp. vii ff.)
3. Arthur Rimbaud, *Une saison en enfer* (Paris: Flammarion, 1989).
4. Nietzsche, letter to Jakob Burckhardt, 5 January 1889, in *Selected Letters of Friedrich Nietzsche*, trans. Christopher Middleton (Chicago: University of Chicago Press, 1969), p. 347.
5. Jacques Besse, "Le danseur," in *La grande paque* (Paris: Editions Belfond, 1969). The whole first part of this book describes the schizo's stroll in the city; the second part, "Légendes folles," progresses to the hallucinations or deliriums of historical episodes.

6. Wilhelm Reich, *The Function of the Orgasm*, trans. Vincent R. Carfagno (New York: Simon and Schuster, 1973), p. 70. For a critique of autism, see Roger Gentis, *Les murs de l'asile* (Paris: Maspero, 1970), pp. 41ff.

7. Maurice Garçon, *Louis XVII ou la fausse énigme* (Paris: Hachette, 1968), p. 177.

14. Becoming-Animal

1. René Schérer and Guy Hocquenghem, *Co-ire, Recherche*, 22 (1976), pp. 76–82: see their critique of Bettelheim's thesis, which considers the becomings-animal of the child merely an autistic symbolism that expresses the anxiety of the parents more than any reality of the child. See Bruno Bettelheim, *The Empty Fortress* (New York: Free Press, 1967).

2. Philippe Vagi, "Les philosophes du fantastique," *Libération*, 31 March 1977. For the preceding cases, what we must arrive at is an understanding of certain so-called neurotic behaviors as a function of becomings-animal, instead of relegating becomings-animal to a psychoanalytic interpretation of behaviors. We saw this in relation to masochism (and Lolito explains that the origin of his feats lies in certain masochistic experiences, a fine text by Christian Maurel conjugates a becoming-monkey and a becoming-horse in a masochistic pairing). Anorexia would also have to be understood from the point of view of becoming-animal.

3. See *Newsweek*, 16 May 1977, p. 57.

4. See Dolfi Trost, *Visible et invisible* (Paris: Arcanes 1953) and *Librement méchanique* (Paris: Minotaure 1955): "She was simultaneously, in her sensible reality and in the ideal prolongation of her lines, like the projection of a human group yet to come."

15. The Signs of Madness: Proust

1. Marcel Proust, "Within a Budding Grove," in *Remembrance of Things Past*, 3 vols. trans. C. K. Scott Moncrieff, Terence Kilmartin, and Andres Mayor (New York: Vintage Books, 1982), vol. 1, p. 568.

2. Marcel Proust, "Time Regained," in *Remembrance of Things Past*, vol. 3, pp. 832–33.

3. Marcel Proust, "The Captive," in *Remembrance of Things Past*, vol. 3, pp. 203-4.

4. Marcel Proust, "The Fugitive," in *Remembrance of Things Past*, vol. 3, p. 613.

5. Proust, "Within a Budding Grove," p. 579.

6. Marcel Proust, "The Guermantes Way," in *Remembrance of Things Past*, vol. 2, p. 298.

7. Charlus' three speeches are: "Within a Budding Grove," pp. 578–80; "The Guermantes Way," pp. 294–306; and "The Guermantes Way," pp. 574–86.

8. Proust, "The Guermantes Way," p. 577.

9. An elementary combination is defined in terms of the encounter of one masculine *or* feminine part of an individual with a masculine *or* feminine part of another. Thus, we may have: the masculine part of a man and the feminine part of a woman; but also the masculine part of a woman and the feminine part of a man; the mas-

culine part of a man and the feminine part of another man; the masculine part of a man and the masculine part of another man. . . .

10. Proust, "The Captive," pp. 202–3.

11. On the distinction between main characters and narrator in *Remembrance*, see Gerard Genette, *Figures III* (Paris: Editions du Seuil, 1972), pp. 259f. Genette introduces to this distinction many corrections.

12. Marcel Proust, "Cities of the Plain," in *Remembrance of Things Past*, vol. 2, p. 976.

16. What is Desire

1. Cf. the article of Roland Barthes on Schumann, "Rasch," in *Language, cours, société: Pour Emile Benveniste*, ed. J. Kristeva, J.-C. Milnes, N. Ruwet (Paris: Seuil, 1975), pp. 218ff.

2. Translator's note: the original is, literally, "Oh, I could tell you, mummy," a line from a French nursery rhyme.

3. René Nellie, in *L'Erotique des Troubadours* (Tours, 1963), gives a good analysis of this plane of immanence of courtly love, in the way it challenges the interruptions that pleasure would like to introduce into it. In a quite different assemblage, similar utterances and techniques are to be found in Taoism for the construction of a plane of immanence of desire (cf., R. Van Gulik, *Sexual Life in Ancient China* [Leiden: E. J. Brill, 1961], and the commentaries of J.-F. Lyotard, *Économie Libidinale* [Paris: Minuit, 1974]).

4. D. H. Lawrence, *Eros et les chiens* (Paris: Bourgois, 1970), p. 290.

5. Ray Bradbury, *The Machineries of Joy* pp. 38–39.

17. Language: Major and Minor

1. On the expansion and diffusion of states of language, in the "patch of oil" mode or the "paratrooper" mode, see Bertil Malmberg, *New Trends in Linguistics*, trans. Edward Carners (Stockholm: Lund, 1964), ch. 3 (which uses N. Lindqvist's important studies on dialect). What are needed now are comparative studies of how homogenizations and centralizations of given major languages take place. In this respect, the linguistic history of French is not at all the same as that of English; neither is their relation to writing as a form of homogenization the same. For French, the centralized language par excellence, one may refer to the analysis of Michel de Certeau, Dominique Julia, and Jacques Revel, *Une politique de la langue* (Paris: Gallimard, 1975). The analysis covers a very brief period at the end of the eighteenth century, focusing on Abbot Gregory, and notes two distinct periods: one in which the central language opposed the rural dialects, just as the town opposed the countryside, and the capital the provinces; and another in which it opposed "feudal idioms," as well as the language of the émigrés, just as the nation opposes everything that is foreign to it, an enemy to it: "It is also obvious that the rejection of the dialects resulted from a technical inability to grasp stable laws in regional speech patterns" (pp. 160ff.).

2. See Michel Lalonde, *Change*, 30 (March 1977), pp. 100–122, where the poem, "Speak White," quoted in text, appears, along with a manifesto on the Quebecois language ("La deffense et illustration de la langue quebecqoyse").

3. On the complex situation of Afrikaans, see Breyten Breytenbach's fine book, *Feu Froid* (Paris: Bourgeois, 1976); G. M. Lory's study (pp. 101–107) elucidates Breytenbach's project, the violence of his poetic treatment of the language, and his will to be a "bastard, with a bastard language."

4. On the double aspect of minor language, poverty-ellipsis, and overload-variation, one may refer to a certain number of exemplary studies: Klauss Wagenbach's study of the German of Prague at the beginning of the twentieth century, *Franz Kafka: Eine Biographie seiner Jugend* (Bern: Francke, 1958); Pasolini's study demonstrating that Italian was not constructed on the basis of a new standard or mean, but exploded in two simultaneous directions, "upward and downward," in other words, toward simplified material and expressive exaggeration (*L'expérience hérétique: Langue et cinema* (Paris: Payot, 1976), pp. 46–47); and J. L. Dillard's study bringing out the double tendency of Black English on the one hand to omit, lose, disencumber, and on the other to overload, to develop "fancy talk" (*Black English* [New York: Random House, 1972]). As Dillard notes, there is no inferiority to the standard language; instead there is a correlation between two movements that necessarily escape from the standard level of language. Still on the topic of Black English, LeRoi Jones shows the extent to which the two conjoined directions approximate language to music (*Blues People* [New York: William Morrow, 1963], pp. 30–31 and all of ch. 3). On a more general level, one will recall Pierre Boulez's analysis of a double movement in music, dissolution of form, and dynamic overload or proliferation: *Conversations with Célestin Deliège* (London: Eulenberg Books, 1976), pp. 20–22.

5. Yann Moulier, preface to Mario Tronti, *Ouvriers et capital* (Paris: Bourgois, 1977), p. 6.

6. Pasolini, *L'expérience hérétique*, p. 62.

7. See the "Strategy Collective" manifesto on the Quebecois language in *Change*, 30 (March 1977); it denounces the "myth of subversive language," which implies that simply being in a minority is enough to make one a revolutionary: "this mechanist equation derives from a populist conception of language. . . . Speaking the language of the working class is not what links an individual to the positions of that class. . . . The argument that Joual has a subversive, countercultural force is entirely idealistic" (p. 188).

18. Minor Literature: Kafka

1. See letter to Brod in Franz Kafka, *Letters to Friends, Family and Editors*, trans. Richard and Clair Winston (New York: Schocken Books, 1977), June 1921, p. 289, and commentaries in Wagenbach, *Franz Kafka, Années de jeunesse* (Paris: Mercure: 1967), p. 84.

2. Kafka, *Diaries*, trans. Martin Greenberg (New York: Schocken Books, 1949), 29 December 1911, p. 194.

3. Ibid., p. 193: "Literature is less a concern of literary history, than of the people."

4. See "Wedding Preparations in the Country," in Kafka, *Complete Stories* (New York: Schocken Books, 1971): "And so long as you say 'one' instead of 'I,' there's nothing in it" (p. 53). And the two subjects appear several pages later: "I don't even need to go to the country myself, it isn't necessary. I'll send my clothed body," while the narrator stays in bed like a bug or a beetle (p. 55). No doubt, this is one of the origins of Gregor's becoming-beetle in "The Metamorphosis" (in the same way, Kafka will give up going to meet Felice and will prefer to stay in bed). But in "The Metamorphosis," the animal takes on all the value of a true becoming and no longer has any of the stagnancy of a subject of enunciation.

5. See Michel Ragon, *Historie de la littérature prolétarienne en France* (Paris: Albin Michel, 1974) on the difficulty of criteria and on the need to use a concept of a "secondary zone literature."

6. Kafka, *Diaries*, 25 December 1911, p. 193: "A small nation's memory is not smaller than the memory of a large one and so can digest the existing material more thoroughly."

7. See the excellent chapter "Prague at the Turn of the Century," in Wagenbach, *Franz Kafka*, on the situation of the German language in Czechoslovakia and on the Prague school.

8. The theme of teeth is constant in Kafka. A grandfather-butcher; a streetwise education at the butcher-shop; Felice's jaws; the refusal to eat meat except when he sleeps with Felice in Marienbad. See Michel Cournot's article, "Toi que as de si grandes dents," *Nouvel Observateur*, 17 April 1972. This is one of the most beautiful texts on Kafka. One can find a similar opposition between eating and speaking in Lewis Carroll, and a comparable escape into nonsense.

9. Franz Kafka, *The Trial*, trans. Willa and Edwin Muir (New York: Schocken Books, 1956); "He noticed that they were talking to him, but he could not make out what they were saying, he heard nothing but the din that filled the whole place, through which a shrill unchanging note like that of a siren seemed to sing."

10. Kafka, *Diaries* 20 August 1911, pp. 61–62.

11. Kafka, *Diaries:* "Without gaining a sense, the phrase 'end of the month' held a terrible secret for me" especially since it was repeated every month—Kafka himself suggests that if this expression remained shorn of sense, this was due to laziness and "weakened curiosity." A negative explication invoking lack or powerlessness, as taken by Wagenbach. It is well known that Kafka makes this sort of negative suggestion to present or to hide the objects of his passion.

12. Kafka, *Letters to Milena* trans. Philip Boehm (New York: Schocken, 1990), p. 58. On Kafka's fascination with proper names, beginning with those that he invented, see Kafka, *Diaries*, 11 February 1913 (apropos of the names in *The Verdict*).

13. Kafka commentators are at their worst in their interpretations in this respect when they regulate everything through metaphors: thus, Marthe Robert reminds us that the Jews are *like* dogs or, to take another example, that "since the artist is treated as someone starving to death Kafka makes him into a hunger artist; or since he is treated as a parasite, Kafka makes him into an enormous insect" (*Oeuvres com-*

plètes, Circle du livre precieux, vol. 5, p. 311). It seems to us that this is a simplistic conception of the literary machine—Robbe-Grillet has insisted on the destruction of all metaphors in Kafka.

14. See, for example, the letter to Pollak in Kafka, *Letters*, 4 February 1902, pp. 1–2.

15. See H. Vidal Sephiha, "Introduction a l'étude de l'intensif," in *Langages*, 18 (June 1970), pp. 104–20. We take the term *tensor* from J.-F.. Lyotard who uses it to indicate the connection of intensity and libido.

16. Sephiha, "Introduction," p. 107: "We can imagine that any phrase conveying a negative notion of pain, evil, fear, violence can cast off the notion in order to retain no more than its limit-value—that is, its intensive value"; for example, the German word *sehr*, which comes from the Middle High German word, *Ser* meaning "painful."

17. Wagenbach, *Franz Kafka*, pp. 78–88 (especially pp. 78, 81, 88).

18. Kafka, *Diaries*, 15 December 1910, p. 33.

19. Henri Gobard, "De la vehicularité de la langue anglaise," *Langues modernes* (January 1972), and *L'Alienation linguistique: analyse tetraglossique* (Paris: Flammarion, 1976).

20. Michel Foucault insists on the importance of the distribution between what can be said in a language at a certain moment and what cannot be said (even if it can be *done*). Georges Devereux (cited by H. Gobard) analyzes the case of the young Mohave Indians who speak about sexuality with great ease in their vernacular language, but who are incapable of doing so in that vehicular language that English constitutes for them; and this is so not only because the English instructor exercises a repressive function, but also because there is a problem of languages (see *Essais d'ethnopsychiatrie générale* [Paris: Gallimard, 1970], pp. 125–26).

21. On the Prague circle and its role in linguistics, see *Change*, 3 (1969), and 10 (1972). It is true that the Prague circle was only formed in 1925. But in 1920, Jakobson came to Prague where there was already a Czech movement directed by Mathesius and connected with Anton Marty who had taught in the German university system. From 1902 to 1905, Kafka followed the courses given by Marty, a disciple of Brentano, and participated in Brentanoist meetings.

22. On Kafka's connections to Lowy and Yiddish theater, see Brod, *Franz Kafka*, pp. 110–16, and Wagenbach, *Franz Kafka*, pp. 163–67. In this mime theater, there must have been many bent heads and straightened heads.

23. Franz Kafka, "An Introductory Talk on the Yiddish Language," in Franz Kafka, *Dearest Father*, trans. Ernst Kaiser and Eithne Wilkins (New York: Schocken Books, 1954), pp. 381–86.

24. A magazine editor will declare that Kafka's prose has "the air of the cleanliness of a child who takes care of himself" (see Wagenbach, *Franz Kafka*, p. 82).

25. "The Great Swimmer" is undoubtedly one of the most Beckett-like of Kafka's texts: "I have to well admit that I am in my own country and that, in spite of all my efforts, I don't understand a word of the language you are speaking."

19. Nomad Art: Space

1. The principal texts are Alois Riegl, *Die Spätrömische Kunstindustrie* (Vienna: Staatdruckerei, 1927); Wilhelm Worringer, *Abstraction and Empathy: A Contribution to the Psychology of Style*, trans. Michel Bullock (New York: International Universities Press, 1963); Henri Maldiney, *Regard, parole, espace* (Lausanne: L'Age d'homme, 1973), especially "L'art et le pouvoir du fond," and Maldiney's discussion of Cézanne.

2. All of these points already relate to Riemannian space, with its essential relation to "monads" (as opposed to the unitary subject of Euclidean space see Gilles Châtelet, "Sur une petite phrase de Riemann," *Analytiques*, 3 (May 1979). Although the "monads" are no longer thought to be closed upon themselves, and are postulated to entertain direct, step-by-step local relations, the purely monadological point of view proves inadequate and should be superseded by a "nomadology" (the ideality of striated space versus the realism of smooth space).

3. See Edmund Carpenter's description in *Eskimo* (Toronto: University of Toronto Press, 1964) of ice space, and of the igloo: "There is no middle distance, no perspective, no outline, nothing the eye can cling to except thousands of smokey plumes of snow . . . a land without bottom or edge . . . a labyrinth alive with the movements of crowded people. No flat static walls arrest the ear or eye . . . and the eye can glance through here, past there" (no pagination).

4. These two aspects, the encompassing element and the center, figure in Jean-Pierre Vernant's analysis of space in Anaximander, in *Mythe et pensée chez les Grecs* (Paris: Maspero, 1971–74), vol. 1, part III. From another perspective, the entire history of the desert concerns the possibility of its becoming the encompassing element, and also of being repelled, rejected by the center, as though in an inversion of movement. In a phenomenology of religion like that of Van der Leeuw, the *nomos* itself does indeed appear as the encompassing-limit or ground, and also as that which is repelled, excluded, in a centrifugal movement.

5. Whatever interactions there may be, the "art of the steppes" had a specificity that was communicated to the migrating Germans; in spite of his many reservations about nomad culture, Rene Grousset makes this point in *The Empire of the Steppes*, trans. Naomi Walford (New Brunswick, N.J.: Rutgers University Press, 1970), pp. 11–25. He notes the irreducibility of Scythian art to Assyrian art, Sarmatian art to Persian art, and Hunnic art to Chinese art. He even points out that the art of the steppes influenced more than it borrowed (see in particular the question of Ordos art and its relations to China).

6. On this question of light and color, in particular in Byzantine art, see Henri Maldiney, *Regard, parole, espace*, pp. 203ff., 239ff.

7. The correlation, "haptic-close-abstract," was already suggested by Riegl. But it was Worringer who developed the theme of the abstract line. Although he conceives of it essentially in its Egyptian form, he describes a second form in which the abstract assumes an intense life and an expressionist value, all the while remaining inorganic; see *Abstraction and Empathy*, ch. 5, and especially *Form in Gothic* (London: Putnam's and Sons, 1927), pp. 38–55.

8. André Leroi-Gourhan, *Le geste et la parole* (Paris: Albin Michel, 1964–1965), 2 vols. *Technique et langage*, 1: 263ff.; *La mémoire et les rythmes*, 2: 219f. ("Rhythmic marks are anterior to explicit figures"). Worringer's position is very ambiguous; thinking that prehistoric art is fundamentally figurative, he excludes it from art, on the same grounds as he excludes the "scribblings of a child" (*Abstraction and Empathy*, pp. 51–55). Then he advances the hypothesis that the cave dwellers were the "ultimate result" of a series he says began with the abstract (p. 130). But would not such a hypothesis force Worringer to revise his conception of the abstract, and to cease identifying it with Egyptian geometricism?

9. Worringer establishes an opposition between the power of repetition, which is mechanical, multiplying, and without fixed orientation, and the force of symmetry, which is organic, additive, oriented, and centered. He sees this as the fundamental difference between Gothic ornamentation and Greek or classical ornamentation; see *Form in Gothic*, pp. 53–55 ("The Ceaseless Melody of the Northern Line"). In a fine book, *Esthétiques d'Orient et d'Occident* (Paris: E. Leroux, 1937), Laura Morgenstern develops a particular example, distinguishing the "symmetrical antithetism" of Sassanid Persian art from the "disjointed antithetism" of the art of the proto-Iranian nomads (Sarmatians). Many authors, however, have stressed the centered and symmetrical motifs in barbarian or nomad art. Worringer anticipated this objection: "Instead of the regular and invariably geometrical star or rosette or similar restful forms, in the North we find the revolving wheel, the turbine or the so-called sun wheel, all designs which express violent movement. Moreover, the movement is peripheral and not radial" (*Form in Gothic*, p. 54). The history of technology confirms the importance of the turbine in the life of the nomads. In another, bioaesthetic, context, Gabriel Tarde opposes repetition as indefinite potential (*puissance*) to symmetry as limitation. With symmetry, life constituted an organism for itself, taking a star-shaped or reflected, infolded form (the radiata and mollusks). It is true that in doing so it unleashed another type of repetition, external reproduction; see *L'opposition universelle* (Paris: Alcan, 1897).

10. Translator's note: Worringer, *Abstraction and Empathy*, p. 33.

11. Translator's note: Worringer, *Abstraction and Empathy*, p. 42.

12. On all these points, see Georges Charriere's very intuitive book, *Scythian Art* (New York: Alpine Fine Arts Collection, 1979), which includes a great number of reproductions. It is doubtless René Grousset who has most effectively emphasized "slowness" as a dramatic pole of nomad art; see *The Empire of the Steppes*, pp. 13–14.

13. Dora Vallier, in her preface to the French translation of *Abstraction and Empathy* (*Abstraction et Einfuhlung* [Paris: Klincksieck, 1978]), is right to note Worringer and Kandinsky's independence from one another, and the differences between the problems they were addressing. However, she maintains that there is still convergence and resonance between them. In a sense, all art is abstract, with the figurative springing from certain types of abstraction. But in another sense, since there are very different types of lines (Egyptian-geometrical, Greek-organic, Gothic-vital, etc.), the question then becomes one of determining which line remains abstract, or realizes abstraction as such. It is doubtful that it is the geometrical line, since it still draws a figure, even though an abstract and nonrepresentative one. Rather, the ab-

stract line is that defined by Michael Fried in relation to certain works by Pollock: multidirectional, with neither inside nor outside, form nor background, delimiting nothing, describing no contour, passing between spots or points, filling a smooth space, stirring up a close-lying haptic visual matter that "both invites the act of seeing on the part of the spectator yet gives his eye nowhere the rest once and for all" (*Three American Painters* [Cambridge, Mass.: Fogg Art Museum, 1965], p. 14). In Kandinsky himself, abstraction is realized not so much by geometrical structures as by lines of march or transit that seem to recall Mongolian nomadic motifs.

20. Cinema and Space: The Frame

1. See P. Pasolini, *L'Expérience hérétique*, pp. 263–265.

2. Noël Burch, *Praxis du cinéma*, p. 86: on the black or white screen, when it no longer simply serves as "punctuation" but takes on a "structural value."

3. Claude Ollier, "Souvenirs 'écran,'" in *Cahiers du Cinéma*, p. 88. It is this which Pasolini analyzed as "obsessive framing" in Antonioni (*L'Expérience hérétique*, p. 148).

4. Dominique Villain, in an unpublished work which includes interviews with cameramen (*cadreurs*), analyzes these two conceptions of framing: *Le Cadrage cinématographique*.

5. Lotte Eisner, *L'Écran démoniaque* (Paris: Ramsay, 1985), p. 124. Translated as *The Haunted Screen* (Berkeley: University of California Press, 1969).

6. Cf. Bouvier and Leutrat, "Nosferatu," in *Cahiers du cinéma*, pp. 75–76.

7. Jean Mitry, *Esthétique et psychologie du cinéma* (Paris: Editions Universitaires, 1990), vol. 2, pp. 78–79.

8. Pascal Bonitzer, "Décadrage," in *Cahiers du cinéma*, 284 (January 1978).

9. R. Bresson, *Notes on Cinematography*, trans. Jonathan Griffin (New York: Urizen 1977), p. 28: "A sound must never come to the help of an image, nor an image to the help of a sound. . . . Image and sound must not support each other, but must work each in turn through *a sort of relay.*"

10. The most systematic study of the out-of-field was made by Noël Burch, precisely in relation to Renoir's *Nana* (*Une Praxis du cinéma*, (Paris: Gallimard, 1986), pp. 30–51). And it is from this point of view that Jean Narboni contrasts Hitchcock and Renoir (*Hitchcock*, "Visages d'Hitchcock," p. 37). But, as Narboni recalls, the cinematographic frame is always a mask in Bazin's sense: this is because Hitchcock's closed framing also has its out-of-field, although in a completely different way from Renoir (not a "space which is continuous and homogeneous with that of the screen" but an "off-space" "which is discontinuous and heterogeneous to that of the screen," which defines virtualities).

11. Bergson developed all these points in *Creative Evolution*, trans. Arthur Mitchell (New York: Holt, 1911), Ch. 1. On the "tenuous thread," cf. p. 11.

12. Bonitzer objects to Burch's view that there is no "becoming-field of the out-of-field" and that the out-of-field remains imaginary, even when it is actualized by the effect of a continuity shot: something always remains out-of-field, and according to Bonitzer it is the camera itself, which can appear on its own account, but by introducing a new duality into the image (*Le regard et la voix*, p. 17). These remarks of

Bonitzer seem to us to be solidly based. But we believe that there is an internal duality in the out-of-field itself which does not merely relate to the working implement.

13. Dreyer, quoted by Maurice Drouzy, *Carl Th. Dreyer né Nilsson Essai de psychocritique* (Paris: Cerf, 1982), p. 353.

21. Cinema and Time

1. Paul Rozenberg sees in this the essence of English romanticism. See his *Le romantisme anglais* (Paris: Larousse).

2. J.M.G. LeClezio, "The Extra-Terrestrial," in "Fellini," *L'Arc*, 45, p. 28.

3. On Marxist criticism on the evolution of neo-realism and its characters, cf. *Le néo-réalisme, Études cinématographiques*, p. 102. And on Marxist criticism in Japan, especially against Ozu, cf. Noël Burch, *Une Praxis du cinéma*, p. 283. It must be emphasized that in France the new wave, in its visionary aspect, was deeply understood by Sadoul.

4. Cf. *Jean-Luc Godard par Jean-Luc Godard*, p. 392.

5. Marc Chevrie analyzes Jean-Pierre Leaud's playing as "medium" in terms close to Blanchot's (*Cahiers du cinéma*, 351 (September 1983): 31–33).

6. Criticism of metaphor is equally present in the new wave with Godard and in the new novel with Robbe-Grillet (*Pour un nouveau roman*). It is true that, more recently, Godard has taken inspiration from a metaphorical form, for instance, in the case of *Passion:* "The knights are metaphors for the bosses" (*Le Monde*, 27 May 1982), but, as we shall see, this form draws on a genetic and chronological analysis of the image, much more than on a synthesis or comparison of images.

7. D. H. Lawrence wrote an important piece in support of the image and against clichés in relation to Cézanne. He shows how parody is not a solution; and neither is the pure optical image, with its voids and disconnections. According to him, it is in the still lifes that Cézanne wins his battle gainst chichés, rather than in the portraits and landscapes ("Introduction to These Paintings," *Phoenix*, ed. D. McDonald (London: Heinemann, 1936). We have seen how the same remarks applied to Ozu.

8. "Lectosign" refers to the Greek *lekton* or Latin *dictum*, which indicates what is expressed in a proposition independent of the relationship of this to its object. Similarly for the image when it is captured intrinsically, independent of its relationship with a supposedly external object.

9. Text of Antonioni's quoted by Pierre Leprohon, *Antonioni* (Paris: Seghers), p. 103: "Now that we have today eliminated the problem of the bicycle (I am using a metaphor, try to understand beyond my words), it is important to see what there is in the spirit and heart of this man whose bicycle has been stolen, how he has adapted, what has stayed with him out of all his past experiences of the war, the post-war and everything that has happened in our country." (See also the text on Eros sick, pp. 104–6.)

10. Noël Burch is one of the first critics to have shown that the cinematographic image ought to be read no less than seen and heard; and this in connection with Ozu

(*Pour un observateur lointain* (Paris: Gallimard, 1982), p. 175). But already in *Praxis du cinema* Burch showed how *Story of a Love Affair* inaugurated a new relation between story and action, and gave the camera an "autonomy," rather like that of a reading, pp. 112–18; on the "continuity grasped through discrepancy," see p. 47.

22. Painting and Sensation

1. Henri Maldiney, *Regard parole espace* (Lausanne: Éditions l'Age d'Homme, 1973), p. 136. Phenomenologists like Maldiney and Merleau-Ponty see Cézanne as the painter par excellence. They analyze, in fact, sensation or rather "sensing," not only in terms of relating sensible qualities to an identifiable object (figurative movement), but also from the point of view of each quality constituting a field which stands by itself without ceasing to interfere with the other's ("pathetic" moment). Hegel's phenomenology short-circuits this aspect of sensation, which, nonetheless, is the basis of every possible aesthetics. See Maurice Merleau-Ponty, *Phenomenology of Perception* (London: Routledge and Kegan Paul, 1962), pp. 207–42; Maldiney, *Regard parole espace*, 124–208.

2. D. H. Lawrence, "Introduction to These Paintings," in *Phoenix*, pp. 551–84.

3. *Francis Bacon. Interviewed by David Sylvester* (New York: Pantheon Books, 1975), p. 18.

4. Ibid., p. 63.

5. Ibid., p. 65.

6. All these themes are constantly present in *Francis Bacon. Interviewed by David Sylvester.*

7. Ibid., p. 58.

8. Ibid., pp. 83–84.

9. Ibid., p. 58 ("coagulation of non-representational marks").

10. Ibid., pp. 76–81 (see also p. 47: "I have never tried to be horrific").

11. Ibid., p. 43. Bacon seems to rebel against psychoanalytic suggestions; Sylvester, in another context, tells him that "the Pope is *il Papa*"; Bacon answers politely: "Well, I certainly have never thought of it in that way" (p. 71). For a more elaborate, psychoanalytic interpretation of Bacon's paintings, see Didier Anjeu, *Le Corps de L'Autre* (Paris: Gallimard), pp. 333–40.

12. *Francis Bacon. Interviewed by David Sylvester*, pp. 75–76, 108.

13. On sensation and rhythm, systole and diastole (and on Cézanne's pages on them, see *Regard Parole Espace*, pp. 147–172.

14. *Francis Bacon. Interviewed by David Sylvester*, p. 74.

23. The Diagram

1. This is very important text of Bacon taken from *Francis Bacon. Interviewed by David Sylvester*, p. 56. "FB: Well, very often the involuntary marks are much more deeply suggestive than others, and those are the moments when you feel that anything can happen. DS: You feel it while you're making those marks: FB: No, the marks are made, and you survey the thing like you would a sort of graph. And you

see within this graph the possibilities of all types of fact being planted. This is a difficult thing; I'm expressing it badly. But you see, for instance, if you think of a portrait, you maybe at one time have put the mouth somewhere, but you suddenly see through this graph that the mouth could go right across the face. And in a way you would love to be able in a portrait to make a Sahara of the appearance—to make it so like, yet seeming to have the distances of the Sahara." In another passage, Bacon explains that, when he makes a portrait, he often looks at photographs which have nothing to do with the model—for example, a photograph of a rhinoceros for the texture of the skin (ibid., p. 32).

2. Ibid., p. 90.

3. On the possibility that involuntary marks offer nothing and spoil the painting, leading it "into a kind of marshland, see ibid, 90.

4. See ibid., p. 56: "And you see within this graph the possibilities of all types of fact." Wittgenstein invoked a diagrammatic form in order to express the "possibilities of fact" in logic.

5. Ibid., p. 56.

6. Henri Maldiney compares, in this respect, Cézanne and Klee. See *Regard parole espace*, pp. 149–51.

7. This tendency to eliminate the manual has always been present in painting, in the sense that we say about a certain work that "we no longer feel the hand." Focillon analyzes this tendency—"ascetic frugality"—which reaches its apex in abstract painting. See *Vie des Formes, suivi de l'Éloge de la Main* (Paris: Presses Universitaires de France, 1934), 5th ed., pp. 118–19. But, as Focillon says, the hand feels itself all the same. In order to distinguish a real from a false Mondrian, Georg Schmidt used to appeal to the intersection of the two black sides of a square, or to the disposition of the layers of color along right angles (see *Mondrian*, Réunion des Musées Nationaux, p. 148).

8. See Elie Faure's famous text on Velasquez, *Histoire de l'Art. L'Art Moderne 1* (Paris: Gallimard, 1988), pp. 167–77.

9. On these new blind spaces, see Christian Bonnefoi's analyses on Ryman in Christian Bonnefoi's "A propos de la destruction de l'entité de surface," *Macula*, 3–4 (1978): 163–66. For Yves-Alain Bois' analyses of Bonnefoi see Yves-Alain Bois, "Le futur antérieur," *Macula*, 5–6 (1979): 229–33.

10. Clement Greenberg (*Art and Culture: Critical Essays* [Boston: Beacon Press, 1961]) and Michael Fried ("Trois Peintres Américains," in *Peindre: Revue d'Esthétique* [Paris: Union Générale d'Editions]) have been the first to analyze the spaces of Pollock, Morris Louis, Newman, Noland, etc., and to define them in terms of "strict opticality." Undoubtedly, the question for these critics was how to break away from the extraaesthetic criteria that Harold Rosenberg had invoked, as he baptized action painting. They reminded us that Pollock's words—although "modern"—are, first and foremost, tableaus, and as such answerable to formal criteria. The question, though, is to find out whether opticality is the right criterion for these works. It seems that Fried entertains doubts but that he abandons them too quickly (see pp. 283–87). The term *action painting* can be aesthetically correct.

11. Greenberg has noted very forcefully the importance of this abandonment of the easel, especially in Pollock. He emphasizes, in this context, the "Gothic" theme,

without giving it, though, the full meaning that the term can assume with respect to Worringer's analyses (one of Pollock's paintings is called *Gothic*); it seems that Greenberg sees no alternative other than that between "painting with easel" and "mural painting" (it seems to us that this would rather apply to the case of Mondrian). See in *Macula*, 2, "Jackson Pollock's File."

12. Bacon often criticizes abstraction for staying "at only one level" and for spoiling the "tension" (*Francis Bacon. Interviewed by David Sylvester*, p. 60). About Marcel Duchamp, Bacon says that he admires him more for his attitude and less for his painting; in fact, his painting strikes Bacon as symbolics or "shorthand figuration" (ibid., p. 105).

13. Ibid., p. 94: "I hate that kind of sloppy sort of Central European painting; it's one of the reasons I don't really like abstract expressionism"; see also p. 61: "I think Michaux is a very, very intelligent and conscious man. . . . And I think that he has made the best tachist or free marks that have been made. I think he is much better in that way, in making marks, than Jackson Pollock."

14. See Gregory Bateson, "Why Do Things have Outlines?" in *Steps to an Ecology of Mind* (San Francisco: Chandez, 1972), pp. 27–32. What used to make Blake mad, incensed, or furious, was for people to think of him as mad; but it was also because of "some artists who paint as if things did not have contours." He used to call them "the slobbering school."

15. *Francis Bacon. Interviewed by David Sylvester*, p. 94: "You would never end a painting by suddenly throwing something at it. Or would you?—Oh yes. In that recent triptych, on the shoulder of the figure being sick into the basin, there's like a whip of white paint that goes like that. Well, I did that at the very last moment, and I simply left it."

24. Music and Ritornello

1. See Fernand Deligny, "Voix et voir," *Recherches*, 8 (April 1975), on the way in which, among autistic children, a "line of drift" deviates from the customary path and begins to "vibrate," "toss about," "yaw."

2. Paul Klee, *On Modern Art*, trans. Paul Findlay, intro. Herbert Reed (London: Faber, 1966), p. 43 (translation modified to agree with the French version cited by the authors). See Henri Maldiney's comments in *Regarde parole espace* (Lausanne: L'Age d'homme, 1973), pp. 149–51.

3. On the musical nome, the ethos, and the ground or land, notably in polyphony, see Joseph Samson in *Historie de la musique*, ed. Roland Manuel (Paris: Gallimard, 1977), vol. 2, pp. 1168–72. One may also refer to the role in Arab music of the "maqam," which is both a modal type and a melodic formula; see Simon Jargy, *La musique arabe* (Paris: PUF, 1971), pp. 55ff.

26. On the Line

1. Heinrich von Kleist, *Uber das Marionettentheater: Aufsätze und Anekdoten* (Frankfurt a.M.: Ingel, 1980).

2. F. Scott Fitzgerald, *The Crack-Up, with Other Pieces and Stories* (Harmondsworth: Penguin, 1965).

3. S. Kierkegaard, *Fear and Trembling*, trans. Walter Lowrie (Princeton: Princeton University Press, 1968). This also shows the way in which Kierkegaard, in relation to movement, sketches a series of scripts that already belong to the cinema.

4. Fernand Deligny, "Cahiers de l'immuable," *Recherches* 18 (Paris: Recherches, 1975).

5. Pierrette Fleutiaux, *Histoire du gouffre et de la lunette* (Paris: Julliard, 1976).

27. Capitalism

1. Karl Marx, "Introduction to the Critique of Political Economy," in *A Contribution to the Critique of Political Economy*, trans. N. I. Stone (Chicago: Charles H. Kerr, 1904), p. 298 (translation modified).

2. On the historical independence of the two series, and their "encounter," see Etienne Balibar in Althusser and Balibar, *Lire le Capital*, vol. 2 (Paris: Maspero, 1968), pp. 286–89.

3. See Arghiri Emmanuel, *Unequal Exchange: A Study of the Imperialism of Trade* (New York: Monthly Review Books, 1972), pp. 13–14, and the following passage he cites from Paul Sweezy, *The Theory of Capitalist Development* (New York: Monthly Review Press, 1942), p. 338: " 'Capital' is not simply another name for means of production; it is means of production reduced to a qualitatively homogeneous and quantitatively measurable fund of value" (whence the equalization of profit). In his analysis of the primitive accumulation of capital, Maurice Dobb (*Studies in the Development of Capitalism*, rev. ed. [New York: International Publishers, 1964], pp. 177–86) effectively demonstrates that primitive accumulation bears not on the means of production but on "rights or titles to wealth" (p. 177; modified to agree with the French translation cited by the authors), which, depending on the circumstances, are convertible into means of production.

4. See the distinction certain jurists make between Roman, "topical," law, and modern, "axiomatic," law of the civil-code type. We may define certain fundamental ways in which the French Civil Code is closer to an axiomatic than to a code: (1) the predominance of the enunciative form over the imperative and over affective formulas (damnation, exhortation, admonishment, etc.); (2) the code's pretension that it forms a complete and saturated rational system; (3) but at the same time the relative independence of the propositions, which permit axioms to be added. On these aspects, see Jean Ray, *Essai sur la structure logique du code civil français* (Paris: Alcan, 1926). It has been established that the systematization of Roman law took place very late, in the sixteenth and seventeenth centuries.

5. Translator's note: Marx, *Economic and Philosophic Manuscripts of 1844*, ed. and intro. Dirk J. Struik, trans. Martin Mulligan (New York: International Publishers, 1964), p. 129.

6. See Jean Saint-Geours, *Pouvoir et finance* (Paris: Fayard, 1979). Saint-Geours is one of the best analysts of the monetary system, as well as of "private-public" mixes in the modern economy.

7. On the tendency toward the elimination of ground rent in capitalism, see Samir Amin and Kostas Vergopoulos, *La question paysanne et le capitalisme* (Paris: Éditions Anthropos, 1974). Amin analyzes the reasons why ground rent and rent of mines keep or assume a present-day meaning in the peripheral regions, although in different ways; see *The Law of Value and Historical Materialism*, trans. Brian Pearce (New York: Monthly Review Press, 1978), chs. 4 and 6.

8. Introductory books on the axiomatic method emphasize a certain number of problems. For example, see Robert Blanché's fine book, *L'axiomatique* (Paris: PUF, 1959) (abridged and translated by G. B. Keene as *Axiomatics* [New York: Free Press of Glencoe, 1962]). There is first of all the question of the respective independence of the axioms, and whether or not the system is saturated, or "strongly complete" (secs. 14 and 15). Second, there is the question of "models of realization," their heterogeneity, but also their isomorphy in relation to the axiomatic system (sec. 12). Then there is the possibility of a polymorphy of models, not only in a nonsaturated system, but even in a saturated axiomatic (secs. 12, 15, and 26). Then, once again, there is the question of the "undecidable propositions" an axiomatic confronts (sec. 20). Finally, there is the question of "power," by which nondemonstrable infinite sets exceed the axiomatic (sec. 26 and "the power of the continuum"). The comparison of politics to an axiomatic is based on all of these aspects.

9. Lewis Mumford, "The First Megamachine," *Diogenes*, 55 (July–September 1966), p. 3 (translation modified to agree with the French translation cited by the authors).

10. Ergonomics distinguishes between "human-machine" systems (or work posts) and "humans-machines" systems (communicational aggregates composed of human and nonhuman elements). But this is not only a difference of degree; the second point of view is not a generalization of the first: "The notion of information loses its anthropocentric aspect," and the problems are not of adaptation but of the choice of a human or nonhuman element depending on the case. See Maurice de Montmollin, *Les systèmes hommes-machines* (Paris: PUF, 1967). The issue is no longer to adapt, even under violence, but to localize: where is your place? Even handicaps can be made useful, instead of being corrected or compensated for. A deaf-mute can be an essential part of a "humans-machines" communicational system.

11. One of the basic themes of science fiction is to show how machinic enslavement combines with processes of subjection, but exceeds and differs from them, performing a qualitative leap. Take Ray Bradbury: television not as an instrument located at the center of the house, but as forming the walls of the house.

12. See Lewis Mumford, *The Pentagon of Power*, vol. 2 of *The Myth of the Machines* (New York: Harcourt Brace Jovanovich, 1970), pp. 236–360 (a comparison of the "old megamachine" and the modern one; despite writing, the old megamachine notably suffered from difficulties in "communication").

13. Marx, *Manuscripts of 1844*, p. 129.

28. The Three Aspects of Culture

1. Friedrich Nietzsche, *Daybreak*, trans. by R. J. Hollingdale (New York: Columbia University Press, 1982); hereafter *D*.

2. Friedrich Nietzsche, *Beyond Good and Evil*, trans. R. J. Hollingdale (New York: Penguin, 1973); hereafter *BGE*.

3. Friedrich Nietzsche, *On the Genealogy of Morals*, trans. by Walter Kaufmann and R. J. Hollingdale (New York: Random House, 1967); hereafter *GM*.

4. Friedrich Nietzsche, *Ecce Homo*, trans by Walter Kaufmann (New York: Random House, 1967).

5. *GM* II 1: On this point the resemblance between Freud and Nietzsche is confirmed. Freud attributes verbal traces to the preconscious, these are distinct from the mnemonic traces peculiar to the unconscious system. This distinction permits him to reply to the question "How to render repressed elements (pre-)conscious?" The reply is: "By restoring these intermediary preconscious elements which are verbal memories." Nietzsche's question would be stated in this way: how is it possible to "act" reactive forces?

6. *GM* II 8, p. 70: It was in the debtor-creditor relationship "that one person first encountered another person, that one person first *measured himself* against another."

7. *GM* II 6, pp. 65–66: "Whoever clumsily interposes the concept of 'revenge' does not enhance his insight into the matter but further veils and darkens it (for revenge merely leads us back to the same problem: 'how can making suffer constitute a compensation?')." This is what is lacking in the majority of theories: showing from what point of view "making suffer" gives pleasure.

8. *GM* II 11, p. 75: "The law represents on earth . . . the struggle against the reactive feelings, the war conducted against them on the part of the active and aggressive powers."

9. *GM* II 10, p. 73: Justice "ends, as does every good thing on earth, by *overcoming itself.*"

10. Friedrich Nietzsche, *Thus Spoke Zarathustra*, trans. by R. J. Hollingdale (New York: Penguin Books, 1961); hereafter *Z*.

11. Friedrich Nietzsche, "Schopenhauer as Educator," trans. by James W. Hillesheim and Malcolm R. Simpson (Chicago: Henry Regnery, 1965), chap. 6—Nietzsche explains the diverting of culture by invoking the "three egoisms," the egoism of *acquirers*, the egoism of the *State*, the egoism of *science*.

12. Friedrich Nietzsche, *Untimely Meditations*, trans. by R. J. Hollingdale (Cambridge: Cambridge University Press, 1983).

Works by Gilles Deleuze

1946   "Du Christ à la bourgeoisie." *Espace*, pp. 93–106.

"Mathèse, science, et philosophie." Preface to Johann Malfatti von Montereggio, *Etudes sur la mathèse; ou, anarchie et hierarchie de la science*. Trans. by Christian Ostrowski. Paris: Editions du Griffon d'Or.

1947   "Preface." To Diderot, *La religieuse*. Paris: Marcel Daubin.

1952   (with André Cresson). *David Hume: Sa vie, son oeuvre, avec un exposé de sa philosophie*. Paris: Presses Universitaires de France.

1953   *Empirisme et subjectivité: Essai sur la nature humaine selon Hume*. Paris: Presses Universitaires de France. English trans. and introduced by Constantin V. Boundas, *Empiricism and Subjectivity: An Essay on Hume's Theory of Human Nature*. New York: Columbia University Press, 1991.

Instincts et institutions. Paris: Hachette.

1956   "Bergson (1859–1941)." *Les philosophes célébres*, sous la dir. M. Merleau-Ponty. Paris: Editions d'Art Lucien Mazenod.

"La conception de la différence chez Bergson." *Etudes Bergsoniennes*, vol. 4, pp. 77–112.

1957   *Bergson: Memoire et vie*. Paris: Presses Universitaire de France.

1959   "Nietzsche, sens, et valeurs." *Arguments*, vol. 3, no. 15, pp. 20–28.

1961   "De Sacher-Masoch au masochisme," *Arguments,* vol. 21, pp. 40–46.

"Lucrèce et le naturalisme." *Etudies Philosophiques,* vol. 16, no. 1, pp. 19–29. Reprinted with modification in the *Logique du sens* (1969).

1962   *Nietzsche et la philosophie.* Paris: Presses Universitaires de France (2d rev. ed. 1967). English trans. by Hugh Tomlinson: *Nietzsche and Philosophy.* New York: Columbia University Press, 1983.

"250e anniversaire de la naissance de Rousseau: Jean-Jacques Rousseau, précurseur de Kafka, de Céline, et de Ponge." In *Arts,* no. 872 (June 6–12), p. 3.

1963   *La philosophie critique de Kant: Doctrines des facultés.* Paris: Presses Universitaires de France. English trans. by Hugh Tomlinson and Barbara Habberjam: *Kant's Critical Philosophy: The Doctrine of the Faculties.* Minneapolis: University of Minnesota Press, 1984.

"Unité de *A la recherche du temps perdu.*" *Revue de Metaphysique et de Morale,* vol. 68, pp. 427–42.

"Mystère d'Ariane." *Etudes Nietzschéennes,* pp. 12–15.

L'idèe de genése dans l'esthétique de Kant." *Revue d'Esthétique,* vol. 16, pp. 113–36.

1964   *Marcel Proust et les signes.* Paris: Presses Universitaires de France (2d enlarged ed. 1970). English trans. by Richard Howard: *Proust and Signs.* New York: G. Braziller, 1972.

"Deux philosophes s'expliquent" (Gilles Deleuze: "Il a été mon maître"; Kostas Axelos: "Il a fai descendre la metaphysique dans les cafés"). *Arts* (October 28–November 3), pp. 8–9.

1965   *Nietzsche.* Paris: Presses Universitaires de France.

"Klossowski et les corps-langage." *Critique,* no. 214, pp. 199–219. Reprinted with modifications in the *Logique du sens* (1969).

1966   *Le Bergsonisme.* Paris: Presses Universitaires de France. English trans. by Hugh Tomlinson and Barbara Habberjam: *Bergsonism.* New York: Zone Books, 1988.

"L'Homme: Une existence douteuse." *Le Nouvel Observateur,* no. 81 (June 1–7), pp. 32–34.

"Philosophie de la série noire." *Arts & Loisirs,* no. 18 (January 24–February 1), pp. 12–13.

1967   "Introduction to E. Zola. La bête humaine." In *Oeuvres complètes d'Emile Zola,* Paris: Cercle du Livre Précieux, vol. 6, pp. 13–21. Modified and reprinted in *Logique du sens* (1969).

(with Michel Foucault). "Introduction générale à Nietzsche." In Frederich Nietzsche, *La gai savoir: Les fragments posthumes (1881–1882).* Trans. Pierre Klossowski. Vol. 5 of *Oeuvres philosophiques complètes.* Paris: Gallimard.

Presentation de Sacher-Masoch avec le texte integral de la Venus à la foururre. Trans. by Aude Willm. Paris: Les Editions de Minuit. English trans. by Jean McNeil and Aude Willm: *Masochism: An Interpretation of Coldness and Cruelty; Together with the entire text of Venus in Furs by Leopold von Sacher-Masoch.* New York: G. Braziller, 1971. Reprinted as *Masochism: Coldness and Cruelty; Venus in Furs,* Gilles Deleuze and Leopold von Sacher-Masoch. New York: Zone Books, 1985.

"Sur la volonté de puissance et l'éternel retour." *Nietzsche: Cahiers de Royaumont.* Paris: Les Editions de Minuit.

"Une théorie d'autrui" (Michel Tournier). *Critique,* vol. 23, no. 241 pp. 503–25. Reprinted with modifications in *Logique du sens.* Trans. as "Michel Tournier and the World Without Others." *Economy and Society,* vol. 13 (1984), pp. 52–71.

"La méthode de dramatisation." *Bulletin de la Société Française de Philosophie,* vol. 61, no. 3: Seance du 28 Janvier 1967.

"A quoi reconnait-on le structuralisme." *Les Foyers de la culture.* November. Reprinted in *Histoire de la philosophie: Idées, Doctrines.* Fr. Châtelet, ed., vol. 8. Paris: Hachette, 1972–73.

"Renverser le platonisme (les simulacres)." *Revue de Metaphysique et de Morale,* vol. 71, no. 4 (October–December), pp. 426–38). Reprinted with modifications in the *Logique du sens* (1969).

"L'éclat de rire de Nietzsche." *Le Nouvel Observateur,* April 5 pp. 40–41.

1968   *Différence et répétition.* Paris: Presses Universitaires de France. English trans. by Paul Patton: *Difference and Repetition.* London: Athlone, forthcoming.

Spinoza et le problème de l'expression. Paris: Les Editions de Minuit. English trans. by Martin Joughin: *Expressionism in Philosophy: Spinoza.* New York: Zone Books, 1990.

"Le Schizophréne et le mot." *Critique,* vol. 24, no. 255–56, pp. 731–46. Reprinted with modifications in the *Logique du sens.* English trans. and ed. by Josué Harari: "The Schizophrenic and Language: Surface and Depth in Lewis Carroll and Antonin Artaud." *Textual Strategies,* pp. 277–95. Ithaca: Cornell University Press, 1979.

(with J. N. Vuarnet). "Entretien sur Nietzsche." *Les Lettres Françaises,* March 5.

1969   *Logique du sens.* Paris: Les Editions de Minuit: English trans. by Mark Lester with Charles Stivale. Edited by Constantin V. Boundas: *The Logic of Sense.* New York: Columbia University Press, 1990.

"Spinoza et la méthode générale de M. Gueroult." *Revue de Metaphysique et de Morale* vol. 74, pp. 426–37.

"Gilles Deleuze parle de la philosophie." *La Quinzaine Littéraire,* no. 68 (March 1–15). Interview with Jeanette Colombel (on *Différence et répétition*).

1970   *Spinoza: Philosophie pratique.* Paris: Les Editions de Minuit. English trans. by Robert Hurley: *Spinoza: Practical Philosophy.* San Francisco: City Lights Books, 1988.

"Faille et feux locaux: Kostas Axelos." *Critique* vol. 26, no. 275, pp. 344–51.

"Schizologie." Preface to Louis Wolfson, *Le schizo et les langues.* Paris: Gallimard.

(with Félix Guattari). "La synthèse disjonctive." *L'Arc,* no. 43, pp. 54–62. Reprinted with modifications in *Capitalisme et Schizophrenie.* vol. 1: *L-Anti-Oedipe* (1972).

"Un nouvel archiviste." *Critique,* vol. 26, no. 274 (March), pp. 195–209. Reprinted as *Un nouvel archiviste.* Montepellier: Fata Morgana, 1972. English trans. by Stephen Muecke: "A New Archivist" in *Theoretical Strategies,* ed. by Peter Botsman. Sydney: Local Consumption, 1982.

1972   *(with Felix Guattari). Capitalisme et schizophrénie.* Tome I: *L-Anti-Oedipe.* Paris: Les Editions de Minuit. (2d enlarged ed., 1980). English trans. by Robert Hurley, M. Seem, and H. R. Lane: *Anti-Oedipus: Capitalism and Schizophrenia.* New York: Viking Press/A Richard Seaver Book, 1977.

"Trois problèmes de groupe." Preface to Félix Guattari, *Psychanalyse et transversalité.* Paris: F. Maspero. Trans. as "Three Group Problems," *Semiotext(e),* vol. 2, no. 3, pp. 99–109.

"Qu'est-ce que c'est tes machines désirantes à toi?" Preface to "Saint Jackie: Comedienne et bourreau," by Pierre Benichou. *Les Temps Modernes,* no. 316, pp. 854–56.

"Helène Cixous et l'ecriture stroboscopique." *Le Monde,* August 11.

"Les intellectuels et le pouvoir: Entretien Michel Foucault–Gilles Deleuze." *L'Arc,* no. 49, pp. 3–10. Trans. as "The Intellectuals and Power: A Discussion Between M. Foucault and G. Deleuze," *Telos,* no. 16 (1973), pp. 103–9. Also trans. by Donald Bouchard, "Intellectuals and Power." In Bouchard, ed., *Language, Counter-Memory, Practice,* pp. 205–17. Ithaca, N.Y.: Cornell University Press, 1977.

"Hume." *Histoire de la philosophie: Idées, doctrines,* Tome 2. François Châtelet, ed. Paris: Hachette.

(with Félix Guatarri). "Sur capitalisme et schizophrénie." *L'Arc: Deleuze,* no. 49 (2d ed., 1980), pp. 47–55. Reprinted in *Pourparlers, 1972–1990* (1990), pp. 24–38. Interview with Catherine Bakès-Clément.

(with Félix Guatarri). "Deleuze et Guatarri s'expliquent." *La Quinzaine Littéraire,* (June 16–20) pp. 15–19. Interview with Serge Leclaire, François Châtelet, H. Torrubia, Pierre Clastres, Roger Dadoun, P. Rose, and R. Pividal.

"Il languaggio schizofrenico." In *Tempi Moderni,* 12. Interview with Vittorio Marchetti. Reprinted in *Una tomba per edipo* (1974), pp. 339–56.

1973 Michel-Antoine Buznier (ed.). *Entretiens: C'est demain la veille.* Paris: Les Editions du Seuil.

(with Félix Guattari). "14 Mai 1914: Un seul ou plusieurs loups?" *Minuit,* no. 5. English trans. by Mark Seem: "May 14, 1914: One or Several Wolves?" *Semiotext(e),* vol. 2, no. 3, pp. 137–47.

"Lettre à Michel Cressole." In Michel Cressole, *Deleuze,* pp. 107–18. Paris: Editions Universitaires. Reprinted in *Pourparlers* (1990). English trans. by Janis Forman: "I Have Nothing to Admit," *Semiotext(e),* vol. 2, no. 3 (1977), pp. 111–16.

"Pensée nomade." *Nietzsche audjourd'hui?* vol. 1. Paris: 10/18. English trans. by Jacqueline Wallace: "Nomad Thought," *Semiotext(e)* vol. 3, no. 1 (1978), pp. 12–20.

(with Félix Guattari). "Le nouvel arpenteur: Intensités et blocks d'enfance dans 'Le château.'" *Critique,* vol. 29, no. 319, pp. 1046–54.

(with Félix Guattari). "Bilan-programme pour machines désirantes." *Minuit,* no. 2 (January), pp. 1–25. Reprinted in 2d ed. of *Capitalisme et schizophrénie.* vol. 1: *L'Anti-Oedipe* (1972).

"Presence et fonction de la folie dans la recherche du temps perdu." *Saggi e richerche di letterature francese, XII.* Rome: Bulzoni. Reprinted in 3d ed. of *Proust et les signes.*

"Le froid et le chaud" (on Gerard Fromanger). Presentation of the exhibition, "Fromanger: Le peintre et le modèle." Paris: Baudard Alverez.

1974 "Introduction." To Félix Guattari, *Una Tomba per Edipo;* A cura di Luisa Muraro. Trans. by D. Levi and L. Muraro. Verona: Bertani.

"Preface." To Guy Hocquenghem, *L'après-mai des faunes,* pp. 7–17. Paris: Grasset.

1975 (with Félix Guattari). *Kafka: Pour une littérature mineure.* Paris: Les Editions de Minuit. English trans. by Dana Polan: *Kafka: Toward a Minor Literature.* Minneapolis: University of Minnesota press, 1986.

"Deux régimes de fous." In *Psychanalyse et Sémiotique,* Armando Verdiglione, ed. 3d colloquim held in Milan in May 1974. Paris: Union Générale d'Editions.

(with Félix Guattari). "Psychoanalysis and Ethnology." *Substance: A Review of Theory and Literary Criticism,* pp. 170–97.

"Ecrivain non: Un nouveau cartographe." *Critique,* no. 343, pp. 1207–27. Reprinted with modifications in *Foucault.*

(with Roland Barthes, Gerard Genette et al.). "Table ronde" (on Proust). *Cahiers Marcel Proust,* new series, no. 7 (*Etudes Proustiennes,* II), pp. 87–115. Proceedings of a colloquy on "Proust and the New Criticism," sponsored by New York University and L'Ecole Normale Superieure, January 20–22, 1972.

1976   (with Félix Guattari). *Rhizome: Introduction.* Paris: Les Editions de Minuit. English trans. by Paul Foss and Paul Patton: "Rhizome," *Ideology and Consciousness,* no. 8 (Spring 1981), pp. 49–71. Reprinted with modifications as the introduction to *Mille Plateaux* (1980).

"Avenir de linquistique." Preface to H. Gobard, *L'alienation linquistique: Analyse tetraglossique.* Paris: Flammarion.

(with Michel Foucault and Félix Guatarri). "Formations des equipements collectifs." Transcript of discussions. In François Fourquet and Lion Murard, *Les equipements de pouvoir,* pp. 39–41, 161–95, 212–27. Paris: Union Générale des Editions. Revised version of the journal *Recherches: Les equipments collectifs,* no. 13 (December 1973).

"Entretien avec Gilles Deleuze." *Cahiers du Cinéma,* no. 271, pp. 5–12. Reprinted in *Pourparlers.* (1990). Trans. as "Three Questions on *Six fois deux:* An Interview with Gilles Deleuze." *Afterimage,* vol. 7 (Summer 1978), pp. 113–19.

1977   "A propos des nouveaux philosophes et d'un problème plus général." *Minuit,* no. 24, supplement (June 5), no pagination. Abridged version reprinted in *Le Monde,* June 19–20, p. 16, as "Gilles Deleuze contre les 'nouveaux philosophes.'" Reprinted in full in *Recherches, Les Untorelli,* no. 30 (November), pp. 179–84. Interview from June 5.

(with Félix Guattari). *Politique et Psychanalyse.* Alençon: Des Mots Perdus.

(with Claire Parnet). *Dialogues.* Paris: Flammarion. English trans. by Hugh Tomlinson and Barbara Habberjam: *Dialogues.* New York: Columbia University Press, 1987.

"L'ascension du social." Postface to Jacques Donzelot, *La police des familles.* Paris: Minuit. English translation by Robert Hurley: "The Rise of the Social," foreword to Donzelot, *the Policing of Families.* New York: Pantheon Books, 1979.

"Nous croyons au caractère constructiviste de certaines agitations de gauche." *Recherches, Les Untorelli,* no. 30 (November), pp. 149–50.

"Le juif riche." Interview, *Le Monde,* February 18. Trans. as "Der Reiche Jude." In Daniel Schmid, *Pro Helvetica.* Zurich: Zytglogge, 1982.

"Gilles Deleuze fasciné par 'Le Misogyne.'" *La Quinzaine Litteraire,* vol. 229. Review of Alain Roger, *Le Misogyne.* Paris: Denoël, 1977.

(with Félix Guatarri). "Le pire moyen de faire l'Europe." *Le Monde,* November 2.

1978   (with Carmelo Bene). *Sovrapposizioni.* Milan: Feltrinelli. *Superpositions.* Paris: Les Editions de Minuit, 1979.

(with F. Châtelet et al.). *Ou il est question de la toxicomanie.* Alençon: Des Mots Perdus.

"Philosophie et minorité," *Critique,* vol. 34, no. 369, pp. 154–55.

"Four Propositions on Psychoanalysis." Trans. and ed. by Paul Foss and Meaghan Morris in *Language, Sexuality, and Perversion*, pp. 134–40. Sydney: Feral Publications. (From *Politique et Psychanalyse* 1977.)

(with Claire Parnet and A. Scala). "The Interpretation of Utterances." Trans. and ed. by Paul Foss and Meaghan Morris in *Language, Sexuality, and Perversion*, pp. 141–57. Sydney: Feral Publications. (From *Politique et Psychanalyse* 1977.)

"Les gêneurs." *Le Monde*. April 7.

"La plainte et le corps." (P. Fédida). *Le Monde*. October 13.

"Spinoza et nous." *Revue de Synthèse*. 3d series, nos. 89–91 (January–September). Reprinted as chapter 6 of *Spinoza: Philosophie practique* (1970), 2d ed.

(with Fanny Deleuze). Preface to D. H. Lawrence, *Apocalypse*, pp. 7–37. Paris: Balland.

1979 "Open Letter to Negri's Judges." *La Repubblica*, May. Trans. by Committee April 7. *Semiotext(e)*, vol. 3 (1980), pp. 182–84.

"En quoi la philosophie peut servir à les mathématiciens ou même à des musiciens, même et surtout quand elle ne parle pas de musique ou de mathématiques." In Pierre Merlin, ed., *Vincennes ou le désir d'apprendre*, pp. 120–21. Paris: Alain Moreau.

1980 (with Félix Guattari). *Capitalisme et schizophrénie: Mille plateaux*. Paris: Les Editions de Minuit. English trans. by Brian Massumi: *A Thousand Plateaus: Capitalism and Schizophrenia*. Minneapolis: University of Minnesota Press, 1987.

" 'Mille plateaux' ne font pas une montagne, ils ouvrent mille chemins philosophiques." *Libération*, October 23, pp. 16–17. Reprinted in *Pourparlers* (1990) as "Entretien sur *Mille plateaux*," pp. 39–52. Interview with Christian Descamps, Diddier Eribon, and Robert Maggiori.

"Entretien 1980: Huit ans après." *L'Arc: Deleuze*, no. 49 (1972; 3d ed. 1980), pp. 99–102. 1980 interview with Cathérine Clement, added in 2d ed.

"Pourquoi en est-on arrive là?" Interview with François Châtelet on Vincennes. *Libération*, March 17.

"Mille plateaux pour combien de chemins?" In *Magazine Littéraire* vol. 167 (December), pp. 58–59.

1981 *Francis Bacon: Logique de la sensation*. 2 vols. Paris: Editions de la Différence.

"Preface." To Antonio Negri, *L'anomalie sauvage: Puissance et pouvoir chez Spinoza*. Trans. by F. Matheron. Paris: Presses Universitaires de France.

Intervention by Gilles Deleuze in Bene, Carmelo. *Otello, o la deficienza della donna*. Milan: Feltrinelli.

(with Félix Guattari). "How to Make Yourself a Body Without Organs."

Trans. by Suzanne Guerlac. *Semiotext(e)*, vol. 4, no. 1, pp. 265–70. (From *Mille Plateaux*.)

(with Félix Guattari). "A Bloated Oedipus." Trans. by Rachel McComas. *Semiotext(e)*, vol. 4, no. 1. (From *Kafka: Pour une littérature mineure*.)

"Peindre le cri." *Critique*, vol. 37, no. 408, pp. 506–11. (From *Francis Bacon*.)

"La peinture enflamme l'écriture." *Le Monde*. December 3, p. 15. Interview with Hervé Guibert on *Francis Bacon: Logique de la sensation*. English translation: "What Counts Is the Scream." *The Guardian*, January 10, 1982.

1982 "Lettre à Uno sur le langage." *Le Revue de la Pensée d'Aujourd'hui*, December, Tokyo.

1983 *Cinéma 1: L'image-mouvement*. Paris: Les Editions de Minuit. English trans. *Cinéma 1: The Movement-Image* by Hugh Tomlinson and Barbara Habberjam. Minneapolis: University of Minnesota Press, 1986.

(with Félix Guattari). *On the Line*. Trans. by John Johnston. New York: *Semiotext(e)*.

Preface. *Nietzsche and Philosophy*. Trans. by Hugh Tomlinson. New York: Columbia University Press.

"Cinema 1, première." *Libération*, October 3, p. 30. And "Le philosophe menuisier." Interview with Didier Eribon. *Libération*, October 3, p. 31.

"Portrait du philosophe en spectateur." *Le Monde*, October 6, pp. 1, 17.

"La photographie est déjà tirée dans les choses." *Cahiers du Cinéma*, no. 352 (October), pp. 35–40. Interview with Pascal Bonitzer and Jean Narboni on September 13, edited by the participants. Reprinted in *Pourparlers* (1990) as "Sur *L'image-mouvement*," pp. 67–81.

"Inédit: Godard et Rivette." *La Quinzaine littéraire*, 404, (November 1).

"L'abstraction lyrique." *Change International*, 1 (Autumn) (From *Cinema 1: L'image-mouvement*.)

"Francis Bacon: The Logic of Sensation." *Flash Art*, no. 112 (May) (From *Francis Bacon*.)

(with Jean-Pierre Bamberger). "Le pacifisme au'jourd-hui." *Les Nouvelles*, December 15–21, pp. 60–64.

Interview. *Cahiers du Cinéma*, no. 352 (October). Reprinted in *Pourparlers* (1990).

1984 "On Four Poetic Formulas Which Might Summarize the Kantian Philosophy." Preface to *Kant's Critical Philosophy*. Trans. by Hugh Tomlinson and Barbara Habberjam. Minneapolis: University of Minnesota Press.

"Grandeur de Yasser Arafat." *Revue d'Études Palestiniennes*, no. 10, pp. 41–43.

(with Félix Guattari). "Concrete Rules and Abstract Machines." Trans. by Charles Stivale. *Substance: Theory and Literary Criticism*, vol. 13, no. 3/4, pp. 7–19. (From *Mille Plateaux*.)

"Books." *Art Forum,* vol. 22, no. 5 (January), pp. 68–69.

"Michel Tournier and the World Without Others." Trans. by Graham Burchell. *Economy and Society,* vol. 131, no. 1, pp. 52–71.

(with Félix Guattari). "Mai 68 n'a pas eu lieu." *Les Nouvelles,* May 3–10, pp. 75–76.

"Lettre à Uno: Comment nous avons travaillé à deux" (on Guatarri). *La Revue de la Pensée d'Aujourd'hui,* September, Tokyo, special issue.

"Le temps musical." *La Revue de la Pensée d'Aujourd'hui.* September, Tokyo, special issue.

1985   *Cinéma 2: L'image-temps.* Paris: Les Editions de Minuit. English trans. by Hugh Tomlinson and Robert Galeta: *Cinema 2: The Time-Image.* Minneapolis: University of Minnesota Press, 1989.

"Les intercesseurs." Interview with Antoine Dulaure and Claire Parnet. *L'Autre Journal,* no. 8 (October), pp. 12–22. Reprinted in *Pourparlers,* (1990).

"Schizophrénie et société." *Encyclopaedia Universalis,* vol. 16, pp. 524–27.

"Active and Reactive." Trans. by Richard Cohen and ed. by David B. Allison. Cambridge: MIT Press, 1985. (From *Nietzsche et la philosophie.*) *The New Nietzsche,* pp. 80–106.

(with Félix Guattari). "Nomad Art." Trans. by Brian Massumi. *Art and Text,* no. 19 (October–December), pp. 16–26. (From *Mille Plateaux.*)

(with Félix Guattari). "City State." Trans. by Brian Massumi. *Zone,* no. 1/2, pp. 195–99. (From *Mille Plateaux.*)

(with Félix Guattari). "Becoming-Human." Trans. by Brian Massumi. *Subjects/Objects,* no. 3, pp. 24–32. (From *Mille Plateaux.*)

"Les plages d'immanence." In *L'Art des confins, Mélanges offerts à Maurice de Gandillac,* ed. by Annie Cuzenave and Jean-François Lyotard, Paris: PUF.

"Le philosophe et le cinéma." *Cinéma,* no. 334 (December 18–24), pp. 2–3. Reprinted in *Pourparlers* as "Sur *L'image-temps,*" pp. 82–87.

"Il était une étoile de groupe" (on François Châtelet). *Libération,* December 27.

1986   *Foucault.* Paris: Les Editions de Minuit. English trans. by Sean Hand: *Foucault.* Minneapolis: University of Minnesota Press, 1988.

(with Félix Guattari). *Nomadology: The War Machine.* Trans. by Brian Massumi. New York: Semiotext(e). Reprinted in *A Thousand Plateaus* (1987).

"'Le cerveau, c'est l'écran': entretien avec Gilles Deleuze." *Cahiers du cinéma,* no. 380 (February), pp. 25–32.

"La vie comme une oeuvre d'art." *Le Nouvel Observateur,* 1138 (September 4), pp. 66–68. Reprinted in *Pourparlers* (1990).

Preface. To Serge Daney, *Ciné-lectures.* Paris: Cahiers du cinéma. Reprinted in

Pourparlers as "Lettre à Serge Daney: Optimisme, pessimisme, et voyage," pp. 97–112 (which refers to the title of Daney's book as *Ciné-Journal*).

"'Fendre les choses, fendre les mots'" (on Foucault). *Libération*, September 2, pp. 27–28, and September 3, p. 38. Interview with Robert Maggiori. Reprinted in *Pourparlers* (1990), pp. 115–28.

"Un portrait de Foucault." Interview with Claire Parnet, *Pourparlers* (1990), pp. 139–61.

"Sur le 'Régime cristallin.'" *Hors cadre* vol. 4, pp. 39–45. Reprinted in *Pourparlers* (1990) as "Doutes sur l'imaginaire," pp. 88–96.

"Le plus grand film irlandais (en hommage à Samuel Beckett)." *Revue d'Esthétique*, pp. 381–82.

"Boulez, Proust, et le temps: 'Occuper sans compter.'" In Claude Samuel, ed., *Eclats/Boulez*, pp. 98–100. Paris: Editions du Centre Pompidou.

"The Intellectual and Politics." *History of the Present* (Spring), pp. 1–2 and 19–21.

1987   "Preface to the English Language Edition." *Dialogues*. Trans. by Hugh Tomlinson and Barbara Habberjam. New York: Columbia University Press.

(with Jean-Pierre Bamberger). "A gauche sans missiles." *Les Nouvelles* (December 15–31), pp. 61–62, 64. Joint interview with Claire Parnet.

1988   *Le pli: Leibniz et le baroque* Paris: Editions de Minuit. English trans. *The Fold: Leibniz and the Barbque* (Minneapolis: University of Minnesota Press, 1992).

Périclès et Verdi: La philosophie de François Châtelet. Paris: Editions de Minuit.

"Foucault: Historien du present." *Magazine Littéraire*, vol. 257 (September), pp. 51–52.

"Signes et événements" (entretien) *Magazine Littéraire*, vol. 257 (September), pp. 16–25. Reprinted in *Pourparlers* (1990) as "Sur la philosophie," pp. 185–212.

"Un critère pour le baroque." *Chimères*, vol. 5/6, pp. 3–9. Reprinted in revised form in *Le pli*.

"'A Philosophical Concept.'" *Topoi* vol. 7, no. 2 (September), pp. 111–12, no translator listed. Reprinted in *Who Comes After the Subject?* (London: Routledge, 1991).

"La pensée mise en plis." *Libération*, September 22, pp. I–III. Reprinted in *Pourparlers* (1990) as "Sur Leibniz," pp. 213–22.

1989   "Qu'est-ce qu'un dispositif?" and ensuing discussion in *Michel Foucault: Philosophe*, pp. 185–95. Paris: Seuil, 1989.

"Preface to the English Edition" *Cinema 2: The Time-Image*, pp. xi–xii. (Minneapolis: University of Minnesota Press, 1989). Translated by Hugh Tomlinson and Robert Galeta.

"Postface: Bartleby, ou la formule" in H. Melville, *Bartleby, Les iles enchantées, le campanile*, pp. 171–208. Paris: Flammarion.

"Lettre à Réda Bensmaïa." *Lendemains*, vol. 14, no. 53, p. 9. Reprinted as "Lettre à Réda Bensmaïa sur Spinoza" in *Pourparlers* (1990), pp. 223–25.

1990 "Le devenir révolutionnaire et les créations politiques." *Futur Antérieur* vol. 1, (Spring), pp. 100–108. Reprinted in *Pourparlers* (1990) as "Contrôle et devenir," pp. 229–39.

"Post-scriptum sur les sociétés de contrôle." *L'Autre Journal*, no. 1 (May). Reprinted in *Pourparlers* (1990), pp. 240–247.

Pourparlers, 1972–1990. Paris: Editions de Minuit. English translation: *Interviews, 1972–1990*. New York: Columbia University Press, forthcoming.

"Les conditions de la question: Qu'est-ce que la philosophie?" *Chimères*, vol. 8 (May), pp. 123–32. Reprinted in revised form in *Qu'est-ce que la philosophie?* English translation by Daniel W. Smith and Arnold L. Davidson: "The Conditions of the Question: What is Philosophy?" vol. 17, no. 3 *Critical Inquiry* (Spring), pp. 471–78.

"Lettre-préface" to M. Buydens, *Sahara: L'esthétique de Gilles Deleuze*. Paris: Vrin, p. 5.

(with Pierre Bourdieu, Jérôme Lindon, and Pierre Vidal-Naquet). "Adresse au gouvernement français." *Libération*, September 5, p. 6.

1991 "A Return to Bergson." afterword to *Bergsonism*, trans. by Hugh Tomlinson. New York: Zone Books, pp. 115–18.

"Preface to the English-Language Edition." *Empiricism and Subjectivity: An Essay on Hume's Theory of Human Nature*. Translated by Constantin V. Boundas. New York: Columbia University Press, pp. ix–x.

"Préface" to E. Alliez, *Les temps capitaux*, vol. 1: *Récits de la conquête du temps*, pp. 7–9. Paris: Editions du Cerf.

"Prefazione: Una nuova stilistica" to G. Passerone, *La Linea astratta: Pragmatica della stile*, pp. 9–13. Milan: Edizioni Angelo Guerini.

(with René Scherer). "La guerre immonde." *Libération*, March 4, p. 11.

(with Félix Guattari). *Qu'est-ce que la philosophie?* Paris: Editions de Minuit. English translation: *What Is Philosophy?* New York: Columbia University Press, forthcoming.

(with Félix Guattari). "Secret de fabrication: Deleuze-Guattari—Nous deux." *Libération*, September 12, pp. 17–19.

1992 Revised version of "Mystère d'Ariane." *Magazine Littéraire*, vol. 298 (April), pp. 21–24.

Index